Alexander McKee was selling aviation articles to flying magazines by the age of eighteen. During the Second World War he wrote for a succession of army newspapers and later became a writer/producer for the British Forces Network. He has been writing and researching aspects of naval, military and aviation history for many years. He first heard of the bombing of Dresden when he was serving with the Army in the Rhineland and Ruhr areas during 1945. The story haunted him, and he spent the following years amassing information, visiting Dresden in 1958 and again in 1980. His aim was to present the story from the point of view of those who took part in it, whether as attackers or victims. In all he has written nineteen books, one of his most recent successes being the Granada paperback *Into the Blue*.

By the same author

ALEXANDER McKEE

Dresden 1945:

The Devil's Tinderbox

GRANADA
London Toronto Sydney New York

Published by Granada Publishing Limited in 1983

ISBN 0 583 13686 9

First published in Great Britain by
Souvenir Press Ltd 1982
Copyright © Alexander McKee 1982

Granada Publishing Limited
Frogmore, St Albans, Herts AL2 2NF
and
36 Golden Square, London W1R 4AH
515 Madison Avenue, New York, NY 10022, USA
117 York Street, Sydney, NSW 2000, Australia
60 International Blvd, Rexdale, Ontario, R9W 6J2, Canada
61 Beach Road, Auckland, New Zealand

Printed and bound in Great Britain
by Cox & Wyman Ltd, Reading
Set in Times

Granada ®
Granada Publishing ®

For Ilse who, born in Saxony, saw the fires of Dresden on the skyline for three days and nights, and has so skilfully and faithfully translated the diaries, narratives and recollections of some of those who survived.

And for Angelika and Sabina, who gave invaluable bibliographic assistance.

Contents

'War is a fire struck in the Devil's tinderbox'

— James Howell, 1655, writing in the Fleet, where he had been imprisoned for his Royalist politics.

Maps

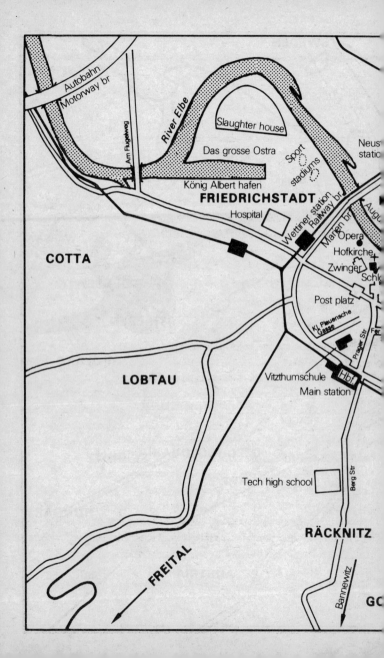

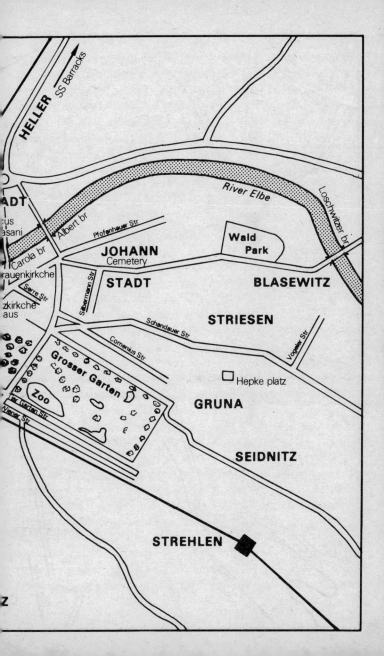

Foreword

Dresden was a famous massacre from the start. At that time I was a soldier with the 1st Canadian Army; I entered Germany in March 1945, about a month afterwards. In the spring and summer, when I was with the British 2nd Army in the Rhineland and Ruhr, I heard the first whispers. Something very terrible had happened over there in the East near the war's end, I was told, but no one could explain why it had been so much more cruel than the fate which had engulfed most of Europe, burnt with fire from heaven or tornadoed into rubble by the passage of the armies.

The Blitzkrieg, theirs and ours, had spared some tracts of countryside and all the Western capitals. Paris, Brussels and Rome were almost untouched; even London was only lightly damaged. But seen from the air, most of the great cities of Europe were jagged scars on the landscape, with the survivors gone to ground, huddled in cellars and under the wreckage, coughing. The bones of dead cattle lay in the meadows by the Channel coast and the towns of Normandy were fields of debris. The Dutch dykes had been bombed and broken, and the sea had conquered Holland. The cities of the North German plain were husks. Warsaw was a pile of bricks and bodies. From the Channel coast and on into Russia, to Kiev, to the Don and the Volga; from the Bay of Naples through Cassino to the Baltic and the Gulf of Finland — the 'red hot rake' of total war had passed over them all. Not with fire and sword as in the old tales of the Thirty Years War, but with thermite bombs, blockbusters, multi-barrel mortars, massed artillery and the stabbing rash of small-arms fire.

The master had read the lesson, and the pupils had learnt it well.

In some towns, such as Emmerich and Arnhem, I was present while their final destruction took place. In Emmerich I saw no building whatever intact, although here and there the gutted shell of a house, one wall of a church tower, still stood. And it was German artillery fire now which vied with the British and Canadian guns in ploughing over the ruins. This process, when the town was an Allied one, we referred to with bitter mockery as 'Liberation'. When you said that such-and-such a place had been 'liberated', you meant that hardly one stone still stood upon another.

But on 8 May 1945, or thereabouts, the guns fell silent, more or less. Officially, peace had been declared, according to the writers of history books, who were not there, or too remote to know the real state of things, or would prefer to forget.

It was a strange peace and, in the great cities, very terrible. In July I was driven through Cologne. We all fell silent as mile after mile we drove through nothing but ruin and still only ruins lay ahead. 'In all that devastation,' I wrote:

I only saw about a dozen buildings which were intact, though several hundred had been damaged and repaired, and still stood. The destruction and damage in the very considerable area of Cologne through which we toured must have been in the neighbourhood of 98 per cent. All through these streets there was a peculiar smell, similar to that borne on the breeze between Elst and Arnhem after the battle, so long stationary, moved on; it was fainter but quite recognizable. The smell of human flesh, long dead, decomposing in the heat.

But in that barren moon-world there was life in spite of death. If you looked closely, you could see that there were narrow paths newly trodden through the heaped hills and mountains of rubble, and when winter came, there was smoke from fires. Men and women were living there, sheltering in caverns excavated in the hillocks of ruin which had been their homes. Apart from a few favoured cities, Europe had been reduced to a continent of cave-dwellers. Against such a background, what could possibly have been so special about Dresden?

The British Zone of Germany, in which I was to work for the next seven years, had an area approximately the size of Ireland and a population far greater — some 18 million people. In 1939 the population had been housed in 5½ million buildings. By May 1945, 1½ million had been totally destroyed and a further 1½ million severely damaged. The German population were starving and many millions of Hitler's former slave workers, ill-treated and armed, were on the loose. The bureaucrats, prim to the last, called them 'displaced persons', but truly, most of them were Russians, Ukrainians and Poles, forcibly uprooted from their homes in the East. War material of all kinds, from Tiger tanks in drivable condition to guns and ammunition, littered the countryside. The sounds of shooting began at nightfall and continued until dawn. Martial law was in force and was enforced. The apocalyptic prewar visions of H.G. Wells and other pacifist prophets had come true, although even they could have hardly imagined the tragic plight of the Ukrainians and Russians, freed from the Nazi slow-death camps only to be sent back, whether they willed or no, to the USSR of Stalin and the Siberian gulags.

It was in these surroundings that I heard those whispers of something unimaginably dreadful having been done at Dresden.

Even when I left the Ruhr and Rhineland and came to Hamburg in the north, even there they spoke of what had occurred in Dresden as having been something cruelly apart. Hamburg was a very great city indeed. Every morning we drove to work through some five miles of almost total devastation, past landmarks such as the collapsed department store under which still lay, they said, some 400 bodies, mainly of children. Out of some 556,000 homes in Hamburg, 455,000 had been destroyed or severely damaged; but there was more beyond that, for the port area lay in ruins also and out of the water reared the wrecks of 55 ships, 3,500 barges, 16 floating docks. It was difficult to compute the area of total destruction, almost impossible to count the dead. Only if nothing much has happened, can reasonably accurate casualty figures be produced (and even those are sometimes suspect). In Hamburg, it took six years of painful detective work to arrive at what was called an 'estimated minimum' figure for the dead. This was not a complete head count, utterly impossible, but included a matching of known previous inhabitants before the raids with present population, taking into account those who had merely moved away. In a fire-storm, people simply vanish into dust and ashes; others again were still under the un-cleared areas of rubble. After six years of counting and calculation, the estimated minimum figures were at last arrived at: 48,000 dead in the raids of July 1943, and a total for the whole war of not less than 55,000 killed. In one German city alone, nearly as many killed as in the whole of Great Britain during the entire war — British losses are more precisely known at 60,595 over 5½ years.

The proud people of Hamburg did not ask for sympathy or pity. They accepted that there had been some reason for the Allies to try to level the city to the ground. But for Dresden, they said, there had been no excuse at all.

This was unusual. I can recall nothing like it in southern England, where we tended to be naïvely boastful. Your bomb was always bigger than the next man's, or nearer, or more spectacular. 'X' had taken far more of a pasting than 'Y', because naturally it was far more important to the war effort; Hitler obviously realized that (and anyway, you lived there). This is the reason why the London 'blitz' looms large in many histories – it was the home of press and radio, the people who were telling the stories. People were proud, not cowed as they should have been, according to the theories of the RAF bomber marshals who, undismayed, looked on and decided to ignore the facts that did not suit.

When for the first time you see and hear – hear because the flames roar and hiss – a city burning apparently from end to end, a great and terrible spectacle in the night, it seems the end of the world; nothing can be worse. Yet, when days later the smoke pall has lifted, although the acreage of ruin impresses, it can be seen that only a shopping centre has been destroyed, a dozen or so unimportant streets turned to blackened skeletons and hills of rubble. Not much mileage for Hitler in that. Hardly worth Goering's petrol bill. That was what I saw at Southampton in November and December 1940, and at Portsmouth in January and March 1941. The civilian casualties in such typical night blitzes tended to be around 100 killed, a little less or a little more. Coventry, with 554 people killed and great damage done to twenty-one aircraft production and other war factories, was exceptional. A combination of circumstances had led to an intense concentration of the bombing, with remarkably effective results. This was to be noted by the RAF bomber marshals, then almost impotent because their small force of defenceless, inefficient aircraft still bombing by 'Stone Age' techniques was not then a factor to be reckoned with in the war.

Goering's Luftwaffe, designed as a force for precision bombing in daylight of targets designated by an army, had not the weight to make much impact on the war economy of the British Isles. When, as sometimes happened, the night bombing went wrong and fell on mainly residential rather than mainly industrial or port areas, the results were unimpressive, particularly where shopping centres were concerned. Burning Woolworths to the ground during the night is unlikely to win anyone a war. The civilian casualties ran at a rate rather less than double that inflicted normally in road traffic accidents.

The difference between these few fire-blitzed streets and a great city which has been almost totally destroyed is titanic, and not to be apprehended by the intellect; it is a matter of emotion. And yet the survivors in the fire-stormed cities of Germany, which had been between 75 and 95 per cent erased from the earth, spoke after the war of what happened in Dresden as if it had been infinitely worse.

I wondered why. My qualifications for asking the question were various. I came from a Service family – navy, army, and connections with the Royal Flying Corps and RAF – and was brought up with the array of values normal to such a background then, but which may need explanation now. One aspect certainly does. A professional soldier, sailor or airman went to war as ordered by his government, presumably in the national interest, regardless of his own opinions and with no distinction made between aggressive or defensive war. His professional contemporaries on the enemy side not only did the same but were expected to do so. The people on the other side were probably splendid chaps. The fact that you happened to be fighting them was purely a matter between your two governments; there was nothing personal in it.

This was the basis of what used to be called 'chivalry', which started to go out of fashion when war came to be waged by mass, conscript armies backed by a vast labour force in munitions factories. To make the masses eager to fight, 'hate' propaganda was widely employed: the entire enemy nation (with whom you had previously been allied, and might be allied again in the war after this one) were devils, fiends incarnate, right down to the babes in the womb. Hitler's antisemitic propaganda was simply a variation on this evil theme. That is, the enemy are not people, they are monsters: destroy them all, utterly.

I learned to fly at the age of fifteen and wanted to become a fighter pilot because I felt that air power would be vital in the war which was almost certainly coming. I wanted to fly fighters partly because I was an individualist but partly also because I was morally soft. I assumed that bombing would be directed only at the key points of an enemy's army or industrial system, but I was aware that the inevitable near-misses must kill women and children, and from this I flinched. Selfishly, I did not want their blood on my conscience.

I was interested in the books of the air power theorists, which I still have on my shelves; but I was naïve. Re-reading them now is like browsing through a British *Mein Kampf*. The horror to come is all there between the lines. What they are really advocating is an all-out attack on non-combatants, men, women and children, as a deliberate policy of terror.

I made then and I make now a distinction between non-combatants killed so to speak by accident − as in a road crash − from the 'overs' and 'unders' aimed for military or industrial objectives, and a policy of making the civil population the actual target of attack. Moreover, I did not then and do not now believe that the latter policy is an efficient method of making war.

Failure to pass an RAF aircrew medical (half-vision in one eye) ensured that I would fly neither fighters nor bombers. I therefore escaped the dilemma of those who volunteered for bombers, believing that they would be serving their country's military aims, and found themselves carrying out mainly massacres of civil populations.

Instead, I was to amass almost five years' experience of air raids in five different countries, topped by seven years' residence in postwar Europe. I didn't just tour the ruined cities, I lived in them, albeit in semi-privileged conditions. My experiences on the receiving end began in May 1940 and continued into March 1945, with the last fling of the Luftwaffe against our Rhineland offensive – the German air force defending Germany itself from invading armies. In between I had witnessed the daylight Battle of Britain, including high-level pattern bombing and Stuka attacks; and also the night 'blitzes' in Southampton, Portsmouth, London and Bristol during 1940 and 1941; sporadic South Coast bombing in 1942 during which my own home was hit; the last London raids of late 1943 and early 1944 (in one of which I was blown twenty feet through the air by a bomb); the first V1 flying bombs into London in June 1944; and the first V2 stratospheric rockets into Antwerp in October 1944.

My reactions were purely personal, and probably bound up with my background. I was unmoved by the interior of a Heinkel bomber drenched with the blood of the bomb aimer – a young man in uniform had died doing his duty for his country, as millions had before him, and millions would in future. And shortly after, seeing two RAF men lying dead on a balloon barrage site which had been dive-bombed and strafed, my reaction was the same as it had been to the Luftwaffe youth. That was the way we would all go. They had just gone a little before us.

When my own house was bombed and my father injured, I felt real rage for the first time. For a week, I hated the Germans, then I went back to normal. (The stick of bombs which did the damage were an undershoot, aimed for a troop train and missing by 150 yards.)

I must confess an apparent illogicality which I shared with many people. During that part of the war when Britain's survival was in doubt, I actually preferred that enemy bombs should fall on shops and offices and houses and kill non-combatants rather than destroy military or industrial targets vital to our ability to resist. This distinction would not have been clear to the air power theorists because they did not accept the judgement that bombs falling on the innocent were simply wasteful. I thought so, however; and still do.

I had no idea of what Bomber Command was doing in Germany (and elsewhere), and would not have believed it had I been told. I believed (mistakenly) that the damage done by the Luftwaffe in Britain represented the high peak of destruction by air power and I told bomb stories with the best of them until in September 1944 I was in an army vehicle bumping over roadways bulldozed through the rubble of Caen in Normandy. I saw what massed heavy bombers could do to a city containing the women and children of our friends. Three Germans had been killed, and 5,000 French, we were told. The figures may have been amended since, but what I will never forget is having to look into the faces of the survivors, standing on the pavements as we drove past, knowing that it was *our* side which had done this.

And in Lisieux shortly after, the same scenes again and on an even greater scale, 90 per cent destruction instead of 80 per cent, with some fire damage in addition to the high-piled ploughed wasteland of stone produced by high explosives in mass; and in the market place the burnt, red-brown remains of a British bomber. For the airmen at that moment, it was difficult to feel sympathy.

Here we stopped and talked to some of the victims and I recorded in my notebook:

Lisieux and Caen are examples of the inflexibility of the four-motor heavy bomber: it cannot block a road without bringing down a city. I'm not surprised that our troops advancing between Caen and Lisieux were fired on by French civilians. No doubt many Frenchmen found it hard to be liberated by a people who seem, by their actions, to specialize in the mass murder of their friends.

This reaction from British soldiers was by no means unusual; it even alarmed the British government, or so one heard. In the battles for the Channel ports, now about to begin, an artillery officer closely related to a future British prime minister refused to obey the fire order on the grounds that the shells were bound to kill many French civilians. This was a brave gesture but had no immediate, practical effect: the officer was removed from his command, court-martialled and sent to serve a spell in an English prison. Someone else fired the guns.

The type of deed causing such a reaction did not have to be on a large scale, as far as I was concerned. The next emotional impression, following a natural progression from these earlier ones, registered when we reached Belgium a few days later and I learned how the Gestapo had actually operated; in one prison they had gutters in the floor to let the blood flow away. This was not a newspaper story; I was told so by someone who had seen it. I think it was the partial insight this gave into the true nature of the

Nazi system which was chilling. With it came the realization that one essential aspect of efficient modern interrogation methods was to take away the dignity of the victim as a first preliminary. I found this horrible, utterly vile. It echoed my violent rejection of the stories we heard of women's heads being shaved in public by so-called Resistance groups.

I thought then and think now that such acts are barbaric, far worse than killing the victim outright. There is a case in British history where the same value judgement was made by a mass of men. In the naval mutiny at Spithead, 1797, an officer was about to be summarily hanged by the mutineers, when a few of the rebels started to jeer at and insult the wretched man. Almost instantly, they were shouted down by the majority. Executing him for his crimes was all right; insulting him at the moment of death was not. These were anything but sophisticated men acting as a result of long deliberation. They spoke from some instinct of what was right and what was not.

I had seen the slaughter-sites of the innocents in Caen and Lisieux during September 1944, had heard about the torture of individuals in the Gestapo prison of Breendonck soon after, and had loathed all these manifestations of the twentieth century. In October 1944 I was in a British military hospital in Antwerp, and still young and impressionable. Yet another V2 rocket, with its sonic double-boom, thunderclapped into the city so close that most of the windows fell in and the walls, floors and ceilings exuded choking clouds of dust. The rocket had exploded in front of a girls' school 300 yards away, and a few minutes later the first, huddled, blood-stained child was carried into the hospital by a soldier. I found myself trembling, for the first time in an air raid. I was full of hate and the desire to hit back. Although I knew the rockets were intended for the docks and was aware of the vital importance the Antwerp port area had for the entire Allied war machine in north-west Europe, I could not forgive this atrocity inflicted on the individual. Given the wide range of error associated with the V-weapons, how could anyone justify such a deed? That was my reasoning, or so I like to think. It may be, however, that my reaction had no rational base, and that it was an emotional response to having been helplessly on the receiving end for so long, because I had not then pressed a trigger in earnest. It may have been that I was, after five years, sick at seeing the results of explosive assaults on cities. There was a wounded German soldier in our ward, along with the Canadians and British, but I did not blame him, nor did anyone else; he was far below the level at which such decisions were taken.

Of the battle area experience I was later to gain, the most horrible by far was the discovery in and around a shattered farmhouse on the Dutch – German border of the long-dead, ruined bodies of Canadian and German soldiers probably killed the previous year. One body at least was booby-trapped, the entire place and the surrounding fields were mined, and there were snipers in the area; I think why I remember this incident above all others was the thought of being shot down or mutilated and left to lie amid this pollution. Like so many, I feared mutilation far more than death. Here was the final degradation, not only to be denied a decent death, but to be used, putrefying, to further the obscene ends of war.

I did not see inside a concentration camp until after it had been cleaned up, but a few weeks before the end of the war the Canadians to whom I was attached interrogated two unusual prisoners – a camp doctor and a high-grade cipher operator. I entered the results in my diary:

The Doctor explained that the concentration camps came under a ministry for the elimination of persons unfit to live. A painful injection, causing death only after several minutes, was the method he used. He had injected 17,000 persons, and ordered the injection of about 100,000 after he had been promoted to chief doctor in the camp. Before injections could take place, the victims had to be passed by a board of doctors as fit to die (or rather, as unfit to live). He remarked, casually, that they could deal with about a hundred a day.

A number of different categories might be considered: those of Jewish blood, of course; but also slave labourers no longer able to work – many nationalities were involved, but most were probably Russian; Germans, too – mental defectives, confirmed criminals, homosexuals, pacifists, defeatists, political and religious opponents, people guilty of 'careless talk', and so on. All to be eliminated by injection, or by gassing or by shooting. It was difficult to think of a parallel to this conception, even in the technological twentieth century; the Russians had a similar machine (later to become widely known as the 'Gulag'), but its aims were more old-fashioned and inefficient.

The final rounds of destruction which I witnessed included as much artillery as aerial bombardment, at the Rhine crossing near Emmerich and in the capture of the Dutch town of Arnhem in April 1945. Arnhem, too, seemed to be on fire from end to end under the hammering of the guns, but like parts of the Rhineland it had been sanitized – there were no civilians there at all.

These forced evacuations of key fighting areas, the one carried out by the Germans, the other by the British and Canadian armies, reflected the orthodox military view – civilians were a damned nuisance but you couldn't very well kill them off. A totally different attitude prevailed at times in some air forces, particularly RAF Bomber Command and, in the war's closing stages, the USAAF. Rarely did they apologize for or excuse what they had done, but in the case of Dresden they made an exception. At once, almost everyone connected with it at a decisive level politically or militarily was trying to prove either that he was entirely innocent or entirely right. Some of the documents were classified for up to thirty-three years afterwards. Amid the categories of common horror, there certainly had been something very special about Dresden.

During the years I was in Germany it was impossible to visit Dresden and ask questions on the spot. The city was 170 miles inside the Russian Zone of Occupation near the postwar borders of Poland and Czechoslovakia. I was able to visit in the West places as diverse as Strasbourg and Heligoland; I was able to see over the remains of Belsen – Bergen concentration camp; I was able to get into Berlin along the Autobahn the Christmas after the Russian block- ade was lifted; I even got back to Normandy to revisit Caen and the beaches where we had landed. But Dresden proved impossible until I was a civilian again and back in England. I was then writing freelance feature scripts for the BBC and in 1956 I put up the idea of a documentary programme on the Dresden raid. It was turned down.

In 1958, this time considering the idea of a book, with my wife I visited Dresden for the first time. Little of the city had then been rebuilt but much of the rubble had been cleared away – ten million cubic metres of it – and so it was possible to look across miles of rough grassland intersected by cracked road surfaces still scarred by the bombs of 1945. This vast, empty space was what remained of the Altstadt, the mainly non-industrial 'Old Town' area of Dresden. Destruction here had been total. The acreage at a guess was less than that laid waste in Hamburg, but Hamburg was by far the larger city. Guidebooks later were to give the area of total destruction in the centre of Dresden as fifteen square kilometres. It was difficult to compare directly with Hamburg because the distinction between total destruction and severe damage was less clear-cut in the Hanseatic seaport; for Hamburg the two grades lumped together amounted to an area of about 22 × 18 kilometres (say 14 miles × 12 miles of perhaps 80 per cent destruction). But it was not the actual area of devastation which had marked out Dresden as special.

In 1958 rebuilding had begun along the sides of the Altmarkt, the Old Town Square, and this too was still scarred, the flagstones bearing the marks of their disturbance. It made me shudder a little to look at it, for I now knew what had happened on this spot during the raids and in the following week. I had talked to people who had seen it thirteen years before. No one then knew what the casualties had been. I was given a number of estimates, each one accompanied by a statement as to how it was arrived at; they varied widely and it was obvious that certain peculiar circumstances would make a firm figure impossible ever to attain. In any case the actual figures, even if known, would not have been very important. The massacre at Dresden was marked out by other factors as a special event. However, it seemed that I had wasted my time, as I could not in 1958 interest a publisher in a book on the subject.

Then in 1963, five years later, David Irving produced his book, *The Destruction of Dresden*. This created a tremendous furore. Undoubtedly there were still some sensitive nerves about. However, Mr Irving's approach was so historically balanced and precise that I felt he had failed to bring out to the full the terrible truths of the story as I had understood it. Even so, some of his many critics accused him of writing at length of horror for horror's sake, particularly as regards the aftermath of the raids. To me, this reaction seemed to show either that the critics had failed utterly to realize what had actually happened in Dresden or, alternatively, that the spectacles it conjured up were simply too shocking to be borne.

What happened there is not for the squeamish to read, although the worst naturally enough will never be told. The people who could have told it died that night: not quickly, and not kindly, but in the most horrible ways. Yet there were some who welcomed the raid − to them, because of their special circumstances, the tragedy was a personal good fortune. Others, again, saw it as their revenge. To many airmen, flying four miles above, the burning city was just a spectacle of awe-inspiring beauty; it was hard to conceive of the loveliness as being a furnace fuelled by people.

The story of Dresden can be told only in the testimony of survivors. Barely half of those who lived through the raids were residents; they consisted mainly of women, children and old people. As many again were refugees trekking in from the overrun lands in the East. There were Allied prisoners of war, also on the march towards the city, or actually working in Dresden for their German masters. And there were wounded soldiers from the battlefronts, some helpless and immobile, directed to one or other of the hospitals in Dresden, many of which were in newly-requisitioned buildings all over the city, such as schools. All these people, together with the crews of the bombers who would attempt to destroy them, were either in or converging on Dresden at the material time. That time was the evening of Tuesday, 13 February 1945. In Dresden it was Fasching night − Carnival Night − when in normal times children dressed up and the adults took a holiday. The Russians were still seventy miles away from a graceful and as yet virtually intact city. It was winter and very cold.

For the Allied war leaders what was plotted for that night and the following morning was to be one of a series of terrible blows struck against German cities on the Eastern Front. Appropriately, the scheme was code-named *Thunderclap*.

Dresden 1945:

The Devil's Tinderbox

1
Thirty-Five Years
CHRISTMAS 1944 – CHRISTMAS 1980

> Maikäfer flieg',
> Mein Vater ist im Krieg,
> Meine Mutter ist in Pommerland,
> Pommerland ist abgebrannt,
> Maikäfer flieg'.
>
> Maybird, fly away,
> My Father's gone to war,
> My Mother she's in Pomeria,
> Pomeria with lance and brand,
> Is burnt,
> There's no hope here.
>
> — Song of the Thirty Years War

Marianne had been twelve years old that last Christmas of the war, a white Christmas then in Breslau, the capital of Silesia, as it was now in Bergisch-Gladbach near Cologne, where she lived with her husband and family in their new house out in the country. We were staying with them for a few days on our way into what I had still to drill myself into calling the 'DDR' (short for German Democratic Republic). It was 1980, and thirty-five years had passed since that Christmas Eve, which was cold, with continual falls of snow. To a child's eyes, Silesia had been still untouched by the war. This was the last normality Marianne was to know.

She was taken to church that day by her parents. It was

crowded. She sensed that the grown-ups were subtly different; there was something in the air which she couldn't understand. No one in England would understand it, because nothing like this had been known there since 1545, and even then the events were on a limited scale and confined to parts of the South Coast. One would have to go back 900 years for anything like a parallel and 1500 years for a more exact one.

Marianne's father was a businessman and they were well off. Nevertheless, there were certain constraints even in the home. Her father was not a member of the Party, and used some of his many contacts to help Jews. In Nazi Germany, that put him on a knife edge all the time, having to watch every word. Marianne was of course in the *Bund deutscher Mädchen* (BDM), the compulsory Party organization for schoolgirls, where any incautious phrase might be heard by the wrong people.

After Christmas, her feeling of childhood security disappeared. On Sunday morning, 21 January 1945, she had to leave her home for what proved to be the last time. A bitter cold of minus 23 degrees Celsius locked in the countryside. As her father drove out of Breslau to the house in the country where her aunt and a grandmother lived, she saw that many people were leaving, in trucks, in carts, on foot. The climate was not kind to the weak. Beside the road already were many dead people and animals. After he had delivered his children to their relatives, her father had to return to Breslau, which Gauleiter Hanke had declared to be a 'fortress' in the path of the Russian advance. Two days later, Marianne in her new home outside the city heard the growl and thunder of the Russian guns. Then she too, with the old ladies, became a refugee, moving south and west before the oncoming Red tide.

It was different thirty-five years later, for my wife and I

were moving in the opposite direction, towards Dresden, which is on the direct routes by road and rail to Breslau. But we could not have reached Breslau even if we had wanted, because the frontiers of Europe had been redrawn by Stalin, Roosevelt and Churchill at the fateful conference held at Yalta in the USSR between 4 and 11 February 1945. Breslau was now a Polish city, renamed Wroclaw (and the eastern third of Poland was now Russian territory). And the new Polish border with East Germany was closed, not just to Western visitors but to Poles and East Germans alike. The conflict between the Polish government and the free trade unions had just begun and the Western press was full of speculation as to a possible invasion of Poland by the massed Russian armoured divisions stationed both in Russia and in the DDR. In one of the 'war maps' printed in a prominent Sunday newspaper, the rear end of a Russian tank marked '1st Guards Tank Army' was square across the location of the town near Dresden which we were headed for.

I had judged that military action was unlikely during the period we would be in Germany, nearly three weeks covering Christmas and the New Year 1981. But one couldn't be sure, and if one is wrong in a guess of this magnitude, one is bound to be very specially wrong. However, the only trouble we had was on the second day in the DDR when a Russian officer tried (unsuccessfully) to barge past us to the head of the money-exchange queue in the bank.

The tension brought about by the internal Polish crisis was extremely useful for my research, however. I am as keen as the next man on unearthing dusty documents, but I wanted much more than that. I had decided to stay, not in Dresden − which has been rebuilt in a way which, although acceptable, gives no idea of what it was like before the RAF erased it − but in a nearby town which had survived the war with its old Saxon and Slav buildings intact. Nothing could rival the Dresden which had been lost, for that had been a showpiece of Europe, a 'Florence on the Elbe', but to live in a similar old town still more or less preserved might give some of the essential atmosphere, and one would get to know the people — I found the Saxons very likeable. A second factor was climate and weather. We were making our visit at about the same time of the year as when many of the important events connected with the decisions to bomb Dresden had taken place, and within about five weeks of the anniversary of the raid itself. The weather pattern did repeat itself, surprisingly warm around Christmas, but with bitter cold marked by heavy snowfalls in January. This was exactly the weather, and very close to the place, where that terrible 'Frostbite March' of the refugees and prisoners of war had begun thirty-five years before. Above all, because of the fear at the back of the mind, that the crisis might result in one's being trapped deep behind the Iron Curtain, a factor one tends to forget was made personally plain. The Nazi regime had ruled only partly by fanaticism and clever propaganda; it had also ruled through fear. One needed to understand that by experiencing it.

All this had come about merely because of a change of fashion in the media. In 1980, and subsequently in 1981, everyone in Britan was doing air raids. Books, radio, TV, museum exhibitions — all recalling air raids. It was not a bad idea, because the world was now peopled largely by youngsters who had never experienced an air raid and could hardly imagine what it was like. Twenty years before, one could rely on there being a great deal of background knowledge available to your audience. But in the 1980s, most would be innocent; they would have to be told everything, including the awesome fact that while bullets and bomb splinters bounce off the cast-iron-and-cardboard characters who re-enact the war nightly on their screens, in real life those shining heroes would be little heaps of bloodied rags in the gutter.

Quite early, a publisher asked me to keep my eyes open for an air raid subject: either a 'new' one which had never been done as a book before, or an old one which had been indifferently done or could be treated in a different way. As I was then in the middle of writing something else, this was an irksome chore, but dutifully I labelled a file 'Bombers'.

The story I really wanted to write was Dresden. It wasn't just an air raid. It had shape and inevitability. Everything appeared to conspire against the doomed city. It was like one of those old-fashioned films in which you see the heroine tied, screaming, to the railway track while the great big engine thunders nearer and nearer. Only, in this case, there was no hero to dash out and cut her bonds at the last moment. Instead . . .

2
'Frostbite March'

'The icy days pass slowly, sometimes it's cold, and at other times it's very cold. The world seems to have been forever under a carpet of snow and ice, gripped by winter for all time. The skies are sullen and snow-laden; the mail doesn't come through for days, sometimes weeks; but always the Doodlebugs go over, headed for Antwerp.'
– Entry for 23 January 1945 in author's diary, Holland

Reichsminister Speer, Hitler's architect and now head of German armament production at the height of the Allied bomber offensive, was riding in the car of a diesel train headed away from Berlin towards Bonn in the Rhineland. It was 16 December 1944, and what he and most of the leadership regarded as Hitler's last card, not a good one, had been played that morning in the mist-shrouded hills and valleys of the Belgian Ardennes. Along ninety miles of what the Americans rated as a quiet and unimportant front, three German armies, apparently conjured out of nowhere, had attacked. They were the 6th SS Panzer, the 5th Panzer, and the 7th Infantry. They constituted virtually the last mobile reserve that Germany had, the only force that could hold up the imminent Soviet offensive in the East or block the impending British, Canadian and American attacks to gain the banks of the Rhine. Speer's task was to help Marshal Model, the reluctant commander of the German offensive, with improvised armaments, for everything from bridging material to fuel was either in short supply or blocked by chaotic traffic conditions.

Speer knew that Hitler dared not fail with this gamble,

that it was in truth the last sensational card he had to play. If his mobile reserve, his three intact, unengaged armies, were dissipated without a decisive victory in the West on the scale he had achieved over the French and British in 1940, then nothing could stop the enemy from flooding into Germany from both sides. The Russians would overrun the Silesian coalfields, the Americans would neutralize the Ruhr. At that point, Germany would cease to be a major power, and three genuinely major powers would dismember her. As armaments minister, Speer could work out better than most how long that might take. Somewhere between four and eight weeks after the loss of the last coalfields.

So, as they came forward through the dawn mists, creeping through the woods, seeping around and between the sparsely-manned American forward posts in small parties of thirty or forty, Model's soldiers carried their Führer's last hope with them.

That same morning, Field Marshal Montgomery, commanding the British and Canadian 21st Army Group, published an appraisal of the military situation which began: 'The enemy is at present fighting a defensive campaign on all fronts; his situation is such that he cannot stage major offensive operations. At all costs he has to prevent the war from entering a mobile phase; he has not the transport or the petrol that would be necessary.'

That day, five-star General Eisenhower (who had been promoted to that rank the day before) had an important engagement in Paris — he had to attend the wedding of his chauffeur, Micky, to a WAC.

Meanwhile, the advance elements of some 200,000 Germans had ruptured the American Front and penetrated deeply. The 106th Infantry Division, which was just out from the States and had never been in action before, lost two of its three regiments. Many of its soldiers were cut off well behind the German spearheads and eventually rounded up. Among them was a young German-American infantry scout called Kurt Vonnegut, who had a destiny as a novelist. When he wanted to write a book on the bombing of Dresden and inquired of the US Air Force for details as to who had ordered it, why, and with what result, he was brushed off by a statement that the raid was still top secret. Mr Vonnegut wondered from whom the secret was being kept, because part of his destiny as a writer had been to witness the massacre at first hand. Nevertheless, he wrote his book and called it *Slaughterhouse-Five*, because that was where he was during the raid – in the Dresden slaughterhouse just north-west of the great Friedrichstadt hospital complex.

Vonnegut's path to Dresden had led first through a POW camp, Stalag IVb at Mühlberg on the Elbe. Claus von Fehrentheil's road to Dresden had begun on the same day as the attack in the Ardennes, 16 December. But his unit, a heavy reconnaissance company of a Waffen-SS division, had been fighting the Russians near Pasto in northern Hungary. As commander of the company, he had been holding an 'Orders' group when Russian shells began to fall. They took shelter behind a wrecked Russian tank, but Claus was wounded by splinters. The wounds were comparatively light, so he was able to get into his car to be driven to the nearest first aid post. On the way there, the Russians put in a surprise attack, and the car went into the ditch. Claus' right hip was now torn open and his spine broken. He was completely disabled, and after a spell in a field hospital he was evacuated to Dresden.

He did not know the city at all, nor could he see out of the window, but the nurses told him that he was in a converted school, the Vitzthumschule, which had been turned into a temporary military hospital, like many more. He assumed that it was in the centre of Dresden, because the nurses said one could see the Frauenkirche from the window of the room he was in. Claus took their word for it. It would be a long time before he would walk again.

By Christmas Eve, everything had been decided on both fronts. In Hungary, the German counter-attack to relieve Budapest had failed; the Hungarian capital had been encircled by Soviet forces. In Belgium, the German offensive had stalled about three miles short of the Meuse and its key bridges; the projected drive for the Allied main supply port of Antwerp would now never take place. The year, after all, *was* 1944 and not 1940, as Hitler had hoped.

As Speer noted, he had great good fortune with the weather, which to begin with was so bad that it grounded the Allied air forces. But there was a severe petrol shortage and traffic chaos on the narrow, badly-graded roads. After three years of Hitler as commander-in-chief, the German army had lost its famous talent for organization, he wrote. On 23 December, Field Marshal Model told Speer that the offensive had definitely failed. In spite of that, Hitler had ordered its continuance, but Speer knew for certain that the war was over; all that resistance could produce now was a slight delay in the date of enemy occupation.

Next day, 24 December, the American counter-offensive began. And on 8 January 1945, Hitler ordered that the last German salient won at such cost in the Ardennes should be withdrawn.

On 12 January 1945 the long-awaited blow fell in the East. The head of German intelligence for the Soviet Front, General Gehlen, had accurate information on the build-up of the opposing Red Army formations. He had reported that the Germans would be outnumbered in tanks by seven to one, in infantry by eleven to one, and in artillery by twenty to one. On some parts of the front, the Russians had been able to mass 380 guns to the mile and bring forward adequate ammunition supplies. The Soviet generals were learning how to organize mass movements of men and material. With Stalin looming behind them, waiting for the results he needed to bargain with at the Yalta Conference in a few weeks' time, they would use them ruthlessly, at terrible cost in Russian lives.

Hans B, a major in a Panzer Grenadier division which had fought at Salerno against the Americans and British as well as on the Eastern Front, gave his Knight's Cross and gold watch to his fiancée to keep, telling her that no one who resisted could survive. The Russians would attack again with boys as young as thirteen in their assault waves, unarmed and ordered to pick up the rifles of the fallen as they went over them, and women and girls, too, in their teens, also unarmed; all coming on in mass 'human sea' advances to overwhelm the Germans, but being mown down in their thousands first. A deeply convinced Catholic who thought of Hitler as Antichrist, this slaughter of the innocent on the Eastern Front made him sick. War was one thing; killing unarmed children another. It was an offence against God. But he would have to do it, not for Hitler, but for Germany. His premonition was right; he did not return.

The Russian group of armies called the First Ukrainian Front, commanded by Marshal Konev, already had a bridgehead over the Vistula at Baranov. After a colossal bombardment, Konev burst through the German 4th Panzer Army in a matter of hours, and let loose the 3rd and 4th Guards Tank Armies towards Breslau and Dresden. Then, to the north, other human tides were loosed. Marshal Zhukov's First Belorussian Front crashed forward in their drive for Berlin. Northwards again, the Second Belorussian Front took the rolling tide of battle as far as the shores of the Baltic sea at Swinemunde. From the Baltic almost to Czechoslovakia, the Red fronts rolled into Germany.

The three German armies which, held centrally, might have slowed or halted that onrush had been wasted in the Ardennes, from which their remnants were now withdrawn. General Hasso von Manteuffel, who commanded one of them, concluded that the American and British new year offensives had not been halted, merely delayed, and that there was no longer any chance of holding the decisive Rhine front against them. On 8 February, a few weeks later than planned, the combined British – Canadian attack began.

The end was now in sight, and it was against this background that terrible events were ordained and brought about by high authorities. The purpose of all the parties was political: they were manoeuvring to win the peace for themselves. Stalin had refused to suggest a date for the next 'Big Three' Conference until just before Christmas 1944, when he knew that his armies were almost ready to sweep through Poland into the German homeland. He suggested the end of January 1945, and the period finally agreed was 4 –11 February.

Among the consequences of the Russian offensive was the expulsion from Silesia of some 4 million people. To those who were engulfed by the event, the tragedy seemed to be on so great a scale as to be unbelievable. There was no precedent, it was unheard of, impossible. And yet it was real, and happening to them.

Walter Thiel was a Wehrmacht officer married to a Breslau girl, Hilde. He had served in the First World War and also in the Polish campaign of 1939 and the French campaign of 1940 as an artillery officer. But in 1941, owing to deafness, he had been down-graded 'GV' and transferred to the Standartbattalion, Breslau. This unit was made up of war-wounded men unfit for the rigours of life in a field unit.

The Thiels had three young children. In addition, they were also looking after Hilde's father, nearly eighty years of age, and her mother, who was also elderly and semi-crippled. This group of people, among many, many others, felt the impact of the battle wave from the East, driving the refugees before it through dark winter days and nights. Walter Thiel recollected:

Until 1944 Breslau had been spared any kind of war activity, and this fact gave it the nickname — 'Air Raid Shelter of the Reich'. When on 12 January the Russians broke out of the Baranov bridgehead, which was the last line of defence on Polish soil, turned up a week later on Silesia's borders, the war became bitter reality for Breslau. From mid-January onwards, overcrowded trains, jammed to the roof by confused, totally exhausted masses of women and children from the conquered lands in the East, entered Silesia. Along the iced-up roads many other refugees were moving in cars, with sledges, and other vehicles towards Breslau, which they believed to be safe. The anxious questions of the townsfolk themselves, about whether Breslau would be declared a fortress or an open town, was answered by an order from the Gauleiter, Karl Hanke, that all civilians, with the exception of men capable of bearing arms, should leave. 'Breslau has become a fortress and will be defended to the last house,' he declared.

On all roads leading to the railway stations masses of people were in flight, panting and sweating under the loads of their emergency packs. Train after overcrowded train moved off, at first going only as far as western Silesia, later as far afield as Saxony and Bavaria. But there were still hundreds of thousands of people in the town when the ground began to tremble with the distant drumfire of the enemy guns. Then on 20 January, to the horror of the entire population, the street loudspeakers blared out: 'All women and children are to leave the city on foot in the direction of Opperau-Kant.'

We were in the middle of a severe winter. The Oder was completely frozen, the temperature was now down to 20 degrees below zero, and yet thousands of young and old women with prams, sledges and little carts were moving along the snow-covered streets into a freezing winter's night. The human cost of this unprepared exodus has never been counted. For towndwellers the ordeal was especially severe, and in particular it was women and children who died. The ditches on both sides of the roads were choked with corpses, mainly of children who had frozen to death and been abandoned there by their mothers. The horror of those nights can be matched only by what happened at the same time in East Prussia. Roughly two thirds of the population followed the orders of the Gauleiter to leave the city. I obeyed, too, as far as my family was concerned.

Hilde Thiel recalled

On the morning of 20 January we could already hear the dull growling of the Russian guns and from nine o'clock onwards the loudspeakers were busy urging all women and children to leave the town. I hurriedly dug through all the contents of the cupboards, filling rucksacks and suitcases with the most necessary items. Silver and other valuables were no longer important. In 20 degrees below zero we loaded the luggage on the sledges. There wasn't a word of protest from the children, but the oldest girl went back into the house and fetched her warm featherbed. Grandpa, nearly eighty, groaned. An uncle shook his head at this exodus of ours into uncertainty. To my dear dressmaker I said: 'Take from our cupboards what you can use yourself,' and then we left to catch a tram to the station.

Luckily, her husband was able to help with the journey, for there were milling crowds at the station, mostly country-folk, who were standing, sitting or lying around in spite of the bitter cold, too far gone to care. There were no trains to be seen — the tracks between the crowded platforms were empty and bare in the bright moonlight. The waiting thousands looked anxiously at the sky for the first sight of enemy planes. Instead, there came an unscheduled train which stopped. Walter Thiel literally forced his family and their luggage on to it, fighting a way through the press of people. A bitter parting followed, for Walter was one of the defenders of Breslau and could not go with them.

Hilde had intended to seek sanctuary with relatives in the Riesengebirge, but when she got there found that no ration cards would be issued if she stayed; refugees had to keep moving. So they continued, having to change trains amid terrific crowds many times, once getting a lift on an army field kitchen drawn by oxen driven by two soldiers. Always there was the problem of accommodation for the night, for it was death to stay outside in the bitter weather. Always they were kindly received, and once they were invited to share the hosts' marriage bed. Other people were worse off − Hilde saw one poor mother with nine children to control while changing trains amid the milling, frightened crowds pushing and shoving; she had tied them together with a rope, so that none would get separated or lost. Her grandfather found the strain too much and was beginning to lose his reason; an unpleasant incident with some Japanese may have helped. He was very weak indeed, and Hilde was advised to find some village where food could be had more easily than in the towns, in which to wait out to the war's end. One village in particular was recommended to her − Rosendorf. In spite of attacks by low-flying aircraft which she thought were British, Hilde at length reached this place and was taken in by an Elbe-skipper. The village was not far from the capital of Saxony − Dresden.

Meanwhile, in beleaguered Breslau, soon to be encircled by the Russians, Walter Thiel had been given command of a half-battalion of fortress troops. He now had 400 men under him. Two hundred were German soldiers and all of a low medical category because of wounds or some natural affliction; the other 200 were Italian soldiers who had been forced into the German army when Italy changed sides. All the entrances to the town were barricaded with overturned trams, railway sleepers, large slab stones, even cobblestones; and whole streets were supposed to be blown up to give good fields of fire, on the orders of the Gauleiter. An artillery officer in two world wars, Walter Thiel judged the proceedings somewhat dilettante: 'It was obvious the barricades could easily be overrun by enemy tanks, but the Party wanted to do something. They felt they were in competition with the army. Gauleiter Hanke, who was as ambitious as he was faithless, wished to impose his will upon the officer who was Town Commandant at that time.'

As a measure to achieve this, he ordered a red poster to be put up throughout Breslau, announcing that the Burgermeister, Dr Spielhagen, was to be shot without trial on the Ringstrasse in front of the statue of Frederick the Second, for trying to leave his post without orders. 'Whoever is afraid of an honourable death must die in shame!' declared the Gauleiter. The two men had known each other for years but there had been serious disagreements between them. Now they were ended.

Reichsminister Albert Speer was touring the Eastern Front at this time, and spoke to Hanke before the Soviet troops closed in. Hanke said emotionally that he was prepared to see Breslau destroyed, if he thought it would fall into enemy hands. Six months before that, with equal emotion, he had warned Speer never to inspect a certain concentration camp in Upper Silesia, for he had seen something there which he was not permitted to describe and which was simply indescribable. This camp must have been Auschwitz, one of the extermination centres.

In the testing time which was coming, three of the Gauleiters were to gain an infamous reputation. The conduct of the three men was to be almost identical, suggesting that the Party produced a certain type of brute at the top, and in some numbers. The trio on the East Front were Erich Koch in East Prussia, Karl Hanke in Lower Silesia, and Martin Mutschmann in Saxony. The latter had his headquarters in Dresden.

Not all the testimony of what happened in those days consists of the recollections of survivors. Sometimes there are letters and even postcards from the dead. In that chaos, the public services should not have functioned, but they did. The K family, living at Wiesbaden in the Rhineland, received a letter from their war-widowed daughter Erika, who was away in Silesia looking after the motherless children of a landowner. It had been written on 7 February and described how they had been fleeing before the Russian tanks for the last ten days. This was followed by a postcard date-marked Dresden, 12 February. On 13 February Erika's brother Udo was taking an evening walk in Wechmar and became aware of a continuous, distant roaring which seemed never to end — the sound of the bomber stream heading for Dresden. 'I didn't know that this had meant the hour of death for Erika,' he commented. Later on, he was able to fit bits of the jigsaw together, for she had not died alone. But it was to be twenty years before the last piece of that puzzle fell into place.

Erika's story began with the words: 'At last a written sign from me that I am still alive after ten days of wandering around and suffering.' She had lived on a large farm which employed a good many workers, and ran the household, which included a nanny and a children's nurse as well as the ordinary servants. On the day before they had come running into the house, blurting out an alarming story: 'We're surrounded by the Russians! All the roads have been cut!

We can't get away now. Tomorrow will be the day we die!'
Erika wrote:

At that moment, we all gave up hope. I cleared my conscience and,
together with everyone in the house, prayed halfway through the
night. As I was the centre of all this, I was surprised to find how
calm I was and fully prepared to see the Russians arrive at any
moment, for their tanks were already rattling along the main road.
But I was desperately sorry for the children.

In her anxiety to save them, other people's feelings and
fears were ignored, and the farmworkers went on strike.
They refused to bring in the horses which Erika required to
pull the carts in which she and her farmer's family and their
luggage would ride. All she managed to find were some
carthorses which were too light for their task and she even
had to harness a riding horse to one wagon. While she and
her family were doing this, she wrote, the farm people were
shouting in unison: 'Make them bite the dust! Shoot them
dead! Don't let them go!' She went on:

Nobody offered to load the suitcases. Everybody wished the
plague on us. The reason being that we were going to save our
things rather than the people of the farm, a feeling for which one
cannot really blame them. The whole thing was a disgusting mess,
and in all this haste and darkness — for the Liegnitzer power
station was already in Russian hands — I could not explain it all
clearly to them. But to calm the people down, I eventually agreed
to take one family and their children. And thus we left with the
curses of the naturally desperate farm people following us, while
the rolling enemy tanks were shooting around us with a loud,
crashing noise, and the sky was dark red because of the fires of
Lüben (we learned afterwards that it was the Germans who had
fired the aerodrome).

Erika was still able to lament in her letter: 'What a lot
we had to leave behind because we were in such a hurry and

the cart so heavy and we so helpless, for there were no men to carry the heavy boxes we had packed.' More important for their survival was that the angry farmworkers had not loaded any oats or hay for the animals, the three horses and two ponies which pulled the wagons. Then, during a halt outside a town, their driver left them, vanishing without a word. A timely German counter-attack, which retook Lüben from the Russians, gave them time to get clear.

Having begun their trek on 28 January, Erika was able to write on 7 February:

And so now we have been moving through the country for ten days, like gypsies, going west. We overcame great difficulties, for we were without a driver for our five horses. The roads are hopelessly blocked. We begged for oats and hay at the farms we passed, a task which was mine and which so far has been reasonably successful, but the horses kept falling because of the snow and ice on the roads and are exhausted to the point of death. We have to have constant halts. Each evening, as far as sleeping quarters are concerned, so far we have been lucky. Very kind farmers took us in with loving care and sometimes put us into minute little rooms. I felt deeply moved by the kindness of those many dear people and it is only because of this vagabond life which I lead at the moment that I have got to know and really like our German farmers. It would be unthinkable to accept that these decent people should be destroyed by the Russian hordes.

Their party consisted of two men, one elderly, two big boys and four small children, a nanny, a children's nurse, and Erika herself. Shortly after the date of Erika's letter, they split up, having reached a town with a main station. On a postcard dated 12 February, Erika wrote her last message:

In [the town of] G, after we had listened to the latest Wehrmacht bulletins, the ground got too hot under our feet, and as the trekking in the cart is desperately horrible, three adults and four of the smallest children travelled by train, that is a slow train, towards

Thuringia. They were half-squashed by the masses of people and there was no question of any scheduled departures. B, with his two big boys, will follow on with the cart, and that will probably take him two or three weeks. I hope we will reach our goal alive and please write soon. I am dying of homesickness for some post from you. God bless. Kiss. ERIKA.

The party which reached the refuge of Dresden, travelling in unheated coaches with broken windows, consisted of the weakest: the four small children, the three women, and the oldest man, Nikolaus B. Later inquiries by a relative established that it was Nikko B who, unwittingly, prevented their leaving Dresden on 12 February. All refugee trains were carefully combed for males apparently capable of fighting, and Nikko was whisked away to a barracks. It took him only one night to get free, for he had excellent papers, and so on 13 February 1945 he arrived at the home of the family who were acting as hosts to this particular party of refugees. Their daughter, by great good fortune, actually worked as a railway guard and she was able to get them a separate compartment on a train due to leave Dresden main station that evening. She went herself and put them safely on the train, ready for their escape to the West, when the preliminary air raid warning was sounded. It was about 9.45 pm German time.

Other refugees who had reached Dresden intended to stay there rather than move on. One of these was Maria Rosenberger, who had fled from Breslau together with her employer, Herr Riedel, and his wife and children. They were heading for Dresden because Frau Riedel had worked for a family called Braune, who lived in Bergstrasse and might take them in. Maria decided to go with them because she herself had a sister living in Dresden. On the evening of 13 February, Maria and her sister had arranged to meet at a restaurant in the centre of the city. They were just preparing to leave when the sirens began to wail. With no further warning, the streets outside were lit up as if it were daylight. 'Ah,' said Maria's sister, 'they are setting up their Christmas Trees!'

Some of the refugees who arrived were sent straight to hospital. Annemarie Waehmann, who worked in a Dresden photographic laboratory and had contracted a skin disease, had been sent to the Friedrichstadt hospital complex not far from the main station, and made friends at once with a fifteen-year-old refugee girl, Hilde, who had been in transit with her mother, her two sisters and an aunt. They, however, had now been put into a refugee camp near the station, to wait until the doctors had diagnosed Hilde's illness. There were four girls in the sickroom, and they were all playing cards that evening when the chilling howl of the sirens began. The nursing sisters began to run along the corridors shouting: 'Get dressed! Get dressed! Quickly, down to the cellar!' There was a great deal of hurrying and scurrying, as bedridden patients were helped into push chairs.

In the Vitzthumschule, a boys' school converted to an emergency military hospital, the lights had already been put out and the patients were trying hard to find a comfortable sleeping position. Claus von Fehrentheil, the SS Panzer officer wounded in Hungary in mid-December, found it particularly difficult. The wound near his right hip had become infected and inflamed, his spine had been fractured, and he had one leg in plaster. Nevertheless, he was drifting off to sleep when the sirens wailed the alarm. Russian prisoners of war who had volunteered for the work came into the sickrooms and began to carry the bedridden down to the small air raid shelter. The other patients had to stand or sit on the ground floor and the stairs leading down to it. There was no room in the shelter for them all, and in any case front-line soldiers instinctively disliked confined spaces. Their experiences made them value the ability to dodge dangers in the open.

That night, a Polish soldier, who had fought the Germans in Warsaw at the war's beginning in September 1939 and had witnessed the Luftwaffe's bombing of the Polish capital, was trying to sleep in a barn somewhere north of Hanover. The Germans were evacuating all the prisoner-of-war camps in the East, so that hundreds of thousands of ill-fed POWs were on the march westwards. This particular group of Polish officers had come from an Oflag in Pomerania. Now, chilled and starving, they could not sleep. Above them was an endless, vibrating roar as formation after formation of Allied bombers passed over towards some target in eastern Germany. The prisoners had a secret radio with them, and when they tuned to the BBC next morning, they learned that the target had been Dresden. They had no sympathy for Germans or German cities. To them, Dresden was a place to be knocked down because of its railway stations.

Jack Myers, who was a lot nearer to Dresden that night, had no sympathy either. He had been in the evacuation from Dunkirk in 1940, the retreat through Greece in 1941, had been wounded in Crete before that island fell to the Germans shortly after, and had been captured in June 1942 while with 64 Medium Regiment, RA, in the Western Desert. After a period in Italian POW camps, he ended up at Stalag VIIIb at Lamsdorf near Breslau. 'There are two sorts,' he recollected. 'Those who survive and those who don't. And I'm a survivor. I intended to live.'

He promoted himself to a local NCO rank, to avoid being sent out on work parties which sapped a man's strength. Even so, he was down to 8 stone by February 1945 (his present weight is 13½). Myers explained:

There was a feeling of perpetual hunger. We were badly fed, but I don't blame the Germans; they were a beaten nation then. We were kept alive only by the Red Cross. The Russian prisoners in and around our camp had no Red Cross parcels; they were in a very bad state. They told us about the concentration camps and because I was Jewish, I was worried about this. But I knew I was to live; I intended to.

Some time in January 1945 the camp was evacuated before the advancing Red army and the 'Frostbite March' began. Jack started off by pulling a small sledge with his kit on it – spare boots, a blanket, a few tins of food. The German guards stabbed the tins to let air in and make sure the food would have to be eaten soon and not hoarded for an escape attempt. It seemed to Jack that they marched for weeks.

A lot of blokes fell out, frozen by the sub-zero temperatures, or shot. I was afraid to take my boots off in case I was unable to put them on again. We looked for barns to shelter in. We fed on roots, grass, tulip roots perhaps. We boiled snow for water to drink. One spoonful of tea made a drink for fifty people. The weather cleared and my foot turned septic. A South African doctor put a drain tube in my heel, and I had to sit on a trolley pulled by a horse. I was taken to a railway siding, possibly Gorlitz or Jauer, I don't really remember. I wasn't so bad as I was making out to be. I remember my old sergeant-major saying: If you can sit down, sit down; if you can lie down, lie down. So I found a corner of the cattle truck to lie down in.

Nobody came near us. The truck moved a little, then it stopped, then moved again. It was closed, unheated, unventilated, with only a bucket at one end for sanitation. There were not three fit people in that truck. I personally was not really conscious most of the time. We'd not had too much to eat for a long while. And for the last few days we'd not been fed or watered at all. Even the biggest lead-swingers were really sick now. It was freezing cold, no food, people dying. We didn't dehydrate because we could suck the snow and ice which entered the truck, although it was enclosed. We stacked the dead at one end, with a bit of no-man's-land in the middle near the doors. There were about eighty in all, of mixed nationalities, and I suppose about twenty or thirty died. The rest huddled together for warmth.

I heard bombs falling, getting bloody near, but didn't realize it was a colossal raid. The Poles and the Russians were in a bit of a panic. The British don't panic. But there was a bit of bad language from them. We were in marshalling yards. Somebody said it was Dresden, although there were no signs to say so, nothing to recognize; and nothing to do in the truck when the raid began, but count bombs.

Like Jack Myers, Rex Wingate too had been in Crete, but he was captured there a year before Jack went into the bag in the Western Desert. It made little difference in the end, for he also arrived at Lamsdorf and eventually passed through Dresden. But his experience was worlds away. As an optician, he was sent with another prisoner, Doctor Frank Haine, from Lamsdorf to the civilian internment camp at Kreuzberg, south of Breslau. The prisoners included Russians, Jews (with British passports, which protected them), a shipping director from Copenhagen, a violinist and a couple of chess-players. When the sound of the Russian guns could be plainly heard, a convenient breakdown in communications prevented Rex Wingate and Doctor Haine from being sent back to Lamsdorf to join the Frostbite marchers. Instead, they managed to be evacuated with all these special civilians. While being marched to Kreuzberg station, Rex noticed groups of girls standing on the street corners weeping, and he wondered if it was from fear of the Russians.

Doctor Haine's diary shows that the date was 24 January, and that although it was a goods train they boarded, they were given seats in a third-class carriage (not second-class, as Rex had remembered it). Their immediate destination was Breslau, where they spent the first night. It was then only five days since Gauleiter Hanke had ordered the women and children and old people of the city to march out on foot, so that they left their dead in the ditches for all the miles towards the West. The civilian internees spent the night in a gymnasium, before catching a train next morning for Austria. Dr Haine was confronted with an unusual case:

It was interesting for me, medically, as a man in his seventies developed acute retention of urine while we were in Breslau. The Commandant let me go out into Breslau to try to get a catheter. I finally found a busy TP, who was packing up to evacuate further west, and he lent me a catheter for an hour. I relieved the old boy, returned the catheter, and we set off by train. When we reached the outskirts of Chemnitz (on 25 January, I suppose) the acute retention was worse than ever, so I persuaded the Commandant to let me go with a guard and orderly in search of a catheter in Chemnitz. We bought a catheter at a chemist, and went to the main station to pick up the train, but it had not stopped on its way to Dresden.

Then followed what might pass for comedy in an early Hollywood film. The orderly got Dr Haine on to another train, then they both got off at a level crossing and the orderly spoke to the signalman, who said that their train had certainly gone on to Dresden. Dr Haine was now distinctly unhappy — marooned in the open in sub-zero weather with only the clothes he stood up in. The medical orderly then said: We will walk down the line after the train! After plodding along the track for a little while there ahead, sure enough, was the train, stopped for some reason, and they both got back on board.

As they neared Dresden, Rex Wingate saw flatcars covered with tarpaulins and speculated that they might be V2 rockets on their way from the factories. In Dresden, there were some signs of bombing, but not much (the Americans had made several daylight raids on railway targets). He remembered principally the huge main station of Dresden with its high, curved roof vaulted far above. This was to be the scene of events so terrible that witnesses find them eluding their powers of description. Rex Wingate escaped being involved in them by some nineteen days, by which time his train had reached Austria on its ten-day journey. But his reaction to news of the raid was that it had been vindictive, done out of desire for revenge. Jack Myers, on the other hand, was to write in 1967 that: 'It gave great pleasure to a group of POWs who were imprisoned in a cattle truck outside the city and who hadn't been fed for five days. Good luck to the raiders and the organizers of the raid.'

Eva Beyer was seventeen years old, the eldest of four children. They were a one-parent family, and both she and her mother had to go out to work. It had been a very poor Christmas. For decoration, three candles. For food, a few scones baked from bits and pieces. Chocolate was unknown, but there was a kind of sugary sweet. There was no coal for heating, only coaldust. But there was still gas. Eva only came home about once a week, because she worked at Junghanns bakery, some distance from the Old Town, and it was her job to get up at half past three every morning to deliver the bread. The baker was in prison, because he had given some of his bread to Polish prisoners of war. His place as the only man in the establishment had been taken by a crippled ex-soldier called Kurt. After she had delivered the early bread and rolls, Eva would clean the shop, dress the baker's children and give them breakfast; then make the beds, do some housework, cook the midday meal, and occasionally help in the shop. In her spare time, she had to give up so many hours per month to the Red Cross. And in January 1945 her Red Cross work had to be done at Dresden Hauptbahnhof, the city's main station.

There were so many refugees from Silesia and Wartegau. My task was to give them soup, bread, coffee and milk. What I saw there of suffering and misery can hardly be described. There were women, old men and children in a condition which was not human any more. After my first day of duty I couldn't eat for two days afterwards and I had nightmares, for I had never seen anything like that in my whole life, or thought that things like that were possible.

As I walked along the train to distribute food, a woman came and begged me for milk for her child. I asked her where her child was, and she unfolded her apron and showed me the child. I wasn't a doctor but I could see that the child was dead; it was stiff and blue and must have been dead for several days. When I told her that her baby was in heaven and wouldn't need any more milk, she replied: 'No, my baby is only sleeping. Please give me milk for my baby.' When we tried to take the baby away from her, so that we might bury it, she turned wild and screamed: 'My child is not dead! It's only hungry.'

We had many women like that. The children died of hunger and cold, and we buried many old people also, who could not stand the stress. For many days the refugees had to travel in goods trains with only a little straw on the floor. For days they didn't get any warm food or an opportunity to wash, so everything they wore was filthy and full of lice. After we had given them some food, we sent them to the showers and that was followed by a delousing action from head to foot. We also gave them clothes from the Winter Help organization. They cried for joy. Many said: 'Thank goodness, at last a warm meal and cleanliness again!' For many, we also had to bandage their feet, for almost all of them were suffering from frostbite. They had wrapped old rags and sacks round their feet in order to get a little protection from the cold. There were also women who gave birth on the journey. In most cases, the babies were dead or in very poor condition. After we had taken care of these people they were either put back on to the same train or put into a Nissen hut camp.

Once in mid-January I was on duty and the train which drew in had been bombed on the way. What I saw there was worse than horror. Not only were the people squeezed together in a goods train, but they had to suffer hunger and thirst and the bombs, too. There were so many injured on that train that we didn't know where to start. The screams and cries for help were almost unbearable. We could bandage their wounds and satisfy their thirst and hunger, but not their emotional suffering. Many died from their injuries, because our help came too late.

I bent down to a woman who had a baby at her breast, to see if I could help, for she was smeared with blood. She was dead but the child was alive. Beside her lay an old man. He was her father. He called: 'Annie, come and help me!' His arm was torn to pieces. When we told him that Annie was dead, he broke down completely and sat crying: 'What is going to happen to us? My son-in-law in the war, my daughter dead, a two-months-old baby, and an eight-year-old boy.' The old man clung to me, asking: 'What can we do next? We have lost our homes, our possessions. Oh God, what have we done, that we are being punished like this? Can there really be a God who allows such things?'

The wounded could only be given minimum bandaging, we were so short of supplies. The doctors were too busy. The hospitals were so overcrowded that we had to use schools to accommodate the refugees who had been injured. Children were searching for their parents, parents were searching for their children, there was constant calling and asking.

A boy of about nine years of age, holding his little four-year-old sister by the hand, asked me for food. When I asked him where his parents were, the boy said to me: 'Grandma and grandpa are lying dead in the carriage and Mummy is lost.' The children had no tears any more, they had reached the lowest point of human suffering. They now doubted the adults who could bring them so much grief and pain.

In one compartment we found a woman. She had twenty-three children with her, and not one of them was her own. She had buried her own child three weeks ago. Her child had died of cold and tonsillitis. I asked her where all those other children came from, and she told me that all these were children whose parents were lost or dead. 'After all, somebody has got to take care of them,' she said. These children were between the ages of seven months and thirteen years. You must see this in order to believe, but those children's faces were not the faces of children any more. They were the faces of people who have gone through hell. Starving, wounded, lice-ridden, in rags. And the most treasured thing they had, security and the love of their parents, they had lost. And that was their worst loss. This is something I would not wish on my worst enemy.

For Eva Beyer, February the 13th had started a day like any other. Get up at 3.30 in the morning, do the last washing-up at 7 o'clock at night, and in bed by 8.15. In the building which housed the bakery lived five other families. In all, there were eleven women and six children, with the wounded soldier, Kurt, the only man. This was fairly representative of the city's population in general, for most of the able-bodied men were away at the war. It was Eva who gave the alarm that night, and woke them all up.

I couldn't go to sleep straight away. I must have had a hunch. I can't tell exactly the time when I had to go to the toilet. This toilet was off the staircase outside the flats and had a window. Then I saw a green light shine through the window. What was this? When I opened the door, I could see what it was. The 'Christmas Trees' were in the sky. As I went to warn the other people in the building, the full alarm sounded without the preliminary warning. I ran through the whole house, calling out: 'Alarm! Alarm!' and waking everyone up. The bombs were already falling.

The refugee trains had continued to come in from the East. The main station was packed with them, the platforms swarming with haggard and hungry people. Dresden's normal population of about 600,000 had now swollen to at least one million. One could hardly move in the streets without falling over wretched 'trekkers' sitting hopelessly on their suitcases and packs, too tired to go on. And they, too, in the main were the women, the children, the old and the weak. The men were at the front or in the factories, and there were hardly any factories in the centre of Dresden.

3
Bombs Away!

IDEAS OF AIR POWER: 1918 –1945

Dresden, the seventh largest city in Germany and not much smaller than Manchester, is also far the largest unbombed built-up area the enemy has got. In the midst of winter with refugees pouring westwards and troops to be rested, roofs are at a premium, not only to give shelter to workers, refugees and troops alike, but to house the administrative services displaced from other areas. At one time well known for its china, Dresden has developed into an industrial city of first-class importance, and like any large city with its multiplicity of telephone and rail facilities, is of major value for controlling the defence of that part of the front now threatened by Marshal Koniev's breakthrough.

The intentions of the attack are to hit the enemy where he will feel it most, behind an already partially collapsed front, to prevent the use of the city in the way of further advance, and incidentally to show the Russians when they arrive what Bomber Command can do.

– from an internal RAF memo, 1945, 'Review of the work of Int I'.

Miles Tripp was a bomb aimer. The map of Europe on the briefing room wall showed their Squadron's track as a long red ribbon beginning in Suffolk and zig-zagging over France and Germany between heavily-defended areas to end at Dresden. A round trip of 1,600 miles, more than nine hours' flying. As a target, Dresden was totally unknown to the RAF, and so Tripp felt almost cheerful; the city could hardly be ringed by the sort of deadly gun and fighter defences which made the Ruhr and Berlin so dangerous.

When the briefing had ended, he felt much less happy. The crews had been told that until lately Dresden had been comparatively unimportant, but now the advance of the Russian army had swollen the population of the city with a million refugees. Conditions in Dresden were chaotic and what was planned was 'a panic raid adding confusion and disrupting communications'. Tripp had a vision of an old newsreel showing German Stukas dive-bombing French refugees on the roads in 1940; vividly, he could see them scatter as the bombs fell. This picture of horror was to determine what he was to do with his own bombs that night. Even that still left him feeling guilty, and he was to write two books about his experiences, one of them in the form of a novel (as Vonnegut was to do also).

Brian S. Blades was flight engineer in a Lancaster of 460 (Australian) Squadron. During a newspaper controversy in 1967, he wrote to the *Sunday Express* that he well remembered some of the phrases used in the briefing he attended: 'Bull in a China Shop', 'Virgin Target', and 'Intelligence reports thousands of refugees streaming into the city from other bombed areas'. Aircrews, he said, had not relished that particular target.

RAF aircrews were volunteers recruited from all over the world, and when the war ended they dispersed back to their homes in Canada, the Caribbean, Australia, South Africa, New Zealand; it was rare for crews to keep in touch and come together again for a reunion. No. 75 (New Zealand) Squadron was an exception. In 1978 survivors came together at Cambridge, many having travelled from the far side of the globe. Four of them, however, lived in southern England between Southampton and Brighton; and three of them had been crew members of the same aircraft, Lancaster AA-P. They were Peter Goldie the rear gunner, Roy Akehurst the wireless operator, and Paul Hill the flight engineer. The fourth man, a mid-upper gunner in another Lancaster of the squadron, was Ken Moore; he was a school chum of Peter Goldie, whose RAF career had marched with his over a period of years in the most extraordinary way. They were all to be over Dresden at a particular time on a certain night, but that was not what they had joined up for; indeed, they had been recruited in very different days, when Bomber Command was (although they did not know it) weak and ineffective. They were all so young then that it was not until just before Christmas 1944 that they saw their names for the first time up on the battle order and flew their first operation. They were all sergeants and their pilots were New Zealanders. AA-P was flown by Flight Sergeant Egglestone while Ken Moore's Lancaster was piloted by Flying Officer Flamank. The New Zealanders were 'fabulous lads' in their British crews' opinion.

Ken's father was a Portsmouth newsagent. In 1938, when Ken was about thirteen and was going to Copnor Road School, the teacher came in one day with a new boy and, unusually, asked Ken to show him the ropes. The newcomer was Peter Goldie and they became friends immediately and walked to school together each day until Peter and his family moved out of the area. Then in 1940 came the daylight bombing of Portsmouth and in late 1940 and early 1941 the night blitzes. Ken lost friends.

In 1942, the 'dirty time' for Bomber Command, as he put it, Ken's sister was going out with Terry, an RAF air gunner, who occasionally stayed with them. Ken can still remember trying on Terry's uniform, with its single-wing 'AG' badge. Four or five months later, Terry was killed. 'From that time on, all I wanted to be was an air gunner,' Ken said. 'And having experienced the raids, I'd rather be on top than underneath.'

In the same year, 1942, Ken went away to become a cabin boy on an army motor launch at Weymouth. Then he joined the Air Training Corps and went back to Portsmouth for a time as a police messenger. Now he began to write verse about the war. One of the most moving poems was written after a visit to the RAF cemetery at Thorney Island, where he saw that there were Luftwaffe graves as well as British, but there were no wreaths or posies to mark the German dead. Most tragic of all, or so it seemed to him, was one German grave lacking identification. When he revisited the spot thirty years later, he was glad to see that the single word 'unknown' on that cross had now been replaced by the man's name.

At that time, as I well remember, an air gunner's life was supposed to be short indeed. Nevertheless, Ken volunteered at the earliest possible moment, when he had reached 17½ years of age, and passed his test. As soon as he was 18½, he was able to join the RAF Volunteer Reserve; in June 1944, when he was nineteen he became an air gunner, and by the time he flew his first operation, on 13 December 1944, he was 19½.

During this period he had met Peter Goldie again, while acting as a police messenger. One day he was riding a bike down a road in Portsmouth, when he met Peter, whom he had not seen for several years, cycling the other way. 'What are you up to?' asked Ken. 'I'm a plumber's mate,' was the reply. 'I've volunteered for the Air Force,' said Ken. 'Strange,' said Peter, 'so have I, I'm going as an air gunner.' 'So am I,' replied Ken. The only difference was in the date, Peter following a little after Ken in the tortuous succession of training courses which led to a squadron. The danger started before then, for there were a number of gruesome fatalities in training. But the road for them both led to Dresden and for Peter Goldie to Hiroshima also, when just after the war he was to be stationed with an RAF unit a few miles from the atom-bombed city in Japan. Dresden and Hiroshima, the two terrible names of the air war.

In sheer numbers of dead, including civilian dead, the

battles of Leningrad, Stalingrad and Warsaw may have taken far greater toll. Hitler's death camps certainly did, and doubtless Stalin's camps also. But all these slaughters occurred over a long period of time, often years. What was special about certain air raids was that they virtually extinguished a city at one blow. All over in at most a few hours. And what accomplished this, regardless of whether the weapons used were 'conventional' or nuclear, was the raising of a fire-storm. In Nagasaki, there was no fire-storm, and the casualties were far less. There was no fire-storm in Berlin, although there was one in Hamburg.

Great massacres indeed there had been in history before (and were to be again in the postwar years), with millions hacked to death. But the instantaneous fire which struck from heaven, that alone was typical of twentieth-century technology at peak efficiency. It would have been impossible earlier in the war.

One could say that Dresden was a legacy left over from the Great War of 1914–18. The city was to die from the ideas which were conceived at that time. One might even indicate a date – 13 June 1917. That morning, a clerk in what was soon to become the Air Ministry building in London looked out of his window and saw what seemed like 'a shoal of little silver fish darting about miles up in the sky'. Another witness thought the resemblance was rather to 'large white butterflies' pinned against the cloudless blue of a summer day. There were eighteen of them up there – twin-engined Gothas (three-man crew, bomb-load 660 lb, maximum speed 80 mph, ceiling 18,000 feet). London had been bombed before, usually by Zeppelins at night, but this was the first time the capital had been mass-raided by day. The inhabitants were caught by surprise – one 100 lb bomb fell into a school classroom in Poplar, where all the children were still at their desks, and slaughtered forty-six of them.

The furious reaction to the raid owed much to horror but equally perhaps to rage at the spectacle of a German aerial parade taking place over London in daylight apparently without any effective reply by guns or aeroplanes. Moscow had been burnt by the Russians, Washington burnt by the British, Paris besieged by the Germans, Berlin occupied by the French, Rome had been sacked many times, but London had been inviolate for 850 years.

On 7 July the Gothas came again − twenty-one of them this time − and dropped three tons of bombs. Fifty-four people were killed, 190 wounded, 27 per cent of them not by bombs but by the defending gunfire; much fewer than in the preceding raid, when no one had thought to take cover. It seemed that the Germans could come and go at will over the capital.

In fact, it was for the last time by day. The Gotha cycle repeated the pattern of the Zeppelin raids: first, bold daylight raids, then a retreat to the cover of darkness, finally, no raids of consequence. Attrition caused by bad weather as much as by improved defences defeated the attackers. In all, only thirty tons of bombs were dropped on London during the whole of the First World War, far less than was dropped by the Allies on unfortunate French and Belgian towns behind the German lines in attempts to hit military transport targets. However, among the momentous results of the London daylight attacks was the setting up of a committee under the South African General Jan Smuts to consider air defence and the creation of the Independent Air Force, a body equipped with the British equivalent of the Gotha, under the command of General 'Boom' Trenchard.

The Smuts Report was futuristic and visionary: 'The day may not be far off when aerial operations with their devastation of enemy lands and destruction of industrial and populous centres on a vast scale, may become the principal operations of war, to which the older forms of military and naval operations may become secondary and subordinate.' It was not only in England that such ideas stirred. The Italian General Giulio Douhet came to the same conclusions, worked them out logically, and was to publish the results in a book, *Air Supremacy*, in 1921.

All this was theory, whereas the defeat of first the Zeppelins and then the Gothas had been fact: the Germans had learned a different lesson. Trenchard, however, became gradually converted to an overwhelming belief in the value of air power exercised independently. His own flying experience was small, his tenure of command of bombing operations lasted only for the last four months of the war, his aircraft were a handful of twin-engined, wood-and-canvas biplanes based in France and loaded with nothing larger than 250 lb bombs, sent out usually against short-range targets such as Metz or Cologne. Nevertheless, he was nurturing grandiose plans to raid Berlin with four-engined bombers as soon as the factories could deliver them. His postwar dispatches (ably analysed by Wing Commander H.R. Allen in *The Legacy of Lord Trenchard*, 1972) show that his intention was to create a large force of heavy bombers which would desolate Germany's cities one by one, and when the terrified inhabitants had fled to the nearest city which was still standing, the bombers would desolate that one too. And so a still greater tide of refugees would flee to another city further away. And so on. And *by this means alone,* the enemy would be forced to sue for peace.

Another result of the Gotha raids had been the creation of the Royal Air Force out of an amalgamation of the army's Royal Flying Corps and the Royal Naval Air Service. The air arm was now a separate service and this doctrine, that a bomber force could pass over fortified zones at will and then win a war on its own, was basic to its very existence.

As if this was not bold enough, the Trenchard doctrine in its purest form envisaged an air force without fighters. 'The aeroplane is not a defence against the aeroplane,' he declared. His reasoning was that the Imperial German air force in 1918 had failed to put up an effective defence against Trenchard's short-range raids by night, and this tended to reinforce his low opinion of the usefulness of the British fighters which had gone up against the Gothas in 1917 and 1918. Trenchard envisaged his bombers — and those of the enemy — passing each other like buses in the street, each intent on its own business. Whoever had the most bombers, would win.

This concept was bolder than it seems, for it implied special status for the air force. It was a claim that the invention of the aeroplane introduced a new factor into war which invalidated all the old principles by which for thousands of years land and sea forces had been governed. One basic principle in particular was the rule that the enemy's main forces must be engaged and defeated before victory could be exploited. Precedents without number could be advanced in defence of this thesis. The Second World War was to show that air forces were no exception to the rule.

However, in the interwar years and even until quite late in the Second World War, the air power theorists were able to avoid all hostile logic by claiming that air operations were a mysterious subject understood only by marshals of the RAF. If pressed hard, they might state their real case: that the object of air attack was the dislocation of the economy of the enemy nation, the production of utter terror and panic in the civil population, resulting in pressures on the hostile government to sue for peace. Armies, navies and indeed fighter aircraft would be irrelevant. Most of the bomber marshals of the Second World War had grown up at the feet of Trenchard, and this doctrine, sometimes in extreme form, sometimes watered a little, was how they saw the war to come and the war itself, when it arrived.

Some air power theorists went further. To defend the integrity of the RAF against the desire of the army and navy to split it up between them, it would be useful to prove that there would be deadlock on both sea and land, as in the First World War. Norman Macmillan in *The Chosen Instrument* (1938) argued that the tank was now 'outpointed' and that battle between opposed mechanized forces was impossible because of the effectiveness of new infantry anti-tank weapons. Likewise, the U-boat was no longer a menace because of new anti-submarine devices. Neither of these propositions, although logical, was in the least true. On the other hand, the same logic was not followed where the effectiveness of new defence techniques against the bomber was concerned, although in this case they proved to have substance.

The motives behind such arguments no doubt owed much to resentment felt at the scepticism of the older services for the ideas of the far-sighted men who had seen a dominant future for aviation in the pioneer days. It would be pleasant to demonstrate that a war could be waged, and won, entirely without the aid of an army or navy. Such claims would be useful also in squeezing out of the Treasury a larger share of the defence estimates for their service.

The older services became alarmed at what they believed to be an RAF plan to conduct a private war on untried principles: that is, against civil populations instead of against the enemy's armed forces. The arguments went on in private throughout the 1920s and 1930s (and were not generally available until 1980, when the Royal Historical

Society published Uri Bialer's study, *The Shadow of the Bomber: the Fear of Air Attack and British Politics, 1932– 1939*). In 1928, the Chief of the Imperial General Staff, Sir G. Milne, opposed Lord Trenchard's doctrine which he said 'put in plain English amounts to one which advocates unrestricted warfare against the civil population of one's enemy'. The Chief of the Naval Staff agreed and in 1932 an internal Admiralty memorandum stated: 'Air bombing is very aggressive and in no way defensive . . . The Army and the Navy do not want [bombers]. Only the Air Ministry wants to retain these weapons for use against towns, a method of warfare which is revolting and unEnglish.'

In the previous year, 1931, the Permanent Under-Secretary of State for Air had privately put the opposite view:

If we really want to work towards the abolition of war we should make it as brutal as possible. I am not sure that a dispassionate and logical review of the problem does not lead one to suggest that if you give the civilian population immunity you are likely not only to precipitate wars but to prolong the one started. This is not a doctrine which I think it would be wise to formulate publicly at the present time.

Instead, the Air Ministry dwelt publicly on the horrors which, it said, *enemy* bombers might visit upon the British civil population; and in this campaign they were joined by the pacifists who wanted complete disarmament. The RAF believed they could frighten the electorate into voting money for a larger air force, while the pacifists, with not dissimilar logic, believed that they could scare the public into giving up warplanes entirely.

A third kind of theorist was typified by E.F. Spanner, who in his book *The Broken Trident* (1929) began by saying:

'Our Air Ministry endeavour to curdle our blood every year by talk of poison gas and bombing attacks directed against the non-combatant population . . .' On the contrary, said Spanner, the real vulnerability of the British Isles was to precision air attacks against key targets, especially those concerned with the sea lanes.

This statement of the obvious was ignored by the air marshals, who did not believe that a defence was possible, only an offence against the enemy's women and children, although their spokesmen paid lip-service to decency. Air Commodore Charlton in *War Over England* (1936) claimed that although armies and navies could not effect complete surprise in war, air forces could do so, and should get in the first blow, making it as overwhelming as possible. 'That is not to say that such barbarism should be condoned,' he added. But we British should have to do it because there were 'barbaric races' prepared to perpetrate just such an 'atrocity'.

In an earlier book, *War from the Air* (1935), the same author showed what might be achieved by such an attack (citing London, but meaning Berlin, Rome, Paris, or wherever). By means of 4 lb thermite bombs (much as were in fact to be used by the RAF against Dresden ten years later), Charlton predicted that a great conflagration could be started, rivalling the Great Fire of London, which had destroyed the city. He foresaw 'undisciplined flight' from the capital, 'disintegrating' the public transport system and 'dislocating' the food supply. Contemptuously, he spoke of the 'labouring masses' herded together in old houses, 'the most difficult people to control (factory employees in particular), who will be more susceptible than most to dismay and stampede'. His conclusion was that 'aircraft form the chief means of waging war'.

This was how the British air power theorists saw the

future war over England, because this was what they were themselves planning to do with their bombers. Not just the factories, power stations and docks, but the factory workers and indeed the civilian population as a whole must be the targets. Burn them out of house and home, send them fleeing into the countryside as refugees to starve and create chaos; this is what 'Mastery of the Air' meant. This is what the Air Ministry planned to do and what the British government prepared to receive from the air in 1939 – ludicrously so, because no other air force in the world was constructed to do such a thing. (Although crackpot theorists existed everywhere, it was only in England that their views were accepted and acted upon.)

The role of the Luftwaffe had been settled in 1936: it was to support the army in mobile and aggressive land operations, not wage a strategic bombing campaign from behind fixed, defensive frontiers (which was the British plan). A Luftwaffe general (Stumpff) actually informed the RAF in 1937 of German views on air strategy, but he was not believed, so obsessed with their own dogma were the RAF marshals. Even in 1939, with a large, technically efficient air force at his disposal, Hitler was sceptical of its strategic possibilities. In private, he stated: 'If the German air force attacks English territory, England will not be forced to capitulate . . . A country cannot be brought to defeat by an air force.' During the next 5½ years these propositions were put to the test, with Dresden as the culminating point in Europe and Hiroshima in the Far East.

Behind the terrible theories, the brutal unconcern for human life, lay the ever-present memory of the Great War of 1914–18, which had consumed the young manhood of Europe in the most selective way. From out of my own family, for instance, no fewer than eleven close relatives were killed in action (including one at Gallipoli, so that among us the name of Winston Churchill was spoken with something less than reverence). The most deadly fact was not the numbers slaughtered (although these were very great) but that all these millions were in the main young men in the prime of life who had not yet had time to marry and have families. What had been destroyed was the future as well as the present. The ghastly logic (and I came to use it myself for a time in my early teens) was that this selective carnage of the trenches was the very worst injury which nations could inflict upon themselves and upon each other. Aerial bombardment of cities, even in its most indiscriminate form, would be far less damaging. It would kill or maim a nearly equal proportion of each element of the population – the women equally with the men, the young equally with the old, the weak equally with the strong, the sick equally with the fit. From such a blood-letting there might be a recovery, whereas to kill for the second time in a century the best of the young men in their prime but without issue would doom Western civilization. There would be no hope. All the combatant nations must decline.

The United States, however, coming late into the 1914–18 war, had been spared much of the frightful manpower losses suffered by the British, the Germans, the French, the Russians, the Italians and some of the Balkan countries. American bombing policy in the interwar years did not envisage carrying out attacks on the civil population, indeed most Americans recoiled from the thought. Also it seemed to them, as it must have to many, that onslaughts directed against the entire populations of great nations resembled rather the death by a thousand cuts instead of the quick kill resulting from shots through vital parts. Indeed, it was questionable whether a decision could be reached at all by widespread indiscriminate bombing.

The Americans planned for a strategic bomber force,

rather than the short-range tactical air power favoured officially by the Germans, the Japanese and the Russians. Where they differed from the British was in the way they intended to use it. The bombers were to be designed for the precision destruction of key targets, which could only be hit by accurate day raiding, so the Americans opted for the 'flying fortress' concept then popular. The bombers were to battle through by daylight. Misled by their own good weather and clear skies, the American theorists had given little thought to conditions prevailing in Europe for many months of the year, with overcast skies hiding the targets from view.

Some theorists wanted the best of all worlds. Major Helders, a German whose ideas were not to be adopted in Germany, in his book *War in the Air* (1936), had predicted the use of 'giant' aeroplanes grouped in massive air fleets which could fight their way through the enemy air defences (the idea adopted by the Americans), and which could also wage aerial battles of manoeuvre against similar formations of enemy 'aerial battleships' (an idea adopted by no one). The use of such a force was to 'terrorize the population and annihilate industries' (which was the plan being pursued by the British). For the purposes of his fictional forecast, Helders made the 'giants' British and the industries they attacked French, and had the French counter the blow by invading England, finding cross-Channel operations rather easier in fiction than the Germans were to do in fact in 1940.

Indeed, the theorists often did find things much too easy. In their minds, in the mental pictures they conjured up of how they would fight the war that was coming, they had it all their own way. The real thing was to prove more intractable, because there were enemy minds bent on thwarting them, often successfully.

An exception was the German practice of the British 'Blitzkrieg' theory of using bombers, tanks and motorized infantry and artillery to effect deep penetrations and so cause defeat by disorganization. That worked like a charm when they tried it in France in 1940, and we tried it later in 1944, also in France. Despite the impression deliberately given by German propaganda newsreels of intimidating and overwhelmingly brutal destruction, it proved a relatively humane method of warfare. Once the initial, critical breakthrough had been achieved (which could be costly) one expended petrol rather than ammunition, sweat rather than blood. Of course, refugees did suffer on the French roads in 1940, choked and mixed up with retiring military traffic; and I saw German ambulances knocked out by our rocket Typhoons of Tactical Air Force when we were speeding through France the other way in 1944.

One appalling result of the breakout of the Allied armies from the Normandy bridgehead in August 1944 was that it put Air Marshal Sir Arthur Harris, who took over RAF Bomber Command in February 1942, in a position to do to Dresden what he had already done to Caen, at the invitation of the British army. Caen was the first city I was to see which had been raided by our own people rather than by the enemy, and I can never forget. Eighty per cent of the city of our friends had been turned within an hour into a wasteland of broken stones. We, not the Germans, had done it. The fact that the raid had been counterproductive, helping the German army more than it helped the British, was an additional bitter irony.

'Sir Arthur Harris made a habit of seeing only one side of a question and then exaggerating it', wrote the RAF official historians Webster and Frankland in *The Strategic Air Offensive Against Germany* (1961). For evidence one has only to go to the 228 pages of Harris's own book *Bomber Offensive* (1947).

Professor Blackett, scientific adviser to the Admiralty for the Normandy invasion, was to say that Harris was 'a very poor strategist but a good commander', because although his aims were wrong he managed to convince his men that they were winning the war and so keep up their morale in spite of cruel losses. In Blackett's view, Harris, a convinced exponent of the Trenchard dogmas, had delayed the defeat of the U-boats by nine months because he would not divert the planes from the German cities. Further, Bomber Command had been the principal opponents of the Second Front. Both Harris and Air Marshal Sir John Slessor believed that the Normandy invasion was a tragic diversion of bombing effort which, if it was allowed to continue, would make the Normandy landings little more than a 'police' action. Incredible as this may seem now, it is amply comfirmed on p. 54 of Harris's book and in Slessor's *The Central Blue* (1956, pp. 389-90).

The RAF policy of attacking city centres which went under the official name of 'area bombing' (often unofficially designated by cynics 'Aiming Point Cathedral') had been approved by the government of Winston Churchill and was carried out by Harris with determination. Trenchard's influence was still present in the background. On 2 May 1940, a week before Hitler's Blitzkrieg in the West was launched, the old veteran was writing to Sir Charles Portal, Chief of the Air Staff, that if the RAF had been used as he, and he presumed Portal also, had wished, 'it probably would have ended the war by now'. In fact, the British bomber force was weak and ineffective, unable even to find its targets, let alone hit them by night. The full extent of its inefficiency was not then fully realized, but Portal had the ultimate aim clear in his mind when he wrote

in 1940: 'We have not yet reached the stage of desiring to
burn down a whole town, but when this stage is reached we
shall do it by dropping a large quantity of incendiaries first
and then a sustained attack with High Explosive to drive
the fire-fighters underground and let the flames get a good
hold . . .'

When Harris took over as a 'new broom' in early 1942,
his command amounted to only 378 serviceable aircraft of
which a mere 69 were heavy, four-motor bombers. In
November of that year, Portal wrote a paper to be
considered at the inter-Allied Casablanca Conference in
January 1943, urging the creation of a fleet of 4,000—6,000
Allied heavy bombers (RAF and USAAF combined) by
1944. Portal calculated that the minimum result must be
the total destruction of 6 million German dwellings, the
rendering homeless of 25 million German civilians, the
killing of 900,000 German civilians and the seriously
wounding of a million more German civilians. His
biographer, Denis Richards, revealed this in *Portal of
Hungerford* (1977, p. 255). In the event, 13 million people
were to be made homeless, 600,000 killed, more than a
million injured, also on minimum estimates.

Under such intense pressure the Germans, like the
British before them, were stirred to resist. In theory,
German industry should have collapsed; in fact, some
kinds of war production very nearly trebled under the
assault. The German air defence system improved and
took increasingly deadly toll of Allied bombers. Bomber
fleets could not pass unopposed over the defences, as
theorists like the Italian Douhet and air marshals like
Trenchard had believed. Nor did civilian morale crack. The
British people under air attack had already shown that the
air marshals' assessment of them, as expressed most in-
sultingly by Charlton, had been a piece of insolent rubbish.

Now the Germans, whom they had referred to even more slightingly, were defying the most terrible air onslaught in history so far, when it seemed at first sight that it must overwhelm them.

The first appalling success licensed by the Casablanca directive was scored at Hamburg in July 1943, when a series of round-the-clock attacks by the RAF and USAAF killed at least 48,000 people. For the first time a 'fire-storm' was identified and, after that, deliberately sought for. Certain conditions had to be present, such as a concentration of high buildings and a concentration of bombers in time and space, which produced so many huge fires so rapidly and so close together that the air above the city became super-heated and 'drew' the flames out explosively, just as will a sheet of newspaper held in front of a small fire burning on a grate. On the enormous scale of a large city, the roaring rush of heated air upwards developed the characteristics and power of a tornado, strong enough to pick up people and suck them into the flames. In a normal fire-bombing it is possible to fight the bombs and the fires, and if you lose, there is still retreat. From a fire-storm there is small chance of escape. The temperatures at Hamburg were estimated to have reached 800 degrees Centigrade, sucking in air at such a rate as to cause an instant howling sound quite different from the normal roar and hiss of burning streets.

Momentarily, the morale of the German leadership wavered. Albert Speer, Reichsminister for war production, wrote that the fate of Hamburg 'put the fear of God into me'. If another six major cities were similarly obliterated, he thought German war production would be fatally affected. Hitler would not accept this. 'You'll straighten all that out again,' the Führer said dismissively. In this case he proved to be right. War production in

Hamburg recovered within months and large numbers of people who had fled the city returned to make homes amid the rubble. In spite of 80 per cent destruction of residential areas, a year later the population had risen to 900,000 (prewar population 1,700,000 before conscription of the males for military service).

Not until February 1945, with the burning of Dresden, was Bomber Command again able to score such a success. The basic reason was the same – lack of effective defence. In the Hamburg attacks, the bombers had for the first time used a radar-blinding device known as 'Window', strips of metal foil dropped from planes to create confusing radar images, which had made both the guns and the night fighters virtually impotent. The bombers had been able to aim without harassment and with few losses. However, there was an answer to 'Window', and the Germans found it.

Two weeks after Hamburg, Speer again had cause for worry, this time from American attacks in daylight on a precision target, the ball-bearing works at Schweinfurt, which were crucial to war production. Had all such plants been attacked repeatedly, the effect would have been serious. There really were key points in the German economy which were vulnerable to precision bombing. The oil-from-coal plants which supplied more than half of German aviation fuel needs were another. Harris regarded them contemptuously as 'panacea' targets.

After devastating Hamburg, the third greatest city in Germany, Harris planned to do the same to the capital, Berlin. If the Americans could be encouraged to take part, as they had at Hamburg, instead of diverting to 'panacea' targets like Schweinfurt, Harris was sure that: 'Berlin could be wrecked from end to end. It will cost us 400–500 aircraft. It will cost Germany the war.' Churchill enjoyed Harris's

Churchillian phrases and approved, but the Americans did not come in – not then.

The 'Battle of Berlin' raged from November 1943 to March 1944. 492 bombers and their crews never came back, 95 were wrecked on home territory, so that the total loss figure was not far short of 600, and a further 859 returned damaged. Berlin, although badly battered, still functioned as the capital of the Third Reich. It was harder to find, harder to aim at, much deeper into Germany than Hamburg, it was winter instead of summer – and the Germans had an answer to 'Window'. The RAF's promise, that the heart of Nazi Germany would cease to beat, was unfulfilled.

What RAF Fighter Command had done to the Luftwaffe in 1940, the German night fighter force had done to Bomber Command – inflicted such losses that the battle had to be called off. The aeroplane had again proved a defence against the aeroplane. Before there could be a decisive bombardment, there had to be a battle, the enemy's fighting forces had to be engaged and defeated. The historic principles of war were still valid.

Harris's chance to prove the opposite had gone. By spring of 1944 the cross-Channel invasion which he opposed as unnecessary had to take priority; all the Allied air forces had to be placed at the disposal of the commander of the ground forces, General Eisenhower. It was an unhappy time because, apart from a few crack squadrons, Bomber Command was a blunt instrument, not always appreciated by the customer. The armies demanded air supremacy – and were given it, largely as a result of the work of the USAAF plus RAF Fighter Command, and the development of aircraft capable of working with them in close co-ordination, such as the rocket-firing Typhoons of

Tactical Air Force. The soldiers were outspokenly grateful for this support.

By 1 July, with the armies bitterly locked into the close-quarters fighting of the Normandy hedgerows, the bloody *bocage* which baffled tanks and used up infantry at a prodigious rate, Harris was writing to Portal to demand better publicity for his Command's part in the invasion. 'They have a right that their story should be adequately told, and it is a military necessity that it should be.' He had 10,500 aircrew in his operational squadrons, Harris pointed out, and in three months they had suffered 50 per cent losses. In August, the American General Omar Bradley was investigating the losses of just one American division, the 30th infantry, as a guide to the reinforcement position. In the fighting around St Lo the division had suffered 3,934 battle casualties, mostly in infantry. The casualties in the rifle platoons had reached 90 per cent in fifteen days (compared to Bomber Command's 50 per cent in three months).

It is necessary to say this because many of his aircrews took their chief's statements seriously, and some still believe that the Command suffered the heaviest losses ever known in warfare, and feel slighted when the effectiveness of its operations is questioned. Most were young men and few were military or naval historians. Harris could make fantastic claims and be taken literally. A bomber commander, he said, had to commit his whole force every twenty-four hours, whereas a naval commander had to fight a major action only *once or twice in the whole course of a war* and an army commmander might engage in *one battle every six months* or, exceptionally, once a month. In Normandy, at this moment, battle was succeeding battle, as the Allies tried to break through first here and then there, while the war at sea was continuous from the first day to the last. Because the Allies were winning that battle, it was possible to invade Normandy, whereas the help given by Bomber Command was negligible, as Portal was to tell Harris. In Harris's view, however, the armies could only advance when 'towed forward' by his bombers, and sometimes not even then.

However, as July merged into August, the Allied armour broke out from the bridgehead and raced for the Seine and Paris. Once again, in a burning summer, a torrent of tanks and soft-skinned vehicles poured through France. They crossed Belgium, taking Brussels and the great port of Antwerp, and were across the Dutch border before their impetus was slowed by lengthening supply routes and stiffening German resistance. The war almost ended that September; but not quite. When winter came almost all Germany's conquests in the West had fallen to the Allies. In one or two places, American troops were confronting the Siegfried Line. From the Nijmegen salient, held by the Canadian army, one could look down the road into Germany.

These enormous gains of ground virtually eliminated the German early-warning radar system and the outer rings of flak defences; from the Channel coast they had been pushed back almost to the Rhine. At the same time, the invasion enabled the RAF to set up its ground stations for navigation far forward into Europe instead of inside England. The result was to totally alter the air war in Harris's favour, enabling him to plan grandly once more, but still to the same old plan of 'area bombing'. The eastern German cities, including Dresden, were now exposed. Even Berlin, that hardest of hard nuts to crack, might now be 'completed', thought Harris delightedly.

By now, even the air staff had abandoned him. To

Harris's request of 1 November, to be allowed to 'devastate' a dozen more cities, particularly those in the East such as Leipzig and Dresden, on top of the forty-five he had already virtually destroyed, Portal replied that he doubted whether area bombing could ever have been decisive, that the air force mainly responsible for the success of the Normandy landings was the USAAF, and that without the land advances gained since, there might have been no future for Bomber Command (*Portal of Hungerford*, pp. 318–22). Portal tried to convince Harris that he too ought to attack oil targets, as the Americans were doing, and as Harris had been ordered to do. There were eleven synthetic oil plants in Germany believed to be supplying 70 per cent of the Luftwaffe's fuel. Bomber Command must join the Americans in knocking them out and keeping them knocked out. Harris continued to argue against being forced to waste time on such 'panacea' targets long into January 1945, and would not change his views one jot; and Portal would not, or could not, sack him.

The British public wanted the RAF to hit back at the Germans for what had been done to them in 1940 and 1941, and again in the form of the V1 in 1944. That they had not the faintest idea of the facts of the air war over Germany can be instanced by a vengeful letter printed in my home paper on 23 July 1944. It was from a housewife living at Fareham, a small but unbombed town at the back of Portsmouth harbour:

A number of residents in this district have signed a petition to the Government for immediate reprisals upon Germany for the flying bomb attacks, in the form of complete destruction of a town or village in the Reich for every day attacks are carried out upon this country . . . In this way we hope to make the continued murder of civilians, chiefly women, children and old people, unprofitable to the Huns . . . Will anyone interested get in touch with me, by letter, as I urgently need help in house-to-house collection of signatures.

The complaint is curious, in that the London area and not the Portsmouth area was the main target of the V1s, but the newspaper editor printed her letter, pointing out that: 'The Government's policy – and we believe it is right – is to hit at Germany's military machine, not to enter into a reprisal competition.'

I was in London throughout the first six weeks of the flying bomb attacks (before leaving for Normandy in the last week of July), and noted that morale was good, military damage small. However, reading the histories and VIP memoirs years later, it is plain that morale at that level had been severely shaken, for reasons quite unclear.

During July, August and September 1944 – the period which saw overwhelming victory in Normandy eventually blocked by defeat at Arnhem, when hopes and fears fluctuated wildly – there is evidence that the Western Allies were contemplating some terrible but swift end to the war by committing an atrocity which would terrify the enemy into instant surrender. Without doubt, the inner truth has still to be prised loose, but the thread of thought can be discerned. In July, the British chiefs of staff minuted the Prime Minister, Winston Churchill: 'The time might well come in the not too distant future when an all-out attack by every means at our disposal on German civilian morale might be decisive . . .'

The British Directorate of Bomber Operations duly made calculations:

If we assume that the daytime population of the area attacked is 300,000, we may expect 220,000 casualties. 50 per cent of these or 110,000 may expect to be killed. It is suggested that such an attack resulting in so many deaths, the great proportion of which will be key personnel, cannot help but have a shattering effect on political and civilian morale all over Germany . . .

In August Portal put before the chiefs of staff what came to be known as the *Thunderclap* plan, a mighty blow to be delivered by the all-out power of the combined air forces of Britain and America in Europe to destroy one great German city, probably Berlin, at a time when, *combined with military events*, this might bring about a formal German surrender. In England, Portal's idea had a dis- missive reception: 'not likely to achieve any worthwhile degree of success' and 'the game is not worth the candle' were just two of the sceptical comments.

Thunderclap reached planning stage at SHAEF, General Eisenhower's HQ, to which Harris was still sub- ordinate. In September, with the American air general Doolittle, he worked out a scheme for a giant combined assault by both air forces to be made in daylight on Berlin. SHAEF's Psychological Warfare Division labelled the plan 'terroristic', a verdict with which the authors of the official USAAF history, *The Army Air Forces in World War II,* agreed; 'frankly aimed at breaking the morale of the German people' was their verdict.

The top American air general, 'Hap' Arnold, and the American Admiral William D. Leahy both went on record as opposing morale bombing in principle, but it was Arnold who suggested what he said was a more humane way of intimidating the civil population; this was for every available Allied aeroplane to be sent out over Germany, attacking military objectives in the many small towns which had never yet seen a bomber. This plan, under the codename *Clarion*, was to be attempted in February 1945, in conjunction with a *Thunderclap* attack on Dresden, and proved equally indiscriminate.

In July, Winston Churchill had asked the chiefs of staff to think about the use of poison gas 'or any other method of warfare we have hitherto refrained from using'. The government seems to have been unduly shaken by the ineffective and short-lived bombardments of London by the V1 flying bombs. Technically, poison gas was a non-starter, and it is surprising that Churchill seems not to have known this. Possibly rumours of the much more deadly nerve gases being experimented with by the Germans may have prompted his suggestion. The Allies did have something at least equally awful in the pipeline but not yet ready for actual use — anthrax — said to be 300,000 times as powerful as poison gas. Some day we may learn what really lay behind all this.

By October the American air general Spaatz, who had opposed Portal's *Thunderclap* plan, himself suggested something superficially similar. If the Allied armies were to be stopped by the Rhine barrier, 'it may still be possible to beat up the insides of Germany enough by air action to cause her to collapse next spring, particularly if the Russians continue pressure against the eastern area'. Spaatz is said to have meant precision attacks on targets of strategic value rather than the wholesale fire-raising of the British, but here again was a thought-process which was to destroy Dresden within five months.

In January 1945, air general Ira Eaker stated: 'We should never allow the history of this war to convict us of throwing the strategic bomber at the man in the street.' This was a fine phrase. What it actually meant remained to be seen. There were only a few weeks now, to wait.

No. 75 (New Zealand) Squadron was to be in the second wave of attack. Ken Moore and the other gunners had taken their parachutes and Mae Wests out to the aircraft for a raid on Wanne-Eickel in the Ruhr, a short-range trip to 'Happy Valley'. They learned that this operation was now 'scrubbed', and they were still out there, chatting idly to the ground crew, when a petrol bowser turned up. The fuel load was to be increased and the bomb load altered to fewer HE, more incendiaries (indicating an unburned, virgin target). 'Christ, if we're going on this one, then we're going a long way!' thought Ken.

He remembered the briefing very well. Unusually, the map showing the route to the target was coverd by a sheet. When that was removed, Ken recalled the long 'OOOOOOOh!' that arose from the crowd of airmen. It was the distance which surprised them; none had been that far before. Although there were a lot of new crews in the squadron then, it was the more experienced ones who had been chosen (not that they were very experienced – many had done less than a dozen trips so far). The reason given for the raid, Ken recalled, was that 'the Russians were pressing forward and there were stacks of German troops moving back towards Dresden'. They were each given a plastic container with a Union Jack on it and notices in English and Russian identifying them as British airmen. If their aircraft was in trouble, they should fly towards the Russian lines, but there was no information available regarding aerodromes in Soviet territory. 'It was a little bit awesome – the length of the trip,' said Ken.

Roy Akehurst was a W/T operator in the same squadron. It was his twelfth operation out of thirty-one. 'I've never forgotten it,' he said thirty-five years later. 'It was the one raid I'd rather not have been on. I felt it was *not* a military target, although, I'm pretty sure, we were told at the briefing that there were many thousands of Panzer troops in the streets, either going to or coming back from the Russian Front, my personal feeling is that if we'd been told the truth at the briefing, some of us wouldn't have gone.'

Peter Goldie was the rear gunner of the Lancaster in which Roy Akehurst flew.

At briefing, we always looked at the board to see what the target was. This time the board was covered over with a sheet. We all settled down and then they pulled the sheet away. I saw one word: 'DRESDEN'. The first thing that came into my mind was Dresden china. I couldn't understand why we were going to a beautiful city like Dresden to bomb it. My New Zealand crew (three of them, that is) had never heard of Dresden and they asked me what it was, what it represented, and I tried to explain.

Then we all stood to attention as the Group Captain came in, the Squadron Leaders, the Flight Commanders, the Navigation Officer, the Radio Officer, the Gunnery Officer. We all sat down again, and they started to explain to us why we were going to Dresden. I think I heard them say that it was Churchill's instructions to destroy the city, but they never really told us what was there. They just said: 'Go in and firebomb the city.' It was the only raid that really mattered to me, it preyed on my mind afterwards. Even walking back from the briefing, talking together, I couldn't understand why this raid.

Paul Hill, the flight engineer in AA-P, which carried Goldie as gunner and Akehurst as W/T operator, did not share their feelings. 'All war is horrible and innocent people get hurt. Nor did the bomber crews fly to Dresden without risk to themselves and many, like me, were fully aware of the damage done by German bombers to our own cities.' His recollection was that the identification material with the Union Jack on was in the form of a silk scarf, and the reason given was the RAF uniform was very similar in colour to German and might cause them to be shot by the Russians. Perhaps fortunately for morale, no one realized even what a Russian army looked like at this time, and what kind of trigger-happy atrocities it perpetrated wherever it went.

Flying Officer Alan Driver, a navigator in 106 Squadron, was to take off with 5 Group, some hours before 75 Squadron. At the briefing he attended, the aircrew were told that 'with the advance of the Russian forces, the German army was in full retreat and that Dresden was occupied by the retreating forces and their supplies. Our task was to destroy the vital railway and other communications in the city and therefore make a new German stand impossible.'

Driver still has his actual plotting chart of the operation, showing the tracks for out and return flights threading their way through the marked hazards of Germany – the heavily defended cities standing out in thick red hatching like rocky islands in a hostile ocean, deadly cities to be avoided. The distance to be covered was nearly twice as long from the English coast as the average trip to Ruhr and Rhine. Just north-east of Leipzig is the pencilled note 'Fires sighted here'. The fires of Dresden.

While they were still on the ground, Driver recalled:

The NCO members of my crew were showing little enthusiasm about the duration of the raid and the two gunners in particular were concerned about spending ten hours in their cramped turrets in low temperatures. There were some pointed comments on whether we would have sufficient fuel to get back to base, especially if a diversion became necessary.

Although their basis was the same, not all briefings were identical, nor did every man remember every point. But Peter Goldie's recollections, as it happens, were both true and basic. Churchill had intervened in the air war to demand that Dresden be bombed. The reasons for that were not revealed to the aircrew because they were on a different level of argument to those of the bomber marshals; they were essentially political, personal and international, and to a certain extent mysterious, and still are. And it was true also that the briefings sounded vague concerning Dresden itself, giving the impression that no one really knew much about the city or what would actually be down there when they arrived above it, four miles high.

4

The Target

Specific military installations in Dresden in February 1945 included barracks and hutted camps and at least one munitions storage depot.
– Top Secret USAAF *Historical Analysis of the 14 – 15 February 1945 Bombings of Dresden*, declassified 13 December 1978

The principal enterprises of the city were medicine and food-processing and the making of cigarettes.
– Kurt Vonnegut, American POW in Dresden, *Slaughterhouse-Five*, 1969

The standard whitewash gambit, both British and American, is to mention that Dresden contained targets X, Y and Z, and to let the innocent reader assume that these targets were attacked, whereas in fact the bombing plan totally omitted them and thus, except for one or two mere accidents, they escaped.

For instance, there was a barracks. It was a Hitler-built structure, centrally-heated, with accommodation to such a standard that British soldiers' eyes popped when they found themselves living in such palaces: single rooms for platoon leaders, double rooms for junior NCOs, six-man dormitories for the rank-and-file. And as this was a Waffen-SS barracks, officers, NCO and privates sat down at the same tables to the same grade 1A meals. There were some 4,000 of them, and they included an odd little party of renegades from the British and Commonwealth armies who had been taken prisoner and for propaganda purposes had been wheedled into joining something called the

Legion of St George. One of them, on sentry-go in German uniform outside this German barracks, proved so careless with his rifle that he accidentally fired a shot and hit a real German soldier. However, this undoubtedly military target was not in the centre of Dresden but on the outskirts of the Neustadt (New Town) area on the fringe of open country, miles away from the area scheduled for burning.

This barracks did contain munition stores, particularly those concerned with military engineering, such as mining. Bridge-building and assault river crossings were also taught there.

It was true also that there were hutted camps in Dresden – and they were full of starving, wretched refugees.

It was claimed that Dresden was a main communications centre for the East. This was very true. But the main road route to the Front was carried by the Hitler-built Autobahn which crossed the river Elbe outside the city limits entirely to the west. If you turn off that Autobahn to the east after a few hundred metres you come to a black-and-orange sign reading 'DRESDEN'. Even then, for the first few miles you pass through industrial suburbs much the same as they were in 1945, with the bomb damage – a few missing buildings here and there – revealing just how little the Allies were interested in hitting any industrial potential.

The railway network was important as a junction, but for historical reasons the tracks did not lead through the city centre; instead they skirted it for a couple of miles. There were no railway stations on the British target map, although 'creep back' would attend to that as far as the main station was concerned. But an emphasis on incendiaries in the bomb-loads meant that only minor damage would be done to the tracks themselves. Of course, if anyone was seriously interested in cutting German communications with the East Front in the Dresden area, they would concentrate on knocking out bridges, especially the Autobahn bridge outside the city and the rail bridge which linked the Hauptbahnhof and the Neustadt station. Even if this had been done, the main effect would have been on the plight of the refugees. The city and its communications network was being used mainly as a clearing centre for the trekkers.

The bomber commanders were not really interested in any purely military or economic targets, which was just as well, for they knew very little about Dresden; the RAF even lacked proper maps of the city. What they were looking for was a big built-up area which they could burn, and that Dresden possessed in full measure. Any ordinary tourist guide made that obvious; indeed this vulnerability was built into the history of the city. At a pinch, an encyclopedia would have sufficed.

Dresden was noted for its fires. Medieval Dresden represented a Germanic expansion into a Slav east. Alongside the native settlements a planned town with a large market square and streets laid out in a grid pattern was built; the houses were of wood, the streets were narrow. Accidentally-started fires were very destructive.

In about 1500 Dresden became the capital of the princes of Saxony. Palace buildings were constructed around the Schloss and strong lines of fortification were raised enclosing the town. That restricted expansion outwards, and so the inhabitants built closely and upwards; in the eighteenth century particularly, many five-storey buildings were erected. Behind its thick, encircling walls, the city stood dense and high. This was the period also when its princes, particularly Augustus the Strong, indulged their ambitions to make of their capital a riot of glorious architecture housing art collections of all kinds. Even the present town guides, written for Communist masters, pay tribute to the results of those ambitions. Dresden, with its fantastic architecture set beside a broad river, was a very pleasant place to be. Many who are exiled from it are homesick, not for what it is now, but what it was, but will never be again.

All this faded with the arrival of the grimy, industrialized nineteenth century. Most of the fortifications were pulled down, and the city advanced into the countryside around, where factories were set up and vast new residential areas created. But the old town centre remained — close-built, high-built, fantastic, housing world-famous collections of paintings, statues and art objects of all kinds. The first expansion of the city across the River Elbe, the Neustadt or New Town, was by the twentieth century an old town too.

The inhabitants did not always accept authority without question. In May 1849 there was an uprising, supported by men like Richard Wagner the composer and Gottfried Semper the architect; but after a week's fighting on the barricades, it was crushed. After the lost war of 1914–18, there was another revolution led by the so-called Workers' and Soldiers' Council, which was more successful; the king of Saxony abdicated and the red flag flew for the first time over Dresden.

During the years with which we are concerned, the successor to Augustus the Strong was the Gauleiter, Martin Mutschmann. He wore the brown uniform of the National Socialist Party, the NSDAP. There was some resistance to it still, but when found, this was stamped on. Those who were lucky were conducted via one escape route or another over the Erzgebirge, the 'Uranium Mountains', into Czechoslovakia; those who were not, faced the public axeman in the yard of the Superior Court of Dresden. From there, during the period 1939–45, a total of 1,069 headless corpses were carted away, often for dissection by medical students.

At the relevant time, Mutschmann was also the head of

the Air Raid Precautions organization of Dresden. Originally, all ARP had been the responsibility of Hermann Goering's Luftwaffe (which also controlled the flak artillery and the paratroops), but later in the war the Party took over civil defence. These were all pirate empires within the Nazi state; indeed, even the Party itself was divided between the brown-shirted SA and the black-uniformed SS. There was also the Waffen-SS, but they wore field-grey because they were fighting soldiers rather than administrators or politicians. The army and the navy were separate empires again, and the security services were divided into at least three competing bodies. Hitler's system was methodically based on the old principle of 'divide and rule'; it was far from being the monolithic marvel of matchless efficiency so admired or dreaded by those outside the Reich. It was also bureaucratically paper-bound to a degree rivalling even that of the British military accounting system of 1900, which it took all the energies of some Boer farmers to demolish. The British army found that either it could account or it could fight, but it could not do both at the same time. In his turn, Speer was to remark on the enthusiasm with which the managers of bombed factories reported that they had lost all their files in the fires lit by Bomber Command and that now, if the Reichsminister so wished, they could devote all their energies to the war.

By the autumn of 1943, with the tide of the war irrevocably turning against Germany and mile after square mile of Hamburg reduced to heaped rubble and the burnt-out shells of buildings, a new emphasis was placed on air raid precautions throughout Germany. The result in Dresden was extraordinary. Ill-informed gossips passed on the tale that the Gauleiter was building himself a superb air raid shelter in the garden of his home in Comeniusstrasse, 100 metres long by 30 metres wide, it was said, and buried metres deep below ground, its steel and concrete ceiling reinforced by four layers of railway lines; it had many rooms, all air-conditioned, with radio and electricity; and worst of all, it was being constructed by public labour at the public expense, that is, by Waffen-SS men from the Pioneer unit out at the Neustadt Barracks. (The German equivalent of the English 'Pioneer' is military engineer; not a low-grade army labourer.) There were better-informed gossips who claimed that this was not the half of it, for the Gauleiter was having a second air raid shelter constructed out in the Tharandter woods at Jagdschloss Grillenburg, also his own personal property, safely clear of the built-up area of the city.

Those still better-informed could point out (and did) that Mutschmann already had a perfectly satisfactory official air raid shelter, for a complete underground headquarters had been set up in the rock cellars of a firm which produced fruit wines at a place called Lockwitzgrund in the south-eastern extremities of the city. Of course, Hitler had issued an order that his Gauleiters, so valuable to the survival of the National Socialist state, should have effective air raid protection, but three first-rate shelters for one Gauleiter, and nothing for the rest of the populace, seemed excessive.

Had the Third Reich been a genuinely monolithic state, the scandal might have been concealed; but it wasn't. Dresden's police chief, SS-Obergruppenführer Udo von Woyrsch, not only had powers equal to Mutschmann the Party boss, but he lived opposite him. Because the Gauleiter's shelter was being constructed by the SS, people at once jumped to the conclusion that he had a hand in it too, and that the shelter was for the use of the police chief as well. Worse still Frau Mutschmann, the Gauleiter's wife, was going round Dresden saying negative things about the SS-Obergruppenführer.

The story reached Himmler, the SS leader, who on 25 August 1943 had been given extensive powers as chief of police for the Reich. Von Woyrsch came under him, so it was von Woyrsch whom Himmler contacted via Dr Brandt, a member of his staff. And von Woyrsch took the opportunity on 24 September 1943 of undermining the position of the Gauleiter. This was a case of the SS using the police organization which they controlled to try to extend their power at the expense of the SA, who controlled the Party apparatus. Himmler's new appointment was a threat to the SA, and Mutschmann was well aware of it.

The SS-Obergruppenführer began carefully, by explaining that all these regrettable events had occurred during July and August, when he was away on his summer holidays. On his return, he had found the Gauleiter building a shelter in his garden, 'while the majority of the population don't have proper shelters for themselves'. The work used 'an enormous amount of people, machinery and material, and this has caused the strongest disapproval by the population'. In spite of protests, the Gauleiter had refused 'in a most unfriendly way' to give up his shelter building, in spite of its effect on the public.

As regards the second air raid shelter for the Gauleiter's use, the one out in the woods at Grillenburg, von Woyrsch was able to state that the place had been camouflaged with expensive netting, instead of paint, and that this project had taken precedence at the factory over army orders for netting.

Having implied that not only was Mutschmann a coward on the grandest scale, but he was defying Himmler's authority as well, the SS-Obergruppenführer tried to show fairness and balance by remarking:

Although I personally believe that Gauleiter Mutschmann is an absolutely decent man, the opinion of the people is almost entirely against him; and this leads me back to the fact that in his personal circle there are people who can be described as 'odd'. But I don't want to finish without mentioning the fact that Frau Mutschmann is a chatterbox who talks more than is good for her. Consequently, I believe she may be afraid of your holding in your hands all the reins of power regarding the SS and the police.

The confusion and intrigue at the level of provincial government was merely a reflection of what was happening higher up; no overriding central authority was created in this supposedly totalitarian state. At one time in 1943 three top people were responsible for civil defence, with the boundary lines unclear. Hermann Goering, head of the Luftwaffe, was running a scheme to prominently signpost authorized open spaces, such as parks, sports stadiums, public gardens and cemeteries, and the flight-paths leading to them, as refuges in case of fire-storm. Joseph Goebbels, propaganda minister, grabbed one post in a newly-created air-war defence organization, while Heinrich Himmler, chief of police and of the SS and much else, held many ARP powers including control of the Safety Police, or Air Raid Wardens. If nothing much had been done in Dresden about ARP, von Woyrsch had at least as much responsibility as Mutschmann.

In 1939, nothing very drastic had been done in Saxony or in the rest of the Reich either. The white lines on the motorways were painted out and a blackout was enforced, but generally people believed what Goering told them – that he had erected a roof over the Reich which would keep out their enemies. In the whole of Dresden there were only two formidably strong shelters, both under factories – the Goehle Werk and Zeiss Ikon – which could withstand 1000 lb bombs. There were a few private shelters such as that built under the offices of the Bramasch company in

Friedrichstrasse. For the mass of the population, there was nothing whatever.

Then came June 1943 and the Hamburg fire-storm. Three places were selected and signposted as safe open spaces: the great park called Grosser Garten where the Dresden Zoo was situated, to the south-east of the Altstadt, or Old Town; the flood meadows of the River Elbe, to the north of the vulnerable Altstadt; and a large open space to the north-west called the Grosses Ostragehege, where several sports stadiums and the city slaughterhouse were situated, as well as the great Friedrichstadt hospital complex. This latter area was right outside the nineteenth-century railway tracks which hemmed in the Altstadt and Grosser Garten in the city centre, following the outside lines of the old sixteenth-century fortifications.

Elementary fire precautions were taken. People were asked to clear their lofts of inflammable material and had to coat the beams with a white anti-fire fluid; sandbags, water buckets and small handpumps were placed inside the houses and flats, the sand to put out incendiary bombs, the water to deal with any small fires. In a few public places — about half a dozen — static water tanks were erected as a reservoir for the fire brigade in case the water mains were cut by high explosive bombs. The Ruhr town of Dortmund had 134 such public reservoirs, but a handful was considered adequate for Dresden.

A work unit was set up to convert the cellars of the houses and flats into interlinked air raid shelters. In Dresden, as in many other German cities, most buildings had useful cellars or basements for storage, for hanging up laundry, and so on. The buildings were two or three storeys higher than an equivalent house in England, and there were few private gardens or large open spaces at back or front, where small shelters might be dug. So the existing cellars were turned to an appropriate use, not so much by strengthening them as by mouse-holing them. Holes were knocked in the walls which divided one set of cellars from another; and then these were lightly bricked over, so that if fires breaking out above trapped the occupants of one cellar, they could knock down the temporary partition, and escape into the next cellar; and from that one into the next one, and so on until they could emerge at street level in an area clear of flames and smoke. That was the theory. But Hamburg had tragically demonstrated that when large areas were set on fire almost simultaneously, interlinked cellars running the length of one street only were insufficient. When the people emerged from the last cellar, they were still enclosed by the roaring, hissing fires and choking smoke. And so they were burnt alive. To be effective, tunnels would have to be driven under the roads connecting blocks of buildings; whole catacombs would have to be constructed, leading down to the Elbe meadows and the river, where surely they would be safe. The task was begun, but it was too great to complete in wartime, and besides, how much real likelihood was there that Dresden would be bombed?

Hugo Eichhorn, then serving in the Waffen-SS with a rank equivalent to lieutenant-colonel, commanded the SS-Pioneer A & E Regiment 1 stationed north of the city at Heller, which was the unit concerned with air raid construction and rescue. He recalled:

In December 1944 the mayor of Dresden, SS-Gruppenführer Dr Nieland, asked me to attend a meeting at the town hall. At that time, people were inclined to the opinion that Dresden was only a cultural city, without any industry worth mentioning, and therefore not a worthwhile target for Allied air raids, which was why no air raid bunkers or any other kind of shelter had been built. There had, it is true, been some very minor raids, when a few bombs had been dropped on railway installations. They were hardly worth mentioning. Nevertheless, the gentlemen in the town hall felt that the time had come to do something for the protection of the Dresden population. One suggestion was to cut down part of the Dresdner Heide and use the tree trunks for supports in some of the cellars of the houses. This project would have had to be carried out by my Regiment. I turned it down for the following reasons: (1) This project would give hardly any effective protection against bombs; (2) to complete the project would take a long time; (3) it seemed inappropriate and irresponsible to carry out a complete deforestation of the Dresdner Heide for a project which ultimately was bound to fail. As a result of my explanations, the whole project was shelved.

The population of Dresden was exposed to the February raids without any protection. The bunker which the General of Police, Ludolf von Alvensleben, had blasted out of the rock near the Mordgrundbrücke served mainly as a secure HQ for the police only. Neither General Freiterr von Gilsa, the commander-in-chief, nor any military units used this bunker.

Hugo Eichhorn's own unit had no proper shelters either; they simply used trenches dug in the parade ground. Such dispersal is quite effective where there is sufficient open space, although light overhead cover to keep off shell splinters, nose-caps, driving bands and half-spent machine-gun bullets or cannon shells is normally a good thing. In Dresden, of course, the rain of hot light debris from the skies which accompanies a normal air raid was missing, as there were virtually no defences capable of firing.

In Germany, but unknown in Britain, were giant concrete air raid shelters and flak towers built to hold thousands of people, which like the U-boat pens and V-weapon sites were effectively impervious to bombs. There were many examples in Berlin, Hamburg and the Ruhr; and they should not be confused with the brick-built surface shelters, cheap cosmetic deathtraps, constructed in England to lull the population into a sense of security.

Where there were large gardens to every house and a low
building density, as was the case where I lived near
Portsmouth in 1940, it was possible to dig family-size
shelters quickly, far enough from the house to avoid burial
by debris, with no profile above ground to catch blast, and
only a light roof to avoid burial under heavy timbers or
beams in case of a near-miss. This is exactly what we did,
and were convinced it would stand almost anything except,
of course, a direct hit. But in a high-built, closely constructed city, self-help is impossible; citizens must rely on
their local authorities; and the local authorities will be
reluctant to spend on civil defence what was lavished without stint on the over-elaborate and often useless V-weapon
sites. In the case of Dresden, there was in addition no clear
case of necessity. As Hugo Eichhorn pointed out: 'The
increasing number of general hospitals and military
hospitals which were being set up in Dresden encouraged
the population to hope that the city would never become
the target of a major raid.'

Even ignoring humanitarian considerations, there were
cultural reasons for not attacking Dresden, particularly at
a time when the war was almost over. Apart from the
baroque and rococo architecture, a catalogue of what one
can only call the 'treasures of Dresden' would run to two
dozen volumes twice the size of this one. The picture
galleries included many works by old masters such as
Holbein, Cranach, Vermeer, Rembrandt, Hals, van Dyck,
Rubens, Botticelli, and Canaletto. Many of the paintings
were too large to be taken out and put in a safe storage
place. The contents of the Dresden galleries had begun in
1560 as the modest private collection of the Elector
Augustus, and had been steadily built up over a period of
almost four centuries. There could be no replacement for
that. Then by the time of the Seven Years War (1756) the

engravings collection numbered 130,000 items; by 1945 there were half a million. Porcelain had been invented by J. F. Böttger in 1707 in his summer house on the Brühl terrace at Dresden, overlooking the Elbe. Although china was mostly manufactured at Meissen a few miles away, Dresden as the home of the inventor came to be represented by the delicate shepherdess, and the image of the city was the skyline of spires and bridges made famous by the paintings of Canaletto. To smash this delicacy seemed unthinkable.

The city held one of the most fantastic treasures of Europe, the baubles of the Grünes Gewölbe collection, wrought from porcelain, gold, silver and jewels, impossible to describe. For the historians, there were famous collections of watches and chronometers, geometrical instruments, arms and armour. Apart from the statuary with which many of the buildings were decorated, particularly the Zwinger (turned into an exquisite place from what had been designed centuries before as a 'killing ground' of the fortifications), there were sculptures and reliefs from the classical age of Greece. Then, for centuries, the city had been a centre for music and musicians on a European scale – Bach, Handel, Telemann, Wagner, Strauss.

It was truly a capital city, with something to delight and interest everyone. It had theatres, libraries, a magnificent circus, a zoo. The animals had not been killed off for safety reasons and to save food, as they had been in more ruthless cities, such as London. Elephants, tigers, apes and antelopes still delighted the children in Grosser Garten, and the best-known keeper was the famous animal-trainer, Otto Sailer-Jackson. Near the waterfront of Dresden Neustadt there had been a permanent circus building since 1912, the famous Sarrasani Circus, with its own stables and down in the cellar an underground pool for Wally the hippopotamus. Wally was to be a most fortunate animal, for although there was a show billed for the evening of 13 February 1945, he did not appear before the bombers did.

In 1942 a policy of dispersal of the Dresden treasures began, but it was never completed. There were too many items, and some were too large or awkward to move in wartime. 196 precious paintings remained in the picture galleries and a further forty-two in the Schloss, plus the antique furniture there. Some of the Greek sculptures and friezes remained in the Albertinum building in the Altstadt.

However, a good deal was removed, and because the treasures were so valuable the people involved were sworn to secrecy and had to sign a paper to that effect. An SS officer, Fichtner, was in charge. Forty-five different locations had been chosen for the dispersal, all of them being castles or large country houses belonging to the aristocracy, deep in the countryside and far from any town. On the way there, the treasures were always at risk, because there were continual delays due to the difficulty of packing the items safely and obtaining the necessary petrol for the lorries (fuel being a very real bottleneck in the German economy even then), and a shortage of guards. The academics asked the Wehrmacht to provide sentries on all the selected storage sites, but were refused; Germany had no men to spare for that purpose.

And then came the Russian offensive of 12 January 1945 and the breakout from the Baranov bridgehead. When it was clear that the advancing Russians were going to over-run many of the hiding places of the treasure, Mutschmann gave a panic order which the East German historians Ruth and Max Seydewitz consider 'almost insane', so chaotic were the conditions, the roads clogged with refugees on foot and in carts and with the inmates of whole prisoner-of-war camps, all on the march westwards. In this situation, the Gauleiter ordered that all of the treasures which had been hidden in castles and country houses east of the River Elbe, on which Dresden stands, should be moved to fresh hiding places west of the Elbe. Apart from the chaos on the roads, cut in some places by defensive ditches hurriedly dug, there simply were not enough fresh storage places to be had at short notice; some of the delicate materials had to go into damp mines and quarries. Other loads came back to Dresden temporarily. In particular, one lorry packed with 154 paintings plus antique timepieces and geometrical instruments which had come from Schloss Milkel and were destined for Schloss Schieritz near Meissen was parked by its driver for the night by the Elbe terrace in Dresden. That night happened to be the night of 13 February 1945. Then there were ten boxes of crated china ordered out of Schloss Rammenau by Mutschmann and temporarily stored in the vestibule of the Residence Schloss in Dresden Altstadt.

Even before the January offensive, the demands of the front lines had stripped Dresden almost bare of heavy anti-aircraft guns, notably the dual-purpose German 88s, which were effective against tanks also, though uncomfortably high for the crews. By December 1944 there were only three batteries of heavy flak left – 24 guns out of sixty-six originally. And no searchlights or smoke apparatus. On 16 January 1945 the last of the 88s had disappeared from the flak sites, and the guns of the last battery to leave, 7./565, were already loaded on rail cars at the Friedrichstadt goods yard. In their places on the empty gun-sites, wooden gun barrels made from tree-trunks had been set up, to try to fool the Allied reconnaissance aircraft. Ironically, Dresden's second air raid, another small one by 8th USAAF, took place on 16 January, the day the last 88s were removed.

All that was left in and around Dresden was some of the light flak for use only against low-flying aircraft – 2 cm guns in single or quadruple mounts – but no records have survived to show how many there were or where. Like the 88s, these guns were partly crewed by children, schoolboys of fifteen or sixteen taken out of school in their last year to learn a practical trade. They were the flak militia, or Luft-waffenhelfer, created back in September 1942 when Hitler had ordered that 120,000 men of the ordinary Luftwaffe gun crews should be taken away from the defence of the Reich to fight on the Eastern Front against the Russians. After the war, Harris's last-stand argument was that Bomber Command had diverted German guns from the fronts to protect the homeland, but there was less in this than met the eye. And for Dresden it must have been near 98 per cent untrue. By February 1945, apart from the night fighters of the Luftwaffe, especially those based only a few miles away at Dresden-Klozsche airfield, the city was un-defended against any high-flying bombers, British or American.

The night fighters scored the most 'kills', but it was the radar-predicted flak which made pilots and bomb aimers flinch, prevented them from flying straight-and-level up to the aiming point, or made them drop short, so that the bombs 'crept back' from the target towards the oncoming bomber stream. In either case, the bombing became scattered, lacking that concentration which alone could allow a fire-storm to develop. Because of 'Window', Hamburg had been momentarily undefended. Now Dresden too was open to the same dire process, unless the night fighters could somehow break up the bomber stream.

In this situation all Mutschmann could think of was moving the Dresden treasures from one side of a river to the other at a time of maximum difficulty and danger. The hope that this move might keep them out of Soviet hands was an illusion. The fate of Germany was at this moment being settled by the 'Big Three' at Yalta in the Crimea. All the hiding places and Dresden itself were to be within the Soviet Occupation Zone of Germany. That had been decided by a few words round a table.

Mutschmann had come out on top in his struggle with SS-Obergruppenführer Rudolf von Woyrsch, who had fallen out with Himmler, and had been replaced by a new police chief, Ludolf von Alvensleben. However, deep inside Soviet Russia, plans were being laid to replace both of them, and all the other chief functionaries of Saxony, with Germans who would serve the USSR. Some were old members of the KPD, the German Communist Party, who had either escaped over the mountains or been freed from the camps — Communists being some of the oldest, indeed original members of the concentration camps, those hard enough and lucky and cunning enough to survive had become 'trusties' and run the camps for the Nazis, concealing their hatred. Others had been recruited inside Russia. Just as Germans went round the Allied POW camps, trying to get Britons and Americans to join their anti-Bolshevik 'Legions', so did Russians tour their POW camps for Germans; soldiers taken at Stalingrad, who often felt that they had been betrayed (they had), were easier game than most. But whereas the anti-Bolshevik SS Legions were a propaganda charade, the Soviet wheeling and dealing was in deadly earnest. The Britons and Americans might be given food, women and drink, the German renegades would have power as well in a conquered land where no one dare call them traitors.

There were sixty-seven working parties in Dresden made up of British and Commonwealth prisoners of war from the camps immediately to the east; like the Americans, who were formed into seven larger parties, most were housed and did their work in the industrial area to the south-west, towards Freital. Many came from Stalag IVb at Mühlberg, which housed all sorts, Americans, British and Russians, and supplied a large area of Saxony, Silesia and Czecho-slovakia with a labour force to make up for the millions of German males who were at the front or under the ground.

Among the Americans was Clyde Smith, a paratrooper who had been dropped in Normandy on the night before D-Day, a badly scattered drop. He took part in the unco-ordinated fighting which followed, when little groups met accidentally on unknown territory, made up their own objectives as they went along. He was cut off and captured, then with other POWs was put into trucks which were strafed by American P47s and RAF Spitfires. He was at Mühlberg when, in September 1944, one hundred Americans were called out to make up a work party to go to Dresden. Supervised by five German civilians, they dug trenches for waterpipes, hard manual labour for twelve hours a day.

We went to work without breakfast, at noon we had a bowl of soup (rutabaga) and at night a slice of bread. Every now and then we would get a Red Cross package. You could take cigarettes and buy bread with them, if the guards didn't see you. Once, one of the men was caught stealing bread — he was taken to the hallway of a school we lived in, put in the middle of a circle of men, and hit from one side to the other; after that, no one was caught stealing.

The prisoners were weak and dazed with hunger almost all the time; the desire for food was continually with them. The work party Kurt Vonnegut was with lived in the No. 5 building of the Public Slaughterhouse on the Grosses Ostragehege, a large area of wild, common land beyond the Friedrichstadt hospital complex, and they worked in a factory producing malt syrup for pregnant women. The work involved washing windows, sweeping floors, cleaning lavatories and packing jars of syrup into boxes. Even after surreptitiously spooning the syrup, which was full of vitamins and minerals, they were still very hungry. Nearby was a sports stadium which was to have a deadly significance on the night of 13 February 1945. Some of these Americans were walking to work at dawn one morning when they saw a crowd gathered outside the stadium. There was a gallows there and a Pole was being hanged on it. He was a farmworker who had had sexual intercourse with a German woman, for which this was the standard penalty. For the woman, the Gauleiters usually prescribed the revolting practice of head-shaving and consequent public exhibition, just as the more barbarous members of some French Resistance movements did with 'collaborators'. The fact that the man had been a farmworker probably explained why he had the energy at all to commit the 'crime'; most of the prisoners thought of food before all else.

Two days before Dresden died, the starving Americans in the slaughterhouse had an extraordinary visitor. He was costumed in a parody of Americanism: a white ten-gallon hat and black cowboy boots patterned with stars and swastikas, shoulder-insignia depicting Abraham Lincoln's profile on a green ground, and a wide red armband carrying a blue swastika in a white circle. His name was Howard W. Campbell, Jr, and he was recruiting for his own unit of the SS, which he called 'the Free American Corps', pledged to fight only against Bolshevism on the Russian Front. He explained to his starving compatriots, who had begun to break out in hunger sores, that the blue of his uniform was for the American sky, white for the race that pioneered the continent, red for the blood shed by patriots in the past;

and that if they would join him and wear a uniform like it, they could have as many steaks as they had room for.

No one said anything. The hundred listless American soldiers gazed apathetically before them. Then one man spoke up. He was a high school teacher, really too old to have been in the army at all. He was to die in the most curiously ironic manner within the week, but just now he was fighting. He said that Campbell was not a snake, because snakes couldn't help being what they were; he was a good deal lower than that, below a rat, less than a blood-filled tick. He said that in America there was freedom and justice for all, and there wasn't one of the prisoners who wouldn't die for those ideals. And now there was a brother-hood between the two great nations, America and Russia, and far from Americans fighting the Russians for the Germans, together they were going to stamp out the virus of Nazism before it could infect the world. Then the sirens began to wail.

All of them, the prisoners, the guards and the would-be recruiter, took shelter in the meat-locker excavated deep into the rock below the ground. It was naturally cold down there, cold as the bitter February snows above, but there were few carcasses of cattle hanging up, just one or two sheep and pigs and horses instead of the thousands there would normally have been. The Germans weren't eating very well, either. Then the 'All Clear' sounded. This was not to be the night.

Clyde Smith, the paratrooper who had been taken in Normandy, was billeted in a school which he thought un-safe in daytime because a battery of light anti-aircraft guns was sited in the street outside. 'Young teenage boys were used as ammunition bearers. I didn't like to be close to those guns in daytime because dive bombers might see them.' What no one knew was that what was planned for

Dresden represented the exact opposite of the pinpoint accuracy of dive-bombing.

Another paratrooper who passed through Stalag IVb at Mühlberg was Eddie Taylor, captured two years earlier. He was with 2 Battalion of the British Parachute Regiment when in 1942 it was dropped near Tunis fifty miles in advance of the British 1st Army, which failed to get through in time to their support. The Battalion had to retreat, losing sixteen officers and 250 men, one of them Eddie. The Germans handed him over to the Italians, who, when he attempted to escape, beat him up and tortured him. Then the prisoners were transported in cattle trucks – no water to drink, no toilet facilities – to Mühlberg on the Elbe. On arrival in the early hours of the morning, they were stripped, had their heads shaved, had a cold or luke-warm shower, had their uniforms fumigated to get rid of the fleas and lice, and finished up with an inoculation.

Mühlberg was an enormous barbed-wire complex, a kind of sorting centre for prisoners. The Russian prisoners were in the majority, and Eddie could see that they were dying off like flies, purely from hunger. There was no Red Cross for them, and they had to exist on German camp rations. Their destination was a covered limepit. Two of their live companions would carry the next dead man on an 18-inch-wide wooden plank and tip him into the pit – 'a frequent occurrence during the hours of daylight,' Eddie recalled.

The newly-arrived British prisoners were lined up. The Germans asked for volunteers to work in munitions factories. The conditions would be much better there, they were promised. Not a man moved. There were no volunteers.

Then the prisoners were told off for various work parties, whether they liked it or not. Eddie Taylor, who is now an architect, was shocked when he heard his destination, the Hercules Mine near Brüx, just over the border in Czechoslovakia. 'I just couldn't believe I was being sent to work in a mine,' he said. (In England, as yet, there was no conscription for the mines, although it was soon to come, enforced in 1943 by a former trade union leader, Ernest Bevin, now Minister of Labour; in wartime, there are no democracies.) As a depressed-looking party of British soldiers arrived at Brüx and were standing in a circle, waiting, a cigarette landed on the floor in front of Eddie. 'Someone [a German] had taken pity on us,' he said. 'We shared it, of course, it was a great time for sharing. That one cigarette went round half-a-dozen men like a pipe of peace. The less one had in the way of possessions, the more one was prepared to share (although self-preservation was always evident). Money didn't mean anything.'

The mine was a deep one with seams of soft coal thirty feet thick; the men stood up to work, but wore loincloths as their only covering because of the heat; there were always fires burning in the seams. They soon realized that they were at the heart of a vital part of German war industry and that they had before them, in the size of the coal stocks which accumulated, a visual indication of the effects of American strategic bombing and, in a smaller way, their own efforts at sabotage. 'Although we were prisoners, we were still British, determined to do as much damage as we could,' said Eddie. They worked out various ingenious ways in which it was hard for the Germans to trace the culprits. 'Our coal was sent to the Hermann Goering works for processing into oil. The three chimneys at that refinery were nicknamed Churchill, Roosevelt and Stalin. Long tanker trains would take the processed material away from the Goering works and the intensity of their activity became a sort of barometer to predict the air raids which gradually became an accepted additional hazard in our lives.'

The refinery, or more properly, coal hydrogenation plant, was eight minutes' flying time from Dresden and by 1944 was surrounded by 266 heavy anti-aircraft guns. At peak, in 1943, Dresden had never had more than sixty-six 88s (8.8 cm), of which many were the comparatively inefficient 'Russian flak', captured Soviet guns of 8.5 cm rebored to take German 8.8 cm ammunition. The defences of Brüx, even at the time of greatest crisis during the Russian offensive of 1945, never dropped below 166 88s.

One man who became expert on the importance of the plant was Ted Ayling of 4 Battalion of the Sussex Regiment. He also had been captured in 1942, at a much more famous battle than Eddie Taylor's, El Alamein. The Bren carrier he was driving had been hit by a 50 mm solid shot and 'brewed up'. He estimated that there were between 4,000 and 5,000 British POWs working at the plant out of a total labour force of many nationalities of about 45,000. The process of extracting oil from coal had been invented by a German chemist, Dr Bergius, just before the 1914–18 war. Hitler had built twelve plants which supplied 85 per cent of Germany's aviation spirit, plus fifty-nine by-products, including margarine, saccharin and aspirin. 'This factory has sprung up since the fall of France and much French, Russian and Czech forced labour had been employed to achieve it,' Ted wrote in his diary.

In three years a shallow lake had been drained and this great factory, 1½ miles square, stood in full production in its place. The factory had eight roads running across it from north to south, and eight also running from east to west, with a railway line beside each road. Quite apart from the element of forced labour, the place was a real achievement to the credit of German technique, and you've got to hand it to the bastards.

Ted's job was lugging stones about for a road contractor on a diet consisting of turnips. 'I soon learned a great deal about the factory, and wished that I knew some way of making sure our people knew, too.' The proof that some of them did was soon to come.

The plant was typical of what Harris with frustrated rage dubbed a 'panacea' target. Portal suspected that the bomber commander might take every opportunity to evade the Allied directive to concentrate on oil targets. Harris denied it. He maintained his views however, even after the war; nothing could shake him from his belief in the wisdom of burning city centres. With some reluctant help from Harris by night, in 1944 the two US Army Air Forces, the 15th from Italy and the 8th from English bases, began to hammer the synthetic plants with precision daylight attacks, and Brüx was high on the priority list. As well as ringing the plants with 88s, the Germans installed 'Nebel' defences – smoke generators consisting of oil drums which quickly masked the plants from the air.

From April 1944 to April 1945 the oil campaign continued. The targets were large, vulnerable and vital to the German war effort. The Allied lives expended in disrupting production were not wasted, although the raids could be costly because they involved deep penetrations in daylight into German territory. For instance, on 12 May 1944 the 8th USAAF from England attacked five oil plants and lost forty-six 4-motor bombers and ten fighters. Ted Ayling was underneath the attack of 21 July 1944 on Brüx by 143 bombers of the 15th USAAF, whose bombing record (according to the American official history) was just twice as good as that of the 'Mighty Eighth'.

Ted wrote in his diary:

The alarm sounded at 11.15 am and we tore out of the factory. I was grateful to get as far as a ditch close to a railway embankment, for I had observed the bombers forming up. The first wave dropped their bombs in and around the factory (and many of our huts at the camp went west). The second wave was right on target, they shoved the lot into the factory itself, damned good show. The third wave silenced the AA guns on the factory outer perimeter. In all, eight waves of Liberators went over. Some bombs, which I could hear rushing earthwards with a terrifying roar, dropped quite close to me and I really thought it was my 'bundle' and that my 'Arbeit' for 'der Vaterland' was about done. Usually in a raid, the terrific hail of shrapnel from the AA guns was a big headache; this time most of the gunners had been put to sleep. I later noted the extent of the damage: many houses, the entire Italian POW camp, much of the Dutch camp, some of ours, and plenty of the factory. Six British were killed and 21 are missing. The 'Nebel' did not save the factory.

Eddie Taylor experienced the same raids from a mile or so away, because the mine where he worked was tied to the hydrogenation plant and supplied it directly with the brown coal from which aviation fuel for the Luftwaffe was made. Some raids came over when he was above ground. 'I don't agree with criticism of the Americans,' he said:

I remember seeing Fortresses turning in the sun, the light reflecting off the Perspex of their cockpits. You'd see one aircraft go down, but the others still coming on; then another aircraft going down, but the others carrying on. One raid straddled us, hit the barracks with Italian, Russian and Ukrainian POWs. A German officer came up with a drawn revolver and I thought he was going to shoot us. But no, he wanted us to pick up the arms and legs. During this episode, the revolver was pushed in turn against my back, chest and head to emphasize the various orders that were shouted at us. That is, for four men to hold the corners of a blanket and one to pick up the bits and pieces of flesh. There were a lot of German bodies in one place, one headless. I heard somebody who'd been shocked stutter: 'I don't think this chap's got much of a chance to live!'

The German officer was furious, shouting at us: 'American gangsters!'

'I'm British,' I said.

'Don't you talk, bloody Englishman . . . bloody Englishman.'

Oil bombs had been dropped, there was the stench of burning flesh, looking like cooked meat; and screaming and moaning. I really thought that German officer would take us round the back and shoot us, he was so furious. Of course, it was hell for the Czech civilians, who were killed or maimed, as in Britain, but 'Lidice' was a word we heard frequently from them and revenge was obviously high in the minds of many. Coal production came almost to a standstill and near the end of the war, there was no evidence of processed fuel being manufactured.

When the oil plant was put out of action, there was no demand for coal from the mine, so the stocks piled up, and the height of the coal dumps was a visible measure of lost German oil production. The Luftwaffe had the aircraft, for area bombing had hardly affected their manufacture, but most of the machines were grounded for lack of fuel. Pilot training suffered, and finally permission to 'scramble' the fighters had to be obtained from higher authority, so precious were the remaining reserves. This was to prove a deadly factor when Dresden, a non-industrial city, was mass-attacked.

The general situation now was grim, particularly for the prisoners in the work parties. 'There was more than one occasion when horses' heads were part of our diet,' recollected Eddie Taylor:

Also frosted potatoes. Rations were right down then. No Red Cross. The Germans were in a bad way too – they were starving. I had a terrific craving for something sweet. I'd dream of food, think of nothing but food. But the soup got thinner and thinner, the ration of Wurst (sausage) disappeared. The coffee was a funny stuff, they said it was made from nuts. Margarine when heated would form a black, oily mass. We smoked any dried stuff – tea leaves, for instance. Nowadays I can't bear to see anyone scrape remains from a plate into the fire. One chap told me: 'A few months after getting back home, and we'll have forgotten.' But I haven't, and I'm sure all the others would say the same. I still hate to see waste and I can't forget the ill-treatment I saw of fellow human beings — hence I have a deep feeling and regard for Jews.

RAF prisoners talked a different language from the army men. Captain Jack Evans, who was doing intelligence work, was in Stalagluft III at Sagan, a camp primarily for airmen. Most non-RAF personnel soon got bored with the RAF stories of how they had got shot down, but Evans was more than bored; he was horrified, sickened by their tales of destruction. They seemed not to realize what had been happening down below (whereas he had been in some of those raids, and did know). Their insensitiveness puzzled him. They talked about their raids, boasted of the size of their bombs and of what the incendiaries had done to people at Hamburg. They expressed no shame, no guilt. The attitude persists, among a few, to this day.

To the shouts of 'Raus, Raus!' on 26 January 1945, Evans left Sagan with the rest for the 'Frostbite March', but slipped away from the columns and, passing himself off as a French forced labourer (although he had no papers to prove it), managed to join various groups of German refugees until on the evening of 13 February he was approaching Dresden. The raid was at least able to give him an excuse for his lack of papers, should he be questioned.

A prisoner whose plans were drastically altered by it was Geoff Taylor, an Australian pilot of 207 Squadron, who had been shot down over Hanover in 1943. As the Luftwaffe camps were then full of captured British aircrews (the Germans told him, smugly), he was to be sent to an army camp at Mühlberg on the Elbe, Stalag IVb, where the other Taylor, Eddie, had been sent after capture with the paratroops near Tunis. Geoff Taylor went there on his own, in a railway carriage with seats, still wearing flying boots, his parachute on the rack above him, and his guard sitting opposite. A large black-clad civilian standing in the corridor began eyeing his flying boots and parachute. Then he spoke to the guard and got the word he wanted: '*Flieger. Terrorflieger! Ach so!*'

Taylor then got a furious lecture, with much fist-waving in his face, of which he understood only a word here and there: 'Hamburg' or 'Essen' or 'Dortmund' or '*Kaput! Alles kaput!*' His final, parting word was 'Scheissen!' The other occupants of the carriage, mostly respectable farmers and their wives, nodded complete agreement. The guard later explained to Taylor that the man's story was that he had been bombed out in three different cities in the last three months and that the rest of his family were missing, presumed dead. This affected Taylor not at all, apparently. He was so proud of his role as a Bomber Command pilot that even after parachuting down, he had not removed the RAF wings from his battledress blouse. For all he knew, the first Germans he met might have murdered him out of hand. They would have had good reason. But, defiantly, he had retained the proud identification.

At Mühlberg he received the same treatment as Eddie Taylor: deloused, clothes put through the gas chamber, X-rayed, inoculated, blood-tested, weighed. The reason, he was told, was that the largest of the exercise compounds was built on the bodies of Russians, buried six deep, who had died of a typhus epidemic which had run through the camp and also infected people in the local villages. The living Russians were in a dreadful state, fighting in the snow for scraps from the garbage bins. A few, a tiny few, of the British prisoners would take amusement from it, by saying 'Watch this', and then throwing an empty bully-beef tin into the Russian compound for the miserable, diseased, starved wretches to squabble over. Geoff thought that the 'evil' minority who did this were showing their fear that they too could be reduced to such degradation if the Red Cross parcels failed to arrive. The official British leadership, however, arranged for a weekly food levy on all British prisoners to be given to the leaders of the Russian POWs.

In the winter of 1943, RAF morale went up as their comrades who were still in the war took advantage of the long nights to raid cities deep in Germany – Berlin, Magdeburg, Leipzig. Berlin was eighty miles away, but Leipzig was much nearer. They could hear the bombs, like the thud of great doors being slammed; feel the ground shake underneath them; see the marker flares, the searchlights, the photoflashes. For the people on the ground, Geoff Taylor had little or no thought, he noticed. Mentally, he was up there with the bombers, with the men he knew. He was stirred by the sounds of hundreds of engines swarming over the camp towards some luckless German city – 'a proud, wild, flooding surge of audible power' he was to write. 'There is a savage, blasphemous pride to be felt in having been one of Butch's boys.'

Without their aeroplanes, they were diminished, incomplete. The grounded pilots watched the operations at the nearby Luftwaffe airfield of Lonnewitz, where night fighters, night bombers and jet fighters were based. Wistfully, they recognized the same sort of routines they were used to, and in the pilots of the various Ju 88s which came to beat up the camp, the same basic types of pilot they knew in the RAF: the cautious, the careless, and the overconfident. It was this similarity, almost a fellow-feeling for their opposite numbers in the German air force, that gave Geoff Taylor his great idea.

First he had to get hold of a diagram of the cockpit layout of a Ju 88 night fighter, and if possible of a Ju 188 as well. He needed to know the layout of the airfield and the procedures, the alignment of the main runway, the positions of the buildings and flak posts. The French prisoners in the camp got him several Ju 88 diagrams; unfortunately, they did not agree exactly. There was also the key question: in a Ju 88 do you open the throttles by pushing the levers forward? (as in British aircraft); or do you pull them back towards you? The question was vital, because the Ju 88 was rumoured to swing violently on take-off, probably requiring quick corrective application of rudder or a chopped throttle − and if carefully built-up instincts were wrong, not only might the take-off be ruined but the Ju 88 as well. Geoff could see himself standing before the commandant of the Luftwaffe airfield, explaining how he had happened to break a German aircraft.

But all of 1944 had to pass before he was ready to break out from Stalag IVb as a prelude to breaking into Lonnewitz airfield and making a first solo on a new type of aircraft, without benefit either of an instructor or an official manual, though first solos on new types were not Geoff's forte. So he and his fellow escapee, Smithy, were still in Mühlberg on Christmas Eve when, as the sun was going down, the first batch of American prisoners from the 106th Division taken in the Ardennes arrived. They were left to sleep in the snow outside the wire that night. It did not occur to Geoff that in the open was where infantry normally slept, but he could see, as they were marched in next morning, that they were in a very bad way, staggering into each other from exhaustion, dirty, unshaven, coughing and frost-bitten. Pfc Kurt Vonnegut, who was among this batch or a similar one from the 106th, described how it felt and how they must have looked to the British in the camp, who had arranged a welcome in advance for the new-comers. One wondered, reading it for the first time in *Slaughterhouse-Five* (1969), if he hadn't injected a little sci-fi; but there it all is, from the hardened inmate's view-point, in Geoff Taylor's *Piece of Cake* (1956). Yet most of the crowd of starving zombies who staggered into Mühlberg recovered in time to go on work parties in still untouched Dresden. They were, many of them, only boys of nineteen or so, and youth is resilient. Most of them had left America only a few months before.

It was the breakout from the Baranov bridgehead that triggered Geoff Taylor's decision not to wait for spring. Previously, his idea had been to fly to Sweden, with thirty to forty minutes over German territory; but now, as the Russians began to overrun Poland and Silesia, their lines seemed to be less than a hundred miles away from Lonnewitz airfield. It was time to go. How to get out of Stalag IVb in the first place proved to be easy, once Geoff had contacted the French escape committee. Whereas the British would sweat away tunnelling and perhaps have the roof fall in on them (as they had at Mühlberg), the French took the easy way – they just walked out through the main gates, using the daily work parties and fiddling the numbers. So Geoff and Smithy dressed up as French prisoners and walked out of camp in the morning.

It was the morning of 13 February 1945.

As the Luftwaffe seemed to be virtually a replica of the RAF, they were going to treat Lonnewitz as any other RAF station. They wouldn't sneak in at night when sentries are most nervous. They would walk on to the field (there'd probably be only one strand of wire on the perimeter), as if they had every right to be there, indeed had an important job to do. Every old soldier knows this dodge: to avoid being detailed for work, pick up a broom and carry it ostentatiously. In their case, they picked up a heavy, fifteen-foot trimmed pine log in a nearby wood. If the German routine was like the British routine then, provided they could start up a Ju 88 and get it airborne, they could take off without permission from the tower and be ten minutes on their way to the Russian lines before anyone suspected that they were anything but a careless crew. Such things happened in England, so why not in Germany?

That afternoon, Geoff and Smithy were walking free as birds along the railway line which connected Berlin with Dresden, with about eight miles to go before they must hide for the night in a wood on the edge of the airfield. Smithy looked thoughtfully along the track to the south. 'You know, if we jumped a freight-train tonight we could be in Dresden in a couple of hours,' he said.

Geoff hesitated for a moment. Then he said they'd stick to their original plan, which would take them over the Russian lines in the same time as it would take to get to Dresden, a dead end anyway. They got into a copse, almost on the airfield boundary, having picked up their pine log, and then settled down for the night in a hole they dug in the ground and covered with branches and brushwood. Darkness came early, and they managed some hours of sleep before waking uneasily.

What had disturbed them was the harsh and sinister noise of an air raid; the vibrating roar of engines, the ringing roar of exploding bombs, the shaking of the ground under them. Close at hand, they could hear the whine and roar of Ju 88 night fighters taking off from Lonnewitz, along a brightly-lit flarepath.

In the opposite direction, southwards, beyond Mühlberg camp, the night sky was an appalling panorama of flickering light: photoflashes from the bombers recording their aiming point, vivid yellow and red gouts of fire from exploding bombs; wavering, glowing, expanding areas of flames as fires took hold. 'It looks and sounds like a thousand thunderstorms run riot,' wrote Geoff Taylor. He had never seen such an intense and concentrated attack since he had been a prisoner. But he was puzzled as to what the target could be. It wasn't any of the usual places: Berlin, Leipzig, Halle, Leuna, Chemnitz, or further south, Brüx. He went to sleep again, without having solved the problem.

The other Taylor, Eddie, who was a prisoner at Brüx, far to the south in Czechoslovakia, was a witness too, and at first equally perplexed.

We were outside the huts, behind the barbed wire; we had no shelters. We stood there looking at the mountain skyline, and we saw a glow coming up behind the mountains. Although it was long after sunset, it wasn't difficult to read print, from the reflection of the glow from behind the Erzebirge. We all realized that something extraordinary was happening – we were used to air raids, both from being in the target zone ourselves and by hearing the bombing of surrounding areas; but this was definitely an entirely different event, not air war as we had known it until now. The glow was not in the direction of Leipzig or Chemnitz. Dresden was forty or fifty kilometres away on the side of the mountain. But this had to be Dresden.

I recall the sound of explosions and of aircraft, as a pounding going on and on. It was as if a machine had gone mad. Enough to turn your tummy over and give you a sinking feeling in your heart. 'My Godfather Dick, this is the end of everything!' That's what we felt. And the German guards, too. The feeling was of *numbness*.

5
The Dresden Decision

THE FATAL MINUTES AND MEMOS

Next morning we took a motor boat across to the Gallipoli peninsula to see the British war cemeteries, where practically everyone has relations, Aunt Dot had a brother there, so she took some red irises for him, and, as we stood by his grave, she began to be angry again, as she had been in 1915 when he was killed, for she had always thought the Gallipoli expedition very stupid, and the most awful waste of her brother's life.
— Rose Macaulay in *The Towers of Trebizond*, 1956.

By 1945 Winston Churchill's interwar reputation as the 'Man of Gallipoli' had been superseded in the popular mind by the image of the bulldog war leader growling defiance at Hitler Germany. Nevertheless, impulsive attraction to large schemes, with insufficient regard to the means available, had remained a basic characteristic of his leadership. Among them were the failed assault on a French colony at Dakar in 1940, the adventures, and evacuations in Greece and Crete in 1941, the loss to Japanese air power of two great capital ships sent out to Singapore as a demonstration of force in 1942, and yet another Aegean disaster in 1943 when an 'ill-trained and ill-equipped' expedition was hurriedly thrown ashore in the Dodecanese as a bid to encourage Turkey to come into the war. This gamble was described by L. Marsland Gander, a war correspondent who only just survived it, as 'preposterous and irrelevant'.

Another Prime Minsterial decision, which had much in common with that, taken in regard to Dresden was not a failure, however; like Dresden, it was technically a success; and, again like Dresden, it succeeded because there was no effective opposition. This was the bombardment of a helpless French fleet in harbour at Mers el Kebir in North Africa after the fall of France in 1940. And the same question was to be asked afterwards as was later to be invoked by the destruction of Dresden: was it necessary?

Of course, no British government could afford then to risk allowing the French fleet to fall into German hands. But the British admirals concerned, according to the British official naval historian, Captain S. W. Roskill, 'viewed the government's orders with something approaching horror; all three believed that, given time for negotiation, a peaceful solution could have been found'. Such time was not allowed, and in a brutally dramatic stroke some 1,300 French seamen died under the guns of the British navy.

The United States Secretary of State, Cordell Hull, was to write that Churchill had told him that he wanted by this action against the French to disprove any idea among people abroad that Britain was about to surrender.

The unwilling entry of Soviet Russia into the war in June 1941, almost a year later, meant that Churchill no longer held the world stage alone with his oratory. In time, this became irksome to him. In 1942 the newspaperman Cecil King learned from the Canadian press baron Lord Beaverbrook, who was a member of the government, that the Prime Minister had been very keen to support Stalin while the Germans were sweeping all before them in Russia, but now that the Red Army had had some successes, Churchill had become 'very jealous of Uncle Joe'. In the nightly meetings of the unofficial war cabinet which sat up over brandy to the early hours, Churchill held forth on the theme that the war was 'Winston Churchill *v*. Adolf Hitler', and that Stalin had no business to butt in and divide the laurels. 'Now that he was buckling on his armour he was not going to have Stalin sharing the glory of his victory.'

By 1944 brute fact had changed his approach. In October, a most curious conference was held in Moscow. Churchill and Stalin met together without Roosevelt (who had an election on hand). Averell Harriman, US Ambassador in Moscow, was to be present for part of the talks but not all. Churchill had previously confided in his doctor, Lord Moran, that he had just had a brilliant idea; that he could 'manage' Stalin as one human being to another. His eyes were popping with excitement and he could hardly get his words out, as he explained this apparently novel idea. He was going to make a great offer of friendship to Stalin.

What the Prime Minister actually did was to bully the representative of the Polish government-in-exile until that unfortunate man had to agree to Stalin's demands on Poland (which meant giving 48 per cent of the country to the Soviet). Then, in Harriman's absence, and without authorization either from London or Washington, Churchill on his own account scribbled down the fate of Europe on a half-sheet of paper. To Russia: 90 per cent of Romania, 75 per cent of Bulgaria, 50 per cent of Hungary and Yugoslavia, 10 per cent of Greece. This referred to spheres of influence, not actual territory, as with Poland. It should be recalled that Great Britain had gone to war with Germany apparently to preserve the borders and independence of Poland, and on behalf of small, oppressed nations generally, so it was said. Stalin made only one concession: he agreed to recognize General de Gaulle's provisional government as the real government of France.

With this 'bargain' Churchill had to be content. He had actually very little to bargain with, as he must have realized. The Red Army, a truly massive land force, was a counter he could not match; it was likely to occupy most of the countries he had signed away, except Greece. The British army in this war was small in comparison and a large proportion of the British effort was invested in its essential navy or locked up in the four-motor bomber force. The Soviet had no such command. The Red air force, like the Luftwaffe, was closely integrated with its army. The Japanese too integrated their air arm with their army and navy.

However, cruel cartoons of the Moscow Conference, which was Churchill's last chance to shape history in any major way, appeared in the world's press. One showed the 'balance of power' with an enormous red Stalin in giant hobnailed boots by far outweighing and hoisting high a tiny, frustrated Winston Churchill. When the most fateful conference of all, that at Yalta in the Crimea, took place in the New Year, this time with Roosevelt sitting down at the table as well, Churchill must have felt very much in need of any bargaining counter he could lay his hands on.

It was Roosevelt who wanted the Yalta Conference; it was Stalin who dictated the date. And he kept Roosevelt waiting. Just before Christmas 1944, Stalin suggested that they meet in a month's time. By now, it was clear that Hitler had committed the bulk of his armoured reserves to the Ardennes in the hope of splitting the Allied armies and taking Antwerp. By doing so, he had exposed Poland, East Prussia and Silesia to conquest by the Red Army. Stalin brought forward the date of the attack to 12 January. And on 27 December he declared that he would no longer recognize the Polish government-in-exile (in London), but instead would recognize the so-called Lublin Committee, consisting of Communist nominees. At the Moscow Conference, Churchill had bullied, threatened, shouted at and waved his fist in the face of the Polish representative from

London, to make him grovel to Stalin; but not even that had been enough. Stalin had intended to take all. He had tricked the Polish underground into a premature rising in Warsaw, so that the Germans would kill off most of them, and as soon as the Soviets had conquered Poland, those few who remained would be hunted down and killed by the 'Polish' government he had constructed.

In spite of this, the Western Allies were very keen to help Stalin with his war, particularly by offering their bombers. As early as 14 December Averell Harriman had assured the Russian leader that General Eisenhower, commanding the Allied armies in Western Europe, was most anxious to assist, and Harriman specifically discussed with the Red Marshal the use of the powerful Allied air forces from the Mediterranean theatre to support the Soviet army in the Balkans. On 23 December came an offer from Roosevelt of the use of the Allied air forces based in the Western theatre of war under Eisenhower, and Eisenhower's deputy, the British Air Marshal Tedder, was sent to Moscow to confer directly with Stalin on 15 January 1945, just as the Red Army was breaking through the German front in the East. Stalin and Tedder agreed that it was necessary to prevent the Germans transferring forces from the West (where they were fighting the Americans, British, Canadians and French) to the East, in order that the Soviet advance might continue. So the emphasis was to be on attacks on communications, specifically oil targets, railways and waterways. If successful, these would decrease the casualties suffered by the Russian army, but increase those of the Western Allies. This was very odd, because the British, Canadians and Americans were due to begin their drive to the Rhine in three weeks' time.

On exactly the same day as the Soviet offensive began, the Allied combined chiefs of staff had issued *Directive No.*

3 for the Strategic Air Forces in Europe, formally regularizing at the highest level decisions to make oil targets number one priority, with 'German lines of communication' as number two. The oil targets were well known and could be precisely defined, as could operations against them, but 'lines of communication' was a vague concept. A third category, the Luftwaffe and particularly the new jet fighters it was using, was mentioned as a 'primary' target, which confused the issue thoroughly. Of 'marginal' importance was U-boat development.

Lots of little notes fluttered about among the dovecotes where the groups of planners nested. There was the RAF air staff, where Portal was lord; there was Eisenhower's air staff, tied in with Tedder the Deputy; there was the US supreme air boss in Europe, General Spaatz, controlling both the 8th and 15th air forces, who was linked for planning purposes with Sir Norman Bottomley; there was the Joint Intelligence Sub-Committee of the British War Cabinet, there was Air Commodore Dawson, Director of Plans; and the Director of Bomber Operations, Air Commodore Bufton; and 'Bomber' Harris himself, who would ignore what anyone else directed, if he saw fit; also Doolittle and Eaker, the two American air generals under Spaatz; there was the Joint Planning Staff in Washington, the Combined Strategic Targets Committee, and so on. After the fall of Warsaw on 17 January, there was a flurry of thought which lasted to the end of the month, four days before the Yalta Conference which in turn would be preceded by a Western Allied meeting at Malta.

It was at this point that Air Commodore Bufton resurrected *Thunderclap*, the 'catastrophic blow' to Berlin, the *coup de grâce* to German morale, conceived in the bright days of August 1944, when it seemed that the end of the war was in sight and that all that now needed to be done was to induce an orderly surrender. This was basic Trenchard dogma, the idea that you could get a city to put out the white flags to an air force, that you could terrorize a whole nation by laying waste its capital. Terror as a weapon of war has a long, if not entirely respectable ancestry. What Trenchard believed was that the morale effect of bombing would be twenty times more important than the physical damage inflicted, and that the Germans were likely subjects for the experiment, for their morale would be poor. In this, he was in tune with the findings of the British official air historian of the 1914–18 war, who wrote, to justify ludicrously small RAF raids projected for Berlin in 1918, that 'Believers in frightfulness are very susceptible to fright'.

On 22 January, Bufton wrote to Bottomley to suggest the time was now right for *Thunderclap,* but in a different context; not the collapse of the Wehrmacht before the Allied Blitzkrieg out of Normandy in 1944, but coinciding with continued Russian successes on the East front now, in January 1945, which would give the appearance of co-ordinated planning between the Russians and the Western powers. 'Such a deduction on the part of the enemy would greatly increase the moral effect of both operations,' he wrote. And he suggested additional attacks, by the 15th USAAF from Italy on both Munich and Breslau, as well as the main, shattering blow on Berlin, which would receive 25,000 tons of bombs during four days of day and night attacks by Anglo-American bombers.

On 25 January, everything happened at once. The Joint Intelligence Sub-Committee of the British War Cabinet put out two papers. The first was for Tedder's guidance, telling him that the Russians ought to be assisted by the heavy bombers during the next few weeks, particularly in preventing movement of German Panzer troops from the West to the East. The second was a consideration of Bufton's suggestion. They did not share the belief that 25,000 tons of bombs on Berlin in four days would break Germany's will to fight on, even with the Russians hammering at the gates as well. This was indeed realism, offensive to Trenchard-followers. But they echoed another Trenchard doctrine, the supposed morale effect of repeatedly causing great tides of refugees to flow out from one bombed city to another. This they thought could be done and would materially assist the Russian advance by creating chaos on top of the chaos already created by the refugee masses fleeing before the Red Army. The British official RAF historians summed up these ideas as follows: 'A heavy flow of refugees from Berlin coinciding with the trek westwards of civilians fleeing before the Russian advance "would be bound to create great confusion, interfere with the orderly movement of troops to the front and hamper the German military and administrative machine".'

When Bottomley telephoned Harris that same day, 25 January, his message was resentfully received. Harris said he had always assumed that Berlin was already 'on his plate'. The sting of Bomber Command's defeat over the city in 1943/44 still hurt. But, Bottomley said, this was not just another attack on Berlin, it was the full *Thunderclap* plan, four days of frightfulness from two air forces. This time the USAAF would be in on it too, as Harris had originally wished. As the official historians put it:

Sir Arthur Harris suggested that the main attack on Berlin should be supplemented by simultaneous operations of a like nature against Chemnitz, Leipzig and Dresden which, equally with Berlin, would share the task of housing evacuees from the East and, again equally with Berlin, were focal points in the German system of communications behind the Eastern front.

Here again was the refugee theme, second nature to any devoted follower of Trenchard, which Harris had been for most of his service life; but also, for the first time, Dresden was mentioned in that connection, and by Harris. After the war, in his book, the bomber commander was to try to evade responsibility for the Dresden massacre by saying that the orders for it had come from above his level. This was true, so far as it went, for Winston Churchill intervened in all this minuting and telephoning on the evening of the same day, 25 January.

He spoke to the Air Minister, Sir Archibald Sinclair, who was a believer in the area bombing policy, and demanded to know what plans the RAF had for 'basting the Germans in their retreat from Breslau'. Next day, 26 January, Portal advised Sinclair that: 'we should use available effort in one big attack on Berlin and attacks on Dresden, Leipzig, Chemnitz, or any other cities where a severe blitz will not only cause confusion in the evacuation from the East but will also hamper the movement of troops from the West'. Once more, the refugees were being suggested as a worthwhile target. But Sinclair's report to the Prime Minister was cautious:

The target which the enemy may offer in a large-scale retreat Westward to Dresden and Berlin is best suited to Tactical Air Forces. This is particularly so now when cloud often makes it impossible to bomb from high level. It would be extremely difficult for our heavy bombers to interfere with these enemy movements by direct attack on their lines of retreat.

These statements accord with army experience, which was that while intervention by the heavy bombers tended to be erratic in its effects, the value of the Tactical Air Force was high because it was precise. Sinclair firmly advocated maintaining oil targets as priority, because their destruction helped both the Soviets and the Western Allies equally, but he felt prepared to consider the use of the heavies for area attacks in Eastern Germany when weather precluded accurate bombing of the small targets (not all that small, really) represented by the hydrogenation plants. He named Berlin, Leipzig, Dresden and Chemnitz as 'administrative' and 'main communications' centres for both military and civil purposes. Churchill replied to Sinclair the same day with a whiplash note:

I did not ask you last night about plans for harrying the German retreat from Breslau. On the contrary, I asked whether Berlin, and no doubt other large cities in East Germany, should not now be considered especially attractive targets. I am glad that this is 'under examination'. Pray report to me tomorrow what is going to be done.

Effectively, that note sealed the fate of Dresden. On 27 January Harris was authorized to carry out the attacks which he had himself proposed on 25 January, specifically mentioning the 'evacuees from the East', and naming the four eastern cities in question. That day also, Sinclair hurriedly told the Prime Minister that he had already complied with his wishes:

The Air Staff have now arranged that, subject to the overriding claims of attacks on enemy oil production and other approved target systems within the current directive, available effort should be directed against Berlin, Dresden, Chemnitz and Leipzig or against other cities where severe bombing would not only destroy communications vital to the evacuation from the East but would also hamper the movements of troops from the West . . . The Air Officer Commanding-in-Chief, Bomber Command, has undertaken to attempt this task as soon as the present moon has waned and favourable weather conditions allow. This is unlikely to be before about 4th February.

That was the opening date of the Yalta Conference, which

was to last from 4 to 11 February. And that was when the Prime Minister required a bargaining counter, or at least something to make him appear important and successful in this gathering of the Great Powers. A number of other planners had to approve the scheme formally and most of them did so on 31 January. Tedder mentioned 'Berlin, Leipzig, Dresden and associated cities where heavy attack . . . will hamper movement of reinforcements from other fronts', according to an American study prepared for the USAF Historical Division. The official RAF history by Webster and Frankland gave the sentence in full: 'Berlin, Leipzig, Dresden and associated cities where heavy attack will *cause great confusion in civilian evacuation from the East and* hamper movement of reinforcements from other fronts' (my italics). The British historians were bold enough to tell the whole truth, that the unfortunate, frozen, starving civilian refugees were the first object of attack, before military movements. The Americans doubtless considered this a dangerous admission, but in the long term one tends to trust those historians who appear to be the more honourable and open.

On the first day of the Yalta Conference, 4 February, Stalin introduced the deputy chief of the Red Army general staff, General Antonov, to put the Western Allies 'in the picture' as regards the situation on the East Front. At the end of his lecture, General Antonov made specific requests of the Americans and British. *Point One* concerned the ground forces in the West: to prevent the Germans weakening their forces in the West in order to strengthen them in the East, the Western Allies should engage them by advancing during the first half of February. We shall return to *Point Two* below. *Point Three* concerned the ground forces in Italy: to prevent the Germans withdrawing troops for the East Front, the enemy should be kept busy.

As regards these two points, there was nothing further to be done by the Western Allies: all the plans were in hand. Although the Americans had suffered 76,890 casualties during the Ardennes fighting, they had pushed the Germans back and were now about to advance from the Roer Dams in the north down to the Colmar pocket in the south. The British – Canadian 21st Army Group, its offensive delayed by the necessity of helping the Americans repel the Ardennes attack, was now in position again and ready to attack in four days' time, out of Holland and into Germany.

My own diary for 8 February 1945 records that the Battle of the Reichswald Forest began at 10.00 that morning with:

five hours counter-battery work by 1,400 guns (400 more than Alamein), then five hours barrage. It's a typical Monty set-up. Bags of guns crammed on a narrow front, all your force at one point, and bash in. Unsubtle but usually successful. Jerry knows you're coming, but he can't do much about it. He can't thicken up his front too much, because the gigantic bomber formations we wield will sweep it like a broom.

On the other hand, no one had any illusions about Bomber Command's accuracy at that time. On 14 February, while on the other side of Europe Dresden blazed, I noted that Cleve had been retaken by 15 Scottish Division. 'The place was hit by 400 bombers on the first day, and pretty well ploughed up. Now that we've got it, Jerry is sending over formations of six Stukas at a time. They'll probably do just as much vital damage as our 400 inaccurate heavies.'

What General Antonov asked for in his *Point Two* referred to the American four-motor bomber force as well as Harris's Bomber Command: 'By air action on communications hinder the enemy from carrying out the shifting of his troops to the East from the Western Front, from Norway, and from Italy. In particular, to paralyse the junctions of Berlin and Leipzig.' There was no mention by the Russians of Dresden as a target, no request for the Allies to bomb the city. Indeed, it seemed that the Russians did *not* want Dresden bombed. Apart from Berlin and Leipzig they were not at all keen on having the heavies unload in their backyard, and General Antonov suggested that a bomb-line should be agreed, which ran through Dresden and would prevent attacks by the British and Americans on targets nearby. After the war, the Soviets alleged that the Allies had destroyed cities in East Germany which were bound to fall into Russian hands with the sole purpose of embarrassing the Russians. It was an understandable view-point. In the Canadian army, with which I was then serving, I can recall considerable criticism at this time of the apparent inability of Bomber Command to do anything but turn a town into a useless heap of rubble, more of an obstacle than anything else. The RAF find this view hurtful, in view of the cost to them in the lives of aircrews, which is sad but irrelevant. The customer is usually right.

Up to this moment, the Americans had prided them-selves that they did not do that sort of thing. An air general claimed that never would they throw the strategic bomber at the man in the street in a frankly terror raid. They would attack only key military or industrial targets and they would hit them precisely, with the minimum amount of suffering to the civilian population. But on 3 February 1945, exactly one day before the conference at Yalta began, they had carried out the first part of *Thunderclap*. To aim accu-rately, the bombardiers in the Fortresses and Liberators needed to see the target; if it was obscured by cloud they had to bomb on radar, and the net result was indistinguishable from an indiscriminate Bomber Command area attack by night. In the full knowledge that the targets might be cloud-covered, on 3 February the Americans launched nearly 1,000 Fortresses at Berlin and 400 Liberators at Magdeburg. In a blind mission, the 8th USAAF had an 'average circular probable error of about two miles'; the 15th USAAF had half that – a one circular mile error. A thousand bombers would drench an area with bombs indiscriminately, and although most of the bombing on 3 February proved to be visual after all, the civilian casualties in Berlin were frightful – perhaps as many as 25,000 dead, in a matter of minutes. The ghastly deed could not be concealed from the world, because the newspapers of neutral countries, particularly those of Sweden, were represented in the German capital, and the German press itself was loud with cries of 'terror bombing', 'child murder' and so on.

General Kuter, Arnold's representative at Yalta, was so alarmed that he queried Spaatz (who all along had said he opposed terror bombing) as to whether the revision of Directive No. 3, made at Malta on 31 January, which formalized the idea of attacking East German cities as part of a bombing campaign to help the Russian offensive, was in fact an official authorization to begin indiscriminate American bombing of population centres. The American official historians summarized Spaatz's reply as: 'The Americans were not bombing cities indiscriminately, but attacking transportation facilities inside cities in missions which the Russians had requested and seemed to appreciate.' That was neat, and had some truth in it, but the basic reasons for making such a raid on Berlin one day before the Yalta Conference opened were political and diplomatic: to make clear to the Russians that, despite some setbacks recently in the Ardennes, the United States of America was a super-power capable of wielding overwhelmingly destructive forces.

Churchill intended to write the same lesson on the night sky on behalf of Britain with the help of Bomber Command, and would have done so already had not the weather been unfavourable for Harris's bombers. He had an additional, personal motive: his jealousy of Stalin on the world stage.

The proposition was an extraordinary one: both the British and the Americans apparently thought that they could intimidate the Communists by terrorizing the Nazis. It seems they naïvely believed that the Russians had never seen a totally destroyed city. This was absurd. The Russians had yet to see a city destroyed from the air, but they had seen many, mostly their own, destroyed in other ways, and were hardened to it. Anyone less susceptible to hints of this sort it was difficult to imagine. Stalin and his henchmen had the deaths of uncounted millions of their own people on their consciences, where the guilt seemed to sit easy. Possibly the miscalculation sprang from Harris's famous photo collection of bomb-destroyed cities in Germany, which he was always proud to show around in the hope of making friends and influencing people to give even greater support to Bomber Command. At one time, it was seriously suggested that he show these to Stalin.

Most of the air strategists no longer believed in the Douhet–Trenchard–Harris doctrines, or that a thousand or two-thousand-bomber raid on Berlin would end the war. The Russians did in the end take Berlin, at the cost of more than 100,000 Red Army soldiers killed and an unknown number wounded, heavy German army casualties and an additional civilian death toll in the region of 50,000 killed. The Germans made them fight for every inch of the way, right up to the Reichs Chancellery, and they only capitulated on 4 May, three months after the Yalta Conference and the great American raid. The 'catastrophic blow' had fallen, but without decisive effect.

It was true, however, that the full *Thunderclap* treatment was to have consisted of a combined USAAF – RAF attack amounting to perhaps two thousand bombers, plus fighter escorts. This blow was made ten days later, but its target was Dresden, not Berlin.

The Americans duly notified the Russians. On 7 February General Spaatz, commanding general of all the United States Strategic Air Forces, informed the US military mission in Moscow, for transmission to Stalin, that the 8th Air Force communications targets in East Germany were, in order of priority: Berlin, Leipzig, Dresden, Chemnitz (and others of smaller importance). The military mission passed on the message next day, 8 February. On 12 February General Spaatz told the US military mission that the 8th Air Force intended to attack the Dresden marshalling yards with a force of 1,200 to 1,400 bombers on 13 February. This gave the Russians very little time in which to object, and besides the stated railway targets must have appeared innocuous. But on 13 February the weather was unsuitable, or so the Americans said, and the American attack was postponed by one day to 14 February. The RAF's two waves of attack, planned for the night of 13/14 February, were not affected. The order of assault was therefore reversed, the heaviest blows being delivered first.

The histories notwithstanding, the 1st Air Division of the 8th USAAF did in fact take off for Dresden on 13 February, many, many hours before the RAF's Lancasters; but what they actually did remains mysterious. At the time, there was much argument about where they had been and what they had achieved. The records of the 381 Bomb Group, a part only of the big formation of B-17s, claimed that this group 'turned what might have been a miserable and costly failure into one of our outstanding combat performances. Dresden was briefed as the target centre, but the field order carried a strict injunction that nothing whatsoever would interrupt the bomber stream, heading for a target very close to the advancing Russians in southern Germany.'

To their consternation, the 381st saw the Bomb Group ahead of them wander off course 'because of foul cloud and contrail conditions over the central Reich'. Realizing that 'the time schedule had already been upset, our Group leader had no other choice but to seek a target of opportunity'. The thirty-seven heavy bombers of the 381st peeled off, 'after sustaining considerable damage from AA defenses, while the Group ahead went plowing on through the cumulo-bango weather and flak prevailing over Munster'. Munster is just north of the heavily-defended Ruhr, and a long way from Dresden.

The Group lead bombardier for the day began looking for a hot target through weather that constantly varied between VACU and fubar. Although he was unaware of the full importance of what he finally selected at the time, he lined up on a vast industrial pile which later proved to be the long-sought-after Sudetenlandische Treibstoffwerke, an A-plus priority synthetic oil plant two miles northwest of Brüx, Czechoslovakia.

(This was the plant where Ted Ayling worked, which was supplied with coal from the mine where Eddie Taylor now spent his days.) The 381st's records continue:

As strike photos later proved, lead and high squadrons did an excellent visual job, with heavy and tight bomb concentrations placed in and near the plant buildings. The 12-plane low squadron, failing to recognize the bomb run, made up for the oversight a few minutes later when they hammered home their explosives on the Skoda arms plant at Pilsen.

It was a rough day, with the formations encountering moderate to intense flak, first at Munster, next at Brüx and finally at Pilsen. On the way out, the crews observed our excellent escort in large dogfights with the Luftwaffe although none of our formations was attacked.

This thirty-seven plane Group landed twenty bombers short. Two crews had bailed out over Belgium, four of the men drifting to land behind the German lines. Thirteen bombers had force-landed on the continent, mostly from lack of fuel or because of engine failures. Five more had got back to England but landed away from base. The diarist of the 381st noted:

It was rough back at base after the remnants of the formation came in, too. The rest of the day was spent trying to determine what it was the Fortresses hit. Grave fears were expressed that the formation was over Chemnitz at the bombs away and that the explosives had fallen on the Russians. When the target had been identified, however, there was great rejoicing. For it developed that the bombs had fallen on an objective which the Eighth had been seeking for months.

The airmen's briefings on the ground situation must have been poor, for the Russians were nowhere near Chemnitz yet, being some 100 miles away to the east. It is curious that although Ted Ayling kept a detailed diary of events at the synthetic fuel plant and recorded a distant raid on 8 February and an even more distant one, said to be Chemnitz, on 15 February, he omits 13 February altogether, and cannot now remember.

And where did the other Groups go?

The roughest experience of the day belonged to 2nd

Lieutenant Hugh D. Robinson, co-pilot of a Fortress whose pilot was wounded. They bailed out over Belgium and Robinson landed just inside the Allied lines, where he was picked up by American soldiers. After a visit to hospital in Liège for X-rays, he was returned to England by air, but the aircraft met heavy cloud and flew around until its fuel gave out, when Robinson bailed out for a second time. Still sold on air travel, he hitched a ride in a B-24 Liberator, but as it was taxiing out for take-off the landing gear collapsed.

The 8th USAAF's Dresden mission having gone considerably astray on 13 February, it was replanned for noon on 14 February, which meant that RAF Bomber Command would hit the city first in two waves. The first wave would attack on the evening of the 13th, while the second would arrive in the early dark hours of 14 February, to be followed by the USAAF in daylight. The total number of bombers was to be 1,299 and the bomb weight 3,906.9 tons (but much of that was lightweight incendiaries). The raid was clearly designed to be heavier than that just delivered against Berlin by the USAAF only, whose bombers carried a smaller load than the British. In detail, the 8th USAAF was to fly 527 four-motor bombers carrying 953.3 tons of HE and 294.3 tons of fire bombs; the RAF were to send 772 four-motor bombers carrying 1,477.7 tons of HE and 1,181.6 tons of fire bombs. The Americans were to attack the marshalling yards by radar aiming, the British were to attack the city centre by the marking method, according to the USAF Historical Analysis from which these figures are quoted. The American bombers would be protected by 288 Mustang fighters, and, to confuse the German defences, other important targets would be attacked at around the same time.

The cynic will ask: why so many fire bombs for railway lines (which don't fire easily)? The super-cynic will point out that railway lines are the easiest things to repair rapidly (even the English Southern Railway could do it in a few hours in 1940), and that the German rail system was one of the most elaborate in Europe. And finally, that despite all the Allied air forces could do, in their overwhelming strength at this time, the Germans in fact transferred from the Ardennes to the East Front the whole of the 6th SS Panzer Army, with its army troops, two corps commands, four SS Panzer divisions, both the Führer Escort and Grenadier Brigades, and all its massive artillery and bridging columns.

The great puzzle is why the *Thunderclap* plan was still pursued. The all-American version had been delivered against Berlin, the original target, on 3 February, perfectly timed for the opening of the Conference at Yalta next morning. The Russians would get the message, such as it was. Churchill, for years sensitive to Stalin's increasing influence over world history, had on 26 January demanded action from his own bomber force against Berlin and other East German cities as well, and been told by Harris that for weather and seasonal reasons nothing could be done before 4 February, and by then the Americans had pre-empted the German capital. For weather reasons, Dresden was not bombed until 13 February, and by then the Yalta Conference had been over for two days. There was no longer any bargaining or prestige mileage to be got out of burning the Saxon capital. Perhaps the Prime Minister simply forgot to cancel the raid.

He may have become immersed at once in the fascinating business of redrawing the map of Europe with Roosevelt and Stalin, in which they jointly legalized the handover of 120 million Europeans to the Soviet Empire. In July 1948, Malcolm Muggeridge was to note 'an extraordinary example of the complete irresponsibility of people in authority'. In a draft of his memoirs for serialization, Churchill had:

> put in a sentence to the effect that the Russians always observed their agreements. When it was pointed out to him that this was entirely and dangerously misleading, he struck out the sentence. What is extraordinary is that he had been concerned in making a number of the many agreements which the Russians have broken, and therefore ought, presumably, to be in a better position than most people to know that these agreements have been broken. I've come to the conclusion that he was so power-drunk during the last part of his period in office that he scarcely knew what was going on — just maundered along.

What can certainly be recorded is the proximity of Harris's underground bunker at High Wycombe, from which he directed the bomber war over Germany, to a Churchill residence; and the fact that he was a visitor there. Much may have been said which was not always put on paper; or the paper would simply be confirmation of something already discussed verbally. In the words of the official historians, in summer 1944: 'Dresden took its place alongside Leipzig and Chemnitz as among the towns which Sir Arthur Harris had for some time believed to be in urgent need of destruction.'

Stalin had asked for Leipzig, which was understandable in military and industrial terms. Even Chemnitz, at a pinch, could be justified: there was certainly a lot of industry there, and much of it was war industry, including important factories making tanks. But Dresden — and especially the centre of Dresden . . . The air historians, both British and American, and indeed the briefing officers for the raids, were to be put to immense trouble in having to depict the city as a sinister cross between Essen, Hamm and some German Aldershot.

In considering the *Thunderclap* suggestion in August

1944, Sir Charles Portal had written one sentence which
was undoubtedly well-founded: 'Immense devastation
could be produced if the entire attack was concentrated on
a single big town other than Berlin and the effect would be
especially great if the town was one hitherto relatively
undamaged.' The attraction Dresden had for Bomber
Command was that the centre of the city should burn easily
and magnificently; as indeed it was to do.

6
'Enjoy the War for the Peace will be Awful'

MARKING-UP THE TARGET: 13 FEBRUARY 1945

But to English visitors particularly, a visit to Dresden is more than a homage to the Sistine Madonna and all the other great treasures of the Zwinger; for the great city of art, set so graciously on the Elbe, was destroyed by British and American bombers partly in retaliation for German attacks on Britain.
— Fodor's 1974 Guide: *Germany*

The attack on Dresden by the RAF was to be carried out in two waves, with a long enough interval to allow fire brigades and rescue teams to come into the city from outside, in time to be slaughtered by the second wave. It had been usual for fire fighters to enter burning cities before the bombing ended, accepting casualties to men and equipment in exchange for beating down some of the conflagrations, just as an attacking force might lose fifty to one hundred bombers in order to inflict the blow.

On just such a night in 1940 I watched the fire brigades from outside rumble into Southampton, silhouetted against a wall of flame-reddened smoke, with the incessant, fluctuating thunder of the Luftwaffe bombers passing overhead at one every minute or so, all night. The firemen, the heavy rescue teams, the dockers, the doctors, the nurses, all were part of the battle in the days and nights of total war; though they did not kill bombers, they fought back. It was their resolution against the courage of the aircrews. Indeed, they were more truly combatants than the soldiers who next morning with bayoneted rifles stood guard over the smouldering, smoking, collapsing wreckage of the city centre, and kept back the crowds of sightseers drifting on idle feet over acres of broken glass.

For the first time in a provincial blitz, for added effect, the Germans came two nights running with 128 planes on the first night and 123 on the second, a total of 251; and in those two nights they dropped 299 tons of high explosive bombs and 1,184 canisters of incendiaries, killing 214 people. As well as the houses, shops, offices and cinemas hit, both the old and the new docks had been battered, the Rank flour mills, the General Motors factory, the works of Harland & Wolff, the Pirelli-General Cable works, the Ordnance Survey, the Civic Centre. Fire appliances from no fewer than seventy-five other localities had been sucked in to fight the flames, some from as far away as Nottingham.

German losses must have been negligible, for the RAF by night, whether on the offensive or the defensive, was then almost totally ineffective; nor were the guns much better. For an air force never designed to undertake strategic tasks, it was a fair effort. The damage done to the British war economy by far exceeded the cost to the Germans of doing it.

The target-finding technique used was far ahead of that of the British. It was based on the Lorenz beam blind-landing system invented before the war and taught in the RAF as well as the Luftwaffe. Guided by sound signals in his earphones, the pilot flew along a main radio beam laid across the target while his bomb aimer waited to hear the sound of the two or three intersecting beams which would tell him in time how far he was from the target and enable him to calculate the exact point at which to release the bombs. Sometimes the British were able to interfere with the beams, so that the bombing went astray; or the Germans used a Pathfinder force both to find the target and then mark it up with flares and fires for the main force, so that they did not need to be equipped with the latest radio systems. But the principal characteristic of the beam method as used was that a single line of bombers played follow-my-leader. If all went well, a good concentration in space might be achieved — that is, most of the bombs would fall into the target area — but they would be falling over a period of some six to eight hours. This gave the defence maximum time in which to react, to fight back by smothering the incendiaries and dousing the fires, before all could spread and become uncontrollable.

Just as the toad beneath the harrow knows best of all where each sharp point goes, so it was the British who realized first that concentration in time as well as space was bound to be the most efficient way of using a fire-raising force of bombers. For Dresden more than four years later, the method had been perfected. Harris planned that the first wave of 244 heavy four-motor bombers, all Lancasters, would pass over the target in the space of from ten to fifteen minutes. Three hours later, the second wave of 529 heavy four-motor bombers, again all Lancasters, would pass over within about twenty to thirty minutes. The concentration would be obtained by forming a broad stream of bombers stacked at various heights. They would carry 1,477.7 tons of HE and 1,181.6 tons of incendiaries. Then in daylight, on two days running, the USAAF would send a total of 527 heavy four-motor bombers. B-17 Flying Fortresses, carrying 953.3 tons of HE and 294.3 tons of incendiaries. And they would be escorted by hundreds of fighters, some of which would be directed to go right down on the deck and strafe transport targets.

The total number of bombers from both air forces would be 1,299, the total tonnage of HE bombs, 2,431, and incendiaries 1,476 tons, over a period of three days. The

German two-day attack on Southampton had involved in comparison only 251 twin-engined medium bombers carrying 299 tons of HE and 1,184 incendiary canisters. In sum, the raids on Dresden would be ten times as heavy as those on Southampton. But this was not all. Whereas Southampton was only just across the Channel for the Luftwaffe in 1940, Dresden could be reached only after an immensely long flight into the heart of Europe. This was the difference both in reach and in power between two strategic air forces on the one hand and an air force designed originally only to co-operate with an army on the other. It was this enormous power, ready to their hands, which made the bomber marshals and air generals vain. Even in the Luftwaffe, in its early days, they had felt something of the same euphoria of power, saying to each other: 'The day that Hermann puts everything up, the birds'll have to walk!' It was impossible to believe an enemy existed who would not be cowed by the sight of such a force.

The bayonets on the rifles of the soldiers at Southampton in 1940 were visible proof of what their leaders thought: that the 'gorblimeys' were unreliable. In Portsmouth, too, the military were soon to be paraded for the same purpose — to the fury of their officers, who saw no signs of panic or of pillage, and felt that the army was being misused by the civil power. At national leadership level, the lesson was never learned: that the led were braver, or perhaps just more stubbornly stupid, than most of the leaders. Those leaders still thought that they could crack German morale at one tremendous blow.

The method of target finding and marking by the RAF was an improved version of those pioneered by the Luftwaffe against Britain: pathfinder squadrons to navigate to the target area by radio beam. A squadron of Lancasters, the flare force, would identify the target area by radar and then illuminate it and keep it lit up for the marker force, eight fast twin-motor Mosquitoes, which would go down on the deck and identify a previously selected aiming point without doubt, and then mark it with large red incendiaries. This process, and the progress of the main force of bombers also, would be controlled by a master bomber in a Mosquito who would orbit the target at low level, check that the aiming point had been correctly identified and accurately marked, and keep on circling the target to maintain tight control by radio of the bombing and check any tendency for it to become wild or 'creep back'. By means of one of three radio-link Lancasters, the master bomber could send messages back to base in England, if necessary.

If the first wave succeeded in their fire-raising, they would also have provided a visual beacon for the much larger second wave to home in on. This wave too would have a master bomber to control the development of the attack from low level; but in this case he would be flying not a fast, frail and agile Mosquito but a souped-up Lancaster four-motor bomber. The master bombers did not have as much latitude as they would have liked: ultimate power lay with the Air Officer Commanding back at High Wycombe, in accordance with current British practice, for naval battles also tended to be run from England even when there were admirals in the far-off ships concerned, who might be thought to know their business best.

The master bombers had to take great risks, offering themselves as targets. Ordinary crews had the protection of flying within a dense stream of bombers, rather as fish will shoal when predators are about. Even so, from what Harris at High Wycombe thought of contemptuously as the 'rabbits' of Bomber Command some crews would tend to drop short — the famous 'creep back' from the aiming point. As one navigator put it, up to the target you were on government business, but after you had dropped your bombs, you were free and could go home. The tendency to get the government's business over and done with as soon as possible was strong in almost everyone. By how much it might be overcome varied not only with the individual's character and circumstances, or with his state of nerves at the time, but also according to the strength of his beliefs. For example, the pilot who would not try too hard against an oil refinery in the early days of the war, because the whole thing was pretty pointless and ineffective, would 'press on regardless' when it came to bombing the invasion barges gathered in the Channel ports. That was worth dying for, while the other wasn't.

In less plain cases, a great deal depended on how much the crews believed in their leaders. Some did, but there were many too who nicknamed Harris 'the Butcher', not so much because he cared nothing for the lives of German civilians but because they believed that he cared nothing for their own either. 'Sending them out for the sake of sending them out' was one Englishman's condemnation of Harris's policies. A Scots-Canadian navigator was more brutal: 'Butcher Harris didn't give a damn how many men he lost as long as he was pounding the shit out of German civilians . . . An air force twin for Haig of the Somme, Ypres, Passchendaele. One thing about Harris, though, he played no favourites. He was just as willing to sacrifice Brits as Canadians.'

Men who thought like this did their job with cold, professional efficiency; pride in self, pride in squadron, pride in Canada, perhaps, or England or Australia, New Zealand or South Africa. From the master bombers even more was required. They had not merely to fly to the target and back, they had to orbit the target throughout the raid, from start to finish, and from low level, within range of even the light flak, because only from low down was it possible often to see what was happening. From above, a burning city soon became a mass of flame-glowing smoke, no landmarks visible. Often, it lingered for days.

Over Dresden, there were to be two master bombers. For the first wave, controlling the attack of No. 5 Group, intended to turn the inner city into a beacon for the second wave, it was Wing Commander Maurice Smith, a very experienced pilot who had won his 'wings' in 1939, spent three years as a flying instructor and had now almost completed his first tour. It was his thirty-third operation, and his tenth as a Mosquito controller or master bomber.

Controller for the second wave, the main attack, was Squadron Leader Peter de Wesselow. In 1939 he had been in the army, but later joined Bomber Command of the RAF, believing that this force was doing something positive for the war effort. Dresden was to be his seventy-second operation, and he was to do two tours and a little more. The force he was to direct was drawn from 1, 3, 6 and 8 Groups, more than twice as many as in the first wave of attack to be controlled by Wing Commander Smith.

Only a minority of aircrews completed thirty operations, let alone seventy-two. The odds against were too great. Originally, Maurice Smith had flown Lancasters with 619 Squadron of 5 Group through the dangerous nights of 1944. There had been V1 sites to bomb, regardless of weather; the targets obvious (and nearly impervious to bombing); and heavy losses with the night fighter flares drifting down above, and the Lancaster beside you falling away as the cannon fire hit. There had been the time he had been coned by the searchlights over Brunswick in a clear sky, pinned there like a bug on a board for the flak and the fighters to see. Mouth suddenly dry, Smith had begun to dive and twist the heavy bomber in the 'corkscrew' evasive manoeuvre which took all the strength of a strong, fit man to manage for more than thirty seconds; and in that emergency had broken free of the blinding beams after more than two minutes of desperate effort at the controls. Worse still perhaps had been the anticipation they had all felt when briefed for the massive daylight raid on Berlin in conjunction with the Americans which the original *Thunderclap* plan of the invasion summer had called for. Smith felt that this plan was an act of desperation, that the losses must be prohibitive; they probably wouldn't even make Berlin, let alone get out again. He did not know — few did until 1981 — of the sinister arguments behind the scenes for the use of anthrax bombs against Berlin and other great German cities, with Churchill urging germ and gas warfare to be begun, if appropriate, against the views of the planners who considered the issue of the war firmly decided now that the Allied armies were established ashore in France. Smith just felt glad that a dangerously unsound operation, from the viewpoint of the aircrews, had been cancelled.

Very often, however, the most intimidating factor for a pilot was not enemy opposition but the necessity of carrying out long, tiring flights in bad weather. The co-pilots had been removed from Lancasters, being replaced by a flight engineer; and the autopilot was usually wired off as being unreliable and unsuitable for rough air conditions. A long journey back through storms could be terrifying, but 'with a really good crew, you felt the support strength of the six men round you. Airborne in a Lanc, the pilot was busy and surrounded, whereas the rear gunners, remote and cold in the tail end, were more likely to be hit and had nothing active to do — nothing but search and wait.'

In October 1944 Maurice Smith was moved from the Lancasters of 619 Squadron to 54 Base HQ at Coningsby as a master bomber on Mosquitoes. 'I felt badly at having to abandon my crew except for the navigator, and I missed their presence tremendously.' He was pretty lonely there, for the only other master bomber was a Wing Commander Woodruffe. As they took turn about to fly operations, they did not see much of each other, and the Base HQ officers did not count as colleagues. But the WAAF officers — signals, stores, catering, equipment — helped to produce a friendly atmosphere with tea, chat and even parties. It was a curious kind of war. 'In an aircraft we were in a relatively clean, scientific environment; there was some mental strain only. Then we returned to wholly civilized surroundings — a hot bath, clean clothes, bacon and egg. This built morale. There was very little worry, once one was in the aircraft. I had tremendous confidence in our planning and in our aircraft.'

Normally, the marker force controlled by the master bomber consisted of five or six Mosquitoes. For Dresden, there were eight. The markers were coloured incendiaries to be dropped in one big blob on the aiming point; they usually burned for about three minutes, so they would have to be kept topped up. For Dresden, the markers were to be red. A few yellow markers were carried also; they cancelled a red and so covered the eventuality of a misplaced marker.

The target area was to be Dresden Altstadt — the old city within the half-circle of railway lines — but the aiming point to be marked was just outside the city to the north-west, one of three distinctive sports stadiums in the open common land between the Friedrichstadt hospital complex and the city slaughterhouse where some of the American prisoners were. Under the light of the flares swiftly dropping downwards below the procession of illuminator Lancasters, the marker leader (who was also the reserve master bomber) would try to identify the right stadium and then mark it with a great blob of red, while the master bomber, circling low down, would check both his judgement and his aim. When the bomb-carrying Lancasters arrived, they would offset their bombsights so that whatever was aimed at the red glow in the stadium would not in fact fall there but beyond, in the built-up area of the Altstadt, which was the target. With a wind in the western arc, the stadium should always be clear of the smoke drifting away to the east from the blazing city, and the tendency to bomb wild would be reduced. Courses and offsets were also to be varied, so that the bombs would fall in sticks like the blades of a fan and effectively obliterate all of the Altstadt, at any rate in theory. Many times in the past, such plans had been frustrated by bad weather over the target or by heavy, accurate flak which had forced the attacking bombers to jink when they should have been flying straight-and-level.

The briefing at Coningsby went to all the squadrons of No. 5 Group; that is, the first wave. Air Commodore Satterly, the base commander, told Wing Commander Smith that the main reason for the raid was that Russian advances on the East Front at that point had made it one of the main communications centres. But Smith recalled:

I had a clear impression that this operation was of special interest to Churchill. Also it was an attack by all the Groups of Bomber Command, so it was represented as an honour to go in first; and that meant we had to get it off right — we didn't want to fail. But I was also given the impression that the destruction of an untouched city of this sort would make a significant effect on the Russians — who were near and would soon be nearer. We had the impression that the Russians discounted what Bomber Command could do. Although we did not regard them like the other Allies, we respected the Russian army and wanted to help them against Hitler.

For the Lancasters, which were slower and would fly

zigzag courses between flak areas to try to confuse the Germans as to the target right up to the last moment, the trip to Dresden would take about five hours. For the faster Mosquitoes, which would fly more directly, it would take 2½ hours.

The main force squadrons began taking off about 6 pm on the evening of 13 February. For Bernard McCosh, a second tour mid-upper gunner of 167 Squadron, it was his fortieth operation. At briefing, they had been told to expect little trouble from fighters on the way, but it was a deep penetration, almost to the point of no return. At one time, McCosh had been a starry-eyed innocent too, but a taste of 'Happy Valley' – the heavily defended Ruhr – had changed his mind. Whereas in the beginning a raid was a wonderful novelty, now he thought: next time we go, we won't come back. The chances of being killed he believed were in the order of 80 per cent. He would have plenty of time to think about it tonight, ten hours in a cramped, icy turret with nothing to do but keep a constant lookout for the fighters which could far outrange him with their cannon and, some of them, could creep in underneath in the Lancaster's blind spot and blow them out of the air with one burst of *'Schräge Musik'* – the 'Jazz Music' of two 20 mm cannon mounted to fire upwards into the belly of a bomber.

The Lancaster of 106 Squadron which Flying Officer Driver was navigating became airborne from Metheringham in Lincolnshire at 6.10 pm with a bomb load of one 500 lb HE bomb and 8000 lb of fire-raising incendiaries, and set course for the Channel coast via Reading. Time on target was to be 2215 – 2219 hours (1015 – 1019 pm). The target was to be illuminated from 10 pm onwards, allowing ten to fifteen minutes for the Mosquitoes to locate and mark up the aiming point. They droned uneventfully over Allied-occupied France, flying first south-east, then east, and then north-east towards the Ruhr. North of Aachen they changed course again to slip between Gladbach and Cologne, here crossing the lines and entering Hitler Germany. Now they could be threatening Kassel, or Halberstadt, or Berlin. Flak sparkled in the sky on both sides, showing where some of the bombers had got off course and had flown over a heavily-defended city.

Back at Coningsby Maurice Smith and his navigator, Leslie Page, had watched the main force go off and seen most of the Station go to bed, although the operations room and flying control were permanently manned, of course. There was just one cold Mosquito out there on the tarmac. They went out to it, alone, using hand torches; then they got in, being careful not to work up a sweat in their heavy clothing. The marker force Mosquitoes had taken off just before them from Woodhall Spa, so they went off completely alone into the night, observing radio silence. They would hear nothing more for 2½ hours, when the target should be just ahead and it would be time to test communications with the marker force.

On 8 February, the day the British and Canadians attacked into the Rhineland, Ted Ayling, still a prisoner working in the oil refinery at Brüx, noted in his diary that:

There was talk of some camps being liberated by the Russians. It sounded too good to be true, although we all fully realized that the end was now really in sight . . . I marvelled at the regularity with which our rations arrived — although small — considering the prevailing difficult conditions. The Huns had to be admired for still managing to issue something, with three invading armies over-running more than half of the starving country.

Although the bomber marshals automatically regarded all rail communications as basically military, this was not so in Germany even at the end, any more than it had ever been true of the railways in England. Much of the traffic was civilian, a multitude of private individuals moving about for their own very personal reasons, although in Dresden refugees from the East still predominated.

One of many people who used the main station at Dresden on 13 February was Mrs Dora Daniel, a chance victim of the USAAF emphasis on bombing railway targets rather than residential areas.

She recalled:

The year 1944 was for us personally a happy year. In October I was expecting my first child by my second husband. We were looking forward to it very much. My first husband had been killed in action on the Russian Front, and therefore I already had a six-year-old girl who was waiting excitedly for her little brother. It was moving to see how she watched over me, so that I wouldn't hurt myself.

We had air raid warnings only now and again, but no attacks. We were firmly convinced that Dresden was too beautiful to be attacked, although the wife of a major once told me that Dresden would become the masterpiece of all air raids. I didn't pass that on. Then on 7 October 1944 came the raid on the Wettiner railway station, not far from our business and our flat, in which some of our acquaintances were killed.

(Thirty-three aircraft dropped seventy-two tons of HE in that first raid.) Three weeks after that, Mrs Daniel's time came and she was taken to the nearby Friedrichstadt hospital for the birth of a son, Holm. A few minutes after his birth, the air raid alarm sounded and she had to go down into the cellar of the hospital among the central heating pipes. Nothing happened on that occasion, but she had him baptized as soon as possible, just in case. The eventuality almost arrived on 16 January 1945, when the 8th USAAF sent 133 bombers to Dresden to attack rail targets with 280 tons of HE and 41 tons of incendiaries. Gretel, their maid, who refused to take shelter, came running down into the air raid shelter, her face blackened with smoke and tears running down her cheeks, to tell them that 'it was all over with the beautiful business and the flat'. Dora's second husband Walter was a cripple, having lost an arm and the use of one leg on the Eastern Front, but together they tried to save what they could from the bombed building, helped by prisoners of war.

Two Russians and two Englishmen carried our piano down the crooked stairs. Together with the foreigners, we made quite a good working team. In spite of friend or foe and language difficulties, we had one thing in common – every one of us could end up the following day under the ruins. And this is exactly what did happen during the great attack. Many foreigners were killed.

It was on the morning of the great attack, 13 February 1945, that Mrs Daniel decided to take the first step in leaving Dresden altogether before the Russians came. She would go out into the countryside of the Erzgebirge, where her sister was living with her baby, and bring them both back to Dresden first, so that they could all leave together. Getting seats on trains was difficult, but she was lucky because she was not weighed down by heavy loads, unlike the refugees.

Masses of people from Silesia with their children and their carts were standing on the platform. As I only carried one bag I walked round the train to the other side and got in there and had a nice seat. The train was jam-packed and many, many people stood outside and wept. I thought: these poor people, now they must wait till tomorrow morning in this awful cold.

For most of them, however, the waiting was much briefer than that.

By going into the country, Mrs Daniel was also hoping to do a little 'hamstering' for her family, because she was visiting a farm. She was already in bed, tired out, when there was the sound of planes, so many that she couldn't hear herself speak. 'It reminded me of the wild roaring of the animals I heard in Dresden Zoo, but a thousand times louder. "Oh, dear God, don't let anyone of my loved ones be killed! I have already lost one man, the business and the flat." ' Her daughter, Bärbel, was with Mrs Daniel's parents in the suburb of Trachenberge, a few miles north of Dresden, while 3½-months-old Holm was with his father and the maids in Friedrichstadt, near the hospital. When she and her sister saw that the bright glow of the fires was indeed Dresden, they 'cried terribly'.

At 1959 hours, that is at one minute to 8 o'clock that evening, Flying Officer Driver had marked the position of their 106 Squadron Lancaster as a little north of Amiens in France, with 2¼ hours still to go before the target.

At almost exactly the same time a fifteen-year-old boy from Leipzig, Gerhard Kühnemund, missed his connection at Dresden. The train he was on, coming from Kamenz, pulled in to Dresden ten minutes after the Leipzig train had gone. Such were the hazards of wartime travel. Gerhard was wearing the uniform of the Hitler Youth, because he had just attended a four-day leadership course at Meissen, and had taken the opportunity afterwards to pay a call on his brother's fiancée, who lived at Kamenz. His brother was serving far to the south in Italy with 26 Panzer Division, and Gerhard had not previously met the bride-to-be. Now what was he to do? His mother would certainly be worried. Miserably, he went to the waiting room in the station with his luggage, prepared to sit there all night until the first train next morning.

Then he recalled that he had an Aunt Else in Dresden, whom he had not seen for many years. She lived some-where out on Serrestrasse, one of the low numbers, he thought. Taking a tram out in that direction, he found the house and of course was offered a bed for the night. He and his aunt had a good deal to talk about, and they were still chatting when the sirens sounded at about 2200 hours (10 pm). 'Dresden will be spared again, of course,' his aunt remarked. 'All the same, we have to go down into the cellar.' But they had hardly left the flat before an HE bomb blew the windows in. Nothing remains of Serrestrasse today, and although Gerhard did get home to Leipzig, his face did not look like that of a fifteen-year-old boy any more.

At 7 pm, an hour before Gerhard Kühnemund missed his connection at the main station by the Altstadt, over the River Elbe in Dresden Neustadt the Circus Sarrasani had opened to an audience of 2,000. The circus was housed in a permanent building and, apart from a few cinemas still open, was almost the only place of entertainment left in Dresden. The artists were men who could not be used at the front, and the animals were those which had still to be evacuated to safety at Bad Schandau; they included nine unfortunate tigers and lucky Wally, the hippopotamus. And there was the young girl equestrienne, Regina Beer, who was to die with her horses, riddled by bomb splinters. Just before 10 pm as the comic Lindströms were finishing their act, and just as Enrico Caroli was about to enter the arena on his unridable donkey, the sirens began to howl. Hugo Rogge, the producer, came to the microphone to announce that the show was over. Neither he nor the resentful audience realized that it was not just for that night, but for ever. Many did not go to the Circus shelters at all, but hurried outside in an effort to get home. They found the streets brightly lit by the flares of the illuminator Lancasters.

*　　*　　*

When Mrs Soldammer went on duty that evening at the
telephone exchange as a night-shift operator, she had met
on the way to work:

people dressed up in the most amusing costumes, ready to celebrate Shrove Tuesday night. Understandably, they were following
the then well-known (but dangerous to quote openly) axiom:
  'Enjoy the war, for the peace will be awful.'
They were probably on their way to a party or fancy-dress party.
There were only happy and laughing faces among them and even I
could not help smiling secretly to myself at the thought which
occurred to me – how much I would like to go with them. But duty
was duty. Towards 2200 hours, as usual, I saw to my air raid tasks
in the upper storeys of the telephone exchange, dressed in denims
with a light helmet on my head. My colleagues and I were all firmly
convinced that this night like all others would pass quietly. Not for
one moment could we imagine an air raid could be made on our
'hospital city'. The Red Cross on a white ground was plainly visible
on the roofs of the great hospitals – the Friedrichstadt, the
Johannstadt, the former Rudolf Hess hospital, the Josephstift, the
Carola and the Burgberg. Then there was the small castle in
Bautzenerstrasse, and four villas and former cafés in the Grosser
Garten park which had been converted to army hospitals or
maternity homes.
  In the railway stations there was maximum activity. A great
number of refugee trains had arrived again from Silesia, which
were waiting to continue their journey and whose passengers were
being taken care of by the Red Cross helpers who gave them coffee
and other necessary things which were still available. And through
the city streets moved the trekkers on foot, and the lorries and
horse-drawn carts of the refugees who were on their way to the
West. They came from East Prussia, West Prussia, Pomerania, all
hoping that they would at least spend a quiet night in Dresden.
  Suddenly a thundering and roaring which made the whole earth
tremble. An earthquake? But immediately the sirens went, short
and eerie through the night; then they were completely silent. The
enemy aircraft were already overhead, suspended like swarms of
bees. Hell broke loose. We in the fourth storey of the telephone
exchange were completely confused. Everywhere in the sky stood
the light-markers ready to show the attackers the way and they

dropped their canisters like torches on the town. Only here and there could be heard the dying sound of a siren, like a last gasp.

In a ward in the Friedrichstadt hospital was a twenty-year-old girl, Annemarie Waehmann, whose family owned a transport business in Dresden, and with her was a fifteen-year-old refugee from Silesia, Hilde, with suspected lupus. Hilde's family — her mother, two sisters and an aunt — had been put into a refugee camp near the main station by the Altstadt which doubtless figured as a 'specific military installation' in American plans — of course the use to which 'hutted camps' are being put is often hard to make out from aerial photographs. Annemarie was suffering from a skin disease on the face, caused either by some ersatz food or possibly from the chemicals of the photographic laboratory in which she now worked.

She had had a privileged youth, happy and carefree, with private schooling followed by technical college, interspersed with visits to the opera, the theatre and musical evenings, and weekend drives out into the countryside. When the time came to do her one year's voluntary service to the National Socialist state, her father had said: 'Go on a farm and learn for once in your life how difficult it is to earn your bread.' She had learned, a lot. When war broke out in 1939, although her father was forty-four years old, he had made a special application to Admiral Raeder to join the navy, which he loved. The application was accepted and her father was killed off the coast of France on 24 January 1941. To his family, it seemed the end of the world.

All day on the 12th, Annemarie had been furious. It was her best friend's birthday and she was having a party in Räcknitzstrasse. Just because Annemarie had a silly sordid little infection, she couldn't go. On the evening of the 13th, she and Hilde and the other girls in her hospital room were playing cards. Then, before 10 o'clock, the sirens went; and not just the preliminary alert but the full warning! That was unusual. It implied that the authorities had been caught napping. Normally, the people she knew didn't bother to go down to the cellar when the warnings were sounded, they just threw a coat over their nightclothes and waited for the 'all clear'. Now, the Sisters were running along the hospital corridors calling: 'Get dressed, get dressed! Quickly, get down to the cellar.' She recalled:

Bedridden patients were put into push-chairs, and there was nothing but hurrying and rushing about. We had hardly been in the cellar for five minutes when hell broke loose. There was a crashing and thundering, whistling and howling as at the last judgement day. Many screamed in fear, and prayed, and we crept trembling under the beds (as if that would do us any good!).

Gisela-Alexandra Moeltgen, who had been born a von Beyer, was the wife of the head of the Friedrichstadt hospital. She was very ill herself at this time with blood-poisoning, contracted while she was evacuating her two baby boys, one four years old, the other 5½, from the threatened city to her parents' home at Murnau in Bavaria, where they would be safe from the Russians. Her surgeon husband fetched her back to Dresden and had her admitted to a clinic at the Friedrichstadt. After treatment she was allowed to go home to rest for two weeks at the house of her grandparents at Grosser Garten, on the corner of Park-strasse and Tiergartenstrasse (the street running alongside the great park where the Dresden Zoo complex was). She now had to learn to walk again. Meanwhile the Russians had encircled Breslau, and if she was to be reunited with her children, Gisela would have to leave quickly. In normal times, nothing would have been easier. Her car stood in the garage in first-class running order and all she needed was a driver and some documents.

Before she could get them, 'a super-National Socialist person' heard about her projected private journey of escape (which was defeatist) and reported the matter to the Gestapo. And that was that. No one now would dare to provide her with travel documents. As far as rail travel was concerned, the doctors considered it impossible for her to undertake such a long journey (the trains were very slow in wartime) without having a sleeping compartment, and such things were not to be had while the refugees were flooding through Dresden. Nevertheless, she decided to go, if Hans, her husband, could accompany her. He, however, was told that if he left his post at the hospital to help his sick wife on her journey he would be treated as a 'deserter' (the penalty for which was summary execution). The best he could do for his wife was to obtain a reserved seat for her on the express train leaving Dresden main station at 10 o'clock in the evening of 13 February, and to arrange for a young doctor who was unfit for war service to go with his wife. He put on his oldest clothes in which to see her off, because he was to help carry the luggage.

Gisela was now able to walk again, although slowly. The men carried between them the two suitcases, the rucksack and a large parcel containing all they could save, including the presents given to the children at Christmas. There was a large, wooden model of a Post Office van, gleamingly beautiful; and a wonderful school satchel made of leather. In one suitcase were all the children's christening presents and the most valuable pieces of Gisela's silver; Hans was going to bury the rest before the Russians came. In the other luggage were some of her clothes — nine sets of brand-new underwear and stockings, three pairs of new shoes, all her warm winter dresses, pullovers and so on, and three pairs of boots belonging to the children. The contents of a recent food parcel had been put into the second suitcase, and this included 6 lb of rice. This was badly needed, because Gisela had lost 26 lb during her illness and now weighed barely 105 lb.

In a narrative written very shortly afterwards, while all the details were clear in her memory, Gisela wrote:

The seats on the train were fine. It stood ready in the main station, when there was a preliminary air raid warning. Everybody's eyes were fixed on the station clock, expecting the imminent departure of the train. Suddenly, information came through the loud-speakers that the train could not leave – someone had pulled the communication cord. Was this sabotage? Or did it happen by accident when people climbed into compartments through the windows? I don't know. In any case, all the communication cords were checked and men with lights feverishly inspected the brake-blocks. In the meantime, the full air raid warning had been given and the station was in complete darkness. The platform had become deserted and only Hans was standing outside the window of my compartment, refusing to go before the train left. I was certain that something terrible was going to happen. After all, it was the 13th! Suddenly, word got around that the train had to be vacated at once.

Accurate weather forecasting so deep into Germany was difficult. Cloud cover was 10/10ths over the continent, as expected, which was why little trouble from night fighters was anticipated; but the forecast was that the skies would clear over Dresden at about 10 pm and stay clear for only a short while, so the timing of the various interlocking moves of the raid was important. And apart from the main raid there were to be spoof and diversionary attacks to keep the German night fighter controllers guessing – and, it was hoped, guessing wrong.

Maurice Smith had lifted his Mosquito off the ground back at Coningsby at three minutes to 8 o'clock. After nearly two hours' flying he was above cloud at around 20,000 feet with a clear sky over him but no sight of the ground below. He and his navigator were searching for the two radio beams which would give them their position accurately in relation to Dresden. At this range, because of the curvature of the earth, they had to be high to pick up the beams, which made straight lines from their source and did not follow the surface of the globe. The beams were also faint, but at 9.49 they picked up the first one and at 9.56 the second. They were fifteen miles south-east of Chemnitz, an industrial city (now called Karl-Marx-Stadt; nobody knows why), which lies at the foot of the Erzgebirge not far from Dresden. Somewhere around them should be the eight other Mosquitoes of the marking force. Wing Commander Smith began to call them up one after the other. 'How do you read me? Over.'

'Clear 5's,' replied the marker leader.

Other Mosquitoes reported reception as 'a little bit distorted' or 'receiving you very faintly'.

Back and forth the clear-speech, uncoded messages went out four miles high over central Germany, to be recorded on a wire-recorder installed in 'Link 1', Flight Lieutenant McConnell's Lancaster of the pathfinding No. 97 Squadron, one of the two squadrons whose duty was to identify Dresden by radar, mark the general area of the city with a 'Primary Green' flare, and then keep it lit up with ordinary flares while the marker Mosquitoes went down one after the other to find and mark the aiming point, that sports stadium on the Grosses Ostragehege between the slaughterhouse and the Friedrichstadt hospital.

Smith called Link 1: 'How d'you hear me? Over.'

'Loud and clear. Over,' came back from McConnell.

'Loud and clear also. Thank you,' replied Smith. Then he called up the Mosquito of the marker leader, also invisible in the solid cloudscape lying below him. 'Are you below cloud yet? Over.'

'Not yet. Out,' replied marker leader. If the cloud was solid over Dresden almost to the ground, no closely-planned, intricate attack could be carried out. Main Force would just have to bomb blind on sky marker flares whose position in relation to the city would be only approximate. The bombing would be badly scattered.

Smith called the marker leader again: 'Do you see that Green yet?' (Meaning the Primary Green to be displayed above the city by one of the flare force Lancasters.) Back came the reply: 'OK I see it.' And a moment later: 'The cloud is not very thick. Over.' 'Thank you,' replied Smith. 'What do you make the base of it?'

'The base is about 2,500. Out.'

'Thank you. Out.'

That decided Wing Commander Smith to come down quick. When he was still ten miles from the target, four miles above it, the weather assessment was that three layers of cloud were moving in, with thin layers at 15–16,000 feet and 6–8,000 feet, with just wispy cloud below that at 3–5,000 feet. 'Having cleared cloud to check position, we were almost on Dresden,' he recalled:

So I had to do a tremendous dive to the target up to about 400 mph. There was a tightening of the controls, no extra engine noises because the throttles were part-closed, but a roar of wind over the aircraft. It was not a consistent angle of dive, I was half-spiralling to see better below. When you throttled back, the exhaust stubs gave off long yellow-blue flames – you made yourself rather visible and you might affect your own night vision. I pulled out just below the lower layer of cloud at 3,000 feet.

Dresden from under the flares at 2,000 feet looked surprisingly like a model. Imagine a big model railway such as that at Beaulieu and with most of the main lighting out, and you in the viewing gallery six feet or so above its level. Light and shadow are accentuated, rivers, lakes and some glass reflect at the right angles. Railway lines snake through the buildings. Big, conspicuous features show up well at some angles but hardly at all at others. Patches of mist or smoke blank out small areas. Markers had to memorize the city plan carefully or risk becoming disoriented as they circled, dived, and pulled up again. At minimum flight levels of about 500 feet, individual vehicles and figures could be distinguished quite well. There was virtually no colour except the red TIs (Target Indicators), and flames as the attack developed. The flares sank and drifted quite quickly so targets were seldom illuminated very brightly and then only for a very short while.

At just after 2205 hours (10.05 pm) the marker leader called out 'Tally Ho!' That was to warn the other pilots that he had identified the aiming point and was diving to mark it with a red TI. Then Marker 2 called out 'Tally Ho!', and then Marker 5. Maurice Smith went down very low to check on where the first red target indicator had fallen. 'I was low enough to see a man by a car on a bridge. I don't remember whether he was being picked up by someone or whether he was a driver who had stopped for a moment and then got away.' He thought this was the Marienbrücke, next to the railway bridge, which was very likely because these adjoined the common land where the sports stadiums were. The one they wanted was the one in the middle, then (he believed) called the Friedrichstadt Sportsplatz, nowadays the Heinz Steyer-Stadion. Circling fast at almost rooftop altitude, Wing Commander Smith could see that the marker leader had missed the sports ground, but that the error was so small as to be irrelevant — about 300 feet. Considering that some people marking by different methods, particularly from high up, made errors of a mile or two, even many miles, this effort was spot-on.

'Hello, Marker Leader,' he called. 'That Tee Eye is about one hundred yards to the east of the Marking point.' Over.'

Marker leader acknowledged and passed it on to Marker 2. 'OK. One hundred yards east of Marking point. Over.'

In his role of master bomber, which was to encourage as well as to direct, Smith came in with: 'Good shot! Back up then, back up.'

Marker leader called all the Mosquitoes with: 'Back up, back up. Out.'

There was a call from Marker 5: 'Clear!' (meaning that he had dived but was now safely clear of the aiming point), and then a shout of 'Tally Ho!' from Marker 2 to warn the others that he in turn was diving to back up the first red TI with another one and so keep the red signal glowing for the arrival of the main force bombers.

Although the 10 o'clock express train from Dresden Hauptbahnhof had been stopped as it began to leave the station, apparently as a result of an accidentally pulled communication cord, Gisela-Alexandra Moeltgen was still on it, talking to her husband at the window.

Word got around that the train had to be vacated at once – but the planes were already over the town. Many optimists stayed in order to secure a good seat, but I broke the window – it was only made of cardboard – grabbed the handbag in which I carried my jewellery, grabbed my fur, too, and got through the window. The others followed suit. We ran along the completely blacked-out platform in the dark and found that all the barriers were closed. Over the barriers, then! The police wanted us to go into the already overcrowded air raid shelter at the station, but we had only one urge – out, and away from the station! How right we were was borne out by the fact that over 3,000 dead were found in the station and 300 dead on my train alone – all burnt to death.

We ran across the road to the Technical High School where, it was claimed, there was a good cellar. And above us – very low – the planes. Masses of people were already in the cellar when we arrived, and I collapsed then. It was my heart. I was still very weak and all the running had exhausted me completely. Somebody asked us to move on, further into the crush in the cellar, and we did so. A few minutes later, the building had a direct hit; the air was full of dust and smoke, and great pieces of masonry came crashing down on the spot where we had been standing at first. This was the first time that we escaped death that night.

While Frau Moeltgen and her husband were still stumbling down the road away from Dresden Hauptbahnhof, with the roar of the diving marker Mosquitoes filling the night sky above them, Wing Commander Smith was checking the progress of the raid, making sure that all the links in the chain were accurately established. He could see clearly the target indicators glowing redly by the sports stadium, but he was low down over the city and there were three layers of cloud above, between him and the height at which the topmost Lancasters of the main force would fly. Could they be seen from that height? So he called up the third of the link Lancasters, which was orbiting at 18,000 feet: 'Tell me if you can see the glow? Over?'

'I can see three Tee Eyes through cloud. Over.'

The words from the Lancaster were distorted and Smith did not hear them clearly. He had to ask again. 'Good work, can you see the Reds yet?'

'Can just see Reds,' came back from the high-flying Lancaster. 'Over.'

Marker 3 cut in with 'Tally Ho!' (meaning that he was diving to back up the existing red markers), and was followed almost immediately by a call of 'Tally Ho!' from Marker 7. There was danger of collision as they dived so close together. 'Take it easy!' called the marker leader, 'take it easy. Out.'

At that moment, Wing Commander Smith had an instant of doubt. It was easy to become disoriented, circling low down, completely exposed by the flares over an empty city. Was that really the right sports stadium out of the three?

He hesitated, then spoke to the marker leader, the man responsible: 'This is the wrong marking point, I believe.'

The story of Udo K's sister Erika is more typical than that of Gisela-Alexandra Moeltgen, although it is clear that they both got seats on the same train, the Thüringer Express. After fleeing from the farm in Silesia they had reached Dresden where they were compelled to change trains, and Uncle Nikolaus had been rounded up by the military. While staying in Dresden on 12 February Erika had written her last postcard, saying: 'I am dying of home-sickness for some post from you.' On the evening of 13 February the whole party had come together again. Erika, the nanny, the children's nurse, and the four small children had been joined by Nikolaus, the eldest person in the party, who had got himself released after twenty-four hours in the local barracks.

The daughter of the family with whom they had been staying in Dresden was a guard on the railways and had used her special connections to get them a completely separate compartment on the express leaving that night. She later told Erika's relatives in the West that she had got them all safely on the train when at 2145 hours a preliminary air raid warning was received. This meant that all the lights had to be put out and the station had to be emptied at once, both of people and of trains. 'Their train also moved off in the direction of Thüringen regardless of schedule, but in the darkness somebody must have pulled the communication cord by mistake, and that brought the train to an immediate halt. Nobody could discover what was wrong.' This girl herself survived the holocaust in Hauptbahnhof, but conditions were so chaotic that she could not say where Erika's party were last seen; they simply disappeared. They might have gone to a shelter, or stayed on a platform or,

outside the station, taken cover in one of the shallow
splinter-ditches.

All these movements, of the passengers in the trains to
evacuate them and get clear of the station if they could; and
the circling Mosquitoes taking it in turns to dive on the
marked stadium and lay more Reds to back up the first one
put down by the marker leader one hundred yards away,
had taken only a few minutes – shorter time in fact than it
takes to tell it. Wing Commander Smith's momentary fear
that the wrong stadium had been marked proved un-
founded. Almost at once he was on the air again to cancel
that remark: 'No. OK. Sorry, Marker Leader, that's OK.'

'OK, Controller.'

'Seven clear!' called the pilot of the seventh marker
Mosquito, to show he had marked up the stadium and was
away.

It was all going remarkably well. Wing Commander
Smith called up the Flare Force Lancasters: 'No more
flares, no more flares.' And then to the markers: 'Very
good work. If you've got any more Reds put them down
and then get clear.'

The marker leader passed it on: 'Hurry up and complete
your marking and then clear the area. Out.'

'Tally Ho!' called Marker 6 as he went down to drop
another Red.

Smith called up the high-flying link Lancaster to check
again on what could be seen from 18,000 feet. 'Can you see
the Red Tee Eyes? Over.'

'Can see Green and Red Tee Eyes,' the Lancaster pilot
called back. 'Over.'

'Thank you,' called Wing Commander Smith. And then,
to the main force, using the codeword 'Platerack', he

ordered: 'Come in and bomb glow of Red Tee Eyes as planned. Bomb the glow of Red Tee Eyes as planned.'

'Clear!' called Marker 6, as he pulled away from the marked stadium.

'Clear!' called Marker 8, as he too roared away from the glowing, heaving mass of red lights around the stadium.

Maurice Smith gave a last command to the marker leader. 'If you stick around for a moment and keep one lad with a Yellow, the rest can go home.' The yellow 'cancellation' marker was to cover the eventuality of the Germans setting up a convincing decoy conflagration, a tactic pioneered back in England nearly five years earlier, under the code name 'Starfish'.

'OK, Controller. Marker Leader to all Markers. Go home, go home. Acknowledge.'

In order, numbers 7, 5, 3, 4, 6 and 8 Mosquitoes called out: 'Going home.'

While Maurice Smith, Wing Commander, RAF, was circling the Alstadt waiting to observe the fall of the first bombs from 'Platerack' Force, another Smith was down below looking up at the flares dropped by the illuminator Lancasters. He was Clyde Smith, paratrooper, ex-82nd US Airborne Division, forced to labour for the Germans in Dresden with a hundred-strong work party. They lived in a requisitioned school with a light anti-aircraft battery down the road.

We had just gone to bed when we heard planes flying over and then you could see a flare drop. We knew what was coming next. The guards opened the doors for us and told us to get out. After the bombs had hit, we jumped into holes; some jumped into the ditches we had dug for the pipes and some crawled into the pipes. Once, some of us fell to the ground when we heard these bombs

falling close to us. After they hit nothing happened, and we
thought it was a dud until we looked up and found out that they
were incendiary bombs. And there were plenty of them dropped,
for the city was starting to burn good then.

Another American prisoner in a Dresden work party was
nineteen-year-old Henry J. Leclair, infantryman. He was
billeted with Kurt Vonnegut's party in the Dresden
slaughterhouse on the Grosses Ostragehege, built on the
same area of wild common land as the three sports
stadiums, and was a mile or so from the marked aiming
point.

It was one hell of a bombing raid, let me tell you, but I survived
them all. The night raid, they dropped incendiary bombs to light
up and burn the city and then different waves dropped blockbusters. We had about forty seconds', not minutes', warning,
because the first wave had dropped their bombs. Then the
Germans came into the slaughterhouse to lead us to the nearby
meat-locker which was about forty to fifty feet underground, and
that is how we kept alive during the fire-storm in Dresden.

The bombs were not in fact to be aimed at the slaughterhouse, or the Friedrichstadt hospital complex or, for that
matter, at any of the railway stations, including Hauptbahnhof, on the half-circle perimeter of the Altstadt. The
crews were to aim off eastwards from the aiming point so as
to obtain a concentration in the old town itself, where the
tall buildings huddled closely together inside the now
virtually invisible line of the original sixteenth-century
fortifications.

As the last Mosquito pulled away from marking up the
stadium, the marker leader called out: 'You have navigation lights on. Over.'

The master bomber was calling out to Platerack Forces:

'Come and bomb the glow of red Tee Eyes as planned. Bomb the red Tee Eyes as planned as soon as you like.'

The marker leader called to all the Mosquitoes: 'Control your lights. Over.'

There was no reply to either of his warnings about lights. Probably the navigation lights were those of a German night fighter, one of the very few to get off from the local airfield at Dresden-Klotzsche, about five miles to the north of the city. Lack of a definite order, coupled with the severe fuel shortage, kept most of the night fighters grounded. Geoff Taylor, who was at that moment in the middle of his attempt to steal a German night fighter from the Lonnewitz airfield further away, was just about to discover that many of the aircraft on the field were locked and immobile. The attacks on the refineries really had crippled the Luftwaffe.

Still orbiting Dresden at low level, Wing Commander Smith now gave a battle order to Platerack Force via the Link Lancaster of Flight Lieutenant McConnell. 'Tell aircraft on the top height band to come below medium cloud.'

A height alteration was within Wing Commander Smith's discretion. What Clyde Smith had seen in the road outside the school where the Americans were kept was a battery of light flak, 20 mm guns, not effective beyond 8,000 feet, manned (if that is the word) by schoolboys. Maurice Smith's aircraft was down comfortably within the range of the light flak, as he had been well aware to begin with. But now he had the measure of the problem. He could take his time. 'There was some light flak around. A minimum amount was squirted from the edges, but there were no defences of note. So I brought the main force down.'

The heavy flak was gone, drawn away to the Russian Front mostly. There was nothing, except perhaps the odd night fighter, to disturb the concentration of the 244 Lancasters of the main force, flying above the range of the little 20 mm cannon.

Dresden was undefended.

7
'The Swine! The Swine!'

Little Eva Beyer, seventeen years old, had got to bed early at the bakery south of Grosser Garten where she lived and worked, because she had to be up at half-past three next morning to make the delivery of freshly-baked bread and rolls in the suburb. A couple of hours later, after a restless sleep, she got up to go to the toilet which had a window facing north-west. A strange green light was shining through it.

This was the glow of the 'Primary Green' dropped at about 10 pm over the bend of the Elbe by radar. Like most people in Dresden, Eva had no experience of air attack beyond the two small daylight raids made by the Americans, so she went outside to see what it was. And now the other flares had been added to the Green by the Pathfinder Lancasters.

The Christmas Trees were in the sky and I knew then what it was. I ran through the house, waking everyone up. Another five families lived in this building and together we totalled eleven women, six children, and one man — Kurt, the wounded ex-soldier. Then I went back to the flat and fetched the children from their beds. They were 2½ and 4½ years old, and they started to scream because they didn't know what was happening and there was no time to explain anything to them.

We all went down into the cellar and I put just a blanket round each child, because there was no time for anything else. I myself was only in my nightgown, but I didn't even feel the cold, for the light went out, the children immediately started screaming again, then three of the women began to scream and rage like mad, while one old woman stood in a corner and prayed from the bottom of her heart to God. It was horrifying.

I got down under an arch and waited for what was to come. I crouched on my knees with my face buried in my arms, and my heart doing overtime out of fear. I experienced an incredible dread of being buried alive, for it is absolutely terrible to lie there and wait for the end when you don't know what the end is going to be like.

Suddenly Kurt was beside me as I crouched. He whispered very quietly into my ear: 'We have fire bombs in the coal cellar, come quick and help me throw the things out!' I gathered all my courage and went with him. Three incendiaries lay there, and we managed to throw out two. The third one we could only throw sand over because it had already started to smoke, and then there was supposed to be only thirty seconds before the thing would explode like a firework.

The bakery was some miles south-east of the Altstadt, so these bombs had fallen very wide; but some of the RAF's incendiary bombs had poor ballistic qualities. In any event, that was what the master bomber was for − to correct any obvious errors and impose discipline in the main force of 5 Group. Generally, he seemed satisfied.

The marker leader called out to him: 'The bombs seem to be falling OK. Over.'

'Yes, Marker Leader, they look pretty good.'

Then Wing Commander Smith called up the main force: 'That's good bombing. Come in and aim at the Red Tee Eyes as planned.'

Susanne Lehmann had celebrated her tenth birthday a month ago, but that evening she had been allowed another party, rather blanketed by the fact that it was a Tuesday night and every Tuesday night was her grandmother's visiting night for coffee. Susanne did not approve of Grandma:

My mother did not like to go to her house in Louisenstrasse and lately she had not even brought a few sweets for us children. It was not that sweets were short. Grandmother was very tight-fisted.

It was Shrove Tuesday, so my friends and I were allowed to dress up — with high-heeled shoes and long skirts which my mother had kept for alteration later on. Actually, it was a bit frivolous of us to think of Carnival in this last winter of the war. We would not have dared to go outside in the streets all dressed up like that. But on our own in the rarely-used, unheated living room, it seemed all right. My mother was so generous as to offer us all some bread and dripping. My grandmother disapproved of everything. But at 1900 hours all my friends went home. One of them, Gisela, ten years old, only lived until shortly before midnight. She had been sent together with her grandmother to one of the catchment camps for refugees, because her own mother, who was an air raid warden, had to help putting the fires out. Neither of them were ever seen again.

Then supper with the family — or was my brother Wilfried, fifteen years old, already at the Circus Sarrasani? I can't remember exactly. What I do remember is a book I was reading by Martin Andersen, a thick, yellow and black book, *Pelle der Eroberer*, which I was not allowed to show to anyone (because it was banned); and I remember I had on my green- and black-dotted flannel nightgown; and that I was allowed to sit at the round table and continue reading until the next news bulletin was due on the wireless.

The first message, *'Enemy aircraft approaching Hannover — Braunschweig',* filled me with a feeling of pleasure. It meant that going to bed would be postponed.

The second message disturbed the adults, but not me. Only at the third one when *'Dresden'* was mentioned did we all become alert and I went to get dressed again.

Next I see myself again in the cellar. At first sitting on a chair leaning against the wooden planks, then lying on the floor with both hands over my ears and my mother murmuring all the time: 'The swine, the swine!' I remember the whistling and crashing, the terrified total silence of all the other people in the cellar. I remember the longed-for break when we believed it was all over. I remember the air raid warden in his blue uniform and the men from the Fire Brigade. They came to open the cellar door from the outside in order to tell my mother that there was an incendiary bomb in our flat. I remember that my mother went up to the fifth storey with them, that I was not allowed to go, but that meanwhile my fifteen-year-old brother had returned home from the Circus and that he was allowed to inspect the damage. Both of them told us that vases had fallen over and the window panes were lying inside on the carpets, but so far nothing serious had happened. I had to stay in the cellar, relieved that we were all still alive.

Fifteen-year-old Gerhard Kühnemund, who was staying the night with his aunt in Serrestrasse because he had missed his train connection to Leipzig, was just leaving the flat with her and she had just said: 'Although Dresden will be spared again, all the same we'll have to go to the cellar!' when the windows blew in and a tremendous blast rocked the building. All the occupants of the other flats poured out in a panic and in all stages of dress or undress and fled down to the cellar. There were about eight or nine women and four children, two of them babies under two years. Beside Gerhard and a very old man, there was only one other male in the cellar − a young NCO in Luftwaffe uniform with pilot's wings and numerous medals.

The building was typical of many in Dresden, butted up against those on either side to save space, and with storage cellars or basements underneath. The walls between them had been pierced to make emergency exits in case of an air raid, and these had been only lightly bricked up again. Now, this exit on one side was broken open and the occupants of the next-door house came pouring into this cellar with screams of: 'Everybody out! The whole of Serrestrasse is on fire!'

The young Luftwaffe 'ace' turned to Gerhard, pointed to the Hitler Youth uniform the boy was wearing, and said: 'Are you a man?'

Gerhard looked at the numerous medals on the other's tunic, noticed that one of them was the German Cross in Gold, and replied: 'Naturally.'

The two men rushed up the stairs to the loft. With

sandbags and a stirrup pump they attacked the two burning incendiary bombs they found there. But the RAF had a surprise for them. Gerhard felt it only as a stabbing pain in his left shinbone and when he grasped it in agony, felt the blood running into his shoe. The Luftwaffe NCO was squatting on the floor with his hands clasping his stomach on the left side, where a splinter had ripped open his abdomen. Even a very small explosion is sudden and violent, totally unexpected. One moment you are all right, intent on the bomb you are sandbagging, aware (if it's 1944 or 1945) that some of them will have explosive charges to discourage you, then you're in mid-air surrounded by brilliant white light until, twenty feet or so away, you hit the ground, hard. Even if injuries are minor, this is not good for morale, momentarily. And so it was in this case.

'Come on, out of here!' shouted the wounded Luftwaffe man. 'Let's get downstairs and leave this rubbish to burn!' As he ran for the stairs, Gerhard looked out through the small attic windows:

The whole of Dresden was an inferno. In the street below people were wandering about helplessly. I saw my aunt there. She had wrapped herself in a damp blanket and, seeing me, called out: 'Come to the Elbterrassen!' The sound of the rising fire-storm strangled her last words. A house wall collapsed with a roar, burying several people in the debris. A thick cloud of dust arose and mingling with the smoke made it impossible for me to see. Then a fist grabbed me by the neck and pulled me away across the rubble. It was the young pilot, who with his calm composure probably saved my life in this chaos. Our uniforms were singed and filthy. Time and again we stumbled over corpses. At Schlageter-Platz we rested for a short while. Then we arrived at a large shelter, it might have been the ARP Centre under the Albertinum, and our wounds were dressed.

Out at the Junghanns bakery, after Eva and Kurt had put out their three fire bombs with sand or water, they both went upstairs to see what the damage was there.

All was dark but for the flames. All the window panes were broken, several doors were hanging crooked from their hinges. My bed and all the other beds had been ripped up by glass fragments, the beds were bristling with glass splinters. I'd have been dead if I hadn't got up to go to the toilet and so been warned in time to warn everybody else. But as I'd just run out of bed in my nightdress, I'd not put on my slippers, and so I found a pair of PT shoes now — no idea who owned them — and put them on, because there was glass underfoot. We'd just lit a candle to see what we were doing when there was a whistling shriek, a bang, and a wave of blast. We didn't get hit by glass splinters, because there weren't any windows now, but Kurt and I were thrown from the window to the door. Before I could get up, I had to straighten my limbs. Next day I could hardly move, a foot and one hand were swollen, I had a black eye and I was bruised all over green and blue.

The bomb which hurt Eva and Kurt had hit a brickworks, but it was far from the aiming point. Several times, Wing Commander Smith, circling the blazing Altstadt which was beginning to sparkle with fires, had to check a tendency to bomb wild.

'Come in and aim at the red Tee Eyes as planned. Careful! Overshoot! Somebody has dropped very wide.'

Then, thinking of the fuel problems all Mosquitoes faced at this distance from base, he told the marker leader: 'Go home now, if you like. Thank you.' And got the acknowledgement: 'Thank you, going home. Out.'

Then the master bomber turned to encouraging the main force: 'Good work, Platerack Force. That's nice bombing.'

Jack Myers, who was twenty-six and had fallen out of the 'Frostbite March' because of a septic foot, had found a kind South African doctor who put a drain tube into his heel and told the German guards that Myers could no longer walk. That had prolonged his life for a few more days. It kept him out of a final billet in a frozen ditch where many of the POWs and uncounted numbers of refugees had ended all earthly care. Dead children, dead mothers, sick and starved soldiers, the weak; they would lie there under the snows, till the spring came.

But now the cattle truck in which he and other fortunate war prisoners were travelling seemed likely to become a more formal tomb, as it jolted, shunted and jerked its way westward in spasms. Out of the eighty or so men of mixed nationalities penned inside, perhaps twenty or even thirty were dead now. The living stacked them at one end, and kept a little 'no-man's line' opposite the central doors which separated the dead from the still living soldiers. They were all sick now, it was freezing cold, there was no food and they had not been fed or watered for days. Dehydration was not a problem, because although the cattle truck was of the totally shut-in kind, there were gaps through which snow drifted in, and sometimes ice formed. On a diet of snow and ice, and nothing else, death was not so far away. They huddled together for warmth.

The cattle-truck train shunted to a stop in marshalling yards.

Somebody said it was Dresden. There were no signs to say so, nothing to recognize. And nothing to do in the truck, when the raid began, but count bombs. It was getting bloody near. The Poles or Russians or whoever they were got in a bit of a panic. The British don't panic. But there was a bit of bad language from them. Very suddenly, after about fifteen minutes of this, there came what was probably a stick of bombs. A crrrrump. And the ground shook. That derailed the truck and it went over on its side. The top of it came off, partly; there was a crack in the roof. A little bloke in our unit, a Scot, took charge of getting enough off to make a gap. People had been hurt, but for the first three minutes after it happened, I don't remember. I found myself wandering about in the open, but I didn't know how I had got out. I do know I was looking for shelter and food. I was down to eight stone, but you get used to perpetual hunger.

I saw London burning. That impressed me more than Dresden. My memory is of an immense amount of noise, of people shrieking and calling. Smoke, wounded, dead, fire. A lot of bells going — ambulances? Or fire engines? I think a domed building on fire. A cathedral? We were well outside the city centre, as far as Wembley is from Piccadilly, say four to five miles. I don't remember well about the burning city, but I think I said to myself: 'I haven't come this far to be killed by the RAF.' I'd been strafed by experts. Now I was dazed from hunger and I was looking for a hole in the ground. I was worried about the Home Guard being trigger-happy. There were the sounds of vehicles and of guns, bit of an AA battery. I was free for perhaps ten minutes — or even half an hour? Then a Home Guard came up, an old man. He was the first man I saw with a gun, and I put my hands up. I couldn't walk then, let alone run. We were eventually fed — I got a potato, a sizeable one, and a piece of black bread.

Jack Myers is convinced that they would not have been fed, had they remained in the locked cattle truck, so that he owed his life to the RAF bombing of Dresden. Although an atheist, he believes that it was a miracle that he got out of the death trap. He doesn't like Germans of around his own age and still won't have anything to do with Germany. 'There were six million of us killed in the camps.'

In the cattle truck with him, ironically, there was an RAF prisoner of war, wearing recognizable RAF uniform. 'We were hobbling along a few days later, when a woman came out of a house and threw a bucket of water over him. She knew what he was.'

Flight Sergeant Bernard McCosh was the mid-upper gunner of a 167 Squadron Lancaster which had taken off from Waddington at 6 pm. The outward trip was 'very, very quiet'. They flew at 15,000 feet but came down lower to 10,000 feet to bomb. He had to keep a lookout for night

Margret Freyer, 1946.

Margret Freyer, 1971.

Maria Rosenberger, 1946.

Frau Edith Beyer with her
daughter Eva, 1946.

Eva Beyer, 1957.

Ruth Pieper on the day of her wedding to Corporal Clifford Leach, 1947.

Frau Kathe Lehmann with her two children Wilfred and Susanne in 1943.

Susanne (left) with her father, Kurt Lehmann, and a school friend Gisela Hubner in 1945, when she was 11 years old.

Erika Simon (centre) with her sister Ursala and brother Jürgen, in the summer of 1944.

Charlotte Mann.

Frau Dora Daniel with baby Holm and 'Bärbel' in March 1946, a year after the bombing of Dresden.

Walter and Dora Daniel with their two children a few years after the war.

Gerhard Kühnemund in May 1945, when his hometown of Leipzig was occupied by the American Army and he was learning English.

Otto Sailer-Jackson, animal trainer and inspector at the Dresden Zoo.

Hilde and Walter Thiel with their family in Breslau. While Hilde took their three children to safety, Walter had to stay behind and defend the doomed city.

Annemarie Waehmann's home (marked with a cross) before the bombing.

Annemarie Waehmann's home after the raid. Note how debris covers both the pavement and the road.

POWs

Paratrooper Eddie Taylor (2nd from right, front row) in training in Manchester. He was captured after a drop with the 2nd Parachute Battalion in North Africa in December 1942.

Paratrooper Clyde Smith of the 82nd US Airborne Division who was taken prisoner in Normandy, June 1944.

Master Bomber for the first wave of attack, 13 February: Maurice Smith and his navigator, Leslie Page, and their Mosquito.

Wing Commander Maurice Smith, Christmas 1944.

Flying Officer 'Alan' Driver.

Extreme right-hand corner of Alan Driver's chart showing the track of his 106 Squadron Lancaster approaching and leaving Dresden. Note: at 2200 hours, east of Leipzig, he has written 'Fires sighted here'. The first wave had only just begun to bomb.

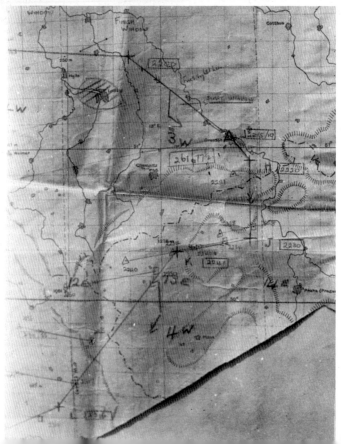

Master Bomber for the second wave of attack: Squadron Leader Peter de Wesselow (centre) with the crew of his Lancaster.

Four pals who flew in Lancaster AA-P: Peter Goldie, Roy Akehurst, D. Egglestone, Jimmy Freestone.

Top Sergeant Harold W. Hall in France after having bailed out following a mid-air collision.

William C. Stewart, ball-turret gunner of B-17 'Round Trip Ticket II'.

The crew of 'Round Trip Ticket II' (Stewart is front row, right) just before leaving for Europe.

Bombs fall away from a Fortress of 527 Squadron, 379 Heavy Bombardment Group, in which Harold Hall was a radio operator.

Colonel Joseph A. Peterburs.

Joseph A. Peterburs in a Mustang of 55 Fighter Squadron, 20th Fighter Group during his tour in Europe from November 1944 to May 1945. The note on the card is to his wife.

Dresden from the Elbe showing the river steamers lying off the Brühl terraces where many people were to take shelter from the fire-storm. On the left, is the dome of the Frauenkirche, on the right the Catholic Hofkirche and the Schloss. *Photo:* A-M Waehmann collection

Zwinger: the wall pavillion. *Photo:* A-M Waehmann collection

The Catholic Hofkirche with its frieze of statues on the left. On the right the Schloss and its tower. *Photo:* A-M Waehmann collection

The Ringstrasse where many corpses were to be laid out for identification. On left, the spire of the Protestant Kreuzkirche, on right the tower of the Rathaus (town hall). *Photo:* A-M Waehmann collection

Zwinger burnt-out and blasted. *Photo:* courtesy of VEB F.A. Brockhaus Verlag

The statue of Martin Luther blown off its pedestal in front of the fallen Frauenkirche.

Beheaded: in the ruins of the Schloss.

Dresden in February 1945, showing the typical effects of a firestorm on a European city: the walls stand, but there is nothing inside them. Every building in view has been burnt out. Destruction is total. *Photo:* Archiv für Kunst & Gerschichte, Berlin

Germany – Year Zero. Refugees from the East camping amid ruins in Spring, 1945. *Photo:* Archiv für Kunst & Gerschichte, Berlin

View from Pragerstrasse to the towers of the Kreuzkirche and Rathaus, 1958. Note road surface still pitted by the fire-storm. *Photo:* Alexander McKee

The city centre of Dresden in 1958: the bulk of the rubble has been cleared away, leaving a jungle of weeds and masonry; in the distance, new buildings rise. *Photo:* Alexander McKee

fighters all the time, protecting his comrades in the bomber.

It was a clear, starry night above. Flares had stopped by the time we got there. I only saw three searchlights. There was very little flak, and only small stuff − cannon mounted on armoured vehicles, that sort of stuff. Over the target, it was one mass of flames. We just dropped the bombs into it. The flames were far greater on this occasion than on any other I had seen. I was on the big raid on Hamburg, and it was bad then; but this was way out of proportion, absolutely. You could see the full city from our position, but there was no way to pick out certain buildings − there was too much fire and smoke.

For me, it was just another target. But once we saw the photographs, some days later, it was another thing altogether. I was sickened. Just nothing there. Just razed.

Margret Freyer lived in the Altstadt. She recalled: 'This attack was real hell, and I believe it was kept quiet at first because there were too many dead. The corpses in the cellars began to decompose and the rescuers were walking about up to their ankles in sludge.' 'Only just twenty-four years old and very impressionable' at that time, it became the most horrible experience of her life.

Before the raid each restaurant, café, pub and bar, as well as the main station, was crammed full of people with suitcases, rucksacks and bundles. You literally fell over these people and their possessions. It was so bad that you did not like to watch it, and it spoiled all the usual happy atmosphere of the Fasching, or Carnival, night. They were refugees − from the East and from the Rhineland. Many believed that Dresden would never be bombed because one of Churchill's relatives lived here.

This seems to have been true. A Captain Churchill was held as a privileged prisoner because he was supposed to have saved the life of a German. A German officer escorted him personally to safety in the Mordgrundbrücke, a still-incomplete air raid shelter.

Margret Freyer blamed 'Herr Hitler and his consorts' for the raid, not the RAF, because:

Not only did Hitler start the war but he always exterminated systematically countless Jews. This fact was better known abroad than here in Germany, although it seems incredible to foreigners. But all these things were kept completely secret here and of course one was punishable even for not using the 'Heil Hitler' greeting. For instance, I was interrogated by the Gestapo in Dresden for eight or twelve hours in 1943, just because I had told political jokes in the cloakroom of the theatre. I only just escaped the concentration camp. I don't think my brain has ever worked so exactly and precisely as it did during this interrogation by three men. My knees were wobbling when I left the Gestapo. They passed it on to a special court and there I was given an official warning: Your name is on the black list and if just one of your colleagues had confirmed this allegation, you would have been taken to a concentration camp. The way I visualized a concentration camp then was cleaning latrines and that sort of work. About the things that really happened in there, we truly had no idea.

On 13 February 1945, when the sirens went, Margaret like so many others in Dresden assumed that the raid was not for them but for some other city in the vicinity. Nevertheless, she took down to the cellar of her home at Ferdinandstrasse in the Altstadt two large emergency suitcases which she kept ready packed. It was more of a basement than a cellar, and it had windows. The first indication that it was now their turn came when the city was lit up by the dreaded 'Christmas Trees'. 'The windows in the cellar looked as if they were covered with yellow paper and lit up from outside,' she recalled.

Including herself, there were forty-four women in the cellar, and no men.

Time and again I gazed at the ceiling, expecting everything to collapse on us. Somehow I had switched off and was expecting the final catastrophe; it must have been for this reason that I did not join in the weeping and praying of the totally terrified women, but tried to calm them down as best I could.

Then at last the 'All Clear'. We were lucky our house was still standing. I took my two suitcases and went upstairs. Everything was in an incredible mess. In every flat, in every room, there was dust, glass splinters, earth, the doors and window frames ripped out, fire-storm and flying sparks everywhere. Completely stricken, we all left our flats, especially because the houses on the opposite side of the street were burning fiercely. I first pulled down the curtains from every window in our flat, thinking that this would stop the place from catching fire. As no one else then remained in the five-storey house, I did not feel like staying myself there alone. It was eerie!

·A friend of mine called Cenci lived two streets away at Struve-strasse 13 (I lived in Ferdinandstrasse 13). I took both my suitcases and went there.

Once in the streets I saw what had really happened − every second house was on fire. And now I also understood why our street was so empty − everybody had fled in order to find shelter away from the fires. I had to cross the Ferdinand-Platz in order to get to Cenci's house. I saw only burning houses and screaming people. The row of houses where my friend lived was intact but all the houses opposite were burning. I left my suitcases with Cenci and returned twice to my own flat to collect a few things. It was frightening − I found myself completely alone, and all I could hear was the roaring of the fires. I could hardly see, due to the flying sparks, the flames and the smoke. I did not dare risk going back a third time. I helped Cenci to remove the worst of the dirt, glass and earth and take down all the curtains. While we were doing this, we asked ourselves if the fire brigade would soon arrive to put out this terrible conflagration.

There are believed to have been about 500 wounded soldiers in the wards of the Vitzthumschule, a boys' school which had been turned into a Reserve Military Hospital, its roof marked with the Red Cross. There was a fire station next to it. Some 200 are thought to have survived the collapse of the building, which trapped hundreds in the cellar. One of those men — who owed their lives to their own determination to survive as well as to good fortune — was the Waffen-SS officer Claus von Fehrentheil, who had been wounded in Northern Hungary while trying to repel the Soviet drive for Budapest. The vehicle taking him to hospital had been shelled off the road by Russian guns, and his right hip had been torn open and his spine fractured. That was on 16 December. He was now recovering from infection of the hip wound, but was partly in plaster and immobile except in extreme emergency. He was also extremely uncomfortable, as were many of the other soldiers in his ward.

The day had come to an end, and we were trying hard to find comfortable sleeping positions, when with a cheerful 'Hello!' all the nurses burst into the room. They had brought us greetings and gifts for Shrove Tuesday Night from the Gauleiter, Mutschmann. They put a carton of sweets on the bed of each one of us, wished us a cheerful 'Goodnight!' and soon disappeared, putting out the lights in the ward. I suppose we could have got off to sleep now, but we were disturbed by a sudden, unexpected air raid warning.

Air raid warning! After all, we understood we were in an open city, world-famous for its works of art, undefended, declared a 'hospital-town'. We patients had been reassured that even the smallest hospital had the distinctive red cross on a white background painted on its roof. It seemed to us as the night went on that these served as excellent markers for the bombs of the English Jabos [fighter-bombers]. With this order to attack Dresden, the Geneva Convention, recognized by all nations except England, had become a farce. One could not help being reminded of the British treatment of the Boer women and of the *Altmark* affair.

Only after very intensive efforts urging us to shelter, did we concede to go into the cellar. Not, naturally, into the air raid shelter proper. For one thing, we regarded the whole affair as probably a mistake at this time. Then also, a soldier who had been on the Front felt too restricted in a cellar, a place where he could not dodge any threatening dangers. In any case the real bunker should be kept for the bedridden sick. And anyway the whole hospital contingent would not all have found room there. So we stood in the passages and on the staircases outside the air raid shelter. The walls trembled as the bombs of the bomb carpets detonated, and although we were used to such things we did not feel very happy about this at all. We were convinced that it was Mr Churchill who was directly responsible for the order to destroy Dresden, no matter what history might say afterwards.

Von Fehrentheil was an experienced 'Front-Schwein' from the East, as his narrative makes clear in subtle ways. The attack of No. 5 Group, although closely packed into perhaps ten or fifteen bombing minutes, was nowhere near a 'bomb carpet' as understood by West Front soldiers. That was something very special. He differentiated between the two very different types of aircraft being used by 5 Group (and none of the Dresden civilians did – they merely realized that some were flying very low, almost over the rooftops). He described the high-level bombers as making a 'humming noise', but thought of them as 'Flying Fortresses'; in comparison, the low-flying Mosquitoes made a 'howling, rather nervous sound', but he did not realize that they were markers and thought them fighter-bombers or 'Jabos'. The Red Air Force was a somewhat primitive organization, using very old-fashioned aircraft in a purely tactical role; von Fehrentheil was unused to the extreme sophistication of the RAF.

But because all the patients in this hospital were soldiers, most of them with battle experience, sometimes years of it, their reactions were very different from those of the Dresden civilians. Apart from the basic fact that most of those were women and children, with few men of military age around, the majority were not inured to war. Whereas the inhabitants of most German cities, and many British towns too, had been 'blooded' in leisurely fashion, starting with weak or ineffective air attacks and gradually working up to something more devastating, the almost untried population of the Saxon capital were to be victims of what air power theorists agree was the greatest, most terrifying technical achievement of the entire strategic bomber offensive of the Second World War.

One of the supreme technicians chiefly responsible at the risky end of the operation was Wing Commander Maurice Smith. What he achieved in certain parts of the Altstadt within fifteen minutes or so was to set half the houses on fire. If the fire brigades could not check that conflagration then the fires would spread with almost explosive rapidity.

Already, the air above the blazing city was superheating and making it difficult for the oncoming bomber stream to identify anything positive except an enormous grouping of fires. The Wing Commander's instructions changed tone. Instead of an encouraging 'Good work, Platerack Force, that's nice bombing', he called up the rest of the bomber stream with:

'Try to pick out the red glow. The bombing is getting wild now. Pick out the red glow if you can and bomb as planned.'

It was more difficult than it seemed.

Flying Officer Driver, navigating Lancaster 'G for George' of 106 Squadron, had got them safely through the Ruhr area with its heavy flak by 2050 hours:

The route took a due easterly heading, passing south of Magdeburg but in a general direction of Berlin. Because we were now beyond 'Gee' radar range and were not permitted to use H2S radar, I had been experiencing difficulty in securing any accurate ground position fixes for some time and had to rely on Dead

Reckoning navigation. When I did achieve a reliable fix it confirmed that although the wind direction was still westerly the velocity had increased considerably to that forecast at briefing, and raised some doubt that we could maintain our correct time over target.

At 2200 hours we turned on our direct heading for Dresden. Shortly after this, the pilot and flight engineer indicated over internal RT that they could see considerable glare ahead indicating that the target area was already well alight and confirming that we were on the correct heading for the target and our timing was OK.

Driver kept his working chart for that night, which shows how they altered course eastward after Kassel, and began to 'Window', then turned again to the north of Halle and Leipzig, confusing the German night fighter controllers as to the target until the final run from near Leipzig down directly south-east to Dresden. As they passed east of Leipzig Driver pencilled in beside the track line 'Fires sighted here'.

It soon became evident as we approached the target that the city was well alight from the earlier bomber waves. The bomb aimer was now passing rapid changes to the pilot to try to line up on the target indicators, which were almost obscured by smoke. Because of the extreme port drift due to the high wind speeds there had been considerable violent manoeuvres to line up before we finally dropped our own bomb load. Extreme turbulence was experienced over the target area due, I assume, to the extreme heat from the fires below. I do not recollect any enemy flak being encountered at this time.

After leaving the target, the rear gunner informed us that the city was well alight until it became obscured by cloud as we descended to a lower height level. Our return trip was south of Nuremberg and Stuttgart without encountering German defences and then north-east across the Ardennes and finally the Belgian coast between Ostend and Dunkirk, and back over the North Sea and East Anglia to base. We landed at 0400 hours on 14 February feeling exhausted but believing we had made a significant contribution to the war effort and acknowledging that we must have taken a heavy toll on the German forces we believed were occupying the city.

After four hours' sleep, we were again called to prepare for another night raid, on an oil refinery at Rositz, which again meant a 9½-hour trip departing that afternoon. Dresden had already become a successful raid behind us, to be put in our log books towards our total tour number. With hindsight though, how wrong it was for this beautiful city to be destroyed together with its occupants who were merely innocent victims of the war and could not be linked in any way to the German lines of defence.

The emergency military hospital in the Vitzthumschule survived the first wave of attack. Claus von Fehrentheil's ordeal was still to come. But the great Friedrichstadt hospital complex was hit early, although it was outside the Altstadt west of the railway tracks which encircled the old city. Annemarie Waehmann had been in a ward with three other girls, including the fifteen-year-old refugee Hilde. Down in the cellar:

There was crashing and thundering, whistling and howling. The walls trembled, swayed by the impact of the bombs. This is the end, we thought. How long it lasted, don't ask me. Minutes? It appeared to be hours. Then some of the doctors screamed: 'Everyone out of the cellar, the whole building is going to collapse!' From a certain distance, the doctors watched the collapse of the houses and as soon as there were a few seconds' respite in between collapsing masses of debris, they shouted: 'Come on, two to three people – out!' And a few shot outside. At the second 'Come on!' I too ran for my life into the next building. Did all of them get out? How many did not manage? I don't know. Everyone was in such a panic that all we wanted was to save our naked lives.

The master bomber was becoming impatient. 'Complete your bombing now – complete your bombing,' he called. 'Aim at the end – try to sort it out from the glow.'

*　　*　　*

Erika Simon was eleven years old, the middle child of the family, for Ursula was thirteen and Jürgen eight. The family had been relatively little affected by the war, until now. Her father, Werner Simon, was a chemist. He had been called up for the Polish campaign in 1939, was demobbed soon after, then contracted a lung disease and spent some years in a sanatorium. In August 1944 he was cured and came to Dresden to manage a chemist's shop. Erika went to the local grammar school and made many new friends. Even the issue of identity discs was fun: these were made of whitish-green metal and had a number on, but no name to go with it; they were supposed to be worn on a cord round the neck at all times. The girls found amusement for a time in calling each other by their new numbers, instead of by their familiar names. It never occurred to them to consider the circumstances in which such almost indestructible means of identification might be of use. The children hardly noticed that there was a war on, until a refugee family, also with children, was billeted on them.

Their flat was surrounded by villas in the Grosser Garten area, and had a cellar prepared as an air raid shelter. Each night when they went to bed, each child had a little suitcase, fully packed, ready for emergency flight, in the bedroom; but they did not expect to have to use them.

On 13 February we were suddenly pulled out of our beds by my parents and very quickly dispatched into the cellar. All hell broke loose over us so suddenly that no one really had a chance to perceive what was actually going to happen. I remember I had my head in my mother's lap under a blanket and was putting both hands over my ears in an attempt to blot out the horrific noise. The outer wall of the cellar was reinforced by sand-boxes. I can see my father leaning against this wall, and I felt that the walls were coming towards us and that my father was trying to stop them from falling down on us. Suddenly, the noise ceased, but we noticed that the house was on fire. We had to leave the cellar. We climbed through a cellar window into the garden with flames metres high everywhere. Our refugee family with their two small children decided to go to a nearby bunker. We saw the owners of the house, too, but it was for the last time.

Our mother had worked for the Red Cross for many years and her first aid post was near our flat. One of her colleagues came to us and told my parents to take us three children there. Somebody took me and my sister by the hand, but my brother Jürgen was nowhere to be seen. The journey to the Red Cross post was endless. Normally, it only took fifteen minutes. Now we had to climb over debris, step over corpses, with fire everywhere and sparks flying, with the air so hot and with so much smoke that it made breathing difficult.

In fact, they never made it. The two girls, fifteen and eleven, were caught in the open by the second wave of attack, not knowing where their little nine-year-old brother had wandered off to.

Wing Commander Smith was calling out his final orders: 'Complete your bombing quickly. Ignore decoy fires. Complete your bombing now.' And the final Lancasters of the stream droned overhead, the engine note seeming to change as the bombs fell away.

Gisela-Alexandra Moeltgen had made the right decision when, instinctively, she had abandoned her seat in the Thüringen Express and with her husband Hans and the young doctor fled from the Hauptbahnhof, Dresden's main station, to the Technical High School. And there again she had escaped death by obeying a suggestion that she come right inside the shelter a minute or two before the building had a direct hit. The masonry came crashing down on the spot where they had been standing, and clouds of blinding dust and smoke almost choked them. The dust seemed to come from the very walls and ceilings, so that those who could wet a handkerchief did so and put it over their mouths and noses.

'The attack continued and the mood among us reached panic pitch. Then a shout — "At once, everyone leave, there is danger of collapse!" Out through the narrow cellar windows we went, flames whipping down the staircase, the whole building alight. It was a gruesome and at the same time impressive picture as one stepped out into the street,' she wrote shortly afterwards when the memories were still fresh. 'Flames, flames wherever one looked. But what should we do now?'

Gisela's instinct was to get back to the train, either to save her luggage, which she had left in the compartment in her hurry to leave the station, or to find a train which would take them out of the city altogether. Although still an invalid, her nerves were screwed up to such a pitch, she said, that she felt neither pain nor tiredness. 'We never reached the station, for it was burning, and Hans promised that he would collect the luggage the following morning. Who could know that this was only the beginning of a horrifying night?' They walked north towards the Altstadt itself, crossing Strehlenerstrasse, into Parkstrasse, then turning left towards the Burgerweisse, a small park just to the west of the great park, the Grosser Garten, where the Zoo was.

It was hardly possible to get through, all the houses were burning fiercely, and there was the smoke and the suction created by the fires. Trees and broken wires blocked the road. People were fleeing to the Grosser Garten, carrying bundles and pushing prams. They had no idea they were walking straight into a death trap. I tried to look along Goethestrasse but it was impossible, there was too much smoke. We hurried on and when I stumbled, for I had hardly any strength left, the men supported me. A hundred times we asked ourselves: 'Is our house still standing?' One could not see more than five steps ahead. The Palais and the

Osramhouse were in flames. The house next to ours on the right was not burning and ours was not on fire either; but the house on the left of it was roaring away. All the doors and windows of our house had been blown out.

I stumbled into our cellar and all the people who lived in our house were horrified to see me come back. The old Junghänse family were very quiet and kept sweeping up the dirt. My God, the work was pointless! But it calmed their nerves and their conscience.

In the meantime, the others took down the curtains, so that they would not catch fire. Hans lugged our mattresses and blankets down into the cellar and made up a bed for me on the floor. But I was totally incapable of lying down. I simply sat on the old camp bed on which the little boy, Frank, had peacefully gone to sleep. There were so many things one could have brought down into the cellar for safety during that time. The radio, the oil paintings, the carpets. Hans did manage to bring down a few of the smaller carpets, but I would not have had the strength even to walk up the stairs, especially as the only light in the house was from the glow of the fires outside. That is why I remember my flat in its original, perfect condition.

Hans's conscience began to trouble him. He wanted to get back to his clinic at the hospital. He went to the Red Cross Post and also to the police to try to hitch a lift back there in an ambulance. They explained to him that it was impossible to get through.

The Zoological Gardens were only a very short distance from Gisela-Alexandra's flat, in the south-west corner of the Great Park, Grosser Garten. They were surrounded by both a wall and a moat, to prevent the animals and reptiles from escaping into the town. One of the senior Zoo inspectors was a renowned animal trainer and former circus performer, Otto Sailer-Jackson, who had served an early apprenticeship in England. Born in 1884 in a small peasant community near Lake Constance, his father was a forester. His knowledge of English, picked up at school, enabled him to get a job on the large country estate of an English nobleman whose hobby was animals. When asked what interested him most, Otto replied: 'Rare butterflies.' He was advised to study them first from books which he could borrow from the estate library, and was then allowed to prepare captured butterflies for exhibition.

Promotion and pocket money came when Otto was transferred to working with the horses, learned to ride and became a stable lad. Then he was taught how to stuff birds, but was sidetracked by opening *Brehms Tierleben,* a book of animals. Immediately he was fascinated, and the idea of stuffing the carcasses of animals for display became repugnant to him. He mentioned this to Mr Smith, the nobleman's agent, and a few days later he was offered the chance to go out to Mexico on an animal collecting expedition, for which he would have to learn how to use revolvers and shotguns and also learn languages.

By the time he was fifty, Otto Sailer-Jackson was with the Berlin Circus, working up to a dozen lions simultaneously in the arena. The critical accident came when he was working with a tiger group. They were very lively, particularly a female tiger called Fatme. She put out a paw and cuffed him lightly, in order to entice him to play with her; but he didn't notice, so she moved closer and cuffed again, unfortunately hurting his right eye. The damage was permanent and made this eye continually water, spoiling the clear vision so necessary with circus work.

He was offered a job as inspector of a newly-opened zoo in Geneva, and was glad to accept in order to continue working with animals. But his wife did not like Switzerland and was unhappy there. One morning when he was on an inspection walk he recognized Professor Brandes of Dresden Zoo, whom he knew well from the time when he had worked for the Sarrasani Circus. When Brandes heard of his problem, he patted Sailer-Jackson on the shoulder and said: 'It's no good for you here. Come to Dresden as Zoo inspector under me, and bring your wife with you.'

What he thought of as Hitler's 'pirate war' brought for
the Zoo a mass of new orders and regulations issued so
hastily that even their originators probably did not know
precisely what they meant. At the same time as the burden
of clerical work was greatly increased, so the staff was
decreased. There were instructions for blacking out the
Zoo and for action at various stages of alert. There were air
raid cellars to be built, one-man bunkers, and a few HQs.
Boxes of sand and buckets of water had to be placed in the
lofts of the buildings and in all the animal houses. There
were three or four hand fire-extinguishers to each building
and also motor pumps. On the evening of 13 February,
Sailer-Jackson made an inspection patrol through the Zoo.
All the ARP men had taken post according to regulations
in the one-man bunkers which had been erected in the
grounds. Then he went back to his office to try and catch up
with the never-ending paper work.

There was no preliminary alert. The sirens howled their
message: Air Raid Alarm – Attack Imminent. As he
stepped outside, the night sky over Dresden became light
as day, sparkling with 'Christmas Trees', the flares drifting
rapidly with the west wind as they sank towards the earth.
Shortly after came the whistle and crrrrump of the first
bombs. With his wife, Sailer-Jackson hurried to the main
control bunker, which was sited in the Zoo restaurant. The
ARP wardens in the one-man bunkers dotted about the
gardens were already telephoning in their reports: the
Wirtschaftshof, a large storage building for the animals'
feeding stuffs, is on fire; the roof of the staff quarters is on
fire; the antelope house is on fire. All the Zoo staff, not just
the wardens, rushed out. The Wirtschaftshof was beyond
saving, for the building included the workshops of the
carpenters and painters, which burned fiercely.

'Save the antelope!' someone called. The men ran until they were out of breath and, panting, tore open the doors. The totally terrified animals, every limb trembling, stampeded to freedom instantly. The giraffe house was burning too, and HE bombs were falling nearby. Ignoring this, they opened the doors easily enough, but the giraffe were too frightened and confused to come out into the open. The men had literally to push the great beasts out from under the blazing roof.

More alarming news came in to the control bunker. The Zoo was separated from the great public park, Grosser Garten, by a wooden fence 2.40 metres high. Incendiary bombs had set it on fire in many places. ARP men and the Fire Brigade succeeded in putting out the flames. Meanwhile, the fire in the loft of the staff quarters had been got under control by three of the women.

Sailer-Jackson went out to look at the antelope and giraffe. They were moving about, frightened and uncertain, but accompanied by their keepers. It was impossible to see whether or not any had suffered serious burns. That would have to wait for daylight. But at least there was a breathing space.

Wing Commander Smith called out for the last time: 'Complete your bombing now. Complete your bombing.' Then he called up the Link 1 Lancaster of Flight Lieutenant McDonnell, No. 97 Squadron: 'How d'you hear me? Over.'

'Strength 5. Over.'

The master bomber then told McDonnell to send back to base on the long-range W/T set in his aircraft: 'Target attacked successfully. Primary plan through cloud.'

'Target attacked successfully primary plan through cloud,' echoed McDonnell.

'That's right, Link 1. Thank you.' And then to Platerack

Force he called: 'Go home now, go home.'

The time of dispatch of the 'success' message was 2225 hours. 'It went well, couldn't be better,' recalled Wing Commander Smith. 'Towards the end I was worrying only about lack of fuel. We could be diverted to another aerodrome by fog or by an aircraft crashing on a runway or, back at base, I could be held up by the Lancasters of the two Pathfinder squadrons then at Coningsby.'

In the burning city, some people went towards the fires, not away from them. One of these was Dr Holzhausen, director of the Historical Museum and Weapon Gallery. Immediately after the bombing ceased, he left his home and went to the Schloss where many of the collections were then housed. The attic of the north-east wing was licking flame to the sky and people were already fighting that blaze. Fires were burning in several departments of the Museum, but it seemed possible to control these also. There were forty-two very large paintings still hanging on the walls of the Schloss, much too large to be conveniently removed for safe storage elsewhere. This was true also of the valuable antique furniture. On the other hand, ten boxes of a china collection, ordered by the Gauleiter to be moved from a safe storage place which was now in danger from the Russian advance, had been stacked temporarily in the vestibule of the Schloss. And parked for the night by its driver on the Elbe Terraces just north of the Schloss was a lorry containing 154 paintings, as well as many other irreplaceable items, which were in transit from another safe storage place likely to be overrun by the Russians, and due to go on to Meissen next day.

Anneliese Richter was a part-time messenger whose duty was to report to the local fire station. That day she had gone to work as usual in a shoeshop in the Altstadt and got back home about 7 pm. Home was a flat at the top of a four-storey block in Schandauerstrasse out at Striesen, some three or four miles from the Inner City, or Altstadt. She shared the flat with her mother and her eighty-two-year-old grandmother, who was bedridden. Anneliese was fifteen years old.

When the first bombs fell, she went to the cellar, where she found herself quite alone, huddled up against the wall, because her grandmother had not left the flat for fifteen years and did not ever intend to leave it again in this life, and her mother had stayed to comfort grandmother, whom they both loved dearly. Then someone broke down the connecting door and the people from next door came into the cellar, the house above them having been destroyed. In spite of the shaking she had received − not only had the house next door been hit but the sandbags placed behind the cellar windows had been blasted into the room − Anneliese set off to go on duty at the fire station as soon as the bombing stopped. Someone gave her a blanket to put round her shoulders as protection against the flying sparks showering across the streets from the burning houses.

But before she got there, Anneliese met a crowd of people coming away from the city who told her that the fire station itself had been hit and put out of action; so she turned back, very relieved. The block of flats where she lived was still standing, although the windows had been shattered and the banisters dislodged. Her grandmother was unhurt, although covered in broken glass. But the house next door was blazing and the fire might spread. The ARP warden passed on the message that the rescue services had been overwhelmed and that it was 'everyone for himself'.

Grandmother was moved down to the cellar, where

Anneliese kept her company. Everyone else had run upstairs to try to save some of their belongings. Sparks from
the burning buildings outside were drifting in through the
broken windows, which had lost their sandbag protection,
and as there was no water available Anneliese tried to
extinguish them with a jugful of coffee. Then two soldiers
from an emergency military hospital arrived and between
them carried her grandmother out of the cellar and down
the road, while Anneliese and her mother carried the bed-
clothes.

This army hospital had earlier been a school; it was about fifteen
minutes' walk away. We had to pass between jets of flame sweeping across the road at irregular intervals. Eventually we reached
the school cellar. Conditions were quite chaotic there, with
wounded soldiers moaning and injured civilians coming and
going. My mother went back to try and save some more of our
belongings, but in vain. Her eyes were affected by the dense
smoke and she, and many others, had to be treated in the school's
first aid cellar.

Superficially, what had occurred in Dresden up to this
point was, except perhaps for its brevity, a perfectly
ordinary air raid such as hundreds of cities and towns in
many countries endured. In many places people were fighting back — and successfully fighting back — smothering a
proportion of the fire bombs (and taking casualties in doing
so), putting out many of the fires before they could get a
hold and spread, even damping down sparks with stale
coffee. And, where they were not on duty or not quick
enough, and the flames here and there began to lick sky-
ward from one rooftop after another, or glowed red and
orange, through bare windows, the fires hissed and roared
upwards.

The first significant hint of a change was not during the
first wave of attack at all, but after it, perhaps as much as

one hour after it. The hint was contained in Anneliese's observation: 'We had to pass between jets of flame sweeping across the road at irregular intervals.' Even at this distance from the city centre, the fires had begun to travel horizontally at high velocity and for considerable distances.

Meanwhile the much greater force of bombers of the second wave were already on their way, three hours behind the first wave.

8
Ways through the 'Witches' Cauldron'

The sirens heralding the first wave of attack on Dresden had howled over the Elbe at 2141.

At almost the same time, at 2140, the Lancaster of No.3 Group in which Miles Tripp was bomb aimer became airborne with a mixed load of one 4,000 lb 'cookie' (a thin-walled blast bomb) and some 3,000 lb of incendiaries for its 1,600-mile return flight which would take 9 hours and 35 minutes. A large part of the load on take-off was petrol. The bomb-load was minimal – some 7,000 lb compared to say 12,000-13,000 lb for the much shorter trips to 'Happy Valley', the Ruhr. Many aircraft carried less high explosive and many more incendiaries. In all, the 529 Lancasters of the second attack wave bore 650,000 fire bombs in their dark bellies. Flying from bases spread over eastern England they were to come together over France into a close-packed bomber stream which would zigzag across southern Germany far from the tracks followed by the first attack wave and would pass over Dresden within half an hour or less, starting at about half past one on the morning of 14 February 1945.

The meteorological experts had forecast that there would be a break in the almost complete cloud cover lying over Europe which would expose the Dresden area of Saxony for perhaps five hours on the night of 13/14 February, and the two waves of attack spaced three hours apart had been timed to fit into the predicted gap. 'Met' was then more of an art than a science, but the timing for the first attack wave had been precisely accurate. The illuminators had been able to light up the target, the markers had been able to locate the aiming point, the high-flying bomber crews had been able to see the markers, and the master bomber had been able to control tightly the progress of the attack. Result: a large part of Dresden Altstadt had been set on fire to become an unmistakable beacon in the night for the massed might of the second wave. If one counted the flare-carrying and marker aircraft as well as the bombers, the total that night was more than 800 machines. Apart from these, many more were being used to confuse the German defences by Windowing or by making spoof or diversionary attacks. It was a brilliant scheme which went almost precisely to plan.

No.75 (New Zealand) Squadron was stationed at Mepal in Cambridgeshire and, like Miles Tripp's squadron, was part of No.3 Group. They had more than RAF organization in common. There can have been few aircrews, ship's crews or army units in which some sort of tribal reunion for 'after the war' was not agreed. The chief bond was the shared experience — many very vivid experiences, in fact, topics for everyone to talk about, which strangers cannot know. But after the Second World War, few such reunions actually took place. The problems of peace were too insistent, and it was necessary to give up the past — forget the war — in order to come to satisfactory terms with them. After 1918, everyone tried to go back to 1914. After 1945, none tried — and few wanted — to go back to 1939. In Britain at any rate there was an appetite for a new future and a determination not to be served by the politicians as the betrayed soldiers of the Great War had been. This feeling was a prime factor in bringing down Churchill, the great war leader, even before the war had ended; at the very first electoral opportunity, in fact.

It was twenty-three years after the war before Miles

Tripp set out to find the other members of his own Lancaster crew – and succeeded. One of the terrible memories they had in common was Dresden. No.75 Squadron came together for a reunion at Mepal in 1978, although many of them had to travel from New Zealand on the other side of the world. And one particular crew – those who had flown in Lancaster AA-P – had remained in touch through a nucleus living in the same small geographical area between Southampton and Brighton on the south coast. Like Tripp's crew, they were divided about Dresden, and in the same proportion. Two felt a horrified sense of guilt afterwards, when they realized just what it was they had helped to do; the others tended to shrug it off as the sort of thing that happens in war.

In both crews, it was what they heard at the briefing which made the difference. Probably not everyone paid uniform attention throughout, but Tripp and one of the gunners were disturbed by the mention of the refugees in Dresden. Tripp in particular recalled the German strafing of French refugees reported and condemned by the British press in 1940. If it was wrong for the Germans to do it to the French in 1940, surely it was still wrong in 1945, even if now the boot was on the other foot? Tripp was the bomb aimer in his aircraft. He would actually have to kill these people, personally.

Peter Goldie was the rear gunner of 75 Squadron's Lancaster AA-P. His role was purely defensive, to sit in a glass bowl for eight or nine hours behind four none-too-lethal .303s and be pulled backwards, seeing only where he had been and with no very good view downwards. 'They started to explain to us why we were going to Dresden. I think there was a hint it was Churchill's instructions to destroy the city. But they never really told us what was there. They just said: "Go in and fire-bomb the city." We walked back from the briefing, talking. We couldn't understand why there should be this raid.'

Roy Akehurst was the W/T operator in the same aircraft, who also did spells as gunner. He is fairly sure that they were told at the briefing that there were Panzer troops moving through Dresden, but in the event it was the one raid he would rather not have been on. It was not a military target, he felt. It was what he saw over Dresden that gave him guilt feelings ever afterwards.

Paul Hill, the flight engineer, who sat beside Flying Officer Egglestone, their New Zealand pilot, was more philosophical. They themselves did not fly to Dresden without risk, and at the back of the mind were the memories of the damage done by German bombers to their own cities. 'All war is horrible and innocent people get hurt,' was the way he looked at it.

AA-P took off from Mepal and set course for Reading, west of London, where they circled as the stream formed up, then headed for the coast between Eastbourne and Beachy Head. Over the Channel, they were climbing, and they had reached 14,000 feet at the French coast. There were three New Zealanders on board: Egglestone the pilot, Gordon Mitchell the navigator, and Jim Freestone the bomb aimer. They had come a long way to be in a Cambridge-based Lancaster that night, bound for Dresden in central Germany. Until the briefing, a few hours before, they had never heard of Dresden. The four English members of the crew — Jack Trueman the mid-upper gunner was the fourth — had had to explain it as best they could. Most of them, like Peter Goldie, thought of the city vaguely as an art centre. Not a military target at all. That is why some of them were uneasy, in spite of those tales of Nazi tanks in the streets.

The master bomber controlling the first attack wave had

flown a twin-engined Mosquito, a machine with a performance equal to that of most German night fighters and therefore unlikely to be caught, although made of wood and very vulnerable to light flak when flying low down in the light of a burning city. But when they kept high, Mosquitoes suffered few losses, and they could carry a surprising bomb-load.

The master bomber who was to control the second wave, Squadron Leader Peter de Wesselow, flew 'U for Uncle', a peculiar aircraft. It was a Lancaster with the 'Universal Power Plant', a development of the Merlin engine designed for civilian use after the war. Two had crashed on a Hamburg 'spoof' raid and de Wesselow had got the third. It was ten to twenty knots faster than most Lancasters and could reach 25,000 feet, a great height for a British night bomber (although the American day bombers flew higher than that, admittedly with a smaller load). But a master bomber had to come down a bit and circle the target throughout the duration of the attack; and even a souped-up Lancaster was big and slow and vulnerable.

Peter de Wesselow saw the bombers basically as the hunted. They were the normal prey of the night fighters and to a lesser extent of the gunners. 'Being human,' he said, 'the top consideration was always to get away with it, subject only to doing the job. And the job (the actual time over target) lasted two minutes (fifteen to twenty minutes for a master bomber, though), and getting away with it lasted on average five and a half hours.' 'Getting away with it' so deep into Germany as Dresden meant eight or nine hours.

De Wesselow had got away with it for a long time. He was on his third tour and Dresden was his seventy-second operation. By inclination, like Wing Commander Smith, the master bomber for the first wave, Squadron Leader de

Wesselow was a team man. His flight engineer, Bill Bamlett, and his wireless operator, Fred White, had done all their tours with him. Bamlett was a North Country farmer, White had worked in a shoe factory. He described them as 'quiet, sterling chaps, duty doing sort of chaps, even if it meant dying'. He believed very much in the importance of the job Bomber Command was doing and had deliberately transferred to the Command from light bombers whose role was to attack targets just in front of the army. De Wesselow wanted to hit the German war effort, and believed that by flying Lancasters he was doing it.

Generally, he took the view that everyone knew before the war that civilians would be involved and anyhow was it really worse to kill a civilian in civilian clothes rather than a former civilian who had just been put into uniform? He didn't particularly like the idea of killing women and children; indeed, emotionally, he hated the thought, but the Germans had done it in Poland, Norway, Holland, England. He thought:

It was better to kill German civilians than let them cause the deaths of other, *entirely* innocent civilians. So if a communications centre, or an industrial area, involved German civilians, that was fate, tragic indeed. Finally, what could German civilians take? If Dresden was worse than Hiroshima, might it not have caused surrender, as Hiroshima did? We didn't know that argument then, but it was in the background. That's how we saw it then.

De Wesselow did once have doubts, which he expressed, when for a raid on the university town of Freiburg the aiming point was to be the cathedral. 'I knew Freiburg from a stay of six months just before the war and had friends there; I knew the industrial area was two miles outside the city centre. When I protested, they put me on another operation, so I never went to Freiburg.'

Normally, everything was very remote, even when there were colossal fires burning down below, as in Hamburg in 1943, which was de Wesselow's first solo trip in Bomber Command.

In general, you saw a light on the ground, which was the fires — but mainly you saw a glowing light in the smoke. Then searchlights above and ack-ack around you. There was always a weird feeling of unreality in Bomber Command. You were living in, say, Cambridgeshire or Norfolk; you were thinking of friends, pubs, girls, even intellectual pursuits. Then you were launched for eight hours into a different world at 20,000 feet over Germany.

Dresden was one experience among many for us. At briefing, we were told it was a communications centre for the Russian Front. I think we knew, and were probably told, that it was to help, and still more impress, the Russians with the power of Bomber Command. Yalta had just occurred. It was deep in, deeper than Berlin, so there was smaller chance of survival. I wished it had been Cologne or even the Ruhr.

The target was lit up a long way ahead, but nothing very special. The weather was good. My main memory is of coming down for a better view. I couldn't identify the aiming point, which must be why I came down to 5,000 feet — just above the blast range of our 4,000 lb bombs. I can still see one picture distinctly: there was a platz flanked by a fine building and some gabled houses suggestive of south Germany. There was a mass of smoke (to the east?) and an industrial area (to the west?) clear of smoke. The city was distinctly lit up. I saw people in the streets, I saw a dog rush across a road — and felt sorry for it (is that absurd?). I was busy, keeping the bombing from going away from the main line and allowing for creep back.

The uniqueness of Dresden for me was coming down, because it needed it. I had a good aircraft, there seemed to be no opposition. So coming down, I saw much more; it was more intimate. All these raids were pretty horrifying though.

We went to Dresden with the usual sinking feeling of personal fear, suppressed by busying ourselves with our technical tasks, in the usual ignorance of why our masters chose this target and briefed on the matter only so far as was relevant to destroying what they wanted to destroy.

The closely-packed stream, 529 four-motor bombers, invisible to each other in the darkness, roared on for Germany.

Death was a lottery that night. Reactions after the first wave of attack often determined one's fate. And the reactions were not those of a canny, war-experienced population capable of guessing what the enemy might do next and knowing what the best counter-moves might be. On the contrary, they were merely the first thoughts of a rather trusting people who had been unable to conceive of Dresden as a target for the massive fire-raids which had reduced most German cities to a wilderness of blackened stones and empty walls.

Some families endured the raids separated among themselves, a prey to anxiety about the others. Eva Beyer did, for instance. She spent most nights at the bakery outside the city centre because she had to be up early on every day except her day off. But her mother, Edith Beyer, lived in Klein Plauensche Gasse near the Annenkirche and Am See, close to the centre of the Altstadt, an area which became a mass of flame from which few escaped. With her was her baby daughter Gertrud, four years old. The two boys were living on the other side of the Elbe in Neustadt, where food was easier to get.

Ruth Pieper was twenty-one and worked as a secretary at the railway hotel next to the Neustadt station.

My father, Heinrich Marcus Pieper, ran a small taxi business, but as he was not a member of the Party, his cars had one by one been taken away from him for the army and he now only had one car left. On this night, he was out at a pub playing skittles, while I was at home with my mother listening to the wireless. I well remember the announcer saying something like: 'Heavy forces of bombers are headed for Leipzig.' I felt they were coming for Dresden and told my mother this.

Their flat was in Pfortenhauerstrasse, in the north-eastern suburb of Blasewitz, and was not affected by the first raid, but Ruth suggested to her mother that they pack some things in case of a second attack. They were still packing when the bombers came again.

I didn't see the flares. Our shutters and blinds were down. It was a fantastic noise, the planes were so low. The cellar shook from bombs and I looked like the ace of spades: a door had been blown open and coal dust had been blown over me from a little flue. But we were lucky, although many houses around us were blasted or burning. My father was seen alive after the first attack but disappeared during the second attack.

Ruth and her mother finished packing and left Dresden to stay with friends in the spectacularly beautiful 'Saxon Switzerland' area nearby. But after a few days, Ruth came back to search the ruins for her father.

Charlotte Mann was thirty-six, and as she was childless had been conscripted for part-time war work. One of her brothers had fought in France and was still on the West Front; her eldest brother, who had been bombed out in Hamburg during the 1943 fire-storms, was fighting the Russians on the Eastern Front. Her husband, who was fifty, had lost an eye in the First World War, but when the army tried to call him up again for the Second World War his firm had succeeded in holding on to him. However, he did belong to the Volksturm, the German Home Guard, which consisted largely of the elderly and the unfit. They lived in a modern, three-storey, centrally-heated house on Hepkeplatz in the suburb of Gruna, next to Grosser Garten, and about fifteen minutes by tram from the centre of the city. That night the Gauleiter, Martin Mutschmann, had ordered the Home Guard and other men also to turn up at the cinemas in the city centre where government information films were to be shown to them. Charlotte remembers:

Consequently we women were almost entirely alone and the men in the town when the sirens went. The sky was already hung with 'Christmas Trees', the coloured lights which fall like grapes. There were not very many of us in the cellar: five families, mostly without men and with only two children. I felt slightly disturbed because I knew that my husband must be out in the streets. We heard crashing and thundering noises for twenty minutes and the house shook. After the 'All Clear' we saw that all the windows were broken and the doors torn off by the blast, but nothing was burning. I got on my way to the town to see if my husband was coming. I met other men but my husband was not among them. I came back and waited and waited and waited. At last, after two hours, he returned and I was glad to see that he was still in one piece.

Now he told me what he had experienced during this short period. From the cinema, which finished shortly before the warning, he had managed to get a tram, although people were already clinging to it like grapes. But two stops later, the warning came and the tram stopped. This was in the centre of the town. My husband knew of a good air raid shelter there and went in. Many people were there and they too were very calm and controlled. But then the first incendiaries came raining down and some explosives. Now they had to get out quick, for the rear of the building collapsed. My husband helped a few people, then he quickly got under way for he wanted to get home. He ran through the Grosser Garten, which was the shortest route, but even there he was stopped several times by people with suitcases and children who wanted to get to the railway station and leave Dresden altogether. He had to tell them that they would not even reach the station, because the fires in the town were spreading and the streets were blocked with people. He helped a few of them, but then anxiety overcame him to find out what had happened at home.

Many people who were afraid had moved out into the open and had settled down for the night on the meadows of the Grosser Garten, the park laid out by Augustus the Strong in baroque style with a little castle in the middle and two lakes. Nobody suspected another raid would come or that the fire would move in a different direction; at that time, it had only just started to spread.

Once reunited, Charlotte and her husband decided to spend the night in their cellar, as the upstairs rooms were uninhabitable due to the broken windows which let in the bitter night's cold. The cellar was clean because they never stored coal in it, but they set about making it more comfortable. Once that was done, Charlotte had leisure to worry about her parents, who lived only ten minutes' walk away. Also, her sister-in-law was staying with them, together with her six-months-old baby and her own mother. She set out with her husband to check up quickly, but they did not get far. 'The roads were blocked with fleeing people.' Then the second raid began, the attack which turned Dresden into an 'inferno'.

The testimony of all the witnesses makes clear that the fire-storm proper did not begin during the first wave of attack, as has been thought, but during the second, much heavier raid. They are absolutely unanimous on that. The deadliness of the results in terms of casualties was partly because, as Charlotte Mann's memories make clear, the streets, the parks, every open space in fact was crowded with people, either fleeing or trying to settle down for the night away from buildings. But there were also very many people who remained sheltering in cellars and basements and underground restaurants, and these were absolutely jam-packed together. The refugees had at least doubled the number of people who were in the city that night.

One of these refugees was Maria Rosenberger from Breslau, who had accompanied her employer, Herr Riedel, and his wife when they sought refuge with friends living in Bergstrasse. Maria herself had a sister who lived in Dresden and on the night of 13 February, Shrove Tuesday, they had arranged to meet at a restaurant in the centre of the Altstadt. They were preparing to leave, just before 10 o'clock, when the sirens sounded, and soon after the Christmas Trees lit the streets like daylight. They scurried round the next corner and down into the air raid shelter beneath the town hall.

We were more carried down the stairs than anything else; we didn't have to walk. The cellar was already filled with women and children, and people were crammed together even on the staircase leading down to it. We were instructed not to speak, in order to save oxygen. A mine must have exploded nearby, for suddenly the rooms were full of dust, the walls trembled, mortar fell down and one could hardly breathe any more. Then somebody screamed: 'Everyone out of here, the place is on fire!' When we arrived upstairs we saw that the street was on fire (later I was told this was due to phosphorus bombs). Near a wall we met some soldiers who said: 'What's happening here is worse than at the Front!' Burning curtain material was flying towards us and glowing pieces of wood came flying down on us from above; also bits of windowpanes. One had the feeling everywhere of walking only on broken glass. It was as if fire was poured from the sky. Where there was darkness at one moment, we could suddenly see flames lick up. As my sister knew the city, she managed to find ways out of this 'witches' cauldron'. The place where I lived was Räcknitzhöhe beyond the main station, and there the fires had been more or less dealt with by the people, but as I looked back to the centre I noticed that it was just one single sea of flames. Now everyone started to make a run for the outskirts in order to reach some open space.

This was true of those living on the outskirts as Maria did, but there were many people who preferred what they felt was the security of the cellars and basements, so long as the buildings under which they had taken shelter were not set on fire. In all these places, one must picture a similar scene to that under the town hall, with crowds of women and children so closely packed that one could move only in the direction in which others moved; and if no one moved, there was no way of getting out, for even the staircases were jam-packed with people and the air was stifling, indeed might shortly become unbreathable. There are very few stories of what happened in such places. Although many experienced them, few survived to speak of it afterwards.

Margret Freyer, an unusually beautiful girl of twenty-four, who had already survived a full day's interrogation by the Gestapo and escaped the concentration camp by carefully considering her answers, was also to survive two cellars in Dresden on the night of 13/14 February. Both were in the Altstadt, where the fire-storm was to develop. She lived at Ferdinandstrasse 13 and took shelter in the cellar there during the first wave of attack, soon to be joined by forty-three other women. The damaged building was abandoned by its occupants at the first lull, and not liking the eerie sensation of being the only person in a five-storey building, Margret set off with her two packed suitcases for the house of a friend, Cenci, who lived a few streets away at Struvestrasse 13. Within an hour or so of the beginning of the lull it became too dangerous to go back again to her own flat to rescue more of her belongings, because the rubble-filled streets were full of sparks and smoke which produced the effect of a thick, hot fog. So the two girls settled down to clean up Cenci's flat, remove the glass and earth which had been blown in and take down the curtains which, in a night of howling sparks, were a fire risk.

'Then we had a cigarette and a cup of coffee,' she recalled.

When the sirens sounded again, my friend and I looked at each other, terrified – surely it wasn't possible? Are they coming a second time? I just caught the radio announcer's message: 'Several bomber units are approaching Dresden.' The voice of the announcer was anything but steady. I felt sick – so they *were* coming a second time. Knees shaking, we went down into the cellar. This time there were forty-one women and one man, Cenci's husband.

I sat next to Cenci on a box while a non-stop hail of bombs seemed to last an eternity. The walls shook, the ground shook, the light went out and our heavy iron door was forced open by blast. In this cellar now, there were the same scenes as had occurred before in the Ferdinandstrasse cellar: a crowd of crying, screaming, or praying women, throwing themselves on top of each other. Cenci and I tried to disentangle them and calm them down. We longed for the 'All Clear', but it never came — the sirens had stopped working. But eventually the earth stopped shaking and now we believed that it was really all over. Cenci and I exchanged a glance of thankfulness. Our cellar had held.

Out of here — nothing but out! Three women went up the stairs in front of us, only to come rushing down again, wringing their hands. 'We can't get out of here! Everything outside is burning!' they cried. Cenci and I went up to make sure. It was true.

Then we tried the 'Breakthrough' which had been installed in each cellar, so people could exit from one cellar to the other. But here we met only thick smoke which made it impossible to breathe.

So we went upstairs. The back door, which opened on to the back yard and was made partly of glass, was completely on fire. It would have been madness to touch it. And at the front entrance, flames a metre and a half high came licking at short intervals into the hall.

In spite of this, it was clear that we could not stay in the building unless we wanted to suffocate. So we went downstairs again and picked up our suitcases. I put two handfuls of handkerchiefs into a water tub and stuffed them soaking wet into my coat pocket. They probably saved my life later on.

But as we went up the stairs out of the cellar, Cenci's husband came up and said: 'Cenci, please stay here, you must help my sister. She's ill.'

I made a last attempt to convince everyone in the cellar to leave, because they would suffocate if they did not; but they didn't want to. And so I left alone — and all the people in that cellar suffocated. Most died down there, but three women were found outside the door, amongst them Cenci. I cried bitterly when I found out that I was the only one who had escaped from that cellar.

I stood by the entrance and waited until no flames came licking in, then I quickly slipped through and out into the street. I had my suitcase in one hand and was wearing a white fur coat which by now was anything but white. I also wore boots and long trousers. Those boots had been a lucky choice, it turned out.

Because of flying sparks and the fire-storm I couldn't see anything at first. A witches' cauldron was waiting for me out there: no street, only rubble nearly a metre high, glass, girders, stones, craters. I tried to get rid of the sparks by constantly patting them off my coat. It was useless. I stopped doing it, stumbled, and someone behind me called out: 'Take your coat off, it's started to burn.' In the pervading extreme heat I hadn't even noticed. I took off the coat and dropped it.

Next to me a woman was screaming continually: 'My den's burning down, my den's burning down,' and dancing in the street. As I go on, I can still hear her screaming but I don't see her again. I run, I stumble, anywhere. I don't even know where I am any more, I've lost all sense of direction because all I can see is three steps ahead.

Suddenly I fall into a big hole — a bomb crater, about six metres wide and two metres deep, and I end up down there lying on top of three women. I shake them by their clothes and start to scream at them, telling them they must get out of here — but they don't move any more. I believe I was severely shocked by this incident; I seemed to have lost all emotional feeling. Quickly, I climbed across the women, pulled my suitcase after me, and crawled on all fours out of the crater.

To my left I suddenly see a woman. I can see her to this day and shall never forget it. She carries a bundle in her arms. It is a baby. She runs, she falls, and the child flies in an arc into the fire. It's only my eyes which take this in; I myself feel nothing. The woman remains lying on the ground, completely still. Why? What for? I don't know, I just stumble on. The fire-storm is incredible, there are calls for help and screams from somewhere but all around is one single inferno. I hold another wet handkerchief in front of my mouth, my hands and my face are burning; it feels as if the skin is hanging down in strips.

On my right I see a big, burnt-out shop where lots of people are standing. I join them, but think: 'No, I can't stay here either, this place is completely surrounded by fire.' I leave all these people behind, and stumble on. Where to? No idea! But every time towards those places where it is dark, in case there is no fire there. I have no conception of what the street actually looked like. But it is especially from those dark patches that the people come who wring their hands and cry the same thing over and over again: 'You can't carry on there, we've just come from there, everything is burning there!' Wherever and to whomsoever I turn, always that same answer.

In front of me is something that might be a street, filled with a hellish rain of sparks which look like enormous rings of fire when they hit the ground. I have no choice. I must go through. I press another wet handkerchief to my mouth and almost get through, but I fall and am convinced that I cannot go on. It's hot. Hot! My hands are burning like fire. I just drop my suitcase, I am past caring, and too weak. At least, there's nothing to lug around with me any more.

I stumbled on towards where it was dark. Suddenly, I saw people again, right in front of me. They scream and gesticulate with their hands, and then – to my utter horror and amazement – I see how one after the other they simply seem to let themselves drop to the ground. I had a feeling that they were being shot, but my mind could not understand what was really happening. Today I know that these unfortunate people were the victims of lack of oxygen. They fainted and then burnt to cinders. I fall then, stumbling over a fallen woman and as I lie right next to her I see how her clothes are burning away. Insane fear grips me and from then on I repeat one simple sentence to myself continuously: 'I don't want to burn to death – no, no burning – I don't want to burn!' Once more I fall down and feel that I am not going to be able to get up again, but the fear of being burnt pulls me to my feet. Crawling, stumbling, my last handkerchief pressed to my mouth . . . I do not know how many people I fell over. I knew only one feeling: that I must not burn.

Then my handkerchiefs are all finished – it's dreadfully hot – I can't go on and I remain lying on the ground. Suddenly a soldier appears in front of me. I wave, and wave again. He comes over to me and I whisper into his ear (my voice has almost gone): 'Please take me with you, I don't want to burn.' But that soldier was much too weak himself to lift me to my feet. He laid my two arms crosswise over my breast and stumbled on across me. I followed him with my eyes until he disappears somewhere in the darkness.

I try once more to get up on my feet, but I can only manage to crawl forward on all fours. I can still feel my body, I know I'm still alive. Suddenly, I'm standing up, but there's something wrong, everything seems so far away and I can't hear or see properly any more. As I found out later, like all the others, I was suffering from lack of oxygen. I must have stumbled forwards roughly ten paces when I all at once inhaled fresh air. There's a breeze! I take another breath, inhale deeply, and my senses clear. In front of me is a broken tree. As I rush towards it, I know that I have been saved, but am unaware that the park is the Bürgerwiese.

I walk on a little and discover a car. I'm pleased and decide to spend the night in it. The car is full of suitcases and boxes but I find enough room on the rear seats to squeeze in. Another stroke of good luck for me is that the car's windows are all broken and I have to keep awake putting out the sparks which drifted in. I don't know how long I sat there, when a hand suddenly descended on my shoulder and a man's voice said: 'Hello! You must get out of there.' I got such a fright, because obviously someone was determined to force me away from my safe hiding place. I said, with great fear in my voice: 'Please, allow me to stay here, I'll give you all the money I've got on me.' (If I think about this now it almost sounds like a joke.) But the answer I got was: 'No, I don't want your money. The car is on fire.'

Good God! I leapt out immediately and could see that indeed all four tyres were burning. I hadn't noticed because of the tremendous heat.

Now I looked at the man and recognized him as the soldier who had put my arms across my chest. When I asked him, he confirmed it. Then he started to weep. He continued to stroke my back, mumbling words about bravery, Russian campaign . . . but this here, this is hell. I don't grasp his meaning and offer him a cigarette.

We walk on a little way and discover two crouching figures. They were two men, one a railwayman who was crying because (in the smoke and debris) he could not find the way to his home. The other was a civilian who had escaped from a cellar together with sixty people, but had had to leave his wife and children behind, due to some dreadful circumstances. All three men were crying now but I just stood there, incapable of a single tear. It was as if I was watching a film. We spent half the night together, sitting on the ground too exhausted even to carry on a conversation. The continuous explosions didn't bother us, but the hollow cries for help which came continuously from all directions were gruesome. Towards 6 o'clock in the morning, we parted.

I spent all the daylight hours which followed in the town searching for my fiancé. I looked for him amongst the dead, because hardly any living beings were to be seen anywhere. What I saw is so horrific that I shall hardly be able to describe it. Dead, dead, dead everywhere. Some completely black like charcoal. Others completely untouched, lying as if they were asleep. Women in aprons, women with children sitting in the trams as if they had just nodded off. Many women, many young girls, many small children, soldiers who were only identifiable as such by the metal buckles on their belts, almost all of them naked. Some clinging to each other in groups as if they were clawing at each other.

From some of the debris poked arms, heads, legs, shattered skulls. The static water-tanks were filled up to the top with dead human beings, with large pieces of masonry lying on top of that again. Most people looked as if they had been inflated, with large yellow and brown stains on their bodies. People whose clothes were still glowing . . . I think I was incapable of absorbing the meaning of this cruelty any more, for there were also so many little babies, terribly mutilated; and all the people lying so close together that it looked as if someone had put them down there, street by street, deliberately.

I then went through the Grosser Garten and there is one thing I did realize. I was aware that I had constantly to brush hands away from me, hands which belonged to people who wanted me to take them with me, hands which clung to me. But I was much too weak to lift anyone up. My mind took all this in vaguely, as if seen through a veil. In fact, I was in such a state that I did not realize that there was a third attack on Dresden. Late that afternoon I collapsed in the Ostra-Allee, where two men took me to a friend who lived on the outskirts of the city.

I asked for a mirror and did not recognize myself any more. My face was a mass of blisters and so were my hands. My eyes were narrow slits and puffed up, my whole body was covered in little black, pitted marks. I cannot understand to this day how I contracted these marks, because I was wearing a pair of long trousers and a jacket. Possibly the fire-sparks ate their way through my clothing.

Margaret Freyer's survival was due mainly to her own determination to live, but partly to the fact, she thinks, that she was wearing boots rather than shoes. Some of the road surfaces melted in the heat and shoes would tend to come off, and then the poor victim would be burning from the feet upwards. Her experiences were so vivid that, like a number of other witnesses, she wrote down what she had seen while the memories were still fresh and detailed, three years after.

In Dresden it was said afterwards (and it cannot have been far wrong) that the temperature generated by the fires in the centre of the Altstadt reached 3,000 degrees; and as 1,200 degrees is as much as sandstone can stand, this explains why the Frauenkirche collapsed and fell in on itself next morning, whereas churches built of harder stone still stood as burnt-out shells. Of course, no one actually measured the temperatures produced by the fire-storm. But the physical results were felt by a great many. Gisela-Alexandra Moeltgen, in another narrative written shortly afterwards when the detail was clear and fresh in her mind, complained of the terrible 'suction' which of itself destroyed lightly-constructed buildings such as garages and greenhouses. As all over the old town almost all the houses lost their roofs and the walled enclosures acted like stoves, belching up great welts of flame and hot smoke, so superheated air rose miles wide and miles high above the flaming city. Even at 20,000 feet the crews of the bombers saw the sky as a rosy bowl above them, saw other Lancasters close to them lit in brilliant detail as though on a stage, and found the heavy aircraft bucking and shuddering in the immense invisible columns of turbulence. And to replace this enormous mass of boiling, heated air, cold winter air rushed in at ground level from outside the area of the fires.

This was the 'suction' felt by Gisela-Alexandra, and this probably, rather than the last ten faltering, stumbling steps taken by Margret Freyer, was the agent which saved her life by bringing her fresh, chill, breathable air when she was collapsing from lack of oxygen.

But for those trapped under the burning buildings (there must have been tens of thousands of them) who could not get out because of the jam of humanity, or who got up to street level and found all the surrounding streets already an inferno of licking, roaring flames – for them there would be slim chance of survival. Their stories can only be inferred from the very fortunate (and determined) few like Margret Freyer who narrowly escaped. Thousands of them probably died of suffocation, not exactly in peace but without the extreme agony of being burnt alive, which was the fate of most of the uncounted masses underneath or at street level in the Altstadt as it went up with a roar, just like the fresh materials already glowing in the fireplace when a newspaper is placed across to create a draught. One must remember too that this was no normal city in normal times. Every household had its large quota of refugees, and many more had arrived in Dresden that day, so that the pavements were blocked by them, as they struggled onwards or simply sat exhausted on their suitcases and rucksacks. For these reasons, no one has been able to put a positive figure to the numbers of the dead, and no doubt no one ever will.

And of course there were the patients in the wards of the maternity homes and hospitals, many of them immobile, some able to move only with difficulty. Claus von Fehrentheil was one of those who, like Margret Freyer, should have been counted among the dead, but survived through luck and determination. To the battle wounds received while fighting with a Waffen-SS armoured formation in Hungary, he had had added a broken spine while in transit to the first aid post, and suffered another injury which became infected and began to suppurate. After the first wave of attack on the night of 13 February, he was brought back to the ward where he was a patient, and found it chilly. The windowpanes were lying in thousands of tiny, jagged fragments on the floor, so there was no potential danger from that source. Through the windows could be seen the burning rooftops of neighbouring buildings, including that of the fire station next door to the Vitzthumschule.

After all the bedridden sick had been made comfortable again, another attempt was made to get some sleep. Any hope we had in this respect faded when a new air raid warning was sounded. Our assumption that this was a kind of precautionary alarm probably set off by returning aircraft was not confirmed. From some unknown source we heard that new and stronger bomber formations were on their way. All the wards had to be vacated again. Russian volunteers were working as sickbay attendants and with untiring zest they carried to the cellar those patients who could not walk. From the sound of the engines we could hear that this time a very large number of aircraft were taking part, definitely more than in the first wave.

Cynical and infamous as the order was, to attack Dresden, so just as cynically was it carried out. We were convinced it was Mr Churchill who was directly responsible for the order to destroy Dresden, but for the shameful way in which it was carried out authorities of a lower rank may have been responsible.

Von Fehrentheil specifically objected to the use of small anti-personnel bombs (a normal tactic used by the Luftwaffe also to discourage the fire-bomb dousers). He conceived the raid as a kind of hunt, the heavy bombs intended to destroy the shelters and set people fleeing and the small bombs to catch them when they did so. And in his rage, he conceived the idea that his enemies were omnipotent, that the pilots of the bombers were actually listening to the German broadcasts telling people what shelters or open spaces to make for, and then deliberately bombing just those places.

In fact, as we know, the master bomber was having trouble identifying the aiming point because of the excessive fires and smoke; and his main preoccupation was the crude one of keeping the bombing concentrated and in particular not allowing it to spread out to the sides. To stop this he was instructing the special flare-carrying aircraft called 'Visual Centerers' which accompanied the bomber stream at intervals and whose job was, on command, to mark the central line of the attack and so prevent the bombing from becoming too widespread. With no opposition over the target, 'creep back' was unlikely to be a significant factor this night.

Many people in an air raid have absolutely no idea what the enemy are up to. In England, there were often rumours of someone seen signalling to German night bombers with a torch. This erratically attractive idea occurred to some in Dresden also, but they could not agree where the English spy really was — some said he had flashed his torch from a house on the waterfront of the Elbe Terraces, others were equally sure that he lived on a surrounding hill and signalled from there. A third story was to fasten suspicion on those British members of the SS who were stationed out at the Wildemann barracks beyond Neustadt. First, they had betrayed England to the Germans, but now that the English were winning, they were betraying Germany to the RAF. The idea of a betrayal produces hate, and hatred is a fine antidote to fear, as far too many politicians have discovered.

Like the good soldier he was, Claus von Fehrentheil was trying to read the battle through his ears, but the techniques being used were complex and unlike those he knew – and besides, being confined in a cellar was restricting to someone accustomed to an open battlefield. 'I am certain that nobody who escaped from this inferno can say with certainty at what time exactly the whole nightmare started or finished. Was it still Shrove Tuesday or already Ash Wednesday? Ash for the crosses on the forehead we had in plenty.' But at length the whistling, whining and – when very near – screaming of the bombs, and the roaring explosions that rocked and shuddered the cellar and seemed to make the walls and floors move, all that ceased. And the sound of the last aero engine died away.

Now they expected to be helped back to the wards and put to bed again. As a general movement began towards the exits, a laconic message stopped it: 'The entire area outside this shelter is completely buried under rubble.' The news that they were trapped would have been intimidating enough to physically fit men, perhaps capable of mining their way up before the fires above came down.

'One first had to digest this information,' wrote von Fehrentheil. 'Assume all of Dresden presents exactly the same picture as we do. In which sequence are the known shelters going to be checked and cleared? No one can say. Right then, it's up to us to get ourselves out.'

He thought first of the air vent. This proved to have climbing irons inside. It was certainly a way of escape, but rather narrow. Unfortunately, his hip was cased in plaster-of-Paris. For von Fehrentheil, there was no way out by the vent.

What about the window? A check revealed a rain of debris, including hot tiles, falling from the roof and upper storeys of the building. If hit by one of those, it would hardly matter to the victim if the tile was hot or cold; but, von Fehrentheil noticed, the fall of debris was not really regular and there was a bit of 'dead ground' sheltered from the wreckage showering down. If he could time his exit right, he might make it. The time to move, he decided, was when a tile had just fallen, and before the next came down. Nerving himself with the drill command: *'Sprung auf, marsch, marsch!'* ('On your feet, move!' would be the English equivalent) he scrambled forward.

Now I was in the open, no longer surrounded by walls, but by flames instead. They had plenty of nourishment in the wooden-beam construction of the houses and the wooden furniture inside them. This started a terrific fire-storm which robbed you of the air you needed to breathe. No path was recognizable between the buildings, no obvious path of escape, because walls were collapsing and adding to the heaps of rubble. The suction of the flames was so strong that the gymnasium next to the Vitzthumschule, in which the desks from the former school had been stored, caught fire. Even the pieces of clothing which I had hurriedly picked up and thrown over myself began to smoulder. Because of the flying sparks my eyes became useless. I was blind. Small holes must have been burnt into the cornea, which were incredibly painful. They made it impossible for me to open my eyes even briefly, just to see where I was.

One could forecast what must happen next: the oxygen in the air becomes completely burnt away, so one becomes unconscious and hardly notices that one is burning to death. Blind, I accepted that this must happen. Suddenly, someone touched my shoulder and asked me to come along. He had found a way through the rubble to the outside. And so, holding on to the arm of a comrade, I was led through burning Dresden.

We walked round unexploded bombs in their craters, and because the craters were so close together it was impossible to use any kind of transport. The dead and injured who were lying around had to be carried, if they were to be brought out. While on our way, we spoke to some of the rescue teams. As an ex-soldier one was not exactly hyper-sensitive, but what I was told sent goosepimples down my spine. In front of the main station, in the Grosser Garten and on the Elbe meadows the bombs had fallen among the refugees whom we had just removed from the grasp of the Soviets. I could see only through the eyes of my companion, but my ears and nose told me what was going on. One could not get rid of the intensive smell of roast pork. This could only come from the bodies of the people who had been buried and trapped in the air raid shelters or cellars, and were now miserably burning to death around us.

Von Fehrentheil lost all idea of time. He thought it was dawn, when he was able to flick his eyes open momentarily in the direction the sound of another great formation of bombers was coming from. But it wasn't dawn, it must have been midday. He could not remember where they bombed, or if they bombed at all. When at last he was led to some place where the wounded were being dealt with, a doctor put some drops into his eyes, but it had no effect on the pain. He was told that the pain would cease only when the blisters which had formed on the cornea had healed. And so it proved, eventually. But his hatred for those who had done this deed did not cease.

In well-informed circles they spoke of 250,000 dead, at least! This number seemed likely, especially to one who had been in the inferno. But it will be impossible to arrive at a true figure because the treks of the refugees had not been registered anywhere. The refined English did the deed, but they left the dirty work of clearing up the mess to the Russians.

Hugo Eichhorn, commanding SS-Pioneer A & E Regiment 1, a unit of Engineers which supplied many of the rescue teams sent into the city, went into action during the first wave of attack. 'The Pioneeer barracks situated north of the city at Heller was in a slightly raised position,' he recalled.

As we had no shelters, my soldiers were taking cover in trenches which had been dug in the exercise ground. My adjutant and I stood on the barrack square and watched the bombing through binoculars. We just had to stand there as the whole city with its 650,000 inhabitants and at least the same number of refugees went up in flames and died. Although there were enough fighter planes and also jet fighters stationed on the aerodromes around Dresden, not a single plane defending the town could be seen in the sky; there was no flak either.

We didn't wait for orders. We had to act at once, while the actual raid was still going on. Each of the company commanders was detailed to go in and take care of particular streets in certain areas, in co-operation with the ambulance and medical personnel they might find there. It would all have to be done in the dark and controlled by word of mouth, for the electricity and telephone cables would be out of action. So dispatch riders were detailed to work with each company, coming back frequently to report position and progress and always able to return to the company to order it to withdraw, if we had warning of another raid. That was good! That worked well! The second raid, which started at 0130 with explosives, claimed no victims from our companies.

Because of the fire-storm, at first it was possible to give help only at the periphery of the fires. I had to look on, helpless, as people who were clinging to iron railings were seized mercilessly by the suction and plucked off into the flames. And not human beings only, but all sort of things, even prams, were seized by this force and sucked into the sea of fire. We could do nothing about this. Advancing into the cellars eventually, we were met by the most gruesome sights. Young girls of the Frauenarbeitsdienst, indeed whole groups of people, dead in cellars without surface wounds, their lungs torn by blast. And other cellars full of water and drowned people. Many cellars had their exits blocked by rubble, so the people had suffocated. I was struck by the fact that whatever cellar we broke into, death in some form or other had visited before us. And in and around the main railway station we found nothing but dead, maimed, torn or burnt people.

How many were there? Figures can only be approximate. I reckon there could have been 300,000, perhaps as many as 400,000 killed. Only a few could be buried in single graves.

The Elbe bridges were only partly damaged and could still be used. The bombs blew holes in the bridge surfaces of roughly three to four metres in diameter, and people who had been partly blinded by the smoke and sparks stumbled across the bridge, failed to see the gaps, and fell in effect down a precipice; that was always fatal. The Autobahn bridge to the west of Dresden remained undamaged, however. Although most of the bridges were blown up when Dresden surrendered, none were blown by my unit.

Susanne Lehmann, the ten-year-old daughter of a civil servant, had spent the time of the first raid sheltering in the cellar of their flat in Silbermannstrasse with her mother, Käthe Lehmann. Her fifteen-year-old brother Wilfried had been out for the evening attending a performance of the Sarrasani Circus, a performance which had been terminated by an announcement from the stage just before 10 pm. Instead of going meekly to the shelters under the Circus, Wilfried had come home in time to see the fire brigade put out an incendiary in their fifth-storey flat. Susanne was jealous that her brother was allowed to watch this, but that she, a mere girl, was not. However, it was all very exciting, so much better than going meekly to bed at the usual time. She was still up and about in the cellar when the sirens howled again.

The same whistling as before − a long, spiralling whistle, then a hard impact and an explosion − sixty, maybe a hundred times. Finally, men came into our cellar − not through the door but through the 'breakthrough' in the left-hand wall − and asked us all to leave. There was no way out through the cellar door, it was blocked by fallen masonry, they said. Our five-storey building had collapsed as far down as the second storey. Go out on the right, through the break in the other wall, we were told. We three, mother, my brother and I, trotted one behind the other through the hole in the wall into the neighbouring cellar which had been vacated long since, and came up under the grocery store which stood on the corner of our street. The white, empty shelves of the shop were bathed in red light. 'Poor Mrs X,' we thought, 'where can she be now?' as we escaped into the street. All the houses around were burning or appeared to be burning.

Under the trees in the Allee we could see the dark shapes of people sitting on bundles and suitcases. One of those hollow advertisement pillars seemed to be the safest place to hide, so I pushed my mother towards it; but she didn't want us to go in. Later, burnt corpses were found inside. Where could we go? There was a cry of: 'To the Elbe! to the Elbe!' for logically we should make for the water. So we struggled over fallen trees, and fallen people and abandoned suitcases to Gerokstrasse. We had just passed our local fish-shop when it crashed into the road behind us, the small tower falling first and then the whole of that corner of the building collapsing. By now, mother had lost a shoe and was limping along, and we realized that the Elbe was too far away.

We decided to go to the nearest open space in the opposite direction to the fires − and that was the cemetery. In there, one building still stood intact − the mortuary. We all hurried inside and I − as the youngest child, still dragging my favourite doll with me by its dress − was even given a place to sit, on top of the big stone slab which normally served to take the coffins. My mother and brother crouched on the floor in front of me. And there we sat all night with many other people.

At dawn, my mother decided to leave and search for families we knew who lived further away from the centre and who might have been spared. I grabbed my doll (rather out of a feeling of obligation than of love) by the corner of its dress, in the same way as I had dragged her to the mortuary; my mother picked up her 'emergency bag'; and we pushed and pulled each other through the crowd out into the street, which was not a street any more.

It was just an up-and-down vista of mountains and valleys of rubble, a tangle of electricity wires hanging down, and crowds of disoriented, confused people who warned us very kindly: 'Be careful with those wires, they still have electric current in them!' It was easy to avoid the fires, for they were in the buildings, not the road, but it was difficult to open one's eyes − they seemed stuck together with soot.

We did not find the first family whose house we went to, because it wasn't there any more. But the second family lived at Pohlandstrasse by a park, and there everything was untouched. They had a little five-year-old daughter who kept saying to me: 'Look over there, that's my nursery school. It's burning, it's burning!' She was very pleased about that. I didn't see anything because I couldn't open my eyes any more. So I was allowed to lie down on the couch in the living-room.

Our cantankerous grandmother, who had been taking coffee with us in Silbermannstrasse, had insisted on going back to her home after the first raid. But she didn't get there for twenty-four hours, because she lost her way and spent the night on a bench. My ten-year-old friend Gisela, who had been at our Shrove Tuesday party, was never seen again.

Gerhard Kühnemund, fifteen years old, who together with the young Luftwaffe 'ace' had been wounded when trying to put out an explosive incendiary bomb, had reached a large air raid shelter underneath some kind of head-quarters. As he lived in Leipzig, and was in Dresden that night only by accident, having missed a train connection at the main station, he did not know just where it was, but guesses that it might have been under the Albertinum in the Altstadt.

After our wounds had been dressed, we were caught here by the second raid. So many bombs were dropped that that whole huge cellar started to sway. This must have been the first and only time in my life when I accepted that I was finished and started to pray. The young NCO pilot saw the fear in my wide-open eyes and patted me encouragingly on the shoulder. Twenty minutes later it was over. Around me, I noticed, everyone was in uniform. A bottle of brandy was handed round and I smoked the first cigarette of my life. Nicotine and that sip of alcohol brought me to my knees.

All in the space of a few hours, he had been wounded in action, had had his life saved several times, experienced his first real terror when at the mercy of the unimaginable elemental force that was tearing Dresden apart, smoked his first cigarette, taken his first drink of brandy, and, before he was sent up out of the cellar with orders to go to the Elbe meadows, given a steel helmet to put on which was two sizes too large. He still had to see a good friend killed by his side. That experience was only hours away now.

Some people went against the fire-storm rather than from it, breasting the masses trying to escape. Dr Holzhausen, who was responsible for the Historical Museum and Weapon Gallery, had reached the Schloss during the first wave of attack and seen the fires beginning to come under control. The second wave attack drove everyone to shelter, and he was successively burnt out of two cellars when the houses above them caught fire. By then he was at the Neumarkt, or new square, surrounded by great fires. The only way clear seemed to be for him to run against the fire-storm in an attempt to reach the Elbe and fresher air with more oxygen in it. On the way, he came to the Schloss, but both wings were fully aflame and it would have been ridiculous to try to save anything.

Herr Graefe, a high official of the ministry responsible for pictures, actually walked all the way from his home in the suburbs to the Schloss, which took him two hours. Before he could reach it the second attack began. He saw a complete street go up in flames in front of him. Nevertheless, he ran on against the fire-storm and against all the people who came flooding back in front of it. He got through to the burning Schloss at last, and the Hofkirche and the Opera, right up to the Zwinger by the Elbe, where he found a total inferno with no sign of the fire brigade and no hope of their doing anything about it even if they had been there. The treasures of art and antiquity still left in Dresden were doomed. Even the lorry, packed with pictures, which had been parked for the night on the Terrassenufer, the road parallel to the Elbe, went up in flames.

One of those who also reached the Zwinger was Mrs Soldammer, who had been on duty on the fourth floor of the telephone exchange. She had noted how the fire of the light flak during the first raid was ineffective and was beaten down; how the sky changed colour and became a red-glowing cloud; how the women on duty who were mothers were terrified for their children at home, and the youngsters who were on duty in the building were grieved for the parents from whom they were separated by duty. Only when the telephone building was well alight and some of its walls collapsing, was the order given: 'Save yourselves if you can.' They all poured down to the basement, which had been designated the air raid shelter. But like many such places in Dresden, it was really no such thing − it housed the central-heating boilers and the maze of pipes carrying the hot water. Not only had the iron doors and windows been torn off their hinges by blast, but the earth-shock effect had ruptured the pipes and flooded the crowded cellar with hot water. The victims had been first burned and then drowned.

When she saw this, Mrs Soldammer was desperate to leave the building. She wanted air, feeling that the biting smoke in the cellar area was suffocating her. Her eyes were burning, yet tears were streaming down her face. Almost blind, holding her hands in front of her, she groped her way outside. Around her was the sound of people moaning and whimpering, but there was nothing she could do. When she got to the Zwinger, where there was a little pond in the centre of the green space between the walls, she took off her light helmet, scooped up water in it and bathed her eyes. Already, the heat was creating that terrible suction which literally seized on everything in its path.

Opposite the Zwinger, across the River Elbe, loomed the blazing dome of the Sarrasani Circus building, designed to seat 5,000 people. The wife of the owner, Frau Trude Stosch-Sarrasani, had discussed with her colleagues what should be done in case of a second air raid, and groups of circus horses had been sent down to the Elbe meadows for safety, in charge of eighteen boys and girls including Regina Beer, the acrobatic rider. A blast bomb mowed them all down except two; Regina Beer's corpse proved to have seventeen bomb splinters in it. Meanwhile, some of the incendiaries also dropped in the second raid proved impossible to put out because they had lodged on the very top of the dome, where there was a small wooden structure. Soon the whole great circus arena was a roaring vault of fire, fed by the contents of the offices, dressing-rooms and restaurants which surrounded it. Below, on the ground floor, were two large cages mounted on carts, holding nine tigers. Desperate efforts were made to save the beasts, and one cart was pushed outside. The other got stuck in the narrow exit. By now, the heat was so intense that the circus people were unable to stand it. The tigers stayed where they were and died of suffocation before the flames reached them. Down below in the cellars there was a water-basin for the amphibious mammals, which held Wally the hippopotamus. At 4 am the whole circus building collapsed in on itself, but Wally survived.

Holm Daniel's father kept a diary, entering in it day by day whatever seemed important. At this time what seemed valuable above all else was his son Holm, born 3½ months before in the Friedrichstadt hospital. He and his wife were deliriously happy, although normal people in normal times might think they had little reason to be. He himself had lost an arm at Kiev, and another wound had made one leg very stiff. His wife had become the breadwinner and was away in the Erzgebirge that night. Their hairdressing salon had been destroyed by American bombs intended for the Wettiner station a month previously, and negotiations for new premises were delayed because of the high asking price, 5,000 Reichsmarks. This night he was on his own, looking after the baby boy and six-year-old Bärbel, his wife's daughter by her first husband, killed in Russia: although there was help from the young maid, Gretel, and her soldier fiancé. He made the diary entries as though writing to his son, telling him that 'Mutti' (his mother) had not come back this evening from Tante Martel's, although she had said she would. 'But she did not turn up, and instead we had the most devastating air raid ever. I have been in raids in Berlin and Essen, they were nothing to this one on Dresden.' As he himself was crippled, Gretel and her fiancé had carried Holm in his pram down to the cellar. 'One could hear the bombs come whistling down and the whole cellar was under air-pressure and was shaking. We all lay on the floor, and I threw myself over your pram in order to protect you. It was nerve-racking.'

When the All Clear went, they discovered that the building next door was on fire and that all their own windows were broken; there was a lot of clearing up to do, which was not finished when the second attack began.

Gretel's fiancé wanted to leave you upstairs. I think he must have lost his nerve and only wanted to save himself — and this from someone who is a soldier in uniform. I couldn't carry you, but Gretel and he did it in the end because you were screaming so. I was terribly worried about Mutti, in case she had arrived by train in Dresden during the raid. I hoped very much that she had decided to return the next day.

She had in fact stayed the night with her aunt in the Erzgebirge, and was staring horrified at the bright glow in the sky over Dresden.

As the fire-storm developed it lit up the heavens so brightly that the burning of Dresden was visible from the ground up to fifty miles away or more. Geoff Taylor, the Australian pilot who had chosen, of all days, 13 February for his attempt to break out of the POW camp and steal a German night fighter from Lonnewitz aerodrome, was camped out with his companion in a wood on the edge of the airfield, waiting for daylight. He crawled out of his hiding place in the wood for a better look. The sight appalled him – the bomb-bursts, the fires, the photoflashes gave the impression of a 'thousand thunderstorms run riot'. He did not know that it was Dresden; could not make out what town it was. But the Luftwaffe flarepath at Lonnewitz was brilliantly lit, allowing a stream of German night fighters to take off into the darkness. The RAF lads would have a long journey home from here, giving the Ju 188s every chance. It was a sinister thought.

Eddie Taylor, the ex-paratrooper POW who was working in the coalmines near the oil-from-coal installations at Brüx in Czechoslovakia, was out in the open behind the barbed wire, looking up at the mountain skyline of the Erzgebirge and seeing the glow that came up from behind it. He was much further away than Holm Daniel's mother, on the wrong side of the mountain from Dresden and some forty or fifty kilometres distant, but the light of the flaming city made it bright enough to read in Brüx. 'My Godfather Dick!' he thought. The pounding just went on and on, like a machine gone mad, turning his stomach over to hear it.

Annemarie Waehmann, the twenty-year-old darkroom assistant who had contracted a skin infection, was in the Friedrichstadt hospital, not far from where the Daniel family were living in temporary accommodation (having been bombed out by the Americans in January). The first wave of attack had gutted the hospital building where she and the refugee girl Hilde were housed. The hospital building she had run to was in its turn set on fire by the second wave of raiders.

Once more the bombs crashed and we had to vacate this cellar also. This time we had to run in a rain of bombs and fire across the big park and into the main hospital building. It was the middle of the night, but the sky was yellow. With all these many different fires burning, a big fire-storm had developed. It tore at the crowns of the trees, pulling them to and fro, and shedding hundreds of glowing branches on to us. I pulled my coat over my head and ran like a mad woman. Slightly singed, I reached the main building. Chaos reigned there. Countless patients with all sorts of different illnesses had been brought together. Moaning loudly, praying, and uttering cries for help, they all tried desperately to push their way down into the cellar. I remained standing on the stairs because the air was a little better there. It was here that I found Hilde again, and we waited for morning.

Erika and Ursula Simon, eleven and thirteen years old respectively, were taken from their burning home near Grosser Garten and led by a nursing sister to the hospital where their mother worked for the Red Cross. Their father, Werner Simon, stayed behind with the children's nanny, a twenty-year-old refugee girl from the East, to try to save some of their possessions from the flat. In the confusion, their eight-year-old brother Jürgen disappeared, and so it was just the two young girls who held the nurse's hands as they stumbled for what seemed hours over a journey that normally took only fifteen minutes to walk. 'We climbed over debris, corpses, there was fire everywhere and sparks flying, the air was hot and the smoke made breathing difficult,' Erika recalled.

It was then we were caught in the second raid. The nursing Sister ran with us to the hospital. So there we were, paralysed by horror and fear, clinging to the Sister in a corridor amongst the dead, the wounded, and soldiers who had just had their legs amputated and were now lying on stretchers, helpless amongst the chaos. Gruesome also is my memory of the Catholic Sisters constantly saying their prayers, murmuring over their rosaries. I am sure nobody bothered to save the screaming soldiers.

I wore the usual protective glasses of man-made material, but they had simply disintegrated due to the flying sparks and the heat. I could not see very well any more and my eyes hurt. All the streets were now blocked by rubble and the way to the place where the family had arranged to meet was impassable due to the fire-storm. For a long time we sat by a fountain, until dawn. The fountain was in the middle of a green. Next to me was an old, dead man. That he was dead, we discovered to our horror only later. The Sister bathed my eyes with water from the fountain. As the sky lightened we attempted to make our way to the prearranged meeting point. We did indeed find the house — or what was left of it — and, what none of us had hoped to find, our parents standing there. They had survived the second air raid — what a miracle — in a burnt-out car. Not so our nanny, who must have lost her reason, for she simply ran into the burning house.

Then the news spread in a most mysterious way, that all those people who were walking about lost and helpless should assemble in the Grosser Garten, the most beautiful park in Dresden. Thus a grey mass of people began to move along in a line. One had ceased to be an individual and was only part of a suffering mass. The grey line of people climbed over debris and over the dead. One's feet stepped on burnt corpses and one didn't even think about it.

I can still see my mother bending down and turning over dead children, or bits of dead children, for she was still desperately searching for my little brother.

Then there was a scream behind us — and suddenly my eight-year-old brother was there. Among all those people he had recognized my father by his black-and-white check scarf. He told us that he had gone with a refugee family and found shelter in a private bunker during the second raid. The word joy cannot describe what we felt.

Those were the memories of a girl who was eleven years old at the time. Another witness living in a flat near Grosser Garten, who took the same path before the fire-storm and wrote down her experiences afterwards, was a mature woman, Gisela-Alexandra Moeltgen, wife of a head surgeon at the Friedrichstadt hospital. Her husband Hans was torn both ways. He felt that he ought to be back at the hospital dealing with some of the thousands of new patients who must be coming in; at the same time his wife, who was sick and weak, would desperately need his presence in whatever new ordeal might fall on Dresden. At length duty prevailed over personal desires. He walked down the street to the Red Cross post, and then to the police, to try and get transport for the journey of some three or four kilometres. They told him it was impossible, and in a way that was a relief.

'There — I thought my ears were deceiving me — the full warning again,' wrote Gisela, while the events were still very close.

Three or four hours had passed since the first one. This was hell, hell itself. Hans threw himself on top of me to protect me. Helga kept asking: 'Herr Doctor, was this noise just now in our garden or in the outhouse?' Little Frank then asked: 'What is all this banging and crashing?' (Our house in Parkstrasse was full of lodgers who had been put in there by order of the government, they were the women and children of men who were at the front or dead.) I thought: 'Surely this will have to stop sometime.' I had the feeling that each individual plane tried to hit our house, because it was not on fire yet but brilliantly lit up by the burning house next to it. The planes flew just across the roofs, or at least, that is what it sounded like. I kept shouting: 'Open your mouths!' The sound of the bombs — 'bschi-bum, bschi-bum' — came wave after wave. There was no end to it. In the end I ceased to care, only the thought of our orphaned children drove me mad. The house seemed to come crashing down and shook continuously. When the direct hit came, no one noticed it, for the whistling noise of the bombs drowned all other noises. In any case, it was the others who confirmed that the house was on fire. From that moment on I felt a little calmer.

My feeling was: 'Thank God they have hit it at last and yet we are still alive.' Hans tried to get out into the hall, but it was already on fire and the roof was gone. Risking his life, he then tried to get the little handcart out of the garage. He had terrible difficulties but managed in the end. Outside the fire-storm and the suction were terrible: the garden-house and the garage were down. One had only one wish – out of this hell, out into the country.

When we reached our fence, we saw a huge soldier in a steel helmet standing there, shaking the fence madly, and screaming all the time: 'Help me, please help me, what can I do on my own? They are all burning to death in that house over there, can't you hear them scream?'

It was horrific. I sat down in the handcart, took little Frank between my legs and wrapped a wet bedsheet all round us. It dried within minutes, for the sparks were whipping against us. Everybody followed. We went up Tiergartenstrasse, where the Junghanns family were left behind. Their suitcase broke open and they stopped to stuff everything back in. We had to go on, for all around us time-bombs were exploding and at any moment there could be another raid. People were running for their lives. Past craters, over tree-trunks and too many times past crushed and shattered corpses. But I didn't see them, for I had the sheet wrapped round me. Again and again we went along streets where we came to a dead end. So back again we came, the circle becoming bigger and bigger, and so did the stream of fleeing people.

At about 4 o'clock in the morning of 14 February, they reached Nöthitz, south of Dresden Altstadt and the Grosser Garten, and well clear of the city proper.

We received a horrible shock. Everything was burning there, too. The entire left-hand wing of the castle was on fire. But there were many who helped put it out, so that it did not spread. Our friends' house was full of people, but nobody recognized us. We were pitch-black. We were received with the greatest kindness and given several brandies, which put back some life into us, but we couldn't eat, let alone sleep. The following day, Hans went to the clinic at the hospital; when he came back to us, he broke down completely. On his way he had seen sights which one cannot describe. Corpses everywhere.

What he had seen had been hidden by the night when they were fleeing out of the city. Even so, for a surgeon to be so affected was unusual. But then, some of the battle-hardened soldiers educated in the appalling holocaust of the East Front, where quarter was rarely given, and atrocious things had been done, were unmanned by the sights in Dresden.

Otto Sailer-Jackson, the sixty-year-old animal trainer turned Dresden Zoo Inspector, saw that the fires were under control after the first raid, and then sat down to read his secret instructions, to be opened only if the Zoo area came under attack. Sailer-Jackson loved animals, particularly the big cats with which he had worked so long in the çircus. This Nazi order was for once unambiguous: if the lives of humans were likely to be endangered, all the carnivores in the Zoological Gardens were to be shot by two named persons, Sailer-Jackson himself and the grey-haired sixty-five-year-old Warden Lehmann, who had spent most of his working life in the Zoo.

Before the order could be put into effect, the second wave of bombers were overhead, apparently flying from the direction of the Altstadt along the length of the Grosser Garten in which the Zoological Gardens were situated. Twice as many bombers as in the first attack swamped the Zoo with explosives and incendiaries, including thermite bombs (which the Germans usually referred to as 'phosphorus' bombs). All the animal houses, with the exception of those housing the elephants, were set on fire. The concert hall was blazing, also the staff living quarters. The staff stormed out to save the animals from the burning buildings, but they were forced to go to ground — and some were blown to the ground — by the blast bombs. The screams of terrified animals of many species mixed with the rumbling

of collapsing buildings; debris roared through the air and
iron girders flew overhead like spent matches. The Zoo
staff, as terrified as their animals, hugged the ground, but
then were up and running forward in what they thought was
a brief pause in the inferno.

The elephants gave spine-chilling screams. Their house was still
standing but an explosive bomb of a terrific force had landed
behind it, lifted the dome of the house, turned it round, and put it
back on again. The heavy iron doors had been completely bent
and the huge iron sliding doors which shut off the house from the
terraces had been lifted off their hinges. When I and some of the
other men, including the elephant warden Galle, managed to
break into the elephant house, we found the stable empty. For a
moment we stood helpless, but then the elephants told us where
they were by their heart-breaking trumpeting. We rushed out
on to the terrace again. The baby cow elephant was lying in the
narrow barrier-moat on her back, her legs up to the sky. She had
suffered severe stomach injuries and could not move. A 90 cwt cow
elephant had been flung clear across the barrier moat and the
fence by some terrific blast wave, and just stood there trembling.
We had no choice but to leave those animals to their fate for the
moment.

I had known for one hour now that the most difficult task my life
could ever bring was facing me. 'Lehmann, we must get to the
carnivores,' I called. (He was their warden.) We did what we
had to do, but it broke my heart. I collapsed physically and
emotionally. Everything that happened after that, happened as if
behind a veil. I was burnt out inside. I acted mechanically, almost
without feeling, as if I had no room for any more pain in my heart.
Ever after, an indescribable feeling of horror came over me when I
thought of that inferno and of the day that followed.

The hippopotamus terrace had been destroyed by a giant
bomb (4,000 lb 'cookies' were supposed to be the largest,
but in fact some 8,000 lb bombs were carried too). There
was a huge bomb crater in the outside water basin for the
hippos. The blast of it had not merely broken the massive
iron bars, as thick as a man's arm, which fenced off the

terrace, but flung some of them a hundred yards away. The three hippopotamuses were still alive in the inner water basin but they were doomed. The iron debris of the collapsed roof had fallen on them and now pinned them down under water. The hippopotamus is a mammal just like us, and needs air to breathe. In their agonizing fear, the great beasts struggled fiercely to free themselves, without success; and they drowned.

In the same building as the hippos was the humanoid-ape house. This also had been destroyed. Not a single ape could be seen except for the gibbon, who crept out from under a corner. The creature held out its hands to Sailer-Jackson, who saw that it had no hands, merely stumps. Haunted by the expression of suffering on its face, he drew his pistol and shot the beast. The chimpanzees had fled into the fruit cellar and then a direct hit had brought the building down on top of them. So they, like the hippos, were suffocated to death − but on land, not in water. Some of the higher apes could be freed from their cages, but none of these creatures were ever caught afterwards, although one was seen months later by a forester in the Erzgebirge.

From the burning aviary, not a single bird could be saved. For a brief space there were shrill and horrible cries, then only the roaring of the flames.

Next to the aviary was a terrace for South American animals, but it had had a direct hit from an HE bomb and no one now could tell, from the shreds of flesh grotesquely splattering the trees, what sort of animals they had come from. The antelope house burnt to the ground, so did that holding the yaks. Some of the animals could be rescued, but those with severe burns died.

Old Warden Lehmann went into the bear house while flames roared up from its roof. His favourite brown bear mother, who had two cubs, was still there, blinded by incendiary bombs. But she knew Lehmann's voice and allowed him to remove the two cubs to safety. They survived, being given to a bitch next day who suckled them. The female polar bear was there too, dreadfully burned on the back by the thermite (or 'phosphorus'), but covering and protecting the two cubs (her first) which she had produced in 1944. Without making a sound, the mother kept the cubs pinned down with her huge paws so that they could not run away and out into danger in the open. It would be a brave man who tried to take them away from her, but the old grey-haired warden managed it. As the mother was in terrible agony, she was dispatched with a pistol shot. Her cubs could have been reared from the bottle, but as there was no milk in the ruins of Dresden, they soon after died of hunger.

Close by was the ape paradise. Of about sixty rhesus monkeys, twenty-one were killed that night. The rest escaped to the trees of the Grosser Garten, but died next day from drinking water polluted by the chemicals from the incendiary bombs. The chimpanzee 'Pitt' was the ace of the apes, a famous creature with his own arena to show off his tricks. There was no sign of him in the wreckage.

The two dwarf hippopotamuses had saved themselves by hiding below ground in a bomb crater, where the wardens threw straw down to them. Later, a time-bomb blew them to shreds.

There were great gaps in the fences surrounding the Zoo, particularly that separating the animals from the Tiergartentrasse, a main throughfare. The stags and reindeer got out, and also dangerous animals such as red buffalo and bison. These mingled with the crowds fleeing the burning city, and neither species took any notice of the other. Great holes had been torn in the big flying cages in which the large birds of prey could stretch their wings, and most of the eagles and vultures had flown. But, like the stags, they came back next day punctually at feeding time, and for a few days after that; and then disappeared. Sailer-Jackson wrote:

On the grey, unhappy morning after the night's terror, the big elephant cow was still standing in the same place where I had seen her the previous night. Galle, her warden, tried to give her some hay. Then I noticed that from a large wound in her side, the intestines were squelching out. I asked the firing squad to liberate both elephants from their sufferings.

On the second evening after the night of terror, the chimpanzee 'Pitt' came back to the Zoo from the Tiergartenstrasse. He carried a glass of preserved fruit in one hand, with the other hand he clutched his body. When he saw me, he screamed and jumped at me. A bomb splinter had torn a wound in his abdomen and he was covered in blood. I bandaged him, gave him his fruit − for I had no hope at all of his recovery − and locked him in a room under the arena. Telephones didn't work any more, but a bicycle was found and a young warden sent in search of a vet. Two days later, the vet came to the Zoo, but by then 'Pitt' was dead from blood poisoning.

Charlotte Mann and her husband lived on Hepkeplatz just east of the Grosser Garten in the suburb of Gruna. He had come home from Home Guard duty after the first attack. During the second attack there was a terrific clap as of thunder directly overhead, and the building above their cellar trembled. They thought it was a direct hit, and crept cautiously upstairs to investigate. Something very odd had happened to the roof, which had been lifted up and then put down again by the blast-wave and suction effect of a big, thin-walled bomb (which the Germans called a 'mine' and the RAF a 'cookie'). Now they had a clear view over Dresden.

We could see that a terrific fire-storm was blowing. It came roaring from the centre of the town towards the east, in our direction, throwing a lot of strange things into our flat, among them a Bible, somewhat blackened. The top of the house on our left was burning and soon everything around us was on fire. We noticed also that the houses which had been spared by the bombs now started to burn because of the curtains which were hanging outside through the empty holes where the windows had been. A few things in our rooms had caught fire, a fact of which we were not aware at once, because we were so busy.

This couple stayed put and began to fight the fires with the small stirrup pumps.

While they were fighting the flames, a nephew of Charlotte's was lying unconscious nearby in the Grosser Garten. Too unfit to serve in the Wehrmacht, he was on duty at a Red Cross post as an orderly, not far from the Zoo.

While he was helping others and was out in the open, he was flung up in the air by an enormous blast-wave which crashed him down to the ground again in front of a tree in the park. He lost consciousness, he did not know for how long, from the impact. When he began to wake up, he felt that somebody was clinging to him. As he came round more fully and looked closer at the person, he saw that it was a large ape, which was trembling and whimpering quietly. My nephew got such a shock that he passed out again at once, and I think also perhaps because he was in great pain from hitting the ground after being thrown through the air such a terrific distance. After a long time, the ape let go and did not move any more, but whether because he was injured or dead, my nephew never found out. He was busy looking after himself, and was so terrified and shocked. He was mentally ill for a long time after, it was about two years before he was normal again.

Lancaster AA-P of No. 75 New Zealand Squadron had an uneventful flight from Cambridgeshire to Saxony. There were 529 four-motor bombers in the stream, which was some twenty minutes long, but in the darkness it was as if each aircraft flew alone. Paul Hill was in the engineer's seat beside the pilot, looking forward through the windscreen, with no view to the rear or downwards. Roy Akehurst was in the astrodome with a good view around the aircraft and above. Peter Goldie was out on his own in the rear turret at the end of the fuselage, behind four guns. Normally, he could see only to the rear and sides — where the Lancaster had been, not where it was going, or what was below. That was the main blind spot of a Lanc, which the night fighters liked to take advantage of. But being a small man and the armour plating having been taken off Lancasters by then (to increase the bomb-load), he could by bending forward look directly down at the earth beneath.

After four hours or so of being dragged backwards through the night sky, while scanning continually for German fighters, he could hear the lads crowded companionably together in the front of the aircraft chatting over the intercom that the target was very well illuminated. Everything seemed to be going well, a good run in, the bomb doors opened, and the master bomber somewhere giving instructions to bomb on the markers.

We went straight in and then everything was illuminated. I could look up in my turret — and there were Lancs above with their bomb doors open. And if I leaned forward in the turret I could see more Lancs swirling below us. It was just like daylight up there; although we were at 20,000 feet, it was more like being at 1,000 feet. There was very little flak, not much trouble with night fighters. Our biggest problem, quite truly, was with the chance of being hit by bombs from other Lancasters flying above us.

We bombed. We took the photograph. The bomb doors closed. The nav gave us a fresh course. By this time, we were travelling *over* the target. Probably, except for the bomb aimer, I had the best view. The whole city was just one raging inferno. Years later, I thought about the people. But at the time it was all very quick. Red TIs, green TIs, white TIs going down. Bombs falling all around us (a lot of panic in some cases, because they just don't look). What I'd call *no opposition* — unlike any other raid. It was like Guy Fawkes Night — fires — and the quivers of bomb explosions in the fires. I felt naked in the glare coming up. I could see those fires burning behind us one hundred miles away. The whole sky completely illuminated. This was the only raid that really mattered to me. It preyed on my mind afterwards.

Paul Hill's estimate was also that the fires could be seen 100 miles away. 'When over the target the fires were so intense that one appeared to be flying much lower than 20,000 feet. It was so light that other aircraft could be seen as if it were a daylight trip.' 20,000 feet is of course nearly four miles high, so there was a degree of remoteness in AA-P between themselves and what they were doing below.

But Roy Akehurst didn't feel that.

It was an uneventful journey for us. Dresden was peaceful. Over the target there was no ack-ack, no sign of night fighters – just the pathfinders marking up and giving orders to bomb. Sometimes we would have a hell of a ten minutes; some targets belted hell out of us, we saw friends go down left and right. Dresden was too peaceful for us. It would have been fair if we'd been fired at. To just fly over it without opposition felt like murder. I felt it was a cowardly war, that there were people down there who were defenceless. I always felt the same way about Dresden and I've never gone back on it.

I can remember that raid, visually, as if it was yesterday. That wasn't so with other raids: I've forgotten them, they've all become blurred in my memory, so similar were they to each other – Hamburg, Cologne, Berlin. But I feel guilty about Dresden. You could have flown low over Dresden, which you couldn't do elsewhere. It struck me at the time, the thought of the women and children down there. We seemed to fly for hours over a sheet of fire – a terrific red glow with a thin haze over it. There was no cloud, but it was like looking down through cloud. It seemed to go on for ever, although in fact it was only for a very short time. I even thought that I could feel the heat – impossible, of course, at our height, but perhaps you could have at 2,000 feet. If you were shot down, you felt you could not survive, because the flames covered so vast an area. I found myself making comments to the crew: 'Oh God, those poor people.' It was completely uncalled for. You can't justify it.

At the time, Roy had a faint impression that Dresden was an art centre, but it was the thought of the people, not the paintings, which appalled him.

Peter Goldie's best friend, Ken Moore, his school chum from prewar Portsmouth, was now serving in the same New Zealand Squadron; indeed, he had got there first, having joined the RAF at the earliest age possible as a volunteer air gunner. Ken was 19½ when he flew his first operation on 12 December 1944, to Witten in the Ruhr. 'I got the mid-upper gun position, after spinning a coin for heads-or-tails. I was young and silly; excited, but with a little bit of foreboding. I had had a friend who was killed in the bombing of Drayton Road First Aid Post in Portsmouth in 1940. I felt it wasn't going to happen to me, but I felt surer at some times than at others.' On a trip to Siegen the Lanc iced up and they had a massive 8,000 lb bomb on board, but miraculously landed safely. Then in an attack on the Reydt marshalling yards, one of the squadron's aircraft was brought down by British bombs.

Peter Goldie joined the squadron just before Christmas 1944, so the friends were reunited in time to fly a dozen or so Squadron raids together (although not in the same aircraft), including the Dresden operation. Ken Moore's reaction to the briefing was that:

It was a little bit awesome — the length of the trip. After take-off there was stacks of cloud below us. Ten-tenths cloud nearly all the way, from France onwards. It was black, ominous down below. After about one hour's flying over France at air speeds varying between 150–200 mph, the navigator called up in a very surly voice: 'Skipper, watch your air speed.' The skipper, a New Zealander, replied: 'We're OK now.'
Within seconds the aircraft felt as though she'd had a big sledge-hammer driven at her. A four-motor bomber falling out of the sky with a full bomb-load aboard. I think the skipper's oxygen mask

was faulty and his faculties were affected; he'd passed out. But the event seemed to bring him round and brought the flight engineer in to help. He put her into a dive and pulled out. This gave us all a shake-up.

We came back to 20,000 feet. It was cold, it was cramped. We had boiled sweets, chewing gum, and a bar of choc. The ground staff lads looked after us — they provided hot coffee, which we could drink only on the way back when we were below 10,000 feet and could take our oxygen masks off.

Then the skipper passed out again, oxygen mask still faulty. By this time, half an hour later, we were over Germany, out of control momentarily.

So we approached Dresden in a rather shaken-up condition — or at least, I did — thinking: Is it going to happen again? I couldn't do anything about it — the gunners were sealed off from the crew, and had to keep a lookout for fighters. Not a pleasant evening at all.

We could see the lights on the clouds. We didn't come into clear air until over the target. So there was first a glow through cloud, then clarity over the target. Then a cry from the crew: 'Bloody hell, look at that!'

Below us was a town well ablaze, giving the impression of flying over a town in peacetime — lights all over the place. But there was only a quick, snatched glimpse for gunners — then you had to go back on sky search. I could see other aircraft, not just as shapes, but clear. Yet it seemed so remote. I was in the Pompey bombings but I couldn't imagine what was happening down there, four miles down. It was like being on a remote platform, seeing landscape unreeling as in a car.

The master bomber was on the air, calling instructions where to bomb. The bomb aimer made his usual run-up. 'Bomb-doors open — left — left — steady — bombs away.' Having delivered the bombs, we only had one thought in mind: 'Let's go home and get the hell out of it.'

We knew the town had really had a pounding, but I can't remember flak over the target. Dresden was not the usual sort of thing, but I'd been to one place before this where the flak was light, maybe decimated from previous bombs. We'd not known before that there was no flak in Dresden. It was a terrible sight, and the sooner the job was done and we got away from it, the better.

I believe the Dresden raid was a warning to Russia. But also, the result of propaganda — 'Germans are beasts' — and perhaps a bit back for Pompey.

The glare followed us back 100 miles or more. When we lost it, 1½ hours later, I started getting a funny old feeling that things weren't quite right. There was an aircraft behind us. In a stream of over 500 bombers, collisions did occur. That aircraft was coming and going behind us for half an hour, and I suppose I was at fever pitch, but I didn't want to shoot one of our own boys down. Later, I found both the rear gunner and flight engineer had seen it too and couldn't make up their minds either. Then it swung away, and in that second I recognized it as a Ju 88. Then it was gone.

Then the flight engineer reported that our brakes were ineffective because the oil pressure was down. So we diverted to Woodbridge, a crash drome three miles long. We handed our parachutes in there — and there in the parachute room was another Portsmouth man.

Back at their base in Cambridgeshire, they were posted as missing. 'Peter Goldie thought we'd bought it, was worried stiff about us. Not many hours later he was off on another raid to Chemnitz, eighteen hours flying in all in the two raids, and only a few hours rest in between.'

At 2140 hours, the same time almost to the minute that the sirens howled their warning in Dresden of the approach of the first wave of 244 bombers, Lancaster A-Able, in which Miles Tripp was the bomb aimer, took off as part of the second bomber stream of 529 aircraft. His squadron was to reach the target towards the end of this second attack, at the climax of the raid.

Over England it was a starlit night, and they could see the Channel coast clearly, but from then on until just before the target there was only white cloud below. Miles Tripp was disturbed on two counts. First, there was what they had been told at briefing: 'a million refugees in Dresden' and a 'panic raid' to 'confuse the disrupt communications'. He felt a 'quiver of outrage' at the thought. Just as distasteful was the implication, that when the Germans bombed refugees it was wrong, but when we bombed them it was right.

There were also the warnings about security which they had just had officially. News about targets was becoming known among the ground staff and even civilians, before the aircrews themselves had been told. If target information should reach the Germans even on one occasion, that would mean disaster for the bomber force because all the night fighters could be concentrated on the approaches. There was a suspicion that the source of the leaks might just possibly be their own rear gunner, Harry, who was a Jamaican. What was much more disturbing was that Harry's apparent ability to predict the future might not have anything to do with knowledge from official sources. Harry had guessed wrong about tonight, he had thought Berlin. But on too many other occasions he had been uncannily accurate. A man who could see into the future from some source inside himself could also foretell the date, the hour and the place of your own death. Couldn't he? In days and nights when death was commonplace, the thought that your own extinction might be ordained and known to someone else was unsettling.

The electronic navigation devices in A-Able went wrong or were jammed by the Germans for much of the flight, but nevertheless their navigator brought them correctly to the run-in point, from which the red glow of burning Dresden was visible forty miles ahead. They passed over the last of the cloud layer and flew in a clear starlit sky. Six miles from the target, the feeling of flying alone through the night vanished – the shapes of Lancasters were becoming visible in the glow from the fires. The city itself looked like some ghastly crossword puzzle, the dark roadways making a grid lit by the blazing buildings which lined them. 'Where do you want me to go, Miles?' asked the pilot.

Miles Tripp wrote that there was no sound of the master bomber on the R/T, controlling the attack. Perhaps Miles was as deaf in both ears as Nelson was blind in one eye.

He told his pilot to turn starboard out over the southern suburbs of Dresden, and when they had passed over the last fringe of the fires, he let the bombs go. Bombs travel forward underneath an aircraft, arcing away towards the ground ahead, to strike miles from where they were dropped, and just as likely to hit a wall as a roof. With the memory of the briefing fresh in his mind, and a vivid mental picture still of old newsreels of German atrocities against refugees, he hoped that the whole load would fall in open country. Perhaps it did.

It is difficult to delineate chaos in an orderly fashion. The wind was blowing from the western arc, but it seems to have veered at least once (although this could have been a local effect). According to their situation, the spread of the flames tended to drive people towards the north-east, where there was hope of reprieve on the open flood-meadows of the River Elbe; to the south-east, where the long vistas of the Grosser Garten were a designated refuge space; or south through a built-up area with many narrow streets, towards Räcknitz, Mockritz, Gostritz, Nöthitz or Bannewitz.

Many if not most of the people caught in the Altstadt, and who took shelter there in cellars and basements, were doomed. The houses were either blown down on top of them, blocking exits, or burnt to the ground above them, killing as much by lack of oxygen as by fire. Those who ran, mostly had too far to run before they could get free of the vast area of flames which had consumed most of the oxygen already. And in each cellar, how many people? Twenty, thirty, forty? Two hundred and forty? And how many might escape, daring to run through the blazing streets as Margret Freyer did? And be lucky enough to succeed? Where she had sheltered the second time, thirty-eight had died in the cellar, and three at the entrance; one had escaped – Margret herself. So who knows how the others died? And then again, groups of people forced up into the open might find themselves surrounded by fires and, there being no way out, would wait. Most would wait in vain. Others would seek a way out, like rats, running this way, that way. And of course the bombs were falling all the time, increasing the chaos and the casualties. And many – at least half – of all the people there were refugees, who did not know their way about the city. Those who died did so most frequently in the company of no surviving witnesses, the exact details of their end unknown.

At the other extreme, there were those far enough away from the spread of the central conflagration to fight back and try to put out the fires – where they also possessed the courage to do that – and people somewhat nearer to the heart of the fire-storm who nevertheless had only a short journey to reach some open expanse safe at least from burning.

Eva Tornow and her family were burnt out in the second raid. They had three children, Steffi, Felix and Klaus, born in 1941, 1942 and July 1944 respectively. Felix had polio. Eva's husband, Klaus Tornow, ran a factory making condensers for radio sets and so was exempt from military service. But Eva's brother, Dietrich Jacobi, had been severely wounded in Russia; and her father, Walter Jacobi, had been arrested in 1939 and committed suicide in prison in June 1940. It was a fated family, and in 1945 Eva's husband was trying to divorce her in order to marry someone else. When the sirens howled on the night of 13 February, Eva grabbed the baby from its cot, pulled the other two children out of their beds, and hustled them all down to the section of the basement they called the red-wine cellar. After a short while they were joined by Eva's husband – and his girlfriend.

Their house, which was in the north-eastern suburb of Blasewitz fronting the Waldpark, and in turn no great distance from the Elbe meadows, suffered only broken windows. It was only the previous day, on 12 February, that Eva and her home help had organized 'a major window-cleaning action – for we had a huge wintergarden with enormous windows and in it we had exotic birds and fish'. The second raid again sent them to the red-wine cellar, which with its vaulted roof was very strong, and once again neighbours came in to share its protection, including a woman with a ten-day-old baby and a husband who had been blinded in the war.

When the house caught fire above them, it was a moment of truth for Eva's husband. Who should he save? He picked up his eldest son in his arms, while Eva grabbed the youngest boy, seven months old. 'I had him bundled up in my arms and I was firmly convinced he was dead, because his eyes were closed, but luckily he had slept through the raid. We just ran along our road until we arrived at a house which was still standing. We went inside and somehow, somewhere found a place to sit or even lie down until the morning.' All they possessed in the world now were some eiderdowns, which the maid and their eldest child, Steffi, had carried away because of the bitter cold.

Charlotte Stiller lived in the Vogelerstrasse, Striesen, the suburb directly south of Blasewitz and the same distance from the city centre. Her husband was a sub-manager of Kunstanstalt Stengel of Striesen, a printing and publishing firm which made war maps for Hitler. She was her husband's second wife, and at this time was looking after two of his three children, a boy and girl between the ages of ten and twelve, and one of her own, her ten-month-old baby daughter Sabina (now a judge in West Germany). Her two eldest children (twins) were safe in their summer house at Gorisch in the Saxon Switzerland district opposite the famous Königstein Castle where some of the evacuated Dresden treasures, including the Grünes Gewölbes, were stored; it served also as POW camp for VIPs.

After the first raid, they found that their house had suffered only broken windows, but Charlotte's husband hurried off to his factory to see how it had fared. Then came the second raid.

This was terrible. We had the feeling that the house was bombed, but it wasn't — only the houses next door. When it stopped, we had the impression of being in a sea of flame, so I told my two stepchildren to go down to the River Elbe, where they would be safe from the flames, while I took my baby to a big school for the bombed-out. We had blankets in our cellar and buckets of water. There was a terrible rain of sparks outside, so we wetted some blankets with water and put them over our heads before we went into the street. I left Sabina with friends at the big school and returned to the house to save what I could, for I had left everything behind, including my money and documents, I collected the most important items and took them to some friends to keep. Then I went back to our house again. It was on fire now, and I met my husband in the hall. He'd returned from the factory, which had *not* been bombed, and found no one in our house. We took down the curtains and put out the sparks and flames.

We stayed there till morning, but there was danger from sparks until 10 am or later. Indeed, my husband's factory was burnt down at lunchtime, having caught fire from the sparks. With my child, I joined a mass of poor people trekking towards Pirna and Königstein, some in nightgowns, some with the hair burnt off their heads. There had been a fire-storm along the Elbe Valley, for in our garden at Gorisch I found half-burnt papers from Dresden businesses — 35 kilometres away.

Charlotte stayed there with baby Sabina until the end of the war, although, by fighting the flames at an early stage, they had saved their Dresden house.

Charlotte Mann, who lived with her husband in the suburb of Gruna, immediately south of where Charlotte Stiller lived in Striesen, had also found evidence of the violence of the fire-storm, when it hurled a blackened Bible through one of the windows. (In some instances, people were actually sucked off their feet and, quite helplessly, drawn into the flames; though there were few living witnesses to such things.) As with the Stillers, so with the Manns: the houses around them were burning, not too seriously at first, but then because they were unchecked, the flames spread.

We saw that the houses which had been spared started to burn because of the curtains hanging out of the empty window spaces. A pity, these houses could have been saved if most of the owners had not run away, but on the other hand one can understand them – panic! We were not spared either, the fire came over to us from the house on the left. But as we had enough water and a small hand pump, my husband and I started to put out the fires. I fetched a second hand pump from a neighbouring house, so that we were both able to work. I had to walk only a very short distance to get that pump, but in that time my head and face came in contact with a burning board. It was only much later that I realized that I had received a rather nasty scratch-wound down one side of my face. One simply didn't pay attention to things like that; the saving of the house came first.

The fire had reached the entire left side of the flat and, in spite of all our efforts, burnt 70 cm deep into the room and right down to the basement. But in the end we won. Although some of the furniture was badly damaged, we kept the flames at bay. It was just the three of us – an elderly man, my husband who was rising fifty, and I. All the others had run away. The fire had to be watched for several days afterwards because it was still smouldering, so one of us always stood guard. After all that, we were pleased to have been able to save the flat from complete destruction, and also the house on our right.

I should like to explain that there seemed to be a border from the Hepkeplatz where we lived stretching north as far as the River Elbe, where everything on one side was burnt and on the other side untouched. It appeared that they had worked according to a plan. Probably they had marked a line on which they flew in a certain width towards the town and then just let the bombs drop. In the west on the other side of the town it seemed to be cut off in exactly the same straight line, so that all the parts of Dresden which had factories remained untouched.

The Junghanns bakery where Eva Beyer lived and worked was at Gostritz, south-west of the Gruna suburb where Charlotte Mann and her husband had been able to fight back against the fire. Here, too, it was the second wave which was worst. They had put out the few incendiaries which had fallen on the bakery in the first attack and were clearing up the mess when the second wave came over.

'There was a crashing and splintering everywhere, and we thought this would be the end,' wrote Eva.

Kurt [the crippled ex-soldier] and I made another tour of the house. I was trembling with fear, for we didn't know what else was going to happen. When we reached the second storey, we saw an enormous gap in the wall and up above, in the attic, a large hole in the roof. The rear of the house was on fire, the wash-house had collapsed, our neighbour's house on the right was on fire, the one on the left had had a direct hit. Luckily the inhabitants of that building were in an underground shelter in their garden. We tried to put out as much of the fire as we could, but we didn't have enough water, so we used sand and earth to contain the smaller fires. Suddenly, I saw a huge bomb sticking out of the ground in the back garden. I was absolutely terrified, for I had heard of time-bombs. We had just put a sandbag in front of the cellar window, when they seemed to drop everything they had in the way of bombs.

It was like an earthquake. We all crouched closely together, and cried, and prayed, and trembled, absolutely terrified. One of the women was so fearful that she had diarrhoea, two other women passed out, the children screamed, the baker's wife started to have a bilious attack. It was like a lunatic asylum.

Kurt tried to put some courage into us time after time, and today I know that it was Kurt who saved us from our panic, for out of sheer fear and helplessness we would have done the wrong things.

The bakery looked afterwards as if an earthquake had hit it. After tidying up a little, Eva packed a small cart and trekked along the road out of Dresden towards Bannewitz with the children, whom she left there for safety with the grandparents of the baker's wife. They were not her children, nor her family. Her mother, Mrs Edith Beyer, had sent the two boys out to Neustadt, but she was at home with her four-year-old daughter Gertrud, Eva's little sister. And home was in Klein Plauensche Gasse, in the Altstadt, by now long since a mass of roaring flame and swirling wind tornadoes and choking smoke and sparks.

Frau Canzler was the wife of a doctor who specialized in gynaecology. They lived with their ten-year-old daughter near a military hospital on a route out of the city which was bombed.

There is only one description which fits – it was like 'The Last Days of Pompeii'. People came crawling on their hands and knees, so as to be near the ground and be able to breathe better, but not knowing, as they crawled, whether they were really getting away from the fire-storm or merely heading into other burning areas of the city. So much fire created not only a cruel storm but much dust. All night we plainly heard under the windows the feet of people passing, because of the dust layers in the streets. Many people had woollen nightcaps and garments over their heads, because otherwise they could not see in the rain of dust which was blowing through the streets.

In the morning, when it got light, she could look out of the window and see that the military hospital had been destroyed. Some of the wounded soldiers had been saved, carried out of the building during the night in their hospital pyjamas. And there they still lay on the ground – in the open, in February – in their pyjamas. Where could they go?

It must have been some hours before this, probably about 4.30 in the morning, he thought, that Sergeant William C. Stewart of the US Army Air Force was woken up by the duty sergeant. All the man knew about the mission was that the B-17G Fortresses were being tanked up with a full load – 2,780 gallons of aviation gasoline. That meant a deep penetration from their base at Podington in England.

I rose, dressed, and made my way to the mess hall and ate a breakfast of bacon and eggs. From there, I took a ride in a truck to the building on the flight line where the briefing was to be held. As I walked in, I could see the map of Europe and the British Isles covering the front wall. On the map was a red ribbon, showing the route to be flown in and out of Germany, held by pins. The target on the map was Dresden. To me, Dresden was just another city in Germany and I didn't recall having heard of it before that time. The briefing officer went over the schedule for the mission and the possible conditions of weather, flak and opposition that we might encounter. Take-off was to be at 0700 hours that morning.

Stewart was a ball turret gunner of a Boeing in 325 Squadron, 92nd Group of the 1st Air Division. The 1st were all going to Dresden. The 2nd Division were going to Magdeburg and the 3rd to Chemnitz, near Dresden. The USAAF were putting up about 1,300 bombers and swarms of fighters in three co-ordinated operations. 316 Fortresses would bomb Dresden.

9
'Mummy, Where Are You?'

THE THIRD ATTACK:
12.15 – 12.25 PM, 14 FEBRUARY 1945

There was terror where families had been separated. Mrs Daniel, who had taken a train out to where her sister lived on the slopes of the Erzgebirge many kilometres from Dresden, in the hope of bringing her back to the city so that the whole family could leave Dresden for the West together, had escaped the raid by half a day. Instead she had watched from the safety of the mountains, as if seated in the balcony of a theatre, as the burning city which held her husband and baby began to turn the heavens above it into a dome of rose-coloured light, beneath the thunder of thousands of aero engines punctuated by the long, ringing roar of exploding bombs. She wanted to go to them at once, but how could she get back? It had been difficult enough getting out of Dresden in an overcrowded train. The trains were not likely to be running after such a raid.

Then came good news. It seemed that the wealthy farmer who lived near them, whom they called the 'Spinach Officer' because he was an ardent Nazi boss, was intending to drive into Dresden, and might take her with him in his car. As they drove towards the glow in the sky, there ensued a bizarre conversation, which in normal times could have been very dangerous. Mrs Daniel was so filled with horror at the thought of what might have happened to her husband and baby that she put no guard on her tongue and began to say the first things that came into her head.

First, she let slip that the object of her visit was to collect her sister so that they might all make their way to safety in the West. Of course, this was an example of what in

England in 1940 would have been called 'spreading alarm and despondency' (and was a punishable offence there, too).

'If all of us wanted to knock off – ' the farmer began angrily. 'Then he followed up with such a highly personal Nazi diatribe as I had never heard the like of before,' said Dora Daniel. (In spite of these splendidly patriotic and politically correct sentiments, the 'Spinach Officer' himself was one of the first to leave the district for the safety of Düsseldorf before the Russians came.)

'Do you really believe in Germany's victory?' said Dora.

'How should I know?' snapped the man. 'I don't have time to think about things like that.'

When he in turn began to question her, he discovered that Mrs Daniel didn't belong to the Frauenschaft (the women's branch of the Party). That really shocked him. 'I ought to put you down right here in the open fields!' he shouted.

Of course, farmers don't fight at the front (unless the front comes to them) and they both knew it. Mrs Daniel had lost her first husband in Russia. Her present husband was a 100 per cent war cripple from the Russian Front who had survived two winters in the East, 1941 and 1942. Bitterly, aware that she was now the family breadwinner, she pointed this out. Her husband, she said, had been awarded the 'Frozen Meat Medal' (the irreverent name the real 'front pigs' gave to this particular decoration, whose real designation Mrs Daniel had long since forgotten). She wasn't trying to take the mickey, this was simple forgetfulness, but it produced in the car a positively sub-zero temperature, and the rest of the journey was made in complete silence.

When Mrs Daniel was set down it was in a part of Dresden which she had known but did not know now. The entire skyscape of the city had changed. The buildings were gutted or down, their fallen stonework and broken bricks blocking the narrow streets. By coincidence, she saw a street sign she recognized — Rosenstrasse — but her way along it was over rubble, corpses, and past people summarily hanged for looting. As all the houses in the road had collapsed, this gave her a long view ahead and she could see that the Massitiusstrasse seemed to be intact, which would make for easier walking. Even so, it was to be another two hours — and the time nearly noon — before she got through to the street in the Friedrichstadt area where they had their temporary accommodation, having been bombed out by the USAAF in January.

Top-Sergeant Harold W. Hall was radio operator in a B-17 of 527 Squadron, 379 Bombardment Group, of the 1st Air Division stationed at Kimbolton near Bedford. Born in 1922, he had tried to enlist in the navy as a pilot, passed both the physical and the mental exams, and then could not obtain his father's consent. So he had to wait until he was drafted into the army in February 1943, and had completed basic training, before going to radio and gunnery school as a preliminary to extensive training for B-17s. Dresden was his thirty-fourth mission, near to the end of his tour overseas, and he was hoping to make it.

Harold Hall kept an occasional diary and any relevant clippings from the *Stars and Stripes* newspaper, but this mission was one he did not need to look up from his records.

The reason I remember that mission is that during our briefing the officer and aide pointed to a small building located on the map as in the centre of Dresden. With a smile, he told us our bombs were to be dropped in 'train'. To me, this was shocking as reason indicated they should be dropped in 'salvo', but I felt it was indiscriminate bombing of all the refugees fleeing the Russians. I have to say that I felt ashamed we had levelled ourselves to the Krauts. During the briefing, no mention of refugees in the city was made, but it wasn't needed and the implication of 'foul play' was strong. Incidentally, that was the only time I ever felt (and others) that the mission was unusual.

Stars and Stripes next day admitted that the city was 'reported to be housing thousands of evacuees from bombed-out areas, some of them even from Berlin'.

Hall's diary retained the technical details of the raid:

Gas load – 2,700 gallons. Bomb load – eight 500 lbs, two M-17s. We took off at 7:55 a.m. and travelled on oxygen for about 6 hours. We flew at 28,500 feet and most of us had a nice case of cramps . . . We encountered no flak over the target but got it coming back over the lines. They got one boy and the ship blew up on our side of the lines. Some reported seeing 4 chutes and others said there were 7. Only two more to go and I sure pray I make it.

From this group of thirty-seven bombers the Fortress flown by 2nd Lieut. Stanley Cubuhar did not return. 1st Lieut. James H. Brown's bomber force-landed on the way back, killing him and half his crew.

Sergeant William C. Stewart ('Stew' for short in those days), in contrast to Hall, was totally inexperienced; but this mission he, too, never forgot. He was nineteen years old and ball turret gunner of a B-17G of 325 Squadron, 92 Bombardment Group, 1st Air Division, based at Podington. He had been woken at about 4.30 am and told that he was to be on a full gas-load mission. At briefing he learnt that the target was to be Dresden, a city he had never heard of, with take-off at 7 am.

By now, as the last Lancasters were coming in to land from the second wave attack, all the American bomber bases were stirring. But it was still dark in England and very cold. Stewart wrote:

I took another truck to the 325th Squadron operations building, and picked up my flying gear: oxygen mask, heated suit, flying helmet, etc. From there, I took another truck to the hardstand where the aircraft '601' was sitting. I prepared the guns in the turret and 'hand charged' a round of ammunition into each. [They were twin .50 calibre guns; with their half-inch bores, much more lethal and longer-ranged than the tinny .303s used by the RAF.] This work had to be done kneeling on the ground. When it was completed I got into the ship and laid down in the waist to wait for take-off time. I recall it being cold and damp there in the ship and hoping the mission might be 'scrubbed' so that I could go back to my barracks. I talked to some of the other crew members I was to fly with that day. I didn't know them, since I was not flying with my regularly assigned crew. We were advised over the intercom by the pilot that take-off had been postponed till 8.00 am.

By now, the darkness was lightening in central Germany but in Dresden the sun was obscured by cloud and by the smoke from the raging fires still blazing unchecked.

It was getting light when the pilot started the engines and we taxied behind a group of Fortresses on the take-off runway. He gave full power to the four Wright Cyclone engines and the ship surged forward. As we reached take-off speed, the plane bounced about four times till we finally were airborne. We flew to the radio 'splashers' and assembled with the Group and proceeded over the English Channel. En route, I put on my heated suit and all the other flying equipment. Before we reached the continent, I turned the turret with the guns downward, and got into it. I plugged in the oxygen mask, intercom, heated suit, etc., and fired a few rounds through the machine-guns.

The ball turret was a spherical turret mounted in the underside of the aircraft. It would rotate 360 degrees in the horizontal axis and translate 90 degrees in elevation. It was mounted with two .50 calibre machine-guns and I was totally enclosed within the confines of the sphere. It allowed the gunner to sweep his line of sight from the ground on up to the bottom of the aircraft. It was like an embryo in an egg that I was over Dresden that day.

If a Fortress was hit, getting out depended on whether or not it blew up, or a wing came off, and a lot of other chance factors. On average, the number of escapes was quite high — 50 per cent. Or put another way, half the crew would probably be unable to get out of their aircraft in time. The ball turret gunner's chance of escape, particularly if the aircraft was spinning in its fall, seemed rather remote. There exist horrifying camera sequences of Fortresses spinning slowly, upside-down, or fluttering down with one wing gone, or breaking apart in mid-fuselage.

'I estimate we reached the Initial Point to start our bomb run somewhere near noon on the 14th,' wrote Stewart.

I was not able to distinguish anything under us except the heavy grey clouds, and only knew we had reached the IP when the pilot announced it over the intercom. I turned up my turret ahead to 12.00 o'clock position (pointing forward, toward the nose of the ship) and could see several black bursts of flak ahead slightly below us. Our ship carried no PFF (radar homing equipment) so all of the navigation for the bomb run was done by one of the lead ships in the Group.

We proceeded on the bomb run till we got to that place in the sky where the flak bursts were and we 'toggled' our bombs, at the same time as the lead ship. I watched the bombs descend through the air till they reached the clouds and there they disappeared from my sight. Because of the poor visibility below, I cannot tell you where in the city our bombs landed.

Lyle E. Keran was co-pilot in a B-17. It was his fourteenth mission and his crew's thirteenth. Over the target, as the bombs fell away, they 'lost' one engine. They were unable to feather the propeller and could no longer stay in formation. The Fortress gradually fell behind and began a slow descent. In a tight, stacked formation of over 300 heavy bombers, they had had the bristling protection of more than 2,000 half-inch machine-guns, as well as being merely one of over 300 targets which an enemy fighter pilot might pick. Now, they were totally exposed deep in the heart of Germany, an obvious lame duck. As they turned on to a compass course for the Rhine, the crew began to strip the plane of all possible equipment and throw it overboard. Finally, that even included the machine-guns and their ammunition. About all they kept were the parachutes.

Joseph A. Peterburs, who retired as a Colonel USAF, had been assigned to the 55th Fighter Squadron of the 20th Fighter Group in November 1944, and served with them to May 1945, when the war in Europe ended. They were equipped with P-51 Mustangs, the very long-range fighters, and were stationed at King's Cliffe in Northamptonshire. He kept copies of the unit's Intelligence Bulletins, which for 14 February 1945 recorded that 1,300 heavy bombers of the Eighth USAAF, escorted by fifteen fighter groups (about 900 Thunderbolts and Mustangs), attacked

the marshalling yards at Dresden and Chemnitz, the synthetic oil plant at Magdeburg and two bridges over the Rhine at Wessel. The Dresden and Chemnitz targets are within 65 miles of the Russian forces led by Marshal Koniev and are vital transportation centres for the German army on this front. The 20th Group was assigned a choice spot – escorting the first 2 bombardment groups of the first force to the target at Dresden.

Within the three squadrons, the 55th, the 77th and the 79th, a further subdivision was made between the 'A' and 'B' groups, with a dozen Mustangs in each. The three 'B' groups were to join the massed formation of Fortresses south of the Zuider Zee in Holland at 1045 and fly close escort all the way from there to Dresden and all the way back as far as Frankfurt, not leaving the bombers until 1425 hours (2.25 pm). In all, the fighters would be airborne between six and a half and seven hours, for most of that time hanging around the bombers. This group was led by Major Nichols.

Joseph Peterburs was flying with the 'A' groups, led by Lt.-Col. Montgomery because Major Meyer had had to return with engine trouble shortly after take-off. Their job was to stay near the bombers only as far as Dresden, then they were to go right down to the deck and shoot up transport targets. They found 'few' of those, according to their intelligence bulletin. 'I was in the group that left the bombers to look for targets of opportunity,' recalled Peterburs.

There were only three of us in my flight, Lt. Skroback having aborted due to engine problems. Major Gatterdam was lead, Lt. Jack D. Leon was number 3, and I was in the number 2 position.

After about half an hour of searching we saw a truck on a side road speeding along. We were at about 10,000 feet and Major Gatterdam called for the attack. He pulled up and rolled over for the attack dive. I should have been second in. However, we were in a turn at the time and Lt. Leon was in position to take number 2, so he did. Gatterdam's attack dive was rather steep and Leon was close behind, too close and too steep. I followed at normal interval and dive angle.

From my position I could see Gatterdam barely miss the ground as he pulled out of his dive. Leon, being too close and too steep, did not make the pull out in sufficient time and smashed into the ground. Being right behind Leon, there was no doubt in my mind as to what happened and how — too steep of an attack and too late of a pull out. If I recall correctly I got the truck with a burst of my fifty-calibre machine-guns. After Leon went in. Gatterdam and I rejoined, looked the area over, and then returned to base without further incident. According to my log book I was in the air for 6 hours and 30 minutes during this mission. The circumstances of Lt. Leon's death is one of those incidents in life that are burned into the memory and are recalled as though they had just occurred.

The Dresden mission was routine from the standpoint of the fighter pilot. As I recall, our pre-mission briefing was standard with the usual warning of heavy flak in the target area. We did anticipate active enemy fighter opposition which did not materialize. There was heavy flak as briefed, but no enemy fighter activity.

There were powerful defences at Chemnitz, on the route to Dresden, which the fighters may have overflown; and also at the hydrogenation plants near Leipzig.

Twenty-year-old Annemarie Waehmann had survived the bombing of the Friedrichstadt hospital complex, running from one building to another, as each was set on fire. And she had been reunited with her fellow-patient, the fifteen-year-old refugee girl Hilde.

Morning came very slowly, and with it into the hospital an endless stream of wounded, burnt and mutilated people. In my head one thought was constantly going round and round: What's happened at home? Is our house still standing? Where is Mummy?

I asked some of the new arrivals: 'What does it look like at the main station?'

One woman replied: 'Are you living there? There's nothing standing. It's all razed to the ground.'

When Hilde and I heard this there was no holding us any more. We had to go there and see for ourselves. A man called out after us: 'Girls, you'll never get there! All the streets are completely buried!'

We didn't even listen to him.

And now began the most terrible hour of my whole life. What we saw on that approximately three-kilometre-long journey to the station was indescribable, horrible. Thick smoke everywhere. As we climbed with great effort over large pieces of walls and roofs which had collapsed and fallen into the street, we could hear behind us, beside us, and in front of us, burnt ruins collapsing with dull crashes. The nearer we came to the town centre, the worse it became. It looked like a crater landscape and then we saw the dead. Charred or carbonized corpses, shrunk to half size. Oh, dear God! At the Freiburger Platz we saw an ambulance, with the male nurses just about to put a stretcher into it. A number of people were sitting on the ground. But why didn't they move? As we came nearer, we saw it all. They were all dead. Their lungs had been burst by the blast.

This macabre frieze would indeed have been caused by blast, which can kill without an obvious wound, although a post-mortem would show perhaps a ruptured spleen or ruptured kidneys where the compressed air had struck with the impact of a motorcar doing thirty miles an hour. The trick, once you know this, is to lie down with your head towards the descending bomb and your arms curled round your head; then the blast strikes no delicate organ. But to know this, and to be able to estimate with accuracy where the bomb will land, requires practical experience which one is lucky enough to survive; and in Dresden most people were novices in all aspects of sudden death.

In my mind, I prayed continuously: Please God, grant me that our house is still standing, and that nothing has happened to Mummy.

There were no streets any more, only heaps and heaps of debris. And when we finally found the broken leftovers of stone, the remains of *our* house, we sat down on the rubble, completely exhausted, and cried and cried and cried: 'Mummy, are you underneath there? Or has a kind fate saved you? Where are you? Why don't you come, you damn bombers, and kill me as well! What's there to live for now? Father is dead in the war, the town is in ruins, and mother . . .?'

A troop of army pioneers, who were clearing up, approached us and their officer called out: 'Girls, what are you doing here? You must leave at once! There's an air raid warning on again. You didn't hear it, because the sirens are out of order. Try to get through the station to Reichstrasse and then up to the Räcknitzer Hohen – and hurry up, for God's sake!'

Desperately, we fought our way through to the station. There the corpses were piled up in heaps: two metres high, five metres wide, five metres long. A sweetish smell came from the heap (which hung over the town for weeks afterwards). Many of them had jumped as burning torches into the water reservoirs, and more and more had followed them one on top of the other, so that they were all drowned.

When we had reached Reichsstrasse, we could hear again in the distance the drone of the bombers, and hoped that we could make it to the Technical High School on the hill. We didn't see a single human being anywhere. In the truest sense of the word, the place was a *desolation*. We hurried on as best we could, falling, stumbling, and reached the Technical High School. There we stood, entirely on our own, and heard the bombs go down into our city. Luckily, a military vehicle came and gave us a lift. They put us down outside the town and here we saw an endless procession of people, hundreds of them trudging along the road, broken, tired, indifferent, to what they hoped was safety.

We joined them. A few minutes later, we could hear the drone of planes come nearer and nearer. We looked up and saw how they flew lower and lower. 'They're coming here . . .' we screamed. A few men took over and gave commands: 'Split up! Scatter! Run into the fields! Down on your faces!' While we were lying in the dirt, our hands clawing at the earth as if we wanted to crawl inside it, they came at us, wave after wave, circling, flying low, shooting with their machine-guns into the defenceless people. Popping noises right and left, clods of earth flying up, screams. Like everyone else, I expect, I prayed: Dear God, please protect me. A few seconds' pause, as the planes circled to come back at us again. The men screamed: 'Up, up! Run on! Run towards the trees!'

Trees? A few, completely bare branches which seemed to reach out to the February sky. But nevertheless, we hoped they wouldn't see us. But again that popping noise as they fired without mercy into the people, and screams and clods of earth flying around. This is a situation which makes one terribly egoistic and self-centred. I took Hilde by the hand and without turning round once, without even looking to see how many people did not get up again, we ran towards the next village. Slowly the drone of the planes was lost in the distance. They had completed their bloody deed. The same kind of massacre was repeated in the Elbe meadows, where thousands of bombed-out Dresdeners had fled. They too were fired at with machine-guns by low-flying aircraft. Who gave such an order?

We ran over the fields until we arrived at my aunt's, starving hungry, crusted with earth, and completely exhausted. My first question was: 'Where is Mummy?'

And the answer? She lives! She's there! Thank God!

My other relatives, who lived near the Falkenbrücke, were both killed. And all of Hilde's relatives who had been in a refugee camp near the main station had been killed. From not a single one of my friends or schoolmates have I ever heard again. I am reminded of the lines by Sergei Yesenin:

'The hurricane swept by, few of us survived, and many failed to answer friendship's roll call.'

Ten to twelve days later, with the aid of three strong men, my mother attempted to dig in our collapsed house. She hoped to find her bag, which contained all our money and jewellery which she had lost during the panic. In vain. The many tons of coal which had been stored in the cellar had been ignited and burned and smouldered for weeks. And the people? All the ones who had been buried down there and were perhaps still alive after the house fell? Did they burn as well? How cruel.

Annemarie only heard about what had happened on the Elbe meadows. Gerhard Kühnemund experienced it. After he and the young Luftwaffe NCO had had their wounds dressed in the cellar of some headquarters, and fifteen-year-old Gerhard had smoked his first cigarette ever, they were advised to go down to the Elbwiesen in order to escape the spreading fires. He estimated that tens of thousands of people had sought refuge on the flat, open expanses of grassland beside the river.

Shortly after midday, we were suddenly and unexpectedly attacked by American planes. No sirens had been sounded. Amongst these people who had lost everything in a single night, panic broke out. Women and children were massacred with cannon and bombs. It was mass murder. Even today, after thirty-five years, there still exist historians who claim that during this daylight

raid no low-flying aircraft were used. This claim is totally false.
While we literally clawed ourselves into the grass, I personally saw
at least five American fighter-bombers, which from an altitude of
approximately 120 – 150 metres opened fire with their cannon on
the masses of civilians. My companion of the Luftwaffe, who had
saved my life during the night raids, was killed beside me in this
attack. There was a hole in his back the size of a palm. Never had
death been so close to me. The First Aid warden of the Waffen-SS
told me that he must have died instantly. Unfortunately, I never
managed to find out who this young pilot was. His Christian name
was Erich, his home was somewhere in North Germany, and he
was twenty-two years old. He told me shortly before, that he had
scored eighteen air victories.

Twelve hours after this horrifying experience I arrived at a huge
catchment area for bombed-out people. From there I was driven in
a convoy of army lorries filled with bombed-out people, in the
direction of Leipzig. Someone had hung over my torn and burnt
Hitler Youth uniform an army greatcoat which was far too large
for me. And on my head I wore a steel helmet which was two sizes
too large. My mother took me into her arms with tears in her eyes.
Weeks later, she told me that after my return from Dresden I
looked as if I had grown many years older. My features had not
been those of a fifteen-year-old boy any more.

In July 1979, I stood for the first time in front of the mass grave
of the victims of 13 February 1945, at the Heidefriedhof in Dresden. I put two bunches of flowers on the huge surface of the grave.
In memory of my aunt Else, who did not survive the raid, and a
young, unknown pilot of the German air force.

American fighter squadrons were divided into flights of
four aircraft. It may have been an organized unit which
came down and attacked the people who had sought sanctuary by the river, but there were also attacks by smaller
numbers – by a pair or even by a single Mustang.

'On the grey, unhappy morning after the night's terror,'
as Otto Sailer-Jackson put it, the staff were dealing with
wounded animals in the Zoological Gardens. The baby
elephant had been blown on to its back in the moat, badly

injured; she had to be shot. The mother elephant had been blown over the moat and stood there trembling, intestines trailing from a severe wound; she had to be shot. The zebras, steppe antelope and white-bearded gnus were all dead from breathing gases let off by a coal dump which had been set on fire nearby. A single giraffe remained, but all the animal houses had been destroyed, so the creature had no protection against the bitter cold of central Europe in February. The keepers decided to erect a special tent for her.

'Round about midday, one low-flying English [*sic*] air-craft turned up,' wrote Sailer-Jackson, mistaking USAAF for RAF.

It came from the centre of the destroyed town. Its target was the tide of refugees flowing along the Tiergartenstrasse ['Zoo Street']. He attacked several times, flying very low, firing from cannon and machine-guns into the refugees. Then he flew low over the Zoo and made several firing runs at anything he could see that was still alive. In this way our last giraffe met her death. Many stags and other animals which we had managed to save became the victims of this hero. So too did the animal-keepers of the Sarrasani Circus who had fled into the Elbe meadows, where they were attacked by low-flying aircraft and miserably killed.

The Zoo was bleeding from countless wounds. Its enclosures and most of its animals had been destroyed; and all the water pipes had been broken, so that it was impossible to put out fires. We ourselves had no accommodation, for all that had been burnt down. We had neither straw on which to lie down nor even a woollen blanket with which to cover ourselves. We had hardly a crust of dry bread for ourselves, and for the animals we had nothing. It nearly broke our hearts to see them come to us, begging for food. Reindeer came, some stags, some apes, and yes, even the shy heron and the big bittern. We had nothing for them. And it soon became clear that the devastated city could not help us. Even our shoes had been burnt in our efforts to save the animals.

Frau Canzler, whose father was a doctor with a surgery which survived the bombing, was kept very busy.

Patients came to us all day. The bell simply kept ringing. Some were blind from fire and dust, and they had to be sent first to an eye specialist. These people had to be guided, so I sent my little daughter with them. She was ten years old. On the way, two American planes dived on them, firing. My little girl saw people fall down and lie still, but did not realize what it was all about; that these people lying down were dead or wounded. She made her way into a cellar and told the family there, who had all been injured, that they could come to see the doctor. Eventually, a man brought her back to us.

We didn't come out of our clothes for two weeks. For a long time there was a cruel smell which is a little sweet, where they burnt the dead. There is nothing like it; nothing smells so; if I smelt it again I could always remember. Corpses lay in the streets for many days. On my way to the soup kitchens I always had to pass a dead soldier without a head. But all organization was falling to pieces, because it was the end of the war.

In the giant meat-safes under Dresden slaughterhouse out to the north-west of the old city, the working party of a hundred American prisoners and their guards had survived the RAF. Down there, the explosions of the two-ton and occasionally four-ton bombs had sounded like the footsteps of giants walking across the ground above them. It was late morning before their guards thought it safe to go up. The sky was dark and overcast, but the clouds were really smoke shrouding the city and rising to the height of the B-17s and Mustangs now approaching Dresden. The guards made the prisoners form fours, then they marched off to the hog barn where they normally slept. The walls of the old pig sty still stood, but the building was roofless, windowless and full of nothing but ashes and melted glass. There was no food or water there.

They would have to go into the city. But as a city,

Dresden no longer existed. The heart of it consisted of shells of buildings and mounds of rubble which appeared smoothly domed when seen from a distance, but were really heaps of hot, jagged, treacherous, unstable rocks which had to be climbed, which often moved or slipped away beneath the feet of the American soldiers and their German guards as they toiled upwards and over this moon-scape. Of course there were a few live people underneath their feet, trapped far down in the cellars, but the Americans did not know that then. Kurt Vonnegut assumed that if anyone was still alive in this devastation, then his survival represented a flaw in the great design. Kindly, so as not to harm Anglo-American relations, he did not write anywhere that this scene was the doing of the British alone, of RAF Bomber Command. But when he said 'American', he meant American.

And he said that it was 'American fighter planes' which came in under the smoke of burning Dresden, saw the hundred American prisoners clambering over the ruins, and dived to attack, spraying them with machine-gun fire. They missed, he recorded (probably because the rubble of broken buildings gives excellent cover to infantry against all kinds of projectiles, explosive or otherwise), but, as he added, they hit some of the people who were easier targets, moving about in the open on the Elbe meadows.

At the main station — where Gisela-Alexandra Moeltgen had been, but had got off the train and left the area; and where Gerhard Kühnemund, having missed his connection to Leipzig, had sat in the waiting room until he remembered that his Aunt Else lived nearby in the Serrestrasse — both the platforms above, and the covered ways and rooms below, were a macabre shambles of the clean dead and the dismembered. Annemarie Waehmann, as she fled through part of the Hauptbahnhof complex, had seen only a glimpse of the horrors around her. And the party of Silesian refugees, mostly women and children, led by Dr K's war-widowed sister, Erika, had caught their train but had now completely disappeared.

An old Red Cross man spent the morning after the night raids searching the platforms for survivors among the heaps of bodies and parts of bodies. In this evil-smelling shambles he found a little boy, perhaps two years old, wandering around on his own among the corpses. There was no sign of any living parent or relative, so he picked up the little child and took him to the square outside the station, where there was a collecting point for lost children. Eventually, he was put on a bus, together with other orphaned children, and driven eastward to a children's home, where he stayed until the Russians began to flood forward once again.

As the retreating lorries of the Wehrmacht rumbled past the orphanage, the Sisters of Mercy who ran the place stood outside on the pavement, begging the soldiers to take the children with them, away from the Red Army. One by one the children were handed up. The soldier who was handed this particular small boy got rid of him fairly soon at a field hospital they passed. He told the Sister in charge that, in his hands, the child was bound to die of cold and hunger. So she took the boy from the soldier and looked after him herself for the next twenty years, in what became the Soviet Zone of Germany and later the DDR.

According to American records, 316 Flying Fortresses took part in the midday attack on 14 February, carrying 487.7 tons of HE and 294.3 tons of incendiaries, a total of 782 tons (as compared to the 2,659 tons dropped in the two RAF raids). Presumably, the American total includes the forty or so B-17s of the 398th Group which should have bombed Dresden but through an error in navigation dropped their load on Prague, the capital of Czechoslovakia, instead. German records timed the attack as lasting ten minutes, from 1215 to 1225. It was certainly all over very quickly, and, apart from the low-flying Mustangs, generally made very little impression on most people in Dresden. Probably, many of the bombs simply disturbed the ruins. Others seemed to have fallen somewhere near the rail targets they were supposedly aimed at. Margret Freyer, who had spent all day searching for her fiancé, was not aware that there had been a daylight attack at all, and had to be told that there was damage in the Neustadt area.

On the other hand, Eva Tornow was very badly affected by this third raid, perhaps because she had three young children to worry about, including one baby and one boy crippled by polio; and also a husband who had been trying to divorce her, although he helped now as best he could. The pram was stolen during the hours of darkness on the morning of the 14th, but her husband borrowed a push-chair from friends, and they started to walk out of the city to Possendorf, where the husband's sister lived. 'It was like an army moving out of Dresden,' she recalled. 'One was delighted if now and then amongst all these people one saw a well-known face. It made one even more thankful to be alive. The only thing I can remember about this third raid is that I was not master of my limbs any more. I shook uncontrollably, and there was nothing I could do to stop it.' They reached Possendorf late that afternoon, virtually with what they stood up in. Everything they had left behind in their cellar had disappeared already. 'This was the beginning of the thieving and looting from empty houses,' she commented.

Mrs Dora Daniel, thanks to the lift she had had from her

sister's place in the car belonging to the fanatical National
Socialist farmer they had nick-named the 'Spinach Officer',
arrived home in time to experience the American raid. The
spectacle of burning Dresden, witnessed from the safety of
the Erzgebirge, had terrified her; it looked as though no
one could survive it, and her husband and baby son Holm
were in the middle of the conflagration. Then had come
two hours of climbing over rubble in burnt-out streets, each
step full of dread, and then, finally, with great relief, the
house still standing. But her husband was lying down in
bed. Had he been wounded again? (He had already lost an
arm, and the use of one leg, in the battle round Kiev.) No,
he was simply tired, having been up all night, had replaced
the broken glass in the windows with cardboard, and was
now trying to get some sleep, like the old soldier he was, or
rather, had been, for he was registered as 100 per cent
disabled.

'Our reunion was an experience,' he wrote in the diary he
was keeping for his baby son, Holm. 'Mummy was at the
end of her strength, her heart gave out and she had to lie
down at once on the sofa.'

'Daddy, I must die, I feel so terrible,' she cried, thinking
of her poor, shattered husband, her baby son, her little
daughter by her first marriage to a soldier killed in Russia
early in the war. They had remade a family together, and
now their recent happiness was at the mercy of the
bombers.

At around noon Mrs Daniel's father, Herr Altmann,
arrived from Neustadt to find out how his daughter was,
and not long after they heard the high-up humming of the
approaching American bomber formations, tight-packed
into a massed procession which would take ten minutes to
pass over the city, unrolling a carpet of bombs from their
bellies as they did so. Nothing could stop them and there

was no way one could run away from them. There was only the cellar, the hole in the ground.

Mrs Daniel stood up, but her legs were too weak to support her. She had to be carried down to the cellar. The serviceman who was engaged to their maid, Gretel, lost his nerve in his fears for her safety, and shouted: 'Gretel, come down at once! Leave the pram upstairs.' Mrs Daniel's baby son was in the pram, and the girl was very fond of him. Bombers or no bombers, she screamed back at her fiancé even more loudly: 'No! I'm not leaving Holm upstairs!' But of course she couldn't manoeuvre the pram, single-handed, down those stairs.

The serviceman cursed and rushed up to help her to carry the pram down, but without much ceremony, nearly pitching the baby out in his haste.

Whistling, the bombs showered on to the street and one struck the roof. They were all incendiaries. The two which landed outside the front door were soon put out, but smoke began to fill the cellar. Old Herr Altmann, who had a weak heart, was the first to be driven out by the unbearable smoke. Mrs Daniel was now lethargically resigned to dying with her baby, but someone grabbed her firmly by one arm, put the pram handle in her hand, and shouted: 'Get out! At the double!' Then, whether she thought she could or not, she was forced to pull the pram up the stairs while the man supported it from the back. Once up at street level they all realized just how thick the smoke really was. The bombers had passed on now, but frequently there was a thudding bang which made the ground shake and smoke rose up; the Americans had dropped a number of bombs with delayed-action fuses, apparently, and there could be one or two time-bombs ticking away dangerously close. So they decided to go to the house of Mrs Daniel's parents in Neustadt, which had been untouched by the night raids.

The Altmanns had only two rooms and a kitchen in the building, but it was a refuge of sorts.

But how to get there? Their street, too, was covered in debris, some of it smouldering. Gretel took charge of a little cart on which they heaped their emergency luggage, while Mrs Daniel tried to manoeuvre the pram up and down over the rubble, pushing hard at it, but without much effect. Someone, seeing her vain efforts, called out: 'Young woman, turn the pram round and pull it after you!' And indeed, that method worked better, because while she went forward, dragging the pram after her, her husband, with a stiff leg and one arm missing, was able to assist by pushing the back of the pram with his stomach. So, laboriously, they dragged pram and baby over the broken bricks and smashed stonework. This was the second time in four weeks in which they had been bombed out. In January they had lost their hairdressing business and their own flat to American bombs. This raid put paid not only to their temporary accommodation but to everything in the way of equipment which they had been able to save from the wreck of their business premises. Now, how were they going to live?

Once clear of debris-strewn roads, they suddenly found themselves looking at an overcrowded lorry which was taking other bombed-out people to Neustadt. That saved them quite a lot of walking, but once they had been set down again, baby Holm began to scream terribly, either because he was hungry or because his stomach had been upset by the endless bumping of the pram over the stony desert which Dresden had become. He was smeared with soot and dust, sackcloth and ashes, as they all were, and it was hard for his parents to get him clean again. However, a woman they met on the way gave him a sugar-dummy and he stopped screaming.

Mrs Daniel was reunited with her mother and her daughter Bärbel, who had been staying with the grandparents, and for a moment they all embraced, beaming. Then her heart began to trouble her again, her legs felt like rubber, and although she was put to bed in her mother's house, she couldn't sleep because of an irrational fear that if she lost consciousness she would die. Then her favourite aunt came to her bed and, not recognizing who it was under the sheets, asked: 'Who are you, then?'

'Aunt Augusta, I'm Dora,' replied Mrs Daniel.

'Good gracious, you look terrible,' said her aunt, and began to pray. Then she said: 'Now sleep well, and in two days you'll be well again.' And it was so.

In his diary, her husband wrote, as if to his son, Holm:

It broke one's heart to think that a little one like you had to go through all this. And Mutti thought she was going to die, it was all too much for her. Indeed one needs nerves as strong as ropes to undergo such experiences, and all of them at home. If life is hard at the front, one accepts it, for that is war and they are all men out there. But this, at home . . . And the English and the Americans call that war? They are not even worth being spat at by us.

Hildegarde Prasse was in her mid-twenties and widowed, her husband having been killed at Stalingrad just after Christmas 1942, leaving her alone with their little son; in 1945, the child was five years old. Hildegarde had a flat in Dresden-Neustadt, east of the Elbe, not far from the river. On the night of 13 February she had just returned from a trip outside the city, to the place where she had stored her most valuable possessions for safety, and had gone straight to the flat to sort out some documents, without picking up the child, who was being looked after by some friends about ten minutes' walk away. When the sirens went, signalling the first wave of the RAF attack, she tore along the road under the light of the flares and was virtually blown

down the stairs to the cellar of her friend's house by one of
the first bombs. She spent the night there, and in the
morning put her son in his push-chair and set off to return
to her flat.

The road was impassable. There were fires everywhere,
sending sparks sheeting across. Crashing and booming
noises came from the roofs. Hildegarde went back to her
friend and borrowed some cloths and blankets, dipped
them in water, then wrapped them round herself and her
son. Carrying him this time, she set out again, climbing
over stones, beams and rubble, making many detours.
When at last she reached the street where her flat was, to
her horror she saw only torn-up tramlines twisted in the air.
The front entrance to the building was blocked, and she
had to go round the back and get in some other way. Doors,
windows and part of the stairwell were down, but at length
she got into her own flat, which proved to be only half-
destroyed. She had not been home for more than an hour,
trying to clear up, when shortly after noon the USAAF raid
took place.

Towards 1400 hours I went with my son in his push-chair to my
parents in Dresden Altstadt, normally a walk of three-quarters of
an hour. I had to cross the Elbe but only the Marienbrücke
(alongside the railway bridge) was still passable. There were no
trams, no telephones; nothing was intact. There was rubble everywhere and when I finally stood in front of my parents' house my
push-chair was moving only on three wheels.

The building was badly damaged, with the middle of it
fallen in, but Hildegarde found her mother sitting in the
cellar with many other people. 'They were all glad to be
alive and only one person was missing – my father. He had
been on night-shift at Dresden main post office on the
Postplatz.' Hildegarde stayed to comfort her mother.

In the evening the family were reunited, for her father turned up, looking very ill (from breathing smoke) and half-frozen from the February cold. The post office building had come down like a pack of cards, he said, but they had got out of the cellar through windows, and run madly down to the Elbe where they had found shelter in a bandstand. Her father looked so terrible that Hildegarde stayed the night with her parents. He was suffering from smoke-poisoning, the doctor said, and died of it a year later. It was not until the next morning that Hildegarde went back to her flat and, detouring past the Postplatz and the Altmarkt, saw that very terrible things were happening in Dresden.

Ruth Pieper's situation was almost the reverse of Hildegarde Prasse's. Aged twenty-one, and single, she worked at the railway hotel in Dresden-Neustadt but lived on the other side of the river in the suburb of Blasewitz, about four miles from the city centre. Whereas the centre of Dresden suffered between 75 and 100 per cent destruction, Blasewitz got off lightly at between 25 and 75 per cent destruction. But her father, too, was missing. As it was Carnival Night in Dresden, he had taken the evening off from his taxi business to go out to a pub and play skittles. He had still not returned when, in daylight on 14 February, Ruth and her mother packed a few things and left the burning city for the security of a friend's house in the Saxon Switzerland area about thirty miles away. But Ruth was young and curious. She was eager to see what had happened in Dresden and fretting about the fate of her father. On the 15th she returned to the city and to her work (for the railway hotel had not been hit) and, like Hildegarde, saw the most terrible sights on the way.

'The news was spread in a most mysterious way, that all

those people who were walking about lost and helpless should assemble in the Grosser Garten, the most beautiful park in Dresden,' recalled Erika Wittig, who as Erika Simon had been eleven years old at the time. In fact, this park, like the Elbe meadows, was a designated refuge area in case of a fire-storm, and some signs had been put up beforehand to show this.

The family had been completely scattered by the night raids. Her mother Ursala was out on duty with the Red Cross at a first aid post. Her little brother Jürgen, aged eight, disappeared. Her father Werner, a chemist, stayed behind at the house to rescue a few things before the flames engulfed them, while she and her sister Ursula, thirteen years old, were taken by a nurse to the hospital where her mother worked, which was soon set on fire also. But in daylight on 14 February they all found each other again, except for the children's nanny, a refugee girl from the East aged about twenty. The little boy, it turned out, had been snatched into shelter by a refugee family when they saw him wandering about as if lost.

The cold was bitter and they walked along until they came to a house which, unlike all the others around it, was intact; or at least was still standing. They simply went in and lay down on the floor, exhausted. They were roused almost immediately by that sinister high-up humming noise made by tightly-packed formations of American bombers approaching. The air filled with the whistling sound of bombs falling, and one particularly loud one rose to a scream followed by a terrific explosion. In the silence which followed, the house seemed to continue vibrating and shaking and settling down for quite a time. When at last they found the courage to go outside, they saw a huge crater opposite the entrance. 'Five metres closer and it would have been the end of all of us.'

Her father, remarked Erika, was 'deeply honest', but now when he found a bicycle in this house, he took it 'without ever suffering a bad conscience' and rode off to friends who lived at Pillnitz on the Elbe, a very distant suburb of Dresden, to get help for his family. They eventually found a lorry which picked up the whole Simon family as well as many other dispossessed people and took them out of the burning, smoking city. Her father's use of the bicycle without asking permission from the absent owner could be classed as looting, and looting was punishable by death, which was just another hazard of survival at that time and in those circumstances.

For over a year we stayed in a lovely villa at Pillnitz, which was occupied by countless people, and had to suffer many more raids. My brother Jürgen, eight years old, once said that he did not want to live any more, which is perhaps the best indication of our situation. Then came the capitulation and the Russians. Plenty of upsets, terrible scenes with the Russians who were billeted there, death by typhus in the house, and one suicide. But also exemplary co-operation amongst this group of people who had been thrown together there after this terrible night of bombing in Dresden. Approximately twenty-five persons of all age groups remained with us living in the same house. Everything was shared, even the burden of grief. We celebrated together and suffered together and even later on, as the group began to break and disperse, we still kept in touch with each other for many years.

Jack Evans, who had escaped from the 'Frostbite March' by posing as a French slave worker, arrived in Dresden between the two night attacks, and 'in a trance of horror' saw people running about like flaming torches. In the POW camp he had been first bored and then sickened by RAF aircrew tales of how they had been shot down or had destroyed this or that city. Now he took shelter in a cellar where there was not a single fit man – all the occupants were women, children or old men. At the All Clear, he went above ground, shaking all over, saw people burning and heard their screams, like those of frantic animals. He joined the trek away from the city and by noon next morning was in a village twenty miles away, where the inhabitants said they had been able to read their newspapers by the light of the flames, and marvelled at his escape. They took him for the Frenchman he said he was and his explanation for his lack of the right identity documents to back that statement, if it was queried, was simply that he had been in the bombing of Dresden. So he calmly went and found a farm to work on, so that he could get some food and build up his strength before carrying on further west. To pose as a foreigner in Germany, provided you had a fair grasp of the German language, was fairly safe; whereas to pose as a German in Germany was asking to be exposed the moment you opened your mouth, even if your clothes had not given you away already.

Two other POWs were at that time also posing as French slave workers, for the same cogent reasons. They were the Australian pilot, Geoff Taylor, who had been shot down over Hanover in 1943, and his companion, Smithy. They had first posed as French prisoners in order to get out of the POW camp at all, for French POWs merely walked out of the gate while the British tunnelled. All you needed was the co-operation of the French, and you were free. But what then? In February, you needed shelter to survive one night, and food to survive more than two or three days. Geoff and Smithy's plan was to steal a German night fighter from the nearby Lonnewitz airfield (their camp was twenty-five miles from Dresden), and fly it to the Russian lines, which would take them about half an hour if they were not shot down. Smithy's German was fairly good, Geoff's was non-existent.

They had studied the Luftwaffe operational style first from a distance at the POW camp and then from shelter inside a wood on the airfield perimeter. Everything they saw convinced them that the Luftwaffe was just as sloppy as their own air force in certain vital respects. Indeed, as the plan unfolded, they began to build up quite an affection for their opposite numbers, and were confirmed in their view that, if you wanted to walk on to a German airfield and steal a machine, you just acted as if you were attempting the same thing on an RAF station. No one would rumble you. Aircraft get stolen in books and films, but in real life no one suspects that that sort of thing is likely to happen.

In this respect, their calculations proved to be completely correct. What their plan did not allow for were the plans of Bomber Command and the 8th USAAF. At the last moment, they had nearly altered their own plan and jumped a train into Dresden on the evening of 13 February. By thinking better of it, they had a grandstand view of the night raids and survived to take an easy stroll on to the Luftwaffe base next morning, carrying on their shoulders that log which they thought should be sufficient excuse for being on German government property. But now, of course, they were no longer protected by the conventions governing prisoners-of-war. The penalty for being caught might be final.

They spent half the morning going down one side of the airfield, stopping for a rest under each aircraft and surreptitiously trying the underbelly hatch. All the likely aircraft, Ju 88s and Ju 188s, were locked; many of the others were unserviceable. That side of the airfield was a dead duck, and the administrative area would be a place to avoid, but there seemed to be a nice little dispersal point for Ju 188s on the other side of the runway, with engines being warmed. Still carrying their log, which was getting heavier by the minute, they walked to the far side of the airfield and chose a waiting spot which overlooked the dispersal point of the machines they were interested in. The only cover available was down inside a weapon pit which, to judge from the smell, had been used as a latrine, but this was no time to be fussy. Then the airfield siren started wailing, and Germans from the dispersal points began running to the perimeter where the weapon pits were. There was the distant drone of B-17s and then with a roar and a crackle of gunfire, a couple of Mustangs went screaming overhead. The next raid on Dresden had begun. Four Germans, three men and a girl, all in uniform, one with a machine-gun, came up to their slit-trench. Now for it, thought Geoff, not understanding a word of their talk.

Afterwards, Smithy explained what they had been saying to each other in German, which being translated boiled down to: 'Here are a couple of Froggies with the twitch. We'll mount our machine-gun elsewhere.' The Germans had thought it funny. Geoff, who had buried his nose in the sewage to avoid being noticed, didn't.

When the Germans blew the whistle signalling everyone to knock off work for the day, Geoff and Smithy decided it was now or never. They got into one of the Ju 188s which they had seen being started and warmed up in readiness for the coming night's operations. Holding his hard-to-get cockpit diagram in one hand, Geoff found that the actual layout was quite different. There was no central pedestal holding all the controls. Instead there was a panel on the left. After some minutes, he had located the fuel cocks when a helmeted German put his head through the hatch in the floor behind him and said: *'Was ist?'*

In books, films and comics, this is where the brave Brit brains the beastly Boche and makes a dash for England, home and beauty. In fact, Geoff and Smithy got out of the night fighter and stood sheepishly facing the German guard, wondering if they would be handed over to the Gestapo. The German snapped at them (in German): 'It is forbidden for foreign workers to enter German aircraft. Clear out!'

So they picked up their log and marched to another part of the airfield, no one taking any notice of them, trying all the Ju 88s on the way. They were all locked, apparently mothballed. This was the result of the American raids on the refineries, the grounding of a large part of the Luftwaffe by fuel shortage.

They were now fairly desperate, because it was sunset, very cold, and they were weak on their feet from starvation. One of the aircraft near them was a Weihe trainer, long out of use apparently and offering shelter for the night. They got inside and made themselves comfortable while watching a squad of Luftwaffe soldiers practising airfield defence tactics 300 yards away. There was no risk of their taking off in the Weihe. It had no fuel. On the other hand, they had no sleep. First German bombers, Heinkels and Dorniers, began to take off with heavy loads for the Russian lines. Then a stream of night fighters got airborne at the same time as the flash and thunder of a heavy RAF night raid disturbed the horizon in the direction of Chemnitz. It was a long time to the dawn.

Apart from the Dresden area, where the enormous fires still burning were sending up smoke clouds to 28,000 feet and the local weather was affected as it often seems to be in these cases, there was sunshine and sometimes cloud-free sky. Not at all an encouraging sight for the crew of the crippled B-17 co-piloted by Lyle Keran on his fourteenth mission, which had 'lost' number one engine over the target and was struggling for home down at 10,000 feet on the remaining three. Not only were they flying back through clear skies, but there was a very strong headwind to bat against now that they had turned for home. Everything portable had been thrown out, including the guns. 'We were very sure the German fighters would come after us,' Keran recalled.

The magnetic compass was all we had for a heading out of Germany, and I have forgotten how long we flew before the Rhine went under us, but it was a very strong headwind. After crossing the Rhine we lost number three engine and all crew members were advised that they were free to bail out if they wanted to do so. No one left the airplane so another descent was begun. Again, things began to happen.

The fuel for number four engine was giving out due to the excessive use of power by the remaining engines. There was a spare supply of about 200 gallons on the left side but the transfer valves were inoperative, so very soon they would have the use of only one engine, which would not keep them aloft but might help a forced landing.

We began looking for a place to land, found a deserted airfield and by this time were down to our number two engine. On a strange field, the procedure was to land with wheels up: and at this time we did not know whether we were in or out of German-occupied territory. I have forgotten the crash air speed procedure, but it was around 130 mph, I think. The rest of the crew got themselves into crash positions. One of the rumours we heard was that on crash landing, the nose turret might come through the cockpit and take the pilot's legs off, and as co-pilot, that was one of my last thoughts before crashing. The idea of the excessive landing speed was to clean the bottom of the airplane off, which it did. No one received a scratch. Switches and electrical power were cut before impact. but when the aircraft stopped we came out the top as fast as we could. However, no fire erupted.

Within five minutes, two jeeps came roaring up to the

crash. They were from an American unit which the day before had moved into the area, now twenty miles behind the American lines. They were taken to Dijon, France, and put on a train to Paris. And there the weather closed in and they had to spend five days in the French capital (which can hardly have been a penance) before a C-47 flew them back to London and another combat mission next day.

The B-17G of the 92nd Bombardment Group in which Sergeant Bill Stewart was ball turret gunner reached Allied-occupied France after a long flight, low on fuel. When they had passed through German air space, Stewart got out of the cramped turret from which, 'like an embryo in an egg', he had watched the bombs go down into the thick smoke clouds over Dresden. The bomber just about made an emergency landing strip on the coast of England, where they refuelled sufficiently to get back to their base at Podington. But on start-up, one engine caught fire. The blaze was extinguished, but the Fort was not flyable in that condition, so they left '601' there and got a ride with another B-17 of the 92nd Group which had also been forced to put down at the emergency strip.

I was completely exhausted when we finally reached Podington that evening. We were debriefed while we were eating our supper. We gave the officer our information: bombing was by PFF, no enemy aircraft were seen, flak was meagre. The 92nd Bomb Group lost one B-17 during the raid, probably due to engine malfunction. There were no casualties in the Group other than this one plane and its crew. Minor, compared to the destruction the people in Dresden saw. I went to my barracks, wrote the mission and date on a sheet of paper, and fell fast asleep on my bunk. I flew 26 missions over Germany and its occupied territories, but the Dresden raid will always stay in my mind even though other missions I flew on were closer scrapes with death. You see, the February 14th raid on Dresden was my *very first* mission.

About the time that the American crews were going to bed, those who had bombed Dresden and those who had attacked nearby Chemnitz, the same RAF bomber crews who had carried out the Dresden night massacre were taking off again. 75 New Zealand Squadron were down to go again, and after only two or three hours' sleep Peter Goldie was woken up for yet another briefing. His best friend, Ken Moore, was still missing from the Dresden raid, and as far fewer people got out of Lancasters than almost any other type of bomber, Peter was very worried. But Ken Moore's Lancaster was down at the Woodbridge emergency strip, three miles long, with an oil pressure drop making the brakes ineffective. After repairs, they got back to their base at Mepal near Cambridge in time to see the squadron take off into the night once more, Peter Goldie's AA-P among them. After debriefing, Ken went to bed. When he woke up it was the morning of 15 February and the station police were in the barrack room removing kit from under a vacant bed. 'Missing airman,' they mumbled to him. Later, he saw the barely concealed anguish in the faces of the man's closest friends, although they tried to put a bold front on it.

In Miles Tripp's squadron, everyone got back safely from Dresden. At briefing, the crews found it difficult to describe what they had seen; there were no words adequate to the task, no comparisons even. Tripp himself was in bed by 9 o'clock on the morning of 14 February, slept for four hours, then got up ready to leave camp and see his fiancée. When, on the way, he stopped at flight office he was told that another battle-order had gone up. And it was another maximum fuel-load, minimum bomb-load operation. All their names were on the board.

By the time he had got back to the crew-hut, the others

were smart in best-blues, brass buttons and black shoes shining, ready for a night on the town. Only Harry, the air gunner from Jamaica, was wearing battledress and was just sitting on his bed, waiting; just as if he knew that there would be no night out for any of them.

This time Miles Tripp came right out with it, asking the dark lad point-blank if he had his hunches from inside his head, or from some leakage of information on the Station? Harry was very, very offended. Of course, the information came from inside himself, why did they not accept that, and not always ask for explanations? He pretended to be amused by their questions, but clearly he wasn't; he was downright angry.

And they, the rest of the crew, were determined this time to know for sure. Did he get his information from human sources or – from sources not human? Or at any rate not understood, certainly not by them.

One asked: 'Where do you reckon we're going tonight, Harry?' But Harry passed it off with a 'Berlin, I hope' (for he always wanted to go to Berlin). They had decided that, informally, without arousing suspicion, there would always be two or three of them with Harry right up to the time of briefing. Only Tripp himself went to the pre-briefing. The red ribbon on the wall led to a town about forty miles south-west of Dresden. He'd never heard of it as a target before.

Then he went back to the room where the rest of the crew were keeping Harry company – and making sure that no one slipped him any information. 'Not much sleep for us tonight,' was the only clue that Miles Tripp gave them.

One of the others turned to Harry and said: 'Have a shot at guessing the target, mate.'

A map of Europe was pinned to the wall in this room also; but a small one and lacking the red route ribbon.

Harry walked over to it, put out his hand and moved it east over Germany until it reached Leipzig, south-west of Berlin. Then he moved his hand further south until a finger pointed to Chemnitz.

'Might be Leipzig, or even Chemnitz . . . I think it'll be Chemnitz.'

'He's right,' said Tripp.

'Christ!' said someone else.

At the main briefing, attended by everyone, they were told that Chemnitz was crammed with refugees who had escaped from the holocaust in Dresden, and that by bombing it they would be spreading the chaos still further. If they were successful, it was unlikely that they would be paying any more visits to the Russian Front. 'Good luck, chaps,' they were told, 'and when you come back don't let there be a Chemnitz.'

'When your target is bombed, and you turn for home with just a glance at the fires you have caused,' ran the Air Ministry's notes for air gunners, 'do not let us read in the following day's newspapers that you said to a reporter "while I was looking at the fires I suddenly noticed a burst of tracer whizzing past the turret". Search keenly and continuously for enemy aircraft all the way back, and do not relax until you have landed at base.'

Four miles high over Chemnitz, invisible under solid cloud cover and with the bombing scattered and the master bomber uncertain, Peter Goldie in the rear turret of Lancaster AA-P could spare a glance at the dull glow in the sky from the flames of Dresden, fifty-five kilometres distant.

Somebody bombed Dresden that night, perhaps Lancasters mistaking the glow for Chemnitz or unable to find Chemnitz at all; or perhaps even a few Russian bombers wandered over from Marshal Konev's front. Once again, it was seventeen-year-old Eva Beyer who gave the alarm to the families in the now battered and half-burnt Junghanns bakery building at Gostritz in the southern suburbs of Dresden. She had had a very, very long day, after a sleepless night.

When daylight came on 14 February, her thoughts had been with her family, wondering if they were still alive, for their home lay in the heart of the area attacked by the RAF during the night. The baker himself was in prison (condemned for the crime of giving bread to Polish prisoners of war) and so his wife ran the bakery assisted by the crippled ex-soldier Kurt. She sent Eva off with her two children, aged two and a half and four and a half, in a cart to Bannewitz, just outside Dresden to the south-west. The journey there and back had taken four hours and used up most of Eva's morning, when she could have been searching for her mother and little sister.

When I arrived back at the bakery, Kurt and a few volunteers were busy baking bread. Everything had to be done by hand, of course, for there was no electricity, and already people were queueing up for bread. We were the only bakers in the neighbourhood who could bake, for we still had a coal-fired oven; many other bakers had changed over to electricity. When I arrived at the bakery, the baker's wife asked me to cook a meal, but I said no. I told her that I was going to search for my family first. She was very angry, but I told her that I had helped her enough, and now it was my family's turn. So I got on my way into the centre of the town.

I had imagined it to be much easier, but the nearer I came to the centre of the town, the worse was the destruction. I wanted to take the quickest way, but it wasn't possible. As I approached the Grosser Garten and the Zoo, air raid wardens stopped me and said, 'You can't go that way, all the animals are running round loose. You could be attacked by a tiger or a snake.' I did see apes climbing about in the trees, so I was forced to make a detour. But that was easier said than done, for where there had been roads before, was now covered with collapsed houses. I had to climb over mountains of stone. When I kicked a charred piece of wood and it slid over to one side, I saw it was a human being. I got such a fright, I screamed. Only fear for my family drove me on.

When I turned into Chemnitzerstrasse I didn't know whether to go on or go back. There were people there who in their desperate need had clawed themselves on to the metal fence. They were burnt and charred; and they were not only adults, there were children of different ages hanging there. I felt so sick I had to vomit. I can't describe the fear I felt. But always there was the thought of my family.

As I approached the paint factory, the smoke and smell of sulphur was so strong that I couldn't breathe any more. As there was no water anywhere, I peed on my headscarf and tied it in front of my mouth. This way, I could breathe and keep on walking.

When at last I arrived at our street, the Kleine Plauensche Gasse, I was totally exhausted. When I came to our house, I saw that it was still standing, but burnt out. I went into the cellar. It was empty. What now?

First, I sat down and cried as I'd never cried before in my life. My tortured body ached all over, my headache was almost unbearable, but the worst thing was the question: Where is my family? Are they still alive? Or are they lying somewhere underneath the debris? 'Mummy,' I thought, 'where are you?' It took an incredible effort to stand up again, but first I wrote on the wall of our house: PLEASE GIVE INFORMATION ABOUT THE WHEREABOUTS OF FRAU BEYER, and put my address at the bakery underneath.

Then I went on my way to my grandma's, for she lived only round two corners. I found nothing there. The house was partly standing but burnt out. I left a message there as well.

I now made my way towards Ringstrasse. When at last I had managed it, for I had to climb across the incredible debris, I couldn't believe my eyes. Dead, nothing but dead. I was almost paralysed with shock. Could my family be amongst them? As I walked along the road I suddenly saw a woman lying there who looked like my grandma. The coat, the shoes, and the handbag looked the same as the ones she used to have. But I couldn't say a hundred per cent, for one side of her face was completely charred. Also, I could not correctly identify her ear-rings. The man who was in charge of the dead said to me: 'I'll put her on one side for you. Come back tomorrow, perhaps you can be surer then, for all those who haven't got anything on them whereby they can be identified, such as papers or identity cards, are going to be buried in a mass grave.'

The handbag of the woman who looked like my grandma was empty. It must have contained papers, money and jewellery. I wondered if it was hers and the contents stolen. Then I felt a strong urge to lie down beside her, for I had come to the end of my tether. I was utterly in despair at not finding my family. But I couldn't really rest. I had a long and difficult journey ahead of me and it was already getting dark. I was also hoping faintly that perhaps my family had found their way to Junghanns.

When I arrived back there, shattered and emotionally destroyed, my family wasn't there. I went into the cellar, sat in a corner, and cried bitterly. The pictures which formed themselves in my mind were gruesome. Then I fell asleep.

Somebody shook me awake. It was Kurt. 'It's your turn to stand guard,' he said.

'Stand guard?'

'Yes. We have formed a guard group, for the sirens aren't working any more and everyone stands guard for two hours in order to give the alarm when the planes come back.'

And so I wrapped myself in a blanket, for it was very cold, and stood guard. After about half an hour I heard the sound of approaching aircraft. Was it friend or foe? I listened intently in order to determine the difference in the sound of the engines. It was the enemy. I went quickly into the cellar and gave the alarm. Most of the bombs dropped into burnt-out houses. Only one did a great deal of damage for it went into the water works. So now we had no water. However, we found an underground water main which we tapped, and then had at least a little water. This enabled us to bake bread, because you can't do that without water.

At 5 o'clock on the morning of 15 February, the Junghanns bakery was in action again, the staff working without cease until 4 o'clock in the afternoon, and long bread-queues forming up outside.

At 4.45 that morning Lancaster A-Able, with Miles Tripp as bomb aimer, had touched down at their base, safely returned from Chemnitz. That attack, too, had taken place in two waves, each wave consisting of some 300 heavy night bombers. Chemnitz was an industrial town, but the raids had been a failure. There had been cloud, flak and lack of concentration. No fire-storm had developed.

At about the same time as the last Lancasters were coming back, the orderly sergeants were going round the American bomber bases rousing the aircrews for breakfast and briefing. Of the mighty daylight force sent out on 15 February, 211 heavy bombers carrying 465.6 tons of high explosive bombs and no incendiaries were given Dresden as their target. Day and night, the city was to be hammered to destruction.

Still shrouded in darkness, what had been its centre was a desolation pervaded by the sickly-sweet stench of unburied corpses, and with many people who had been trapped alive in the cellars now slowly choking or smouldering to death.

10
'Learn How to Weep'

The old man in the sanatorium on the hill of Loschwitz looked out across the Elbe to burning, smoking Dresden. He was almost eighty-three years old and had come back to Dresden, the dream city of his youth, to die. Now he knew that it was a miracle that he was still alive after witnessing its fall. He was a writer, a poet, a dramatist, surely he, Gerhart Hauptmann, could find some words to convey what was in his heart.

'Those who had forgotten how to weep learned again when Dresden fell . . . ' he began. But how to end? He was so helpless, like everyone else surviving in the city whose life had been extinguished. 'I will soon stand before our Lord with my request. It comes from the depths of my heart, but is so useless. I shall beg Him to love and purify mankind more than he ever did before, for their sakes.'

The heights of Loschwitz overlooked the most easterly of the Dresden bridges, popularly known as 'Blaues Wunder'. It was outside the bombed area and was intact. In the city area between the Altstadt and Neustadt there were five more bridges: the Albert, the Carola, the Augustus, the Marien and the railway bridge. All were standing except for the Carola bridge. There were two more bridges outside the city to the west, the Autobahn bridge and the Am Flugelweg, and both were intact.

Dresden was indeed an important communications centre with a single key point which, if knocked out, would bring rail traffic to a halt for months. That key point was the railway bridge over the Elbe. Not only was it intact but it had not even been an RAF target. In the past, where the destruction of bridges had been essential for military reasons, they had been duly destroyed by the air forces. Those over the Seine are examples I personally can recall.

The second most important rail target in Dresden was the marshalling yards, because much rolling stock was there. They survived the RAF attacks and indeed were outside the RAF target area.

The third most important communications target was the Autobahn bridge outside the city to the west. That was not attacked.

Access to the internal road bridges was difficult for a time because of the rubble in the streets, but in terms of the Eastern Front communications network, road transport was virtually unimpaired.

The railway lines eastward from Neustadt were in operation on 15 February. Double-track working throughout Dresden from west to east was established two days after that, three days after the RAF raids. Bombed railway lines, like cratered airfields, are easily and rapidly repaired as, in this sixth year of the war, everyone knew. A specialist force of 40,000 men under General Erich Hempe was available to repair bomb damage to railways. The knocking out of a railway bridge over a major river would have set them a considerable task, but making good bombed track was no problem at all.

However, they were presented with no such problem because no attempt had been made to effectively interfere with communications. In my view, Dresden had been bombed for political and not military reasons; but again, without effect. There was misery, but it did not affect the war.

*   *   *

An anonymous witness wandering through the ruins the day after the raid told a German historian:

I simply had to go back and see what had become of my family in the cellar. I went to our house in Wettinerstrasse. It was deadly still there, only the hot, scorching ruins gave a crackling noise. Now and then flames shot up and died down again. The smoke was so thick that I could see only three metres ahead of me. I crawled on all fours towards the walls, looked into one of the basement windows and shouted the names of my relatives. Nothing moved, only little flames leaping up when some oxygen reached the cellar rooms. It looked like a heap of burning coal.

Everyone, I was sure, got killed in there. I staggered on across the rubble and suddenly heard someone sing. At first I thought it was an hallucination, but no, the singing came nearer. Slowly, out of the smoke and dust, a young girl moved into sight. She was about twenty-two, dirty, with distorted face. Her clothes were scorched. She staggered across the rubble, a bicycle-frame flung across her shoulder, completely shapeless, and she sang, sang with a brittle voice: '*In der Nacht ist de Mensch nicht gern allein* . . .'

This was a popular wartime ditty — 'In the night, people don't like to be alone.'

In 1958, when my wife and I talked to Frau Canzler she remembered what others interviewed later forgot — the rain.

After a fire-storm, followed by blowing clouds of dust, came the rain always. So the ruined city became a sea of mud and dirt and wreckage and half-hidden corpses.

The First Aid Sections, staffed by nurses, saw horrible sights. A young man fell over something in the dark, and turned on his torch. There lay a woman with burnt, blackened arms, crying out for the help he could not give.

The wild animals broke loose. Mad for food and drink, they came into houses. An ape came suddenly into our house, into a room where a girl was sitting typing at a desk. The ape picked up a bottle of ink, and drank. An ostrich was found, dead in the snow eighty kilometres away, with bits of a fox in its beak.

When the Schloss caught fire, the people were trapped in the cellars. Young men with axes tried to break through to reach them, but the walls were too strong. They did not get out, and the building burned above them. Outside, copper from the blazing roof of the Schloss melted and fell like rain on people who were escaping from other cellars.

The first bombs of all came when the famous Dresden choir were singing, and fell among the young boys.

My father (who was a women's doctor) went to fetch two of his patients from a bombed hospital. They had just had operations (Caesarian-section). They were not in the hospital, however. That morning, they had got up and gone out, still bandaged from their operations, to look for their children in the ruins of the building. It was impossible to find them, for few came alive out of that hospital.

People were evacuated in ships and boats along the Elbe to Pirna. Once there, they lay in bare, empty rooms, on the floor, in the cold, in their winter clothes, their wounds covered with paper because there were no proper bandages.

We didn't come out of our clothes for two weeks.

All the centre of the city was cordoned off and the dead burnt on grids, set on fire by army flamethrowers. For weeks, men passed our house with carts, with wooden boxes, with cardboard boxes, with paper parcels, with suitcases – all containing human remains they had found. They were taking them to this crematorium.

At the Junghanns bakery on 15 February they baked without cease from five in the morning until four in the afternoon, and were then so exhausted that they could hardly eat their own meal. Most of the modern electric bakeries were out of action, so the pressure came on to Junghanns and its old-fashioned equipment. So great was that pressure that the owner, Herr Junghanns, was 'sprung' from prison by his brother on grounds of national emergency, to help run the business. The brother was a very great contrast to the owner, who had gone to prison for taking pity on Polish prisoners; this man was a member of the Gestapo and proud of his uniform.

Eva Beyer recalled:

That day at midday I went off again to search for my family. This time the journey was worse than before. I shall never forget it as long as I live. People were running around searching for a father, a mother, for children, for relatives. They got down on their hands and knees and tried to scrape away the earth and stones of the rubble of homes in the vague hope of finding a beloved human being. Again and again, I heard children screaming for mummy or daddy, and nobody could help them. As I made my way towards the centre of the town, I arrived at the Altmarkt, I got such a shock that my legs refused to carry me on.

What my eyes saw can hardly be described. Nothing but parts of bodies, arms, legs, heads, hands and torsos, being shovelled up into a big heap with forks by men of the ARP, the army and the Red Cross. Then petrol was poured over it and the whole heap was burnt.

Lorries came all the time and brought more of these dismembered people. I became incapable of walking away. The only thing I could think of was, could it be that mother is amongst these mutilated things? Mesmerized, I stared at the heaps of human remains in the hope of finding an answer. Mentally, I started to put together these parts of bodies in order to see whether they could be any of my family. How long I stood there, completely motionless, I don't know. I cannot even remember passing out.

When I came to I was lying on a stretcher. A Red Cross man gave me a cup of coffee and a tablet. He told me that they had watched me for quite some time, but when I sank to the ground screaming they had come to help me. I told them that I was looking for my family and that when I saw this terrible sight I imagined that I had seen them there. The Red Cross man neither agreed nor disagreed, but said he felt that it could have been my nerves which led me to imagine all this. Perhaps none of my family were really there. After all, what we had gone through during the last forty-eight hours was such that it would be hardly surprising if someone lost their sanity. So, with this hope in my mind, that Mutti and little Gertraud and the two boys were not lying there in the Altmarkt, I continued on my way to search for them elsewhere. But if I had not seen all this myself, I would have said it was just the one hundred per cent horror film of our century.

As I made my way over heaps of stones, slid down into craters here and there, I sustained scratches and sprains, but eventually reached the Kleine Plauensche Gasse. There was no news, and I became desperate.

Suddenly, I thought of the nursery in Cotta. It is on the outskirts of Dresden, beyond Friedrichstadt. When my parents divorced, my father had been in charge of that nursery. I got up and went there, and when I reached the outskirts of the town I could use the tram. That saved me time, and above all I didn't have to walk, which did my legs the world of good. When I arrived there, it was deserted. No bomb damage and everything in order, but overgrown. It looked as if my father had not done any work in it for a long time. There was no trace of my family there, either. I was terribly disappointed. I went round the neighbourhood and asked. Nobody knew anything about my family. Deprived of yet another hope, I started on my return journey, racking my brains trying to think where they could be.

Halfway, I was surprised by an air alarm. I stood under the arch of a gate and waited for I don't know what. When I couldn't hear planes any more I continued on my way. Wherever one looked, there was destruction, suffering, despair.

Back at Junghanns again, I went into the bakery and helped. I couldn't sleep. My heart and soul were so raw that I simply couldn't rest. I was obsessed by images of my family. I found no peace, and although there was now trouble with the baker's wife and her brother-in-law, I completely ignored it, put on my coat, and went out again searching for my family.

Hildegarde Prasse had been fortunate, finding her parents' home badly damaged but her mother alive, and although her father was missing, he had staggered home late on the evening of the 14th. She was not to know that he would die from smoke poisoning within a year. She stayed with her parents in their cellar (for the house above them was a ruin), then next morning returned with her child in his push-chair to her flat in Neustadt. She took a route which led through the Postplatz, past the ruins of the post office from which her father had escaped, and so on to the Altmarkt, the old market square of Dresden.

What I saw at the Altmarkt was cruel. I could not believe my eyes. A few of the men who had been left over [from the Front] were busy shovelling corpse after corpse one on top of the other. Some were completely carbonized and buried in this pyre, but nevertheless they were all burnt here because of the danger of an epidemic. In any case, what was left of them was hardly recognizable. They were buried later in a mass grave on the Dresdner Heide.

These were terrible days and nights and one does not like to reflect too much on them. The time following the raids was also terrible. One could not get anything. The shops were all bombed out, and besides many people had left Dresden altogether. What little stock of foodstuffs was still available was soon exhausted, and there had not been enough to go round anyway. We even had to fetch our water at the nearest street crossing where someone had turned on a hydrant. Later came the Russians and that was the last straw. What little we had was stolen and they had, as we said, 'liberated us from everything'.

Ruth Pieper worked in Neustadt at the railway hotel but lived in Blasewitz with her mother and father. Father, who drove a taxi, was out that night playing skittles. Ruth and her mother got out of Dresden on the morning of 14 February and went to stay with friends in the beautiful Saxon Switzerland stretch of the Elbe.

Ruth did not have much air raid experience. She used to go to the Baltic for seaside holidays, where an occasional Allied fighter would machine-gun the beaches; from Travemünde too she had seen V2s fired over the island of Rügen. The take-off of the rockets was like 'a flash of lightning, with a rumble like thunder'. And twice she had been caught in raids while passing through Berlin, but there she had been in good shelters. One guesses that it was her mother's influence which had induced her to leave their damaged house, for she returned to Dresden on 15 February.

'I was young and curious to see what had happened,' she recollected.

In the city most streets were impassable, filled with piles of rubble. In those streets were what looked like tailor's dummies (which undressed are white). But these were people with their clothes blown off. At some places I saw piles of dead people all heaped together; they may have come out of their houses and been caught by the second attack. I didn't see any burnt ones.

The area of Neustadt station had not been hit. There were no trains that day, I think, but we went back to work at the railway hotel and tried to be as normal as possible. I slept there at nights, because I didn't want to go back home and live there alone. Father had not come back.

I couldn't do much about finding father. The people who shouted so much before – the ARP crowd – you didn't see them now. Conditions were chaotic, there was no organization. I went round the town on my own. I knew he had had his car with him, and I knew the pub he had gone to. I discovered that he had been seen alive after the first attack, with his taxi. But not after that.

As a result of the raids, I heard people attack Hitler, but not the British. He certainly was a troublemaker.

I was quiet, though frightened, during the raids, but three years later I started to wake up in the night, screaming. That was embarrassing. Was it the raids – or the Russians? I don't know which was the more scary.

Ruth was twenty-one at the time of the raids. Anneliese Richter, who was only fifteen years old, also suffered later, and still does (although she has a British husband and lives in England). Sometimes she becomes ill with the memories, reliving it all again in dreams – seeing lights, and the flames sweeping across the road in gusts and the fires burning again. Perhaps it will never go away, she thinks. 'When I was younger, I thought I'd come to terms with it, but not now. I think it may be because of having to be brave at the time, when really I needed protection.'

*   *   *

For the prisoners in Eddie Taylor's camp near the mine at Brüx in which they worked, the pounding of Dresden was a terrible spectacle. 'You got a sinking feeling in your heart,' said Eddie. But it was also a victory in their undeclared battle with the guards and the German war effort, which by their forced labour they were supposed to be assisting.

As would be expected, the camp guards were a mixed bunch. I would say a number of them appeared to still have confidence until the raid. They could hardly believe it had happened. It was beyond their comprehension. I remember a big German chap shaking his head and saying: 'This is the beginning of the end, we can't survive.' Up till then, other guards had thought the V-weapons would win the war for Germany, so now we taunted them, asking: 'Why can't you stop this raid then?'

We were able to ram home the fact that their defences were obviously most inadequate to cope with enemy aircraft flying right across their country almost to its Eastern border. To be able to put over some undeniable propaganda on behalf of *our* country was a most satisfying occupation.

The other Taylor, Geoff, the Australian pilot, who with his companion Smithy had spent all 14 February on the Luft-waffe airfield of Lonnewitz, trying to steal a German night fighter, spent some of the 15th on it also. Finally they gave up, worn down by hunger, cold and loss of hope. Most of the planes were locked, or had no fuel, and the only opera-tional, ready-to-fly machine they had got into had seen them spotted and turfed out by a sentry who had taken them for what they seemed to be, French slave workers. Solemnly, they picked up their pine log and walked off the airfield with it.

Later that day, they walked back into Stalag IVb at Mühlberg-on-Elbe, forty-three kilometres from Dresden. The sentry in the striped guardbox gave them a nod, an officer came out of the guardroom and interrogated them briefly but was satisfied with their story of being French prisoners who had taken some soup to a comrade lying ill in the sickbay just outside the camp. The British POWs, busy with their own escape plans, were surprised to see them back, but dumbfounded to learn that they had just walked through the gates, French fashion, instead of tunnelling under the wire, which makes far better filmic material but takes months instead of minutes.

In the camp, they had access to the Leipzig and Berlin newspapers with their reports of the Dresden raids. 'Terror-fliers', 'Air-gangsters', 'Child-murderers' were some of the emotive phrases they used, but this was not reflected in the attitude of the German guards, even though some had lost relatives or whole families in Dresden. They appeared too dazed and shocked to be capable of hatred or revenge. One guard was given leave to visit the city but told them on his return that he was unable to find the street, let alone the house, where his family had lived.

They also had the BBC news on a hidden receiver and learned, according to this source, that the Russians had asked for Dresden to be eliminated as a vital communications centre. The RAF POWs in the camp were quite convinced that the raids had achieved this object. It was not an academic question, for the faster the Russians advanced, the sooner would they be freed from the camp.

There was yet another Taylor for whom the bombing of Dresden meant a good deal. He, together with a fellow-member of the so-called British Free Corps, supposedly soon about to fight in the ranks of the Waffen-SS against the Russians, had gone into Dresden on an evening leave pass from the Neustadt barracks on 13 February. Neither of them returned to answer roll-call on the morning of 14 February, when the British SS were paraded to go into the city to relieve the first SS Pioneer detachments which had been sent there to do rescue work during the night and were now due to be relieved.

The rescue services, including ARP, the Red Cross and the Fire Brigade, had suffered heavily in the second RAF attack and so their efforts were less successful than they might have been. But sometimes there was help from unexpected quarters. For instance, the Johannstädter hospital and the Women's Clinic next to it were badly hit and burning, with the electricity cut and the wards in darkness, lit only by the fires. Some of the patients were bedridden or recovering from recent surgery. The first people to the rescue were French forced labourers whose Nissen-hutted camp in a nearby park had been set on fire in the early stages of the attack. They could have fled to safety on the banks of the Elbe nearby, but they did not. They went into the burning buildings, amid collapsing walls and the whistle of falling bombs, to rescue the sick. It was the Germans, their enemies, who praised them, so there can be no doubt of their courage. Later, some squads of SS Pioneers got through from Neustadt and reinforced the French. So slave workers and SS worked together. But this time the French were not slaves — they risked their lives to save the women and children of their enemies, because they wanted to; because they thought it right.

Eva Beyer went out continually, searching for her family, and a few days later passed by these two hospitals and the Vogelwiese park (where in peacetime the funfairs used to be), and which had housed the French slave workers.

The journey became more difficult every day. Also it became more dangerous, for low-flying aircraft were beginning to give us a lot of trouble. Will I find them or not? I wondered. As I climbed my way into the centre of the town I had to pass the Women's

Clinic. The air raid wardens were busy loading the corpses.

I went down on my knees, trembled and cried, for there really and truly lay women with new-born babies. Several women lay there with their bellies burst open, probably by the blast, and one could see the babies for they were hanging half outside. Many of the babies were mutilated. In their terror the women must have been running into the park, which received a direct hit.

Several men were running around, looking for their wives. One man found his wife, and it was heart-rending how the man bent over her body and cried and moaned. Apparently, what he was saying was: 'Oh, my God, what's going to happen!' Scenes like that one saw everywhere and very slowly one became numbed. One acted like a zombie. The people I was most sorry for were the men who had the task of shovelling corpses the whole day.

The whole of this day I walked around the town looking for my family. Emotionally, morally, I was so exhausted that I would have liked to lie down and die myself. I wasn't sure how much longer I would last. The uncertainty tormented me.

When I arrived at Junghanns bakery in the evening, Herr Junghanns had arrived from the prison, where he had been released. He asked me if I had had any success in my search. I said no. He replied: 'Go and sleep now. Tomorrow is another day.' I was very grateful for his words. They gave me some strength.

In the morning the baker asked me if I would help him to fetch some flour from the mill. I said yes, and together we went off with a little handcart. We had been under way for approximately half an hour when low-flying aircraft attacked us. I cannot describe the fear I felt. We lay flat on the ground and the planes roared above across us and fired their guns.

When, two days later, we went again to fetch some flour, we weren't so lucky. I knelt under the cart, but all the others had thrown themselves flat down on the ground. Bullets were flying left and right around us. If I had lain down flat I would either have been dead or I would have had many shots in my legs, for the cart was perforated with holes at the back. We had two dead and three seriously wounded. That I survived was a miracle.

This went on day after day. There seemed to be no end to the horror, and still there was no news from my family. I couldn't sleep properly and I could hardly eat. The uncertainty made me ill.

These two ground-strafing attacks perhaps took place as part of the *Clarion* operation (successor to *Hurricane*, turned down in 1944 as a 'terroristic' idea), which involved many small groups of heavy bombers operating all over Germany in a dispersed effort, plus the use on ground-strafing of all the 8th USAAF's fighters. 22 and 23 February were the two big days for this idea, during which, it was claimed, 'the German people received an unforgettable demonstration of Allied air power'. So, too, did the neutral Swiss, for the Americans hit the town of Schaffhausen on 22 February, following it up on 4 March with raids on Basle and Zurich.

Of the 210 (or it may have been 211) Fortresses supposed to have attacked Dresden on 15 February, not even the American official historians claimed to know where their bombs went, dropped blind through overcast, the negation of strategic bombing. People in Dresden seem not to have noticed them, although some, like Eva Beyer, heard aeroplanes at some time during the day. The USAAF historians hinted that they must have fallen into the ruins or caused damage not ascertainable by reconnaissance later, but German records show a little disturbance in outlying districts and a lot of holes in fields.

Winter weather in Europe proved a better defence to the still smoking city than did the flak and the fighters. The 381st Bomb Group which had failed to find Dresden as briefed on 13 February tried again on the 15th, putting up only twenty-four aircraft instead of the usual three dozen. The Group's historian reported:

Although the formation was briefed for clear weather over Dresden, Capt. MacNeill in the lead ship was informed by the weather scout that it would be 10/10. There was no flak at the target but the formation encountered anti-aircraft fire both at Brüx and at the bomb line. It was meagre and inaccurate although it covered a wide area. The formation bombed Dresden, using PFF methods. Two of our aircraft hit other targets.

Both the 41st and the 379th Bomb Groups had Bohlen, not Dresden, as their primary target. 'Buckeye Red', the weather scout aircraft, didn't exactly get lost, but 'said he couldn't pinpoint himself exactly but it was 10/10ths over the entire area of the Primary Target (Bohlen), that it looked as if it might be 7 to 10/10ths at the Secondary and he advised us to go to the Secondary, which we did,' reported the historian of the 41st. 'We bombed by squadrons at 1151. There was 10/10ths undercast at the target and bombing results were unobserved. There was no flak at the Secondary Target.'

The 379th Bomb Group had weather trouble already, back in England, before take-off.

Due to fog and a heavy ground haze at the base, only five planes were able to take off for the mission. The primary target was completely undercast, and the secondary target at Dresden was bombed by Pathfinder. As the 'mickey' equipment in the lead aircraft of our five-plane high squadron was inoperative, the squadron dropped off the group leader's release. No anti-aircraft fire was encountered over the target, and only light flak was met on the route.

Dresden, with little left in it to defend, was still defenceless.

Of course, there were Americans in the city as prisoners. The working party, of which the paratrooper Clyde Smith was a member, were billeted in a school on the southern outskirts. Of the RAF night raids, he wrote:

We were lucky not to be burned or hurt, but we knew God had to be with us. The next day around noon (14 February) American bombers came over and I said: Here we go again! But we were lucky. They seemed to have certain targets, like the railway station, where a lot of people went for shelter but plenty were killed there.

We didn't work for four days after that because the city was still burning. The stench was awful with bodies burning. They took us in to dig out underground lines. For what, I don't know; the city was gone. They were digging out the dead, you could see legs or arms under rubble and a lot of families died in the cellars or basements of their homes from lack of oxygen. We saw an American plane down between the streets and the Elbe River, but we couldn't get close to it.

One day our guards were soldiers from the Russian Front and they made it hard on us; we didn't get much rest that day. The people took the bombing out on us; they cursed and spit on us. We heard that there was some prisoners from other groups that was shot for looting. If you picked up anything they would call it looting.

It was several days after the RAF night raids before another working party of Americans, the one that contained Henry Leclair and Kurt Vonnegut, and which had survived because they had been sent into the meat-lockers under the slaughterhouse, was also ordered into the ruins. Prisoners of war of many nationalities were working there, brought together from all over the world to dig for bodies under the hot, smoking ruins of the city on the Elbe. Many times they struck pavement or huge blocks of sandstone too huge to lift, because no machinery could be manoeuvred across the rubble mountains. Then for the first time they came across timber beams holding up the debris over a dark hole under the ruins. Holding a torch, a German soldier clambered down into the dark. There was a long wait. When he came up, he reported that the dark hole was a cellar which had been under a house. It was still lined with benches all round the walls and on the benches dozens of people were still sitting. An officer ordered the entrance enlarged, a ladder put down, and the bodies brought out. 'Thus began the first corpse mine in Dresden,' wrote Kurt Vonnegut, who had helped to dig it.

At first, the stench was not too bad. But then pools of evil, greenish liquid began to form and spread out from under the bodies; all the bodies in all the cellars all over the city. After that, the SS Pioneers brought in flamethrowers and burnt out the cellars with their contents. Of all people, they knew best what the next stages of decomposition would be, as the days went by and the weather warmed. The clouds of giant flies, the heaving mass of maggots moving where it would no longer be possible to tell flesh from cloth. For it is only in this semi-liquid way that dust actually returns to dust.

Somewhere at this time in the obscene landscape of rubble, the old high school teacher who had stood up to Campbell, the recruiter for the Free American Corps of the SS, found a battered teapot and rescued it from the debris. Of course, technically he was guilty of looting rather than salvage. Certainly, the court which tried him thought so. So, amid tens of thousands of unburied corpses, they formally sentenced him to death. He was forty-five, far too old ever to have been a foot soldier, which in fact he was; he was old enough to have a son in the Marine Corps. But they told off a firing squad of four, and tied a piece of paper to his breast as an aiming mark, and afterwards Kurt Vonnegut helped to bury him, remembering how he had faced the rifle muzzles, glassy-eyed and silent. Perhaps they had doped him up a bit.

There was nothing discriminatory about the shooting. Germans were getting the same treatment, and if they were civilians, then often without the formality of a trial and firing squad. The unlucky ones were hanged. The bodies of 180 of the more fortunate were later found in a shallow grave. They had been dispatched by the method long since proven by the Soviet NKVD and now confirmed by the Nazis — the bullet in the back of the head. Their offence, it was supposed, had been either to criticize Hitler or to express doubts about Germany being able to win the war.

Charlotte Mann, thirty-six, and her fifty-year-old husband were now living in the cellar of their house, because although they had managed to put out the fires which had ravaged the upper storeys, the rooms above were still open to the elements. They stayed in the cellar for two weeks, hardly taking off their clothes. The wound on Charlotte's face, which she had received from a blazing timber, slowly began to heal. Her parents stayed with them for the first few days after the raid (they had been bombed out of their house, some ten minutes' walk away, and had lost almost everything). But they became very nervous because of the continual daylight raids and decided to trek out of Dresden to a refugee camp for the bombed-out which had been established on the Elbe, upriver.

My heart nearly broke as I watched them walk away, without my being able to do anything for them — my mother bewildered and confused and my father carrying a little rucksack with not very much in it.

In the streets lay many completely charred bodies, all people who had been too exhausted to go on or had been caught by the fire-storm. I myself got on my way after a few days in order to check up on my firm, but it had been destroyed. Then I went to see my boss, who lived in the southern part of Dresden. There was a lot standing there. I made this journey on my bike, and I saw so many sad things that to this day I find it difficult to talk about. I had to ride past the main station, getting off my bike many times because of the rubble. There at the railway station lay heaps of dead people. Some held under their arm a little package, or a child. Burnt, or asphyxiated, or lungs torn by blast, they were gruesome sights. People were already beginning to tidy up but did not quite seem to know how and where to begin.

My boss was starting up his firm again in a small way from his home and he gave me leave, so that I could put my flat in order again. We repaired our roof as best we could, put cardboard in the windows where the glass was missing, straightened up the doors so that they would open and close, and finally made two rooms livable. But the long-distance central heating system had been destroyed, so in order to make the place just a little warm with a small stove we went out searching for wood among the wreckage.

In our search we came to a house which was partly shattered. We heard voices and screaming. I fetched some more helpers and we dug and shifted stones and did indeed find some people who had not been able to get out of the cellar in time. Some of them were slightly injured. And this rescue after four days and four nights down there. The joy was so great that we had found and freed them despite all the sadness and despair around us. And this was not an isolated incident!

For the first two weeks, when we lived in the cellar, we received our lunch in a nearby school which had been turned into a public kitchen. We had no coal for our own kitchen range in the flat, but we had a tiny emergency stove called a Hexe on which we could cook and heat a little. Only a long time after the war, when the situation had eased, were we able to get some craftsmen who could repair our houses and flats properly.

Maria Rosenberger, who had fled from Breslau as a refugee with the Riedel family, had a sister who lived in Dresden. On the night of the RAF raids they had been caught sitting in a restaurant in the city centre. Knowing all the ways and short-cuts through the beautiful old town, her sister had found a way out of the 'witches' cauldron' of blazing streets, had led her beyond the main station and put Maria on the road to her lodgings on the Räcknitzhöhe, a height on the way south to Bannewitz. From there, next day in daylight, she heard the massed USAAF Fortresses go over, but escaped injury from a low-flying fighter; she just heard the sound of its engine and whistling noises of things going over her head as she stood by the garden fence. This decided the Riedels, who had two children, one seven years old, the other only 1½, and, carrying their belongings on an overloaded pram, they trekked further out to the refugee camps which had been set up at Bannewitz.

But Maria wanted to find out if her sister still lived, for she had taken advantage of the lull after the first wave of RAF bombing to go to her own flat, which was in the opposite direction to Maria's temporary lodging.

A person who knew the city somehow managed to direct me to her flat. The walk there — it was some days after the raid already — was horrifying. All those corpses, some of them in the most dreadful condition and in almost unreal circumstances.

One woman was still sitting in a destroyed tramcar as if she had merely forgotten to get out. But many of the corpses were naked. For instance, a completely shrivelled corpse of a man, naked, his skin like brown leather, but with a beard and hair on his head. All this was simply terrible.

On the carbonized door-frames of the burnt-out houses were little bits of paper with addresses written on them. There were some of these also in my sister's house, which was also an empty, burnt-out ruin. I stuck on it a message of my own, asking her to let me know if she was still alive.

After three days, at last I had word from her. After we had left each other behind the main station, she went on to the bank of the Elbe where she was surprised by the second raid which — thank God — she survived. After that, as her house was on fire, she managed to get out to the suburb of Klotzsche where she remained until the end of the war.

The Daniel family had been overjoyed to be able to escape across the rubble to Neustadt, Dora pulling baby Holm in his pram, the crippled husband pushing, and her daughter Bärbel walking. They went to her parents' place, which was already full of aunts and uncles who had been driven out of Silesia by the Russians. In all, there were now thirteen of them, living in two rooms and a kitchen.

'Later on,' Mrs Daniel recalled, 'our chemist joined us and offered us her four-roomed flat.'

She wanted to go with her family out of Dresden as far as Radebeul, but she didn't want to leave the flat empty. When I heard that, I didn't trust my ears, and when I saw the flat, I didn't trust my eyes. A four-roomed flat complete with beds new-made with sheets, a dining room, a store of baby foods and all the other things a chemist has a stock of. And they were willing to let us in.

After we had all had a bath and got into our clean beds, my husband said, what every refugee who has gone through smoke, dirt and danger will confirm is true: 'No, really, it couldn't be more beautiful than this in heaven!'

Unfortunately, in those days I didn't pray. But after a hearty and honest 'The Lord be thanked', we all slept deep until next morning. Even our little Holm slept right through with us.

The only thing that spoilt the beauty of our paradise were the rows and rows of farm carts, loaded up high with corpses, which coming from the town passed through Grossenhainerstrasse where we now lived to the Waldfriedhof cemetery. I had to fetch Bärbel away from the window so that she wouldn't see that terrible sight. But nothing could disguise the fact that the air was heavy with the smell of rotting corpses.

Her husband, who was keeping an occasional diary at this time, wrote:

They have counted 256,000 dead, and that is without the ones who were killed outright without a trace. First they brought them in wagons to the outskirts of Dresden for burial. Then they burnt them in the Altmarkt. The recoveries and burials took weeks, and there was the danger of epidemics breaking out. It was a miracle we survived. What misery existed. There were children dead whose parents were still alive, and parents dead whose children were left behind. For them, life is hardly worth living any more. We are very grateful that we are all still alive and together. When the war is over, all we have to do is build everything up again.

Gisela-Alexandra Moeltgen, the wife of the surgeon at the

Friedrichstadt hospital, was actually sitting in a train in the main station, the Hauptbahnhof, when the sirens howled for the first time, and only survived the holocaust of burning trains and people trapped below in the underground rooms because she decided to flee the station altogether, and got out in time. She went to her flat near Grosser Garten, but that also was set on fire by the RAF in the second wave of attack. All the wonderful paintings and fine carpets, gone. With her husband and a colleague, she reached the southern suburb of Nöthitz, a mile or so before Bannewitz, by the early morning of 14 February. There were fires burning there, too, though they were soon put out, and she knocked up some friends living nearby. They gazed at her blankly, for she and her husband were pitch-black with dirt and soot, two unrecognizable apparitions.

We stayed with our friends, and all night − and for the following eight days − these good people cooked soup and food from morning till night for the refugees passing south along the road. The spectacle on that road was heartbreaking, those few who had survived moving along with their last possessions, all they had in the world. On the next and the following day we had one heavy day-raid each day directed at the outskirts of the city. It was terrible sitting and waiting in those stone cellars from which there would have been no escape. Our nerves were at breaking point, the fear of death was constantly with us. Now we knew what war was like. For eight days we did not take off our clothes, not even at night, so that we could be ready at a moment's notice. No lights at night, many more air raid warnings. Hans had gone to his clinic on the following day, but when he returned he broke down completely. On the way he had seen sights which one cannot describe.

On the 19th February, Mrs G. and I made a second attempt to get to Murnau (where my two little boys were living in the house of my parents). We were taken by horse and cart to Freital from where, it was said, some trains would leave. My state of health was no better but at least I could see a goal now − my children. We travelled for three days, a gruesome journey. At Hof, there were three full air raid alarms in one night, which we had to spend lying on the ground waiting for trains, and with refugees, nothing but refugees everywhere, in an atmosphere of panic. But we reached Murnau — and I held my children in my arms.

11
'Acts of Terror and Wanton Destruction'

INTERNATIONAL REPERCUSSIONS:
FEBRUARY–APRIL 1945 AND AFTER

Where then is Germany's weak point? It is to be found in precisely the sphere in which I began this paper by stating that we had a great strength. All the evidence of the last war and this shows that the German nation is peculiarly susceptible to air bombing. While the ARP services are probably organized with typical German efficiency, their total disregard to the well-being of the population leads to a dislocation of ordinary life which has its inevitable reaction on civilian morale. The ordinary people are neither allowed, nor offer, to play their part in rescue or restoration work; vitually imprisoned in their shelters or within the bombed area, they remain passive and easy prey to hysteria and panic without anything to mitigate the inevitable confusion and chaos . . . This, then, is their weak point compared with ourselves, and it is at this weak point that we should strike and strike again.
– Lord Trenchard, 19 May 1941

On 16 February 1945, an odd happening occured at SHAEF, the Supreme HQ of the Allied Expeditionary Forces under General Eisenhower, which had a part-share in the strategic bombers of the RAF and USAAF and might therefore be assumed to have some responsibility for their actions. The recent very heavy air attacks on Berlin, Magdeburg, Dresden, Chemnitz and other cities behind the Eastern Front, supposedly at the request of the Russians, could be interpreted as intervention in the ground battles with the object of aiding an ally; or, alternatively, as strategic rather than tactical bombing, designed to cripple or terrorize the German into surrender. Within the US Strategic Air Force command structure at this moment an inquiry was going on to try to establish whether the USAAF's part in the recent operations was precision bombing or in reality an indiscriminate attack on cities, and if the latter, under the authority of which directive? The recent deliberations of the Allied leaders at Malta on 31 January, just prior to meeting Stalin at Yalta, has resulted in a directive which could be read as a licence to kill at random in large numbers. And on 3 February, just one day before Yalta, the 8th USAAF had indeed killed as many as 25,000 people in a single raid on Berlin. Against the background that the USAAF up to now had proclaimed that it 'did not intend to throw the heavy bomber at the man in the street', a suitable formula was devised. As the USAAF official historians were to put it: 'The Americans were not bombing cities indiscriminately, but attacking transportation facilities inside cities in missions which the Russians had requested and seemed to appreciate.'

In these highly delicate high-level circumstances, SHAEF on 16 February put up an RAF Air Commodore to tell a press conference all about the recent change of Allied air policy. The American official historians recorded that 'an RAF officer described how the air forces planned to bomb large population centres and then attempt to prevent relief supplies from reaching and refugees from leaving them – all part of a general programme to bring about the collapse of the German economy,' but that this press talk was exaggerated and misrepresented by Associated Press, which accused the American air commanders but 'clear SHAEF' of responsibility.

The Associated Press report of the conference was cabled to America on the 16th and widely used the following day. It read:

Allied air chiefs have made the long-awaited decision to adopt deliberate terror-bombings of German population centres as a ruthless expedient of hastening Hitler's doom. More raids such as those recently carried out by heavy bombers of the Allied air forces on residential sections of Berlin, Dresden, Chemnitz and Kottbus are in store for the Germans, for the avowed purpose of heaping more confusion on Nazi road and rail traffic, and to sap German morale. The all-out war on Germany became obvious with the unprecedented daylight assault on the refugee-crowded capital, with civilians fleeing from the Red tide in the East.

The news came as a shock to the American public who believed that their own air force attacked only military objectives, never mind what other people's air forces did. In England, too, the report produced disquiet, but not so widely, because it was instantly and effectively suppressed. But of course, the report came in to the newspaper offices in London, where Cecil King, director of the *Daily Mirror*, saw it:

The most shattering item was put out tonight by SHAEF, saying that at last the long-expected orders had been given and that to shorten the war we were resorting to terror bombing. Recent attacks on Berlin, Dresden, and Chemnitz had been directed at the refugees swarming into these cities and were part of this policy. This is entirely horrifying. Not only does it make nonsense of all our protestations about our war aims and about our bombing policy: it gives official proof for everything that Goebbels ever said on the subject. It is wicked as well as being typically un-British . . . I cannot help feeling that the price, political and moral, we shall have to pay for all this will be a grievous one. We rang up the Ministry of Information as soon as the news came in, to urge that it be suppressed – a very forlorn hope – and in any case did not print it.

In due course, the RAF's official historians, while admitting the 'serious embarrassment' caused to the British Air Staff and Air Marshal Harris by the AP dispatch, admitted that RAF policy generally could be 'not inaccurately, described as "terror bombing" ', and that the AP message 'accurately, though, perhaps, injudiciously, described the aims of the attacks on Dresden and the other towns which it mentioned'. They quarrelled only with the statement that a 'radically new kind of bombing policy had been adopted'. They pointed out that nothing had changed and that the bombing policy, which could be called terror bombing, had been initiated by the politicians, especially Winston Churchill. There was no question of unnamed 'Allied Air Chiefs' deciding for themselves.

The USAF historians were equally candid in admitting that, in respect of the American air forces (unlike the British), there had indeed been a notable change of policy at around this time. They cited the launching of the city-burning raids by B-29 Super Fortresses on Japanese cities and the use of unmanned, radio-controlled B-17s packed with ten tons or more of high explosive against German towns back in January.

On the other hand, when it came down specifically to the raids on Dresden, the same American historians, a few pages later, stated: 'The Secretary of War had to be appraised of Dresden's importance as a transportation center and the Russian request for its neutralization.' (There had been no specific Russian request for the bombing of Dresden, regardless of what anybody might have told the Secretary for War.) Perhaps the Americans felt that it was the RAF which had carried out most of the terror bombing, and they were able only to hint that the RAF communiqué had grossly exaggerated Dresden's industrial importance. However, they concluded with a soothing statement of their own that, although 'casualties were exceptionally high and damage to residential areas great, it was also evident the city's industrial and transportation establishments had been blotted out'. But it was far from evident in Dresden, whatever may have been reported on the distant side of the Atlantic.

Only in Britain was it possible to keep the massacres from becoming public knowledge, and then for a time only. Representatives from neutral coutries such as Sweden and Switzerland were present in Germany, especially in Berlin. In Britain, the American services newspaper *Stars and Stripes* circulated; one edition admitted the presence of 'thousands of evacuees' in Dresden. The German press was full of anger against the bomber crews: *'Terrorflieger'*, *'Luftgangster'*, *'Kindermörder'*. Nevertheless, the German leaders were themselves, quite clearly, gangsters who ruled by terror and slaughtered children; indeed, one of their most effective methods of dealing with opposition was to see to it that a man's family suffered with him for what he had done.

In the atmosphere of 1945, it took a brave man to speak up publicly in Britain and to accuse the British government of war crimes in terms similar to those employed by the enemy's propagandists. However, on 6 March Richard Stokes did this in a debate in the House of Commons. Together with a small group, which included the Marquess of Salisbury and the Bishop of Chichester, Dr Bell, he had been opposing the area bombing policy since 1942, suspecting that it was both inefficient and inhumane. Now, he referred particularly to reports of the bombing of Dresden (obtained by a British newspaper from German sources) and asked if it was wise to perpetrate deeds such as these in the closing stages of the war:

What are you going to find, with all the cities blasted to pieces, and with disease rampant? May not the disease, filth and poverty which will arise be almost impossible either to arrest or to overcome? I wonder very much whether it is realized at this stage. When I heard the Minister speak of the 'crescendo of destruction',

I thought: What a magnificent expression for a Cabinet Minister of Great Britain at this stage of war.

The minister concerned, Sir Archibald Sinclair, had pointedly left the Chamber before Stokes rose to speak, and his official denial was given only hours later and through the mouth of a depty, Commander Brabner:

We are not wasting bombers or time on purely terror tactics. It does not do the Hon. Member justice to come here to this House and suggest that there are a lot of Air Marshals or pilots or anyone else sitting in a room trying to think how many German women and children they can kill.

But of course, that was exactly what some officers had seemed to be trying to do at High Wycombe for years. Had they been Germans, and guilty of such deeds against their enemies, they would almost certainly have faced a trial for war crimes.

The officers concerned were no doubt too firm in their beliefs for this sad thought to occur to them. The politicians proved a good deal more sensitive. The Prime Minister himself was to demonstrate this three weeks later.

On 6 March, the same day as that on which the debate had taken place in London, Dr Joseph Goebbels, propaganda minister of the Third Reich, recorded in his diary that he had been visited in Berlin by Ludolf von Alvensleben, Dresden's SS and police chief. This was the more tactful man who had replaced Rudolf von Woyrsch, the outspoken SS Obergruppenführer who had lost his internal Party feud with Gauleiter Mutschmann of the SA. Goebbels wrote: 'He painted a horrifying picture of the Dresden catastrophe. This was a real tragedy such as has seldom been seen in the history of mankind and certainly not in the course of this war. Life in Dresden is slowly beginning to emerge from the ruins.' And this was only three weeks afterwards. What was being contemplated by Hitler at this moment was intended to make destruction final; and throughout Germany.

On 18 March a fateful Führer Conference took place in Hitler's command bunker in Berlin. Speer had sent the German leader a memorandum which might cost him his head — and also the lives of his wife and their six children. He had included in his text the warning that 'the final collapse of the German economy' could be expected 'with certainty' within four to eight weeks — an accurate prophecy.

To illustrate the personal risks that Speer took in merely stating facts, that day's Wehrmacht communiqué had included the news that four officers had been shot for allegedly not doing their utmost to prevent the American army from capturing the Rhine bridge of Remagen. Field Marshal Model, who commanded on that front, told Speer in confidence that the four officers were totally innocent; Hitler was merely shooting them in order to 'encourage the others'.

That very morning of 18 March, the German newspaper least favoured by Dr Goebbels, *Das Reich*, had commented in restrained terms on the Dresden catastrophe. As recently as 2 March, the propaganda minister had written that he was 'very vexed' with this paper, which 'plays the role of a sort of outsider'. He was going to take 'energetic steps to stop this'. On this day, the paper picked up the spate of Allied denials which had followed the unfortunate Air Commodore's comments as reported by Associated Press and used in newspapers and on radio around the world (except in Britain). *Das Reich* rejected the Allied protestations that the bombing of Dresden had been merely an ordinary air raid aimed at military objectives and that the presence of refugees, which had rendered the results far more frightful, had been a fortuitous circumstance.

The Dresden attack, they pointed out:

has two features which distinguish it from other happenings of a similar nature and of recent date. (1) the three raids − two during the night of 13 February and one the following midday − have, in so far as it is possible to draw comparisons, resulted in the most absolute destruction of a large town area and by far the greatest number of civilian casualties of any air raid. A city of perfect architectural harmony has been lost to Europe. Tens of thousands of those who lived and worked under its spires and turrets have been buried in mass graves without any attempt at identification being possible. And (2) Allied headquarters in Paris (SHAEF) countered the news of the destruction of Dresden, which would have a dreadful impact if realized at once, by spreading slowly and by degrees a denial of unbelievable cynicism. They said that it was untrue that the Allied air chiefs had decided to bomb residential areas deliberately.

The writer had put his finger on a facet of the destruction which, he can hardly have realized, was to long outlast this almost-finished war and endure for more than thirty years of peace. In both the UK and the USA a high level of sophistication was to be employed in order to excuse or justify the raids, or to blame them on someone else. It is difficult to think of any other atrocity − and there were many in the Second World War − which has produced such an extraordinary aftermath of unscrupulous and mendacious polemics.

The journlist in *Das Reich* then gave his own version of what had happened:

In the late hours of 13 February, strong Anglo-American bomber forces bombed the centre of the city on both sides of the Elbe and also the encircling ring of residential streets, and reduced them to blazing ruins. What had stood there previously can be seen on any map of the city printed in 1944: dwelling houses, streets of shops, a few dozen public buildings . . . That evening there must have been one million souls within the city: several hundred thousand bombed-out people and refugees from the two neighbouring Silesian provinces in addition to the 600,000 population. Sheets of flame consumed the narrow, closely-built streets, where many people found a quick death from lack of oxygen. At midnight a second enemy air fleet appeared in the red sky of the Elbe valley and bombed the masses of people who had fled to the green, open spaces in a way that no one but Ilya Ehrenburg could conceive. Twelve hours later, on Wednesday, when the sirens were out of action, a third attack laid a fresh belt of destruction upon the periphery of the city where the streams of homeless humanity might be expected to be. And on the following day, at midday again, enemy formations bombed the villages further along the Elbe valley where the long columns of refugees were seeking shelter. Those are the four acts of a coldly calculated plan of murder and destruction.

On the evening of the day in which this edition of *Das Reich* appeared, to condemn the infamy of the Allied air leaders, the Führer Conference took place. A plan was put forward, and confirmed, which would wreak upon the German people a havoc far more serious than anything Churchill or the air marshals and generals had ever been able to create. What they had merely tried to do, the Nazi Party organization would actually do to Germany on Hitler's order. This order was issued next day, 19 March, as the first of the 'Nero Commands'. Speer had survived the conference because he was a long-standing friend of Hitler, who admired him as an architect, and by means of a device: at the same time as he submitted his pessimistic memorandum, he asked Hitler for an autographed photograph. When the conference ended in the early hours of 19 March, Hitler told Speer in icy tones:

This time you will receive a written reply to your memorandum! If the war is lost, the people will be lost also. It is not necessary to worry about what the German people will need for elemental survival. On the contrary, it is best for us to destroy even these things. For the nation has proved to be the weaker, and the future belongs solely to the stronger eastern nation. In any case, only those who are inferior will remain after this struggle, for the good have already been killed.

This was an admirably honest expression of Hitler's basic beliefs: that the German nation was not worthy of him; he had failed only because *they* had let *him* down.

Speer and those who felt like him were now left with a decision to take: not whether to oppose Hitler openly, because that was certain, instant death, achieving nothing; but whether or nor to obstruct, sabotage and delay the deadly 'Nero Commands' at the risk not merely of their lives but the lives of their families also, for Hitler, like Stalin, used this dreadful lever to obtain obedience. With few exceptions, the Allied pilots had obeyed their orders, although with some reluctance; but they were ordered only to destroy their enemies. Speer and the remaining functionaries of the Third Reich were being commanded to make any future at all impossible for Germany, for their own people.

The most amazing turnabout of Winston Churchill's long political career was represented by the memorandum he wrote on 28 March 1945 to the Chiefs of Staff Committee, composed of the leaders of the three services — Admiral Cunningham, Field Marshal Brooke, Air Marshal Portal — plus General Ismay as the Prime Minister's deputy. An additional copy of this letter went to the Chief of Air Staff, Portal, who must have been both astonished and infuriated when he read it:

It seems to me that the moment has come when the question of bombing of German cities simply for the sake of increasing the terror, though under other pretexts, should be reviewed. Otherwise we shall come into control of an utterly ruined land. We shall not, for instance, be able to get housing materials out of Germany for our own needs because some temporary provision would have to be made for the Germans themselves. The destruction of Dresden remains a serious query against the conduct of Allied bombing. I am of the opinion that military objectives must henceforward be more strictly studied in our own interests rather than that of the enemy.

The Foreign Secretary has spoken to me on this subject, and I feel the need for more precise concentration upon military objectives, such as oil and communications behind the immediate battle-zone, rather than on mere acts of terror and wanton destruction, however impressive.

Rarely can a more astounding, not to say intimidating, message have been received by an air marshal, except perhaps on that occasion when it was Portal telling Harris that it was the American air force which was winning the war, not Bomber Command. The bold statement that Bomber Command was carrying out 'terror' attacks, just as Goebbels said, and disguising the fact by telling untruths, must have been particularly galling to Portal, who was to continue to the end of his life to justify the bombing campaign. The Prime Minister's 'mere acts of terror and wanton destruction' was a bold slap in the face, while to write that 'the destruction of Dresden remains a serious query against the conduct of Allied bombing' could, in the climate of the time, hardly be construed in any other way than that it might be ranked as a 'war crime' by any disinterested observer. The references to the utterly ruined, diseased land the Allied forces would inherit was not taken quite word-for-word from Richard Stokes's speech in the House of Commons three weeks earlier; and indeed, was all too true, as the British army was very shortly to find out.

Portal had a reputation for calmness and conciliation which was severely strained by this memorandum. It was only two months since Churchill, on 26 January, the eve of the Yalta Conference at which he had wished to impress Marshal Stalin, had sent a 'hurry up' minute to Sinclair, the Air Minister, which read:

I did not ask you last night about plans for harrying German retreat from Breslau. On the contrary, I asked whether Berlin, and no doubt other large cities in East Germany, should not now be considered especially attractive targets. I am glad that this is 'under examination'. Pray report to me tomorrow what is going to be done.

That minute had resulted in the decision to bomb Dresden, although it is true that Harris had wanted to do so for some time. It was the Prime Minister himself who in effect had signed the death warrant for Dresden, which had been executed by Harris. And it was Churchill, too, who in the beginning had enthusiastically backed the bomber marshals in carrying out the indiscriminate area bombing policy in which they all believed. They were all in it together, Portal himself, Harris of course, Trenchard too, and the Prime Minister most of all. And many lesser people.

It took Portal some thirty-six hours, but at length he made Churchill reconsider the memorandum, withdraw it and issue a less damning indictment of his bomber marshals. All references to 'wanton terror' bombing disappeared; the very name of Dresden vanished. Instead there appeared 'area bombing' and a recap of Mr Stokes's views on the disadvantages of distroying a land you are shortly going to occupy.

In his autobiography *Bomber Offensive*, published in

1947, Harris was to disclaim responsibility for the policy of area bombing, and in this he was correct, although he was to become its most ardent and ruthless practitioner. He also denied having a hand in the Dresden decision, commenting: 'the attack on Dresden was at the time considered a military necessity by much more important people than myself'. So it was indeed, but, as the RAF official historians commented: 'Dresden took its place alongside Leipzig and Chemnitz as among the towns which Sir Arthur Harris had for some time believed to be in urgent need of destruction.'

Much later, in *The RAF and Two World Wars*, Portal was to attempt to justify Dresden by arguments which relied for their success on the ignorance of the audience regarding matters outside their normal sphere. 'Early in 1945, it seemed to the Allies that Germany was far from beaten. The Ardennes offensive had a profound impact.' In sober fact, it was clear at least as early as July 1944 that Germany was irrevocably beaten, and although the Ardennes offensive produced some red faces on the Allied side, that gambler's throw had failed before Christmas, and all the Allied armies – Russian, American, British, Canadian, French – were building up prior to pouring over the last river barriers and flooding forward into Germany in overwhelming power.

But Portal had a second 'crisis' argument to deploy, writing profoundly: 'There was the threat of other new weapons; there was even the risk of nuclear attack.' The sober truth was that the Allies had been so concerned about German nuclear research that they had pinpointed Strasbourg as an important research centre and captured the city by an unexpected thrust, with nuclear scientists following close behind the leading troops. That had been in November 1944. They were able to report: 'Germany has no atom bomb and is not likely to have one within any reasonable time.' And the scientific head of the mission added that the German effort was still on a purely academic level: 'They were about as far as we were in 1940, before we had begun any large-scale efforts on the atom bomb at all.' In short, the Germans were four years away from making a bomb, and the Allies knew it months before Dresden.

Britain was fortunate in her official historians for the RAF, Sir Charles Webster and Noble Frankland. Although Harris would have nothing to do with them, because he thought them ignorant of the bomber offensive, Frankland was in fact a decorated navigator of Lancasters. In Harris's background world, people died in theory; but Frankland had been over Germany where they died in fact. Their work impresses as open and fair, with all said and nothing to hide. It was they who first found and then printed the key documents showing Churchill's hand in the bombing of Dresden.

In the United States, however, one is left with the feeling of there being a very great deal more to tell. The official history by W. F. Craven and J. L. Cate indicates that there was concern both before and after Dresden about the terror aspects of air war, and at the highest levels in the States (General Arnold of the USAAF and Admiral Leahy) and in Europe (Air General Spaatz and General Eisenhower). Spaatz in particular could oppose it on grounds of inefficiency and waste, as compared to the precision bombing of oil targets. By 1944, Portal also had come round to this belief, but he felt that he could not get Harris to obey his orders; the British bomber chief could deploy too many apparently reasonable excuses for evading oil directives.

An inhibiting factor on the American side may have been a diplomatic unwillingness to condemn an ally publicly, for the British share in the atrocities committed far outweighed that of America. The USAAF came late and perhaps reluctantly into the mass-murder business. Possibly this was the reason why a specially commissioned report on the Dresden affair remained secret in America until 13 December 1978. Titled the *Historical Analysis of the 14–15 February 1945 Bombings of Dresden*, it was prepared by Joseph W. Angell for the USAAF Historical Division of the Research Studies Institute of the Air University at Maxwell air force base. Its opening sentence, however, indicated that Dresden was causing concern because of its use by the Russians in the Cold War:

The *reasons* for and the *nature* and *consequences* of the bombing of Dresden, Germany, by Allied air forces on 14–15 February 1945 have repeatedly been the subject of official and semi-official inquiries and of rumor and exaggeration by uninformed or inadequately informed persons. Moreover, the Communists have with increasing frequency and by means of distortion and falsification used the February 1945 Allied bombings of Dresden as a basis for disseminating anti-Western and anti-American propaganda. From time to time there appears in letters of inquiry to the Unites States Air Force evidence that American nationals are themselves being taken in by the Communist propaganda line concerning the February 1945 bombings of Dresden.

This report is specially valuable because it gives the numbers of bombers taking part in raids on various dates, from the 13th to the 15th of February, with their bomb-loads. Other parts of this report, though, I would dispute. For instance it states that 'Dresden was protected by anti-aircraft defences (various types), anti-aircraft guns and searchlights in anticipation of Allied air raids against the city', yet in fact the bulk of these defences had been withdrawn before 1945, and effectively Dresden lay undefended against high-level air attack.

However the report accurately summed up the object of the RAF raids: 'to devastate the city area itself and thereby choke communications *within* the city and disrupt the normal civilian life upon which the larger communications activities and the manufacturing enterprises of the city depended'. This was indeed the rationale for area bombing, which the American author justified by adding: 'Further, the widespread area raid conducted by the British entailed bombing strikes against the many industrial plants throughout the city which were thus to be construed as specific targets within the larger pattern of the area raid.' I part company with the author's conclusions here, because the centre of Dresden could not be construed as an industrial area, and it was the centre of Dresden which was selected by the RAF as their target.

The American author thought that the casualties had been minimal, no greater in proportion to the weight of attack than those suffered in other great German cities:

Contemporary British estimates were that from 8,200 to 16,400 persons were killed and that similar numbers of persons may have been seriously injured. Most of the latest German post-war estimates are that about 25,000 persons were killed and about 30,000 were wounded, virtually all of these being casualties from the RAF incendiary attack of 13–14 February . . . The most distorted account of the Dresden bombings – one that may have become the basis of Communist propaganda against the Allies, particularly the Americans, of recent years – was prepared by two former German general officers for the Historical Division, European Command (USA) in 1948. In this account, the number of dead from the bombings was declared to be 250,000. That this figure may be the *probable* number of dead, multiplied by ten for the sake of exaggeration, became apparent by comparing the weight of the Dresden bombings with the total tonnage expended by the Allies against the six other largest German cities and by comparing the various estimates of the Dresden casualties with the best estimate of the total casualties suffered by the Germans from all Allied bombings during World War II.

However, in my opinion the basis for this calculation is quite erroneous, regardless of what the actual figures for Dresden may be. Three factors are left out of the reckoning: that a fire-storm occurred; that when it happened, it engulfed a population swollen to perhaps double its normal size by refugees; and that defences and shelters even for the original population were minimal.

Mr Angell came to the conclusion that: 'With communications through Dresden made impossible as a consequence of the Allied bombings, the Russian salient in that area was rendered safe through the ensuing months of the war.' In actual fact rail communications were halted only for a few days and the Autobahn route bypassing Dresden was untouched. However, the author went on to make claims in the more cloudy area of morale:

Again, the death and destruction inflicted on the largest German city that had not before undergone large-scale bombing was almost certainly a major contribution to the final weakening of the will of the German people to resist. While the Americans, happily, cannot and would not claim credit for this aspect of the Dresden bombings, the fact remains that the RAF area raid on the city was the last of the instances during World War II in Europe when the shock effects of area bombing resulted in nearly total demoralization of a great enemy city.

However, it was claimed for Dresden that the decision to bomb was for tactical as well as strategic reasons. The author gave a hint of SHAEF involvement on his page 10, where he said that on 31 January 1945, Air Marshal Tedder, the British deputy to the American supreme commander, General Eisenhower, had listed as second priority targets for the strategic bombers: 'Berlin, Leipzig, Dresden and associated cities where heavy attack will . . . hamper movements of reinforcements from other fronts.' Two pages later, where Mr Angell was able to list in great detail the actual specific requests made by the Russians, the only rail targets the Soviet wanted 'paralysed' were 'the junctions of Berlin and Leipzig'.

A major reason for the preparation of the report may be contained in pages 13–14, where the complicated inter-force and inter-Allied organization controlling the strategic bombers is explained. Mr Angell makes it clear that in his view the 'ultimate responsibility' was held by General Eisenhower at SHAEF and that it was on his behalf that Tedder had listed Dresden as a target on 8 February 1945. Furthermore, in Mr Angell's interpretation the whole procedure came tidily under Directive No. 3 as laid down by the combined chiefs of staff (who were in effect the leading half-dozen home-based war policy makers of Britain and America).

This seems at odds with SHAEF's apparent repudiation of responsibility for the Dresden raid, and makes strange reading to anyone familiar with the documents printed by the RAF official historians, Webster and Frankland. Churchill's initiatives of 25 and 26 January 1945 do not appear; nor does Harris's desire to add the city to his list of major population centres to be erased by fire. Instead we have only Tedder on 8 February, two weeks later and a few days before the raid, mentioned in such a context as to suggest that it was his idea. The two prime movers, Churchill and Harris, appear to have vanished from the scene.

It may be that, strictly speaking, they were outside the proper chain of command and perhaps might be said to have improperly exerted their influence. Harris could, and did, plead superior orders; but Churchill could hardly hope to succeed in such a tactic, although he tried to shift the blame on to others. It may be that there is a suspicion of illegality about the command procedures which led up to the decision to destroy Dresden. If so, the reason why the subject is still regarded in some quarters as a sensitive issue would be explained.

The distaste for what was actually done there, regardless of the question of technical legality, became widespread. The condemnation of the British official historians was restrained. Having quietly equated area bombing with a policy of terror, they referred to 'the vast havoc of the continuing area offensive culminating in the devastation of Dresden'. That was the verdict of Webster and Frankland published in 1961.

Wing Commander H. R. Allen. DFC, in his book *The Legacy of Lord Tenchard* published in 1972, concluded: 'The final phase of Bomber Command's operations was far and away the worst. Traditional British chivalry and the use of minimum force in war was to become a mockery and the outrages perpetrated by the bombers will be remembered a thousand years hence.'

Allen was a former fighter pilot, but Flight Lieutenant G. D. Linacre, DFC, whom I interviewed in 1963 regarding the use of the heavies in daylight during the Normandy campaign, was a navigator in a Lancaster of a Pathfinder squadron, 635. In passing, he mentioned Dresden. 'I was glad I was not on the Dresden raid, although I had been briefed for it,' he told me, 'because this was an unnecessary massacre. But generally we did not feel like "terror bombers" because we were just doing what we were told.'

Kurt Vonnegut must have thought long and hard before making his one oblique comment on the men who bombed Dresden. He used one of his fellow prisoners, a former Mafia gangster, a hard character capable of torturing a dog simply because it bit him − he gave it a steak which he had carefully filled with sharp little bits of clock-spring, and he told how he watched the animal die in agony. But Dresden shocked him. He was proud of his record of never having killed an innocent bystander. 'No one got it from me, who didn't have it coming,' he said, sadly, gazing on the ruins.

There are many people still who will defend the Dresden massacre, mostly by claiming (falsely) that it was them or us, or, more widely, that it was just tit for tat — didn't the Germans do a lot of horrible things, too? In most cases, these people will not have the faintest notion of what really occurred in Dresden, nor why. But some, who do know, still maintain that view. Knowing that the city contained mainly women and children and old people, they still think it right to burn them all.

For them, perhaps, Christ's words recorded by Matthew: 'Whoso shall offend one of these little ones who believe in me, it were better that a millstone were hanged about his neck, and that he were drowned in the depth of the sea.'

The RAF claimed that the Russians did not really appreciate the work of Bomber Command, and that it was to educate Stalin that they bombed Dresden. Mr Angell was to insinuate that any suggestion at all of the slightest impropriety in the decision to bomb Dresden, and the deeds done there, was to follow the Communist line. But the Russians captured Dresden and they are in Dresden today. What did they and their Commie stooges really think of what they found there?

12

'Activists from the First Hour'

THE RED ARMY REACHES DRESDEN: MAY 1945

Zabashtansky: 'Above all, the soldier must hate the enemy, that is why he wants to take his revenge, and not just a little but in such a way that everything is exterminated, rooted out. And besides this it is essential for him to have a vested interest in the battle, to know why he is climbing out of the trench and exposing himself to machine-gun fire and mines. So now everything is clear and intelligible, he comes to Germany and everything there belongs to him — everything he finds, even the women, and do with it what you like — get rid of it, so that their grandchildren and great-grandchildren may still feel the terror.'
Kopelev: 'What? Does that mean killing women and children?'
Zabashtansky: 'Now wait a minute. What you're saying there about children, you crazy fellow you, that's extremism. Not all of us will kill children, you won't and I won't. But to be honest, if you like, let those who *will* do it also kill the little Fritzes in their frenzy until they've had enough — that's war, Comrade, and not philosophy or literature. Of course in books there are such things as mortality, humanism, internationalism. All OK, theoetically correct. But right now we want to let Germany go up in smoke, and when that's done we'll behave correctly again, we'll write nice little books about humanism and internationalism. Right now it's essential for the soldiers to want to fight, for them to go into battle, that's the main thing.'
— Lev Kopelev, *No Jail For Thought* (1977)

2 March 1945 was the date of H. R. Manuel's thirtieth and final mission. He flew as co-pilot to Lieutenant James Baird in 710 Squadron of the 447th Heavy Bombardment Group. There were 406 other 'heavies' in the vast formation and they carried 940.3 tons of high explosive as well as 140.5 tons of fire bombs. The target was Dresden,

specifically the marshalling yards. 'From the air, the city looked to be in a very torn-up condition. There were large areas that were flattened to the point that no building cast a shadow within those areas,' he recalled.

We ran short of fuel on the return trip and were forced to land at Mereville, France, where we borrowed 750 gallons and took off for our own base located at Rattlesden, England. Night caught us over the Channel and we were hopelessly lost when a searchlight battery picked up our call on the radio and guided us to our base where we landed at about 10 pm. We had been listed as down in flames over the target due to mistaken identity by some of our friends. One ship did go down in flames over the city, but fortunately it was not us. I left the base on 6 March and was subsequently discharged from the Air Corps.

Although the target was the marshalling yards, among the rail targets left virtually undamaged by the February raids, German records report no hits, merely a scatter of distant misses in an arc to the north (some of the bombs landing on the far side of the Elbe), and groupings of explosions at three places many miles outside the city and some miles from each other. However, it was enough to panic the Daniel family from the cosy flat which had been lent to them after they had been bombed out. There was an ammunition factory nearby and they assumed, like many innocents in many countries, that airmen never made mistakes: that the bombs which rocked their cellar had been intended for the factory.

Mrs Daniel declared with hindsight:

We should have stayed there, for neither bombs nor Russians would have touched us. But then in March came another one of those horrible raids with many bombs directed at the Göhlewerk ammunition factory nearby. Our cellar shook, and from sheer fear we decided to go back to my sister's place in the Erzgebirge. We had no idea what a frighteningly bad time was ahead for us there, in Freiberg. One morning at half-past two, we started with hand-cart and pram for the station, two and half hours' walk away. Even little Bärbel with her thin little legs managed it. She was happy and singing, so much so that my husband and I looked at each other in surprise.

At her sister's, conditions were very cramped; neverthe-less, there were proper beds for the parents and Bärbel and the baby, Holm. The change occurred when the Russians came nearer. 'My sister began to act very strangely. She walked around all the time with razor blades in her hands. My husband watched her carefully. We all decided that we would much rather die by the side of the road than fall into the hands of the Russians. After all, what can one disabled man do to help such frightened women? He has one arm amputated, and the other he can use only to a limited extent.' So they made preparations to flee from the village.

The stories of Russian atrocities which produced such suicidal tendencies in her sister, Mrs Daniel had heard only at second or third or even fourth hand. But she believed them. They all did. One of those who really knew was Major Lev Kopelev, operating a Red Army propaganda unit partly staffed by Germans for Marshal Rokossovsky's Second Belorussian Front in East Prussia. These Germans had been recruited by the National Committee for Free Germany, formed in 1943 in Moscow and headed by Erich Weinert, a German Communist poet. They were the Soviet equivalent of the Nazis' British Legion of St George, or British Free Corps, the Free American Corps, and so on. While the Nazis were intriguing against each other in Dresden, the SS against the SA as to who was to rule the city, the Russians were incubating their own nominees, who would join Marshal Konev's First Ukrainian Front when the city seemed likely to fall.

Oddly enough, and probably a major factor in Lev Kopelev's fate, was that although the Germans had recruited units of 'Free' soldiers from many nations, the number of volunteers rarely exceeded a battalion in size and often consisted of no more than a company; but from Russians and Ukrainians and all the other races and nationalities inside the USSR, the Germans had raised a complete army of something like a million men to fight on their side. Marshal Stalin's regime *needed* political indoctrination, political police, political spies, terror and torture, suspicion and denunciation, in order to function. When they entered Germany, the results proved appalling.

The job of Kopelev's unit was broadly that of a 'fifth column': to encourage retreat by sending ahead their own Germans dressed in Wehrmacht uniform with tales that the Russians were all around them and so create a panic; and by broadcasting locally to opposing German units, to secure surrenders – to take towns without fighting. But, all too often, the drunken, pillaging Russian soldiers would set fire to the captured towns and villages, slaughtering on suspicion or mere whim. The unit's third job was to explore the political attitudes of the conquered Germans and to uncover any cells of Nazi underground resistance. But at first, Kopelev noted bitterly, the only German civilians they found were corpses. The first he saw was an old woman, her dress ripped up, incongruously a telephone receiver between her thighs, where some drunken conquerer had tried to ram it up her vagina. 'They got her by a telephone booth, a spy see? So they didn't fool around,' a soldier told him.

Then they found him a local Communist, or at least a man who claimed to be one. He had all his papers, including concentration camp certificate (freed 1938), Communist Party card, valid to May 1933, and a Nazi draft card marked 'unsuitable for military service'. But it was his speech which convinced Kopelev that the man was a real Communist − Nazi turns of phrase were distinctive, so too were those of Communists. The man kept asking about his wife, who had been taken away by Russian soldiers. He had no suspicion then of what must have happened to her, and Kopelev awkwardly tried to reassure him that she had probably only been evacuated.

And then another scene. A woman with bloodied, bandaged head walking down the street, leading by the hand a little girl with tear-stained face and blood running down her legs. The little girl is thirteen; and she has been raped twice, the mother many times, and her son, aged eleven, beaten up, perhaps dead.

And another scene. A blonde Russian girl, a freed slave labourer for the Germans and now employed as a waitress in a Red Army mess, cheerfully walking down a German street, expecting soon to go home to Russia. A drunken soldier accosting her with 'Hey, Fritzie, hey, you bitch!' And the brittle, popping noise as he put a burst into her back from his submachine-gun.

Indiscriminate, often alcoholic vengeance was wreaked on everyone in sight. Kopelev found himself intervening to save Poles, Frenchmen, Dutchmen, Italians, as well as Germans. The most appalling thought for him was that these criminals would soon be going back to Russia as heroes in their thousands, to Russian women and children.

There were embittered arguments within the Red Army. Major Kopelev remembered one night particularly, when they discussed it over captured cognac. There was one captain who spouted stock newspapers phrases (you find him in all countries, all armies) – in this case: 'Our sacred vengeance' and Comrade Ilya Ehrenburg's immortal threat: 'Tremble, cut-throat nation!'

Then the young engineer officer spoke up:

We're supposed to be a Socialist army! We're supposed to be internationalists! How can you talk of vengeance on the German *people*? Remember what Comrade Stalin said: 'Hitlers come and go, but Germany goes on for ever . . . ' Ever since I was in the Pioneers I have been taught that the workers of all countries are brothers. Marx and Engels were Germans, so were Liebknecht and Thälmann; and today among the Germans there are plenty of Communists and plenty of good ordinary people. It's impossible for a whole nation to be Fascist. Only People who are Fascists themselves can think so!

If Kopelev took a similar line, often enough they would turn on him with: 'What's the matter with you? You're a Jew. How can you love the Germans? Don't you know what they've been doing to the Jews?'

Major Kopelev knew only too well, for his grandparents had perished at Babi Yar, but he hated what this uncontrolled vengeance was doing to the Red Army itself. On 5 April he was arrested and stripped of his rank, 'for gross political errors, for showing pity for the Germans, for bourgeois humanism, and for harmful statements on questions of current policy'. Probably there was hidden antisemitism behind the arrest. As an intellectual, Kopelev seems to have aroused the jealousy and resentment of his Russian superiors, who were of the peasant type which had replaced the Tsar's officer corps. One of his bitterest experiences had been to find and read a German propaganda book detailing all the atrocities committed by the Imperial Russian armies in 1914. The German author, desperate for material, had uncovered two cases of rape, a few murders, and a number of robberies and beatings – and that was all, and in every case the Russian officers had stepped in to stop it and to punish such behaviour. But then, they were the Tsar's officers, not Stalin's.

Rokossovsky, the Soviet army group commander, did

issue an order allowing immediate execution in cases of rape and pillage, but it was not enforced at unit level. I still have a copy of Field Marshal Montgomery's order of March 1945, demanding 'non-fraternization' with the Germans, but explaining that this 'implies no revenge'. The soldiers of 21 Army Group were advised: 'Be just; be firm; be correct; give orders, and don't argue.' Nobody complied with the 'non-fraternization' order unless they positively couldn't help it, but for the rest of the items, the advice was really unnecessary – unless very sorely tried, British soldiers normally behave decently.

In the West, all the armies were now across the Rhine. The Americans crossed on 23 March, meeting little resistance, only 'old men with old rifles and hearts full of hate'. The British and Canadians got over on 24 March, meeting stiffer resistance initially, but then breaking through. Leaving German-occupied Holland on their left flank, they drove north for basically anti-Russian objectives – to make quite sure they forestalled any Soviet attempt to snatch Denmark, a key geographical factor. In Holland itself, the German governor, Seyss-Inquart, opened secret negotiations with the British and Canadians designed to negate Hitler's order to blow the dykes and flood the country. Shortly afterwards, No. 75 New Zealand Squadron, which had carried fire and high explosive to Dresden, were to fly their last operations of the war to Holland with a different cargo – dropping food supplies on the Dutch capital, The Hague.

Hitler's 'Nero Command' should have ruined the Ruhr for ever, by flooding the mines and blowing all the bridges, but Speer spent a great part of March visiting generals, Gauleiters, industrialists, and other men of power, encouraging them to negate Hitler's last wish – that Germany should go down with him. Sometimes it was by bold speaking, at others by suggesting that this or that industry or target might be needed still for defence, or might be re-captured. Sometimes, it was a near thing − all the remaining buildings in Düsseldorf were within hours of being set on fire in accordance with the Führer's 'scorched earth' policy. Although the damage done to the German cities by the bombers was frightful, it was incomplete, and the effects on industry and transport were far less than Harris had hoped. The 'Nero Command' was designed to remedy this state of affairs. 'The nature of this struggle permits no consideration for the population to be taken,' the Führer emphasized on 30 March.

But Speer had already taken his decision. He had been visiting Field Marshal Model, who was proving difficult, and went for a walk over the hills. 'I could see far out over the hills of the Sauerland, the land lying between the Sieg and the Ruhr rivers. How was it possible, I thought, that one man wanted to transform this land into a desert . . . The execution of that order must be prevented.' It is indeed a beautiful place and I remember it well, for 2½ months after Speer's visit that was where I was to be, playing a small part in running occupied Germany, and it was here that I first heard whispers of something terrible having been done over in the East, at Dresden.

As the RAF official historians said, Dresden had been the culmination of the area bombing offensive waged by Harris. It had also been the most technically perfect, the raid where everything went right. Partly, that was practice and skill acquired by Bomber Command after years of operations; partly it was because there were no defences in or around the city worth the name − Dresden was defence-less. So everything worked as it should, a fire-storm re-sulted and, the morning after, Dresden lay in ashes. Of those who survived, great numbers were fleeing from the still-burning city towards the countryside. The apocalyptic visions of the air power theorists had at last come true. What followed then was the breakdown of law and order, chaos, anarchy, the loss of the government's will to fight, the collapse of all resistance. The triumph, single-handed, of air power.

But it did not in fact turn out quite like that. Certainly, the citizens of Dresden were terrified. Indeed, the more ignorant Germans now realized that the war was lost (the others had realized it quite some time ago). The Russians, of course, pursuing the Germans in their retreat from Breslau, should have swept into Dresden before the ruins had time to grow cold. But it didn't happen like that, either.

First, the German garrison of Breslau did not retreat from Breslau. They defended the city. Frau Hilde Thiel, who was born there and had left her husband Walter there, had found refuge near Dresden at the village of Rosendorf. Walter at last went into Russian captivity on 7 May, when Breslau surrendered. Even then, the Red Army was still not in Dresden, which it entered only on 8 May, the last day of the Second World War.

It is difficult to discern what effect the bombing of Dresden had on the conflict, apart from helping Dr Goebbels to whip up last-ditch hatred. Certainly, the desired terror effect was produced. For instance, the Daniel family lost their livelihood with the destruction of their hairdressing salon and finally fled the city for the safety of the Erzgebirge. But in the sum of world history, how important to the war aims of the Allies were one burnt hairdressing salon and an apprehensive family? Then again, there was Eva Beyer, who wasted day after day of her free time from the bakery in searching fruitlessly for her mother, her little sister and her brothers, who had all disappeared after the bombing. Her grief and tears were real, but by how much, if at all, did they shorten the war?

The USAAF, however, had still not finished with Dresden. On 17 April they sent out their largest force yet to the city: 572 bombers carrying 1,690.9 tons of bombs to drop on the marshalling yards, plus a further eight bombers carrying 28 tons to unload on industrial targets. They followed this on 19 April with attacks on rail targets near Dresden and on towns like Pirna, to which many refugees from Dresden had fled. But the Luftwaffe was not quite done. The Germans put up some Messerschmitt 262 jet fighters which destroyed a number of Fortresses, including five from one formation.

Meanwhile, the American fighters – Thunderbolts and Mustangs – ranged widely at low level, seeking targets of opportunity. They made life exceedingly dangerous for the POWs at Stalag IVb. During April there were many spectacular flying displays above and around the camp. On one occasion a pair of Mustangs came down and strafed a fatigue party which had been out gathering wood, killing four American prisoners, one Russian prisoner, and a German guard. In the camp itself there were further casualties. Another spectacle which had the RAF prisoners staring in amazement was the sight of three low-flying Mustang fighters repeatedly trying to kill one Russian slave worker who was trying to plough a field with oxen.

The arrival of the Red Army was frequently incongruous, particularly for the British, who were not aware of its true nature: that it was less an army than one of those human tides which from time to time submerge Europe from the East. At Stalag IVb they arrived in the middle of the night, with something much more ominous than artillery or tanks – small-arms fire close at hand in the darkness. The first

Russians Geoff Taylor saw next morning were three Cossacks — horsemen slung about with guns and bandoliers and ration-sacks. Within a few days, he wrote: 'Rape, murder, pillage stalked Saxony in the bright spring sunshine.'

For Eddie Taylor, in the work camp near the mines at Brüx which the American air raids had virtually closed down, the event was more dramatic. The Germans withdrew behind the camp as the Russians approached, so that the prisoners were in the middle. A friend, a prisoner for a long time, had both legs blown off in this last squabble; then Russian tanks drove across the wire, flattening it. But still they were not free, for the Russians did not seem to want to let them go.

The local Czechs had a private vendetta, and now was the time to settle it without interference from anybody. They hunted down two of the most hated of the German mine managers who had not been quick enough to get away, and killed them.

At about the same time, on 8 May 1945, the day the armistice was supposed to come into force at midnight, Ted Ayling's POW work party, which was employed in the nearby refinery at Brüx, was on the road with the rest of the refugees. British soldiers in old, stained battledress, German soldiers in grey-green uniforms, and civilians, all headed west in a dismal procession of defeat. Ayling wrote in his diary:

Rifles, steel helmets, and all kinds of military equipment were strewn all the way along the sides of the road, and many tanks, lorries and guns were being abandoned as the vehicles ran out of petrol, their occupants continuing on foot. A Czech boy of about 14 years of age picked up a rifle out of idle curiosity. An SS storm trooper (probably thinking of the Czech rising) observed him, paced up to him quickly, and without ado, shot him through the head at point-blank range, with the unfortunate victim's young sister as witness. This action was the most hideous piece of cold-blooded barbarism I had come across in the war.

That night, Ted arrived at Komotau, where a New Zealand doctor was manning a Red Cross post. He saw his first Russian soldier next morning, a man on a German motorbike who dismounted, rushed into the post with a submachine-gun, shook hands all round, and roared off again. When Ted went outside, the place was in Soviet occupation.

Russian vehicles of every description were travelling in every direction — to the onlooker, with no apparent system. The Russians seemed to have commandeered, apart from motor vehicles, all the horses and wagons in the district, and there was a continual din of the iron tyres of the heavy wagons and of the horses' hooves over the cobbled streets. I felt for the horses in those rough hands and hoped that they would get a drink of water and some grub. The Russians did not interfere with us in any way but we were careful, as the majority were in different degrees of drunkenness, and appeared generally uncouth and ignorant. I personally doubted if the rank and file were capable of discerning the difference between khaki and field-grey uniform when sober, and felt certain that they could not when drunk. We took care to salute all officers. Russian conduct towards females of all ages was outrageous, but I won't go into that.

Clyde Smith, the American paratrooper who had originally been in Stalag IVb too, before being put on a work party in Dresden, was also in Komotau at this time. On 14 April they had been marched away from Dresden, and somehow he and two other American POWs had got in with three British POWs and, boarding a German civilian bus, had made the last stage of the trip in comfort. Four or five days after the war, they marched out of Komotau to the west and were picked up by a convoy of American trucks.

*   *   *

'About these terrifying and often dangerous experiences I do not wish to write anything,' was the comment of one witness when it came to describing the end of the war and the arrival of the Russians. Others, having promised to talk about the bombing of Dresden and its aftermath, found when they came to the point that the memories it conjured up were too terrible, and asked to be excused. One witness, Gerhard Kühnemund, who lived in Leipzig and had merely been passing through Dresden on the night of the raids, saw his home town captured in mid-April not by the Russians but by the American army. Leipzig was in fact deep inside that area of Germany which, it had been agreed at Yalta, should be given to the Soviet Union. But, after their initial breakthrough and the bombing of Dresden which followed, the Russian army had been held well to the east of Dresden and only further north, opposite Berlin, and further north still, in East Prussia, had the Soviets been able to sweep forward. Eventually the Russians came into Leipzig too, for the Americans drew back to a line well to the west which, it had been agreed, should be the boundary of the Communist world. But that was after the war.

Marianne Hennicke, twelve years old, who had been evacuated from Breslau privately and not on one of the doomed government trains which had gone to Dresden, had fled south to Czechoslovakia. She was lying in bed, exceedingly ill with dysentery, when a Russian soldier came through the door, demanding alcohol. This was the first Red Army man she had ever seen who was not a prisoner. Seeing only a bottle of ink, he picked it up and drank − just like the ape which broke into Frau Canzler's house after the bombing of Dresden Zoo. Some of the Russians drank petrol, she recalled.

Her father had remained behind in Breslau after it was encircled early in February. He was besieged there for three months, and although the town was reduced to ruins their family home remained intact until 6 May, when Russian infantry reached it and, tossing hand grenades down into the cellar, set the house on fire. 'My parents were happy that everything in our house was burnt rather than looted,' said Marianne. She added that when the Gauleiter, Kurt Hanke, fled the city by plane, her father was the first into his cellar. He found it full of food and everything else which he had kept others short of.

Walter Thiel, who as an officer in the Wehrmacht had defended Breslau to the end, while sending his family away to safety in a village near Dresden, wrote down his impressions shortly after. He noted how the Gauleiter who had executed anyone whom he could accuse of 'defeatism', starting with the Burgermaster, had not himself manned the barricades to the end. On 5 May he had got into a Fieseler Storch, the last aircraft left in the city, and fled to safety. His final heroic message had been that he was flying away to get help, and would be back. On 6 May the garrison capitulated, and next day, 7 May, the first Russians entered. And, of course, the day after that, the war ended.

Erich Koch, the Gauleiter of East Prussia, behaved similarly. He fled in an icebreaker, broadcasting messages to suggest that he was still defending Königsberg, where he had condemned a general to death for wanting to surrender the city. Then from Admiral Dönitz he demanded the loan of a U-boat to take him to South America. The request being refused, he went underground as a civilian with a false identity. Fritz Sauckel, an even more notorious Gauleiter, fled south to the mountains. Both were caught eventually.

Eva Tornow, whose first marriage was going wrong, had left her bombed home in Dresden with her children and, accompanied by her husband, had eventually found refuge at Johnsbach in the Erzgebirge. Here, her husband should have been roped into joining the Volksturm, or Home Guard, but he evaded his call-up papers by being always absent from 'home'. Living on a farm out in the country, they found the food situation better than in Dresden, where it was appalling.

Then, over the radio came the rather hasty news that Dönitz had taken over and Germany had capitulated. We were so afraid of the Russians that we packed our two-wheeled cart with all our belongings, a sack full of rusks, and the two young boys on top of that, and marched in the direction of Czechoslovakia, where rumour had it that the British were. It must have been a few days before the armistice that we were going through the Müglitztal valley. Past us drove the functionaries and high party members of the National Socialists in their cars loaded with suitcases, furs and other loot. At some time there was another raid, this time by low-flying aircraft, allegedly British fighter-bombers: during this raid, on the bank of the River Müglitz, I threw myself on top of my children. Though terrified, we survived this, too. We all reached the top of the Erzgebirge, my mother included (she had joined us at Johnsbach).

Here we found that many of the things the fleeing Nazis had taken with them, they had later thrown away as ballast. At times, we literally waded through raisins. Sacks of sugar and flour were standing by the roadside and piles of fur jackets (to some of which we helped ourselves). Soldiers who had thrown away their weapons were slaughtering pigs and cows in the ditches. We were offered horses free – they were standing around, saddled and without an owner – but because of the children we could hardly take anything. We went on towards the south, where we found a beautiful ski-hut in one of the winter sports resorts, and intended to stay there. Then we saw some cars and jeeps driven by Russian soldiers.

Eva Tornow went back to Dresden later.

My brother's girlfriend survived the raid with her mother; but she returned afterwards to see if anything of their house was standing — and nobody has ever seen or heard of her again. The same thing happened to a relative of my second husband, Herr Studeny. I myself, when I returned to Dresden, walked for kilometres through the destroyed centre and residential areas. It was in the summer and it was like walking through a yellow desert. The yellow sandstone from the Elbsandsteingebirge in its blinding brightness made the terrible insanity of war, destruction, murder and extermination only the more obvious.

Susanne Lehmann, who is now Mrs Pates, but was just ten years old at the time of the Dresden raids, had found refuge with friends living in Pohlandstrasse.

The lady of the house possessed piles of *Illustrateds*, which my brother and I spent hours reading. All through the 5th, 6th and 7th of May, with all the noise and the thunder of guns, we spent lying on the beds, reading. The mothers were frightened, we were not. When we heard that the Russians were coming, we went to the Elbe bridge 'Blaues Wunder' and watched the tanks slowly thunder across the bridge. Men with guns sat on top of them. One heard neither applause not cries of terror. It was rather quiet. Before that, my brother (like all boys) had 'organized' some food for us with the help of a friend. I remember a bucket full of jam which fed us for weeks. Life in those days was an adventure — a little bit Wild West.

Ruth Pieper, who was twenty-one and worked as a secretary at the railway hotel in Dresden-Neustadt, had taken to living in the hotel with some of the other girls. Although their damaged house still stood, it was empty now; her mother had fled to the country and her father was still missing with his taxi after the night of 14—15 February, and she was frightened to sleep there alone.

The Americans had come as near as Chemnitz. Then the sound of Russian guns, nearer and nearer. Late one afternoon tank troops came in; they were not so bad. Then came the infantry and it began. Our boss at the hotel wouldn't get rid of the wines and spirits, although I'd advised him to.

The Russians got drunk and became completely stupid; they smashed everything. However, the Mongols among them went for rings and other items of loot. I heard screaming. Even fifteen-year-old *Russian* kids didn't escape being raped. I kept with the French, Belgian, and Dutchmen and girls for protection; I was the only German among them. It was the French and Belgian men who prevented me from being raped. The Russians wrecked the hotel and all the surrounding houses. They threw beds out of the windows. Everything they didn't understand, out the window! I found a Russian with his feet in the lavatory bowl. When not drunk, they played harmonicas – mournful songs. Commissars came in and kept them in order with whips; they feared the commissars.

Most of the Russian troops were dirty, and their baggy trousers made them look untidy. Only a few were smart. The Russian women were even more dangerous than the men; they could handle their guns, my God! There were some smart officers among them, someone suggested they might be German. They didn't smile, one felt they could shoot anybody. I remember one very handsome one on a horse as handsome as he was; he spoke German.

I left after three weeks, at the end of May 1945. Some American vehicles had crossed by accident into the Soviet Zone. They looked different somehow, then I saw these soldiers had different helmets, and that some were negroes, so they must be American. They had had a job on the border. Did they get lost or were they just curious? We spoke to them and they agreed to take out half of the French and Belgian people, men and girls, and me. There were three Russian border posts for them to cross. I sat beside a negro.

The Russians at the first two posts were so intrigued by the negro that they never even asked me for my papers. The negro was quite a cultivated, very kind man, but the white sergeant in charge was a common dare-devil who helped me nevertheless. There were three trucks and one jeep and normally the jeep led. But for the third Russian barrier, I think he put one of the bigger trucks in the lead. He told them not to stop but to charge it, and they smashed the barrier to pieces. A few shots were fired after us, then we were away.

The smart, German-speaking Soviet officer Ruth Pieper saw may well have been German. For instance, Stefan Doernberg, who had been born in Berlin in 1924 and fled the country in 1935, two years after Hitler came to power, returned in 1945 as a political officer of Marshal Zhukov's First Belorussian Front. Serving in Soviet uniform with the Soviet troops, he took part in the final advance to Berlin, which the Germans contested yard by yard. Air Marshal Harris had lost the first Battle of Berlin in 1943/44, but although it was the Russians who finally secured the German capital, it was only after bitter street fighting. The Allied air raids, even the ghastly American attack in February 1945, did not seem to have affected matters on the Eastern Front. The Battle for Berlin lasted from 16 April to 2 May. Promptly, Stefan Doernberg was sent to Dresden, then being approached by the armies of Marshal I. S. Konev's First Ukrainian Front. But a number of other Gemans from the anti-Fascist front being formed by the Moscow-based National Committee for Free Germany, had already been flown out from Russia to help administer Dresden when it was captured.

Helmut Welz had been taken prisoner during the great German disaster at Stalingrad and, not unnaturally, he felt betrayed. So he turned from being a Wehrmacht officer into a political soldier against Hitler, as the Comrades put it. Welz was one of a group selected from a POW camp, put into civilian clothes, and flown out of Russia to Sagan, where there had been a POW camp for RAF personnel, Stalagluft III. Jack Evans had been there before the camp had been evacuated in face of the advancing Russians on 26 January. Now, in late April 1945, Welz was told to report to First Ukrainian Front HQ, where he would get his documents from Guards Major-General Jaschetschkin.

From Sagan they all drove to Kunau, twenty minutes

away, where at the Soviet headquarters they were given quartering forms and told to go to these billets and meet their landladies. Later, they would all meet again for lunch in the Russian officers' mess dining hall. Welz was given a very comfortable billet in a farmhouse, but the little old lady who greeted him was very suspicious of him because, although he was clearly a German, the billeting form was Russian. (In the zones controlled by the Western Allies, there was a different policy of no billeting; entire buildings were requisitioned instead, a policy designed to keep the democratic troops pure and unsullied from contact with Nazis.)

Welz freshened up, then went to the officers' mess. It was 1400 hours and the Soviet officers had already eaten, but places had been set for the twenty passengers from the special plane from Moscow. Their main topic of conversation was the suspicion and distrust they had all now met from the population, because they were German civilians working for the Russians. This was not a good augury for their work, the setting up of a German anti-Fascist front, but they decided to celebrate their new mission in vodka. They had to be very careful, because this was the first alcohol they had had for years, but the talk became very gay and lively. Then a white-haired man in his forties, with thick, horn-rimmed glasses hiding clever eyes, joined them. This was Kurt Fischer, a Communist since the street-fighting of 1919 with the Red Front bands against the Counter-Revolution. His activities had so upset the authorities that he had been forced to flee twice from Germany, even before Hitler came to power. He had joined the Red Army, risen to the rank of Lieutenant-Colonel, and later served in the East as consultant to the Chinese People's Army of Mao. He gave them the latest piece of news from the Soviet HQ, possibly the most important news of the war: 'Hitler is dead. It seems that he's committed suicide, but no one can yet be certain.' There was utter silence for a minute. Hitler's war had been going on for 5½ years. Could it really be over at last?

Then there were outbursts of hatred. 'Brutal' . . . 'insane' . . . 'irresponsible' . . . 'seducer of the people' . . . 'loudmouth' . . . 'coward' . . . So the whole German nation had sworn fealty to a man who, discarding his responsibilities to the people he led, had taken his own life . . .

In his book *Die Stadt, die sterben sollte* ('The town that was meant to die'), published in the DDR in 1972, Helmut Welz wrote:

We wondered what was going to happen and if the war really was going to finish, because Dönitz had taken over from Hitler. Then we 20 men were joined by one woman, Elsa Fenska. In 1923 she had stood trial in a class court; in 1933 she was arrested for the first time and put into the Altona concentration camp. Released, but illegally active again, in 1936 she fell into the hands of the Gestapo for the second time. A Fascist People's Court accused her of high treason, and she was condemned to death but later reprieved and given instead a life sentence in a strict-severity prison. She had spent almost nine years behind walls, but those years hadn't broken her. After a few hours, the men realized that they could learn a lot from her. Now, out of our group of 21 people, four of us were going to be sent to Dresden: Kurt Fischer, Heinrich Greif, Elsa Fenska and myself.

On 7 May we got our travel papers and on 8 May drove through Lausitz towards Dresden. The road was completely jammed with refugees, units of the Soviet army, hordes of Polish forced labourers who were walking home . . . so that you had one stream of people going west and another stream of people going east, and the roads were completely blocked.

We reached a small town situated near the Autobahn bridge on the Dresden – Berlin motorway which, until a few days ago, had been desperately defended by the SS. Now only Red Army soldiers were to be seen, for the inhabitants were sitting tight inside their houses, afraid of what Goebbels had told them to expect from the Red army. One old workman told us how people were denounced and arrested by the SS, who created a sort of end-of-the-world mood. Young people especially fell victim to this; schoolboys were drafted into Werewolf groups, while the girls were misused by the SS in other ways. Thus this German provincial town became a focus for the lowest instincts.

All through into 9 May the jeep rolled on along the road to Dresden. The driver had to be hellishly careful, to get undamaged past all the obstacles. Burnt-out Panzers and destroyed or damaged assault-guns, and deep craters, also had to be circum-navigated.

The brakes screeched! Greif and I slid forward, but the next moment, the driver accelerated again. We were in a hurry.

The Fascist leadership had capitulated, the war was over. And the others were already waiting for us; they were four or five hours ahead, in order to use the first minutes straight away. People would have to be found on whom one could depend and who also knew Dresden. The time for mental preparation was over, the situation required quick action.

I only knew Dresden from a short visit before the war, but I wondered how much of it was left after the terrible air raids, which did not aim at strategic points, nor at war factories, but at streets, whole districts, of houses where people lived. Already, yesterday, we had heard a more detailed report about that night of terror . . . During the dark February days of 1945, millions of German women, children and old men found themselves on the roads, chased out by the orders of Ortsgruppenleiters gone mad. The first of these queues of misery had already flooded into Saxony. Nobody had counted the people, nobody had taken care of them; it was everyone for himself. Dresden was completely blocked up with refugees, who all hoped to get a little bit of rest and respite here. These poor, tired, shivering people were crowded together in the centre of the city – from the Madonna painting to the Pillnitzer Schloss, from the Technical High School to the Town Hall – and there the taboo was broken. Raphael and Pöppelmann, Semper and Bähr, stood at the point of the climax of a drama whose strategic importance is nil, and which neither decided nor sped up the finish of the war, for the deciding moves had already taken place on the East Front. Why then this barbaric attack without any military necessity? In retrospect it is not difficult to judge. During the last months of the war the targets of the Anglo-American bombers lay increasingly in the future Soviet zone of occupation. The intention was: to increase the chaos and make rebuilding more difficult.

Some bomber pilots thought the Dresden raid was laid on because the Russians did not really appreciate what Bomber Command was doing in the war. Alas, it seems that even when they saw the results, they still did not appreciate it.

'Then we were driving through the destroyed city,' wrote Welz.

We were stopped once by officers asking for documents. No other vehicles were to be seen anywhere, but some Cyrillic letters had been painted in white on the walls of the houses. Then we came to the Riesar flats, where we stopped, this was an old school which now served as the Kommandantur building. Lots of people were already about (it was early), moving furniture, taking down information boards, organizing conferences. A German nurse came up the cellar steps and asked if anyone knew where a Soviet doctor might be, because there were still wounded and dying in the cellar.

We went through the door and there was Hermann Matern, an old Communist, with a group of other old Communists, workers, socialists, refugees, who had been in there since yesterday; some, quite obviously, very recently-freed political prisoners. They had come to the Soviet Kommandantur to find out what was going to happen and to see if they were needed. They reported in detail about the situation in the city and decided that the first thing to do was to get a new mayor, who must be both able and an anti-Facist. Within hours, outside in the corridor, a row of grey-haired prospective mayors were sitting waiting. Hermann Matern (having just consulted the Soviet commander) came along with a man, introducing him with: 'Here's our new Mayor. His name is Rudolf Friedrichs and he is an old social democrat.'

Welz spoke to him and was told that Dresden needed water, electricity and gas, the bridges must be restored, there was a big food shortage, and they needed many specialists and someone who could co-ordinate it all.

To lend a heroic tinge to what they were doing, this group of people were dubbed in the current Communist jargon, 'the Activists from the First Hour'. But when Welz had finished work and went outside, the prospect of the broken city was sombre indeed:

The houses look grey and friendless, and so do the people. Their faces are like stones, I try to speak to one of them, but the man turns away. Obviously, they are still trying to get over the capitulation. Some arrows are painted on a wall beside the words

ZUM DIVISIONSGEFECHTSSTAND REMER

which is a Waffen-SS HQ sign and next to it is another one saying

KOMMANDANTURA

which is Russian. On a front door I read:
'Am at Tanta Meta's, come to Eisenach'
and underneath that hangs a piece of paper with the message:
'Dear O, if you come here, finish and go to your mother, we have lost enough!'
The signatures are missing. One can understand that, for who would want to be brought before a drumhead court-martial at the last moment of the war. Gauleiter Mutschmann was still threatening death from an advertising hoarding – his picture was still up there, threatening death and destruction to anyone who surrendered. Whoever opposes orders, whoever listens to foreign radio stations, whoever spreads enemy propaganda, whoever sabotages, whoever hides deserters . . . who this, who that . . . anybody could be shot down on the spot, or hanged, without trial, let alone trial with a jury. Just a suspicion would be enough, for human life never counted for anything in this State.

But where was Martin Mutschmann, the Gauleiter of Dresden who, like Erich Koch of East Prussia and Karl

Hanke of Lower Silesia, had executed all those who were not prepared to defend to the last the sacred soil of Germany?

Annemarie Waehmann, aged twenty, who had survived the bombing of the Friedrichstadt hospital where she was a patient, but found that both her home and her place of work had been destroyed, went away to the Erzgebirge for several weeks' rest during April. On 4 May she decided to return to Dresden because it was her mother's birthday, so she journeyed out to the southern suburb where her parents had found lodging with an aunt. She found the place swarming with refugees hourly expecting the arrival of the Russians. The inhabitants who still had some valuables left got busy hiding them in various ingenious places. She and another girl called Vera pulled on headscarfs, put on old overalls and smeared coal dust on their faces, generally making themselves as unattractive as possible.

Hide quickly!' someone called.

Already a few Russian vehicles were drawing into the yard and a number of Mongolians jumped out. We quickly grabbed half a loaf of bread and a sugar bowl from the table, and bolted behind the house into an empty chicken-run. We stayed there, trembling with fear, until dark, listening to the Russians shouting and laughing and firing their pistols. The family had managed to slip away and disappear into neighbouring buildings through a secret passage, at a favourable time, but we had missed that opportunity.

As we didn't feel safe, we decided to use a ladder and climb on to the roof of the stables and get from there on to the roof of the house. It was a daring thing to do. In the dark, much handicapped by our thick clothing and heavy boots, and with the bread and sugar hanging from our necks in a sack, but winged by fear, we managed it. And then we lay all night flat on the roof, and heard and saw what went on among the totally drunk Russians. They raged through the house, smashing everything, and relieved themselves into the cupboards and on to the beds.

At dawn, while the Russians were sleeping off their hangovers, the girls crept down from the roof and found a more secure hiding place, until slowly life became more normal.

But around June another event took place which I shall never forget. A long train with hundreds of wounded soldiers from the East arrived at Dresden, having been held up for weeks in Czechoslovakia. The Czechs had taken out of the hospital train the doctors, the nurses, the medicines, the bandages, the mattresses, the beds, the blankets and the food, so that the poor soldiers were lying on the bare wood, their wounds covered with paper, and without food or drink. Many died. An appeal was made for help with food and clothing from among the inhabitants, and every family which could manage it took in one or two soldiers and looked after them.

I worked again in a photo laboratory, but it was like living only half a life. So I decided in the summer of 1946 to flee from the Russian Zone. Eventually I reached the North Frisian island of Sylt and worked in Westerland as a photo-laboratory assistant until 1953. A good friend who had lost her home in Pomerania had emigrated to Canada in 1952, and although her letters from the new country sounded discouraging, I decided to give it a try. In 1953 I came to Toronto, and here I had to start again from square one. Germans were not liked very much and had to swallow many a nasty remark. One settles down, but the homesickness remains. How glad and thankful I am that I knew Dresden in all its beauty and glory. Every time I go to visit there I walked from the main station, the Hauptbahnhof, a little to the north and count my steps. So, now a little bit to the left: and here exactly is where once our house had stood.

4 May 1945, the day on which Annemarie had decided to leave the Erzgebirge to see her mother, was also the last day on which lorries carrying some of the Dresden treasures reached the caves of Pockau-Lengefeld in the Erzgebirge, where they were supposed to be safe from the Russians. One of Gauleiter Mutschmann's last orders had

been to evacuate the art treasures and paintings from hiding places east of the Elbe to new storage tunnels and caves on the 'safe' side of the river. Some of these places, such as the Rottwendorfer tunnel near Pirna, were hardly suitable as stores for the paintings which were brought there.

On 27 April, the first lorry moved off towards the Erzgebirge. It was not an easy journey which lay ahead of the lorry crews and guards. They had to travel by night for fear of American fighter-bombers and with their lights almost blacked out because Soviet troops were already lying on the far bank of the Elbe opposite Albrechtsburg, where the paintings were stored. The lorries came under fire at times from the Russians, and some of the shots penetrated the boxes and did damage to the contents; and then again, the lorries could not use the direct road to the Erzgebirge because of Soviet troops and had to crawl along bad minor roads, and that caused more damage. Then, when the treasures were unloaded, they had to be stored in primitive hiding places, so that many more pieces suffered damage. The last lorry convoy containing forty-nine boxes of china arrived at Pockau-Lengefeld from Rothschönberg on 4 May.

4 May was also the day on which the German commanders in Northwest Europe, including Dönitz's government, signed an instrument of surrender to Field Marshal Montgomery's British-Canadian 21st Army Group, anticipating the general surrender and saving thereby many thousands of lives.

When the Russians entered Dresden four days later, they had with them, in addition to 'the activists from the first hour', a recovery commando for the Dresden treasures, headed by Major Perewostschikow, which included a Lieutenant Leonid Rabinowitsch, a painter in civil life who was also a German speaker. The Russians made a film about their exploits in what was literally a 'treasure hunt', for the value of the collections was beyond price.

It was Martin Mutschmann who, in senseless obedience to his Führer's last order, had organized these futile, doomed moves of the treasure. He had also ordered the blowing up of bridges and the destruction of food supplies and stores, exactly in accordance with the 'Nero Command'. Then in the last days he had changed his SA uniform of brown with red and gold facings for ordinary civilian clothes under a raincoat, and joined the refugees in his turn. Walking along rough country roads and paths through the woods, his shoes became scuffed and the soles worn thin, the raincoat dusty and shabby. Mutschmann soon looked just like any other unfortunate refugee, of whom there were millions all over Germany at that time. He had with him just one companion, Schmiedel, manager of an electricity works and a 'Werewolf' leader.

They were heading in the general direction of the American army when on the night of 16 May they came to a farmhouse in Tellerhäusen near Oberwiesenthal, and asked for accommodation. And here the Gauleiter paid the penalty for having had himself protrayed on all the hoardings threatening death to anyone who ran away from the Russians and so betrayed his nation and his Führer. At that farm, he was recognized as Martin Mutschmann, whose reputation was well known. He was not among friends, and was swiftly arrested.

In June a letter reached the evacuated Riedel family from Breslau, brought by a wounded soldier. The husband of Frau Agnes Riedel has also been a soldier, on leave from the Front, when Breslau was declared a fortress city and the women and children were sent out to the West. Frau Riedel, their two children aged one and seven years old, a little nephew one year old, and Maria Rosenberger, whose sister lived in Dresden, had all survived the Dresden raid. Now they learned that Herr Riedel was still alive after the 2½-months-long siege of Breslau by Colonel-General V. A. Glussdowski's 6th Army, and that the defenders under General of Infantry Hermann Niehoff had surrendered on 6 May. Better still, he had been allowed to set up in his civilian job with his father, who was also a qualified baker, so there was a living for them.

Frau Agnes encouraged her sister, Frau Hedwig Grundei, and Maria Rosenberger to take the older children back to Breslau to join their father immediately, while she remained in Dresden with the two little ones. 'It was a most adventurous journey,' recalled Maria. 'For the whole journey we were sitting in open freight-wagons which carried dismantled railway tracks from Germany to Russia. There were some nuns with us whose caps were constantly ruffled by the wind. Eventually, we were accepted by the Russian paymasters and were allowed to move into our former flat.'

This proved to be only a temporary refuge. More great movements of population were being forced upon Europe as a consequence of Yalta. Polish militia came into Breslau and turned them out of their flat, installing a Polish baker instead. Then, from 4 October onwards, the Poles began systematically to clear the suburb of Breslau-Bischofs-walde street by street of its German inhabitants. The eastern part of Poland had become part of Russia and the eastern part of Germany was to become Polish. Breslau was to become Wroclaw, behind the new border, the Oder-Neisse line. On 6 November the Polish militia drove them to the Neisse bridge, and at midnight that night the train they had managed to catch arrived in Dresden, which was to remain a German city.

Frau Agnes Riedel died in August 1960. Fifteen months later Maria Rosenberger married Herr Riedel.

Ruth Pieper, who had escaped from the Russian Zone in an American army truck at the end of May, bursting through the Red army barrier in the process, had found no trace of what had happened to her father, still missing since 14 February, like so many others. She made her way to Bonn, on the Rhine, which was to become the capital of West Germany much later. This was 1946, still the time of the military occupations, and she got work with a British engineer unit. A year later she married her immediate boss, Corporal Leach, who had served in 4 Commando at Dieppe, with the Northants Yeomanry at Anzio, and with the Hampshire Regiment at Salerno, where he was badly wounded in the back. In 1953, she went to live in England with him in the small village of Liss in Hampshire.

She never did find her father, but she learnt that his body had been discovered a year and half after the raid, and had been identified by his teeth and some papers which he had on him.

Eva Beyer, still only seventeen, had spent all of her off-work hours during the last months of the war in scouring Dresden for news of her mother, Edith Beyer, and little four-year-old Gertraud, who had been at their home near the centre of Dresden in the Klein Plauensche Gasse. The two boys, Peter aged eleven and George aged fourteen, were away staying with friends in Neustadt. All the area where her mother had lived was a wasteland. Many of the houses were still standing, but mere burnt-out shells with pitiful messages tacked to carbonized door frames or written on blackened walls from relatives seeking missing families. Eva had written her own messages, giving her own

address out at the Junghanns bakery, both on the burnt
walls of her home and on the ruins of another house where
her grandmother had lived. She had journeyed out to the
place where her father used to work, and there was no trace
of him either, or of anyone who knew him, or even knew of
her family. No trace at all. Eva wrote:

I couldn't sleep properly, I could hardly eat. The uncertainty made
me ill, and yet weeks passed, the war approached its end, and I was
still without news of my family. It was shortly before the Russians
came to Dresden when my aunt visited me. She was almost blind
and had to depend on other people, and that's why it wasn't until
now that she'd heard of the messages I'd put on the wall of our
house. So she'd come to bring me the wonderful news that
my mother and brothers and sister were alive, evacuated to
Nieschutz. I can't describe how happy I was. But before I could go
to my mother, everything happened so quickly. The Russians
came, no woman or child was safe from them. The baker had great
support from the Polish workers, who told the Russians how kind
we had been to them, so we were safe at first. But when the next lot
of Russian troops entered, things started to happen. I, with several
other women, were taken as far away as Wassa where we had to
work for the Russians. My health had been weakened so much by
all the emotional and physical stresses that I soon got TB and was
sent home. I saw my mother again in August. She had heard that
the Russians had taken me with them, and worried very much. I
could write a lot more about this, but my night's rest and peace of
mind are gone. The wounds which had healed have broken open
again, and I can't go on. I pray to God that the hell we had to go
through will never return.

Her mother, Frau Edith Beyer, had had several
miraculous escapes during the February raids, not least
because the area where she lived was engulfed by the
fire-storm, although admittedly it was in the upwind area of
the conflagration; probably that, and some other chance
factors, led to her survival.

She worked for a firm in Am See, not far from where she lived in the Altstadt.

I returned home from work on 13 February at half-past five. A day like any other, but this day would go into the annals of history, for ruin and iniquity. Gertraud was four years old. We had our evening meal, played a little together, then at half-past six I put her to bed. After that I prepared food for the following day, because the two boys were expected back home. They had stayed with friends for a few days, as all the schools were closed because of the imminent danger of terror raids. After I had laid everything out, I found that I was so restless that I could not go to bed myself.

Suddenly the sirens went. I fetched Gertraud, dressed her, picked up our raid luggage, and went to the cellar. Everybody was there and the first bombs were dropping already. I lay down by the door with Gertraud under me. The blast pushed open the heavy door, which I tried to keep closed with my foot. My thoughts went to my daughter Evi, who was working in a bakery in Gostritz, and to the two boys. I prayed that God would protect them. A quarter of an hour later it was all over, and we went back to our flats. In our flat the bomb tremors had burst open the electricity meter and the money was all over the floor – so I picked it up. The double-glazed windows in the kitchen had been half torn out; the top tiles of the big china stove in the living-room had been blasted off; and the wall between that room and the bedroom had sprung a gap from top to bottom. I thanked God the damage was not worse.

I took 'Traudel' (our nickname for Gertraud) to the air raid warden and told her that I was going to see how my mother was (she lived two corners away from us) and that Frau Bobe would look after Traudel while I was gone. The warden agreed. When I arrived at mother's, she was just sweeping masses of glass splinters off her bed. I fetched some nails and a hammer and repaired a door which had been pushed outwards. The windows were half off their hinges, and to pull them up was too much for me, so I got help from two ARP men. Then I ran back home, got some cardboard, went back to mother's and glued the cardboard into the empty window frames. Then I looked round the back of the house – it was on fire!

'You can't stay here, mum,' I said. 'I'll just pack your bedding and then you come to my place. The whole Seilergasse is on fire and the gables are all coming down.'

At that moment uncle Hans called out to ask if his wife was with us, just as I was putting on my mask against the smoke and phosphorus fumes. I replied:

'No, but it's a good thing you are here! You take mum and I'll carry her bedding.'

So off I went, but Hans didn't seem to be following with mother. The alarm sounded again as I entered my own house. I wanted to go back and fetch my mother but the air raid warden would not let me go out. Then, just as before, there was I lying down with Traudel by the door, and it flew open with the blast. A woman lost control and declared she had to get out, she couldn't breathe.

'Don't be so daft, you can't get out now, pull yourself together!' I said.

She flew into a rage and in the end we all said:

'All right, let her run outside, straight into the hail of bombs!'

That calmed her down. We didn't feel the tremors in our cellar because the walls were made of stone several metres thick; not one crumb of mortar flaked off the walls. A young girl sat there knitting. Everybody was very quiet. Even the children kept silent. Then a very heavy bomb seemed to fly straight over our house. For a moment, we had the feeling that everything was collapsing about us, that this was the end.

Easy breakthroughs had been prepared in all the cellars to link the houses in case of emergency. There was no emergency in our cellar, but the son of the woman who had previously lost her nerve suddenly declared that he was going to open the breakthrough. Everybody disagreed, but he took no notice. But as the next-door building was burning furiously, all the smoke came pouring into our cellar. We got out fast, otherwise we would have suffocated.

They came up to street level to find themselves already encircled by fire. The house was burning at both back and front and the only escape from the heat was to break open a gate leading to a school yard. There were no schoolboys using the school now; instead it housed maladjusted people, and they were still sheltering down in their cellar, unaware.

We went first to the far end of the school yard, but then the fire blazed up there, and we tried another direction; but all around us it was starting to burn. So we all got into the centre of the school yard where it seemed comparatively safe, and sat down. Suddenly a woman screamed:

'Traudel is on fire!'

Flying sparks had set the trousers of her tracksuit alight. I took the corner of a blanket and beat out the flames with it. Luckily, she wasn't harmed.

We all settled down there, out in the open, terribly exhausted. From the other side of the street, screams for help began to come out of one of the cellars of a burning building. The poor people were trapped. It was cruel and terrible, their screaming was gruesome. But there was nothing we could do.

The army rescue teams from the Neustadt barracks were unable to penetrate deeply into the heart of the fire-storm, but some of the rescue companies were able to find fire-clear paths into burning areas on the periphery, as they did in this case. Here the open space of the school yard had preserved an oasis of life in the centre of which the little group from the cellar huddled, and the soldiers found a path to it by clambering over solid, incombustible debris.

Some soldiers came and said they would guide us out of the town centre. We were very thirsty and hungry. The soldiers explained how all the children and sick had to be carried, while the rest followed on foot. It all went wrong the first time. Too many gables lay smashed on the ground and the piles of rubble were so high that we had to come back. Then some of the soldiers went ahead and with great effort cleared some of the rubble and made a path. 'Now!' they said. 'Be quick! No stopping or turning around to look!'

We still had to climb over lots of stones, and were incredibly lucky to get through at all, for just as the last of us escaped, the rest of the gables came crashing down. Those in other groups behind us had not yet reached that spot, so they too were safe. They waited until all the dust had settled and they could see again; then they ran quickly after us, and all were saved. It took us almost three-quarters of an hour to climb over the rubble and reach a road.

Failing to find any relief post in operation, the soldiers took the bombed-out people down to the banks of the River Elbe and left them there, in some sort of safety. They had arrived at a part of the waterfront where the pleasure steamers moored, and they found shelter from the cold in a damaged ticket office which was also very wet. The time must by then have been around noon on 14 February, for Frau Beyer recalls that they had hardly got inside the splintered building when low-flying aircraft came at them, firing. This was the same attack as that experienced by Gerhard Kühnemund. He actually watched them do it. Edith Beyer, however, pushed Traudel flat on the damp floor of the damaged ticket office and attempted to shield the little girl with her own body.

Arched terraces fronted the Elbe meadows and the river at this point. They offered some protection.

Officials from the shipping company turned up and put us into the bunkers under the Brühlsche Terrasse. There we stayed for two days and two nights without food or drink. The screams of the thirsty and hungry children were cruel, for we had no chance of getting anything for them. And there were babies and toddlers among them! There were at least 200 of us in there; the smell soon became almost unbearable. But the low-flying aircraft came and shot at us and others dropped bombs. Four bunkers were hit and there were dead and seriously injured.

On the third day the officials from the shipping company returned and told us that we had to leave, as it was obvious that the enemy had discovered that there were people in the bunkers and that was why they were dropping bombs now. A ship was ready to take us to Meissen or Blasewitz. But I decided to walk to Gostritz, where my daughter Evi was working in a bakery. We were stopped by Post Office officials before we had gone ten metres. They advised us to go back. There were still some wild animals running around loose in the Grosser Garten which they had not yet been able to shoot; and anyway the Zoo was still burning.

What could we do? To go to Blasewitz was pointless, for Blasewitz had also been bombed. Meissen then. And it was high time! The ship would have left without us had it not been that two stretcher-cases had to be carried on board. The captain told us:

'Go below and hide, and don't let anyone see you at the windows. Please do as I say. Yesterday, a ship was attacked because the passengers did not follow instructions, and there were a lot of them hurt.'

The low-flying aircraft came this time also, but as they did not see anyone on the ship (we were all below and away from the windows) they turned away, and we reached Meissen safely. At the gallop the NSV ladies led us to a school where the children were given milk and some food. We were so relieved that we all burst into tears. Then we were given coffee and a clear meat soup – it was delicious! I said a prayer of thanks to God and Traudel came to me afterwards and said: 'That tasted really good, Mum!' Straw had been put down on the class-room floors, so we could sleep.

Next morning the children were given milk to drink and soup with bread to eat; and we had cold sausage, jam, bread and coffee. Then we were taken to another school on the Altstadt side of the river, where we stayed until the following day and were well looked after. After that, we were put into carts drawn by horses and distributed all over the countryside, for Meissen too was being bombed. It was freezing, and we were shivering like young dogs, particularly the children, who felt the cold terribly. It took two hours to get from Meissen to Nieschütz. We were told we would be put into a guesthouse with a fire blazing and a hot meal straight away. But no, the hall was ice-cold, the landlord refused to light the fire.

The surly, grasping landlord was an exception, however; mostly the refugees were met with great kindness.

It was not until the war was almost over that Frau Beyer learnt that her eldest daughter, Eva, was alive; and it was August 1945 before they were reunited as a family. Later, Eva escaped to the British Zone of Germany, crawling through fields and swimming a river. She came to England in 1959. Now Mrs Eva Smith, she lives in a Hampshire village and in the same street as Bernard McCosh, who flew the Dresden raid as an air gunner with 167 Squadron.

Peter Goldie, who flew the raid as an air gunner of 75 Squadron, was transferred to 45 Squadron in India when the war in Europe ended. When Japan surrendered after Hiroshima and Nagasaki had been A-bombed, he volunteered to serve with the occupation forces because it was an opportunity to see Japan. He was stationed at the former Japanese air force base of Iwakuni, where all the hard and dirty labour was done by gangs of Japanese POWs. The nearest city, just down the road, was called Hiroshima.

It was a week before I went into Hiroshima in a jeep. As I approached it was like Portsbridge used to be with lanterns — you just looked out to South Parade Pier from Portsbridge and there was nothing in between. For four or five miles everything was flat and charred, except the railway, which was in jolly good condition. There were impressions on the concrete roads where people had thrown themselves down. People were wandering round in a daze still (it was May 1946), dressed in old clothes, with a black market by the station and the odd sniper in the hills. Couldn't show yourself against a light or you'd draw a shot. I saw Tokyo, Kyoto, Kobe, Kure — and they'd all been terribly bombed.

Although Peter had flown over Dresden, it was at night and four miles up; he had not been able to walk through the Saxon capital and make comparisons with Hiroshima. The difference in destruction was not in extent but in the height of the debris. You could see right across the devastated area of Hiroshima, because the flimsy buildings had burned to little more than charred ashes, but the solid stone and brick of Dresden made great mounds of debris which had to be cleared before, like Hiroshima, it was possible to look right across the city for miles with nothing in the way to obstruct the view.

So the war ended in the Far East as it had some months before in Europe. There was no sense of exultation or victory (except perhaps among those who had been far from the fighting). Confronted by the reality one felt soiled by the evil which had been done; distinctions between opposing forms of atrocity seemed meaningless, when in effect one had been an unwilling part of it. That is what I felt, anyway. It was many years before I came across an American author who had felt exactly as I had but had expressed himself rather better. *Combat: The War with Germany* had been published by Dell in 1963. It consisted of extracts from various war books, including one of mine on the Battle of Britain, which was why I received a copy. The final extract was from the American, Captain Laurence Critchell:

This strange state of mind which fell upon us for a little while after the guns had been silenced was a vague obscenity. It was the faint, lingering aftertaste of having achieved something monstrous. We had unleashed powers beyond our comprehension. Entire countries lay in waste beneath our hands — and, in the doing of it, our hands were forever stained. It was of no avail to tell ourselves that what we had done was what we had had to do, the only thing we could have done. It was enough to know that we had done it. We had turned the evil of our enemies back upon them a hundred-fold, and, in so doing, something of our own integrity had been shattered, had been irrevocably lost.

We who had fought this war could feel no pride. Victors and vanquished, all were one. We were one with the crowds moving silently along the boulevards of Paris; the old women hunting through the still ruins of Cologne; the bodies piled like yellow cordwood at Dachau; the dreadful vacant eyes of the beaten German soldiers; the white graves and the black crosses and the haunting melancholy of our hearts. All, all were one, all were the ghastly horror of what we had known, of what we had helped to do . . .

Face it when you close this book.

We did.

13
'Who Knows Us?'

DRESDEN: 1956 – 1980

'The German people survived the wars with the Romans. The German people survived the Great Migrations. The German people survived the later great battles of the Early and Late Middle Ages. The German people survived the wars of religion at the dawn of modern times. The German people survived the Thirty Years War. The German people later survived the Napoleonic Wars, the Wars of Liberation; it even survived a World War, even the Revolution — it will survive even me!'
— Adolf Hitler, 1938

Hitler did not survive his war, he died by his own hand in Berlin on 30 April, a little over two weeks after Roosevelt. Churchill lost his first postwar election and in his own constituency an independent candidate with no organization polled 10,000 votes against him; almost every memoir or serious work of history has adverse judgements on his handling of the war, but in the popular mind his image is confused with that of Britain and therefore revered. Stalin flourished hugely and went on to kill a great many more people and secure the borders of a vastly expanded Soviet Empire, but after his death his memory suffered through the harsh revelations of Khrushchev, who gave the simple Russian people some idea of the real nature of that monster.

Unlike other service chiefs, Harris was not awarded the customary honours after the war. Some said it was because he was made the scapegoat for Bomber Command, but more likely it was the consequence of the disagreements with Portal over policy. He outlived most of his contemporaries, and in 1981 was writing to the *Daily Telegraph* to complain that farmers were spoiling the summer by a campaign of stubble burning. No one made the appropriate retort.

West Germany, which I thought would take fifty years to recover, rebuilt in ten, followed closely by the Netherlands, France and Italy, with England lagging last because (I always thought) there the damage was least and the necessary spur to get on with the task was therefore lacking.

Out of the Second World War came the Cold War, but it was Soviet policies in its protectorates which caused the population to flee across the frontiers by the million, voting against Communism with their feet. To keep a captive work force safely corralled in, the Iron Curtain was erected. First there were temporary timber towers, now there are permanent structures of concrete and glass, backed by the same ugly scar across the landscape, the so-called 'death strip'. All of the East, including Dresden, lies locked away behind all that.

At Christmas 1949, just after the Russian 'Blockade' had been lifted, I got into Berlin along the Autobahn from Helmstedt which passes over the Elbe at Magdeburg. The countryside was frozen with ice and snow; all the checkpoints were manned by Red army men in fur hats with red stars; but I was wearing British army uniform in a British army vehicle and was bound for the British Sector of Berlin. So, although there was an atmosphere of international tension, one felt secure.

In September 1958, when I visited Dresden for the first time, although there was still considerable tension (this was the year of the 'Great Trek' when tens of thousands of East Germans were escaping, mainly through Berlin, at the rate of one person every two seconds), my wife and I were entering the DDR as British civilians. The good advice we received was: Don't express in public any opinion about anything – not even the architecture of the local town hall. And remember always to call it the 'DDR', not 'East Germany', let alone the 'Russian Zone'!

Leipzig station hall had not been rebuilt and was still a maze of scaffolding, although the city was decorated with red flags and slogans for the annual trade fair. The train for Dresden left at 1014 and was due in at 1230. I suppose the average speed was about 30 mph, and I noticed that there was only one track – the Russians having removed the other as reparations in 1945. The war had been over for a dozen years, but it is now nearly twenty-three years since that visit, so I will use the words I wrote down at the time, in 1958.

We did not know quite what to expect; we had seen so much reconstruction in the West – bright, gleaming new cities rising like mushrooms from the rubble. Up to Dresden-Neustadt, there were hardly any signs of bombing; just Russian officers singing in the corridor. Then the train drove over the Elbe bridge with the river curving away in what used to be the famous view of the city (and which is still used on the china): gardens and meadows going to the river on the left bank, the cluster of spires, towers and turrets rising on the right bank. What came into view now made one gasp. It was all shabby and stained, and the corner of a large building was still collapsed, the flat roof hanging down like the corner of a blanket draped over a fence. It was as though a woman reputedly the most beautiful in Europe turned out to be an old hag, wrapped in rags, with a cigarette dangling from her lips.

The train sped on, to show the historic buildings of the Old Town from a different viewpoint – as an oasis of

darkened stone in a desert of wild green. Between the train
and the spires was a distance of perhaps one and a half
miles. It was all green-covered earth, grass and bushes
growing on what had been houses; the cellars filled in.
Beyond this waste the historic buildings, with new pinkish
structures clustering around their base, hid what was
beyond. We were looking across the rectangle of total
destruction (7×4 kilometres), of which the Old Town was
virtually the centre. The very flatness of the wreckage —
and the extent of it — at once recalled photographs of
Hiroshima.

Hauptbahnhof had been rebuilt. We bought a town map
and then walked along the Pragerstrasse towards the Old
Town. Between the main station and the Altmarkt there
was nothing; except that, over towards Grosser Garten,
some barrack-block flats were going up, and a few buildings had started to creep out towards the station from the
Altmarkt. Apart from this, what had been the centre of the
city looked like an unkempt, untidy park. The rubble (18
million cubic metres of it, I learned later) had been cleared
away, so that the land was in its bare and natural state.
From Pragerstrasse it was possible to see a mile or more in
every direction uninterruptedly, the view obstructed only
by bushes, for it was quite clear of buildings.

The side roads, though broken and cracked, seemed
passable; they led, sometimes past broken statues, through
the horrible greenery. But large areas seemed to be without
roads, or gave that impression from a distance. Where the
roads did wind through the wasteland, the occasional figure
of a man walking, solitary and alone, seemed incongruous;
as though the road and the place itself was dead, and he was
trespassing there. These few figures — they were on the
left: nothing moved on the right — made the place horrible,
because they made plain that this had been a city. The

whole atmosphere was inexpressibly and quietly horrible. One suspected that the cellars still held their packed, burnt, suffocated dead. Knowing what had happened was perhaps a disadvantage; these roads, the morning after, and for many days after, had been deep in filth, carpeted indiscriminately with corpses in their thousands, 9,000 of them carried down to the Altmarkt ahead for disposal. Yet, in its detail, the picture did not recreate itself, perhaps because the mind rebelled. At one corner was a memorial to some hero of the proletariat murdered in 1945 by the Nazis on that spot; it seemed more real. The death of one man may be grasped, the death of so many, never.

After about twenty minutes walking through this we came to the Altmarkt. At the time, we were not quite sure where we were. The spires of the new Rathaus and the Kreuzkirche had been in clear view all the time, leading us towards them. These seemed to have been reasonably repaired, at least the outside fabric, which presumably had stood. There was a square, on its right a ruin, but on the south side brand-new government offices decorated with flags, the old spires rising behind them, and on the north side brand-new stores, nightclubs and restaurants built of pinkish stone in a style which fitted quite well with the dignity of the historic structures; although somewhat new and unweathered at the moment. In quality, too, the standard was exceptionally high for the DDR.

Directly ahead, between the two rows of new buildings, was a brand-new open space; and beyond, as a continuation of it, the Altmarkt. The lamp-posts were quite recognizably those which showed in the photographs of the hundreds of smouldering corpses, hideously charred and mutilated, being burnt there on the grids. The atmosphere now was so sad and unreal that it was difficult to realize that 9,000 bodies had been burnt in that place. As backcloth, there was a row of propaganda hoardings topped by flags along the road renamed Ernst-Thälmannstrasse, and beyond that again the burnt-out shells of the Schloss and the Hofkirche. Between the hoardings and these was another open green space with cut stone and marble blocks lying among the grass, weeds and bushes.

The Frauenkirche, which we now slowly approached, was a total loss, fallen in upon itself; but Luther's statue had been raised from the ground and was back on its plinth. The raised arches of the collapsed dome, like the arms of a horseshoe, reaching over the pile of central rubble made a pathetic and curiously compelling picture.

There was more traffic here than on the Pragerstrasse, but it was still very quiet. One was uncomfortably aware of a number of contrasting emotions which battled each other, muffling any vivid reaction. The square, with its brittle aura of bright flags and hoardings, was vividly DDR; the reaction to that was compounded instinctively of hostility and fear. One was aware, too, most uncomfortably, who the authors of this disgusting tragedy had been. These feelings served to put at a distance any actual imaginative reconstruction of the scene as it was nearly thirteen years ago. Consequently, there was no immediate, violent feeling of revulsion; only a pervading, disquieting sadness.

We walked slowly north from the Frauenkirche, with burnt-out historic buildings all along the eastern horizon flanking the Elbe. The roads here were buckled and signed 'DANGEROUS FOR TRAFFIC'; some of them were barred off. An occasional cyclist and one very ancient car were all the traffic we saw. Here and there, some piece of statuary or a carved door surviving made one gulp at the realization of what this must have been like. All destroyed, presumably to let the Russians in a bit quicker.

At the Zwinger, a fairly good job of reconstruction appeared to have been made and part of the building (which is an art gallery) had been reopened. We passed what appeared to be part of the Schloss, judging from the elaborately-wrought staircases, battered and charred, within the empty fabric. This hint at a former more gracious existence assorted weirdly with the bushes and grass which grew inside the bare walls, open to the sky. I had not realized the Schloss was so central. It had had charming aerial corridors connecting, in bridge-fashion, the main buildings of the complex; these had been covered in copper and must have looked like golden fairy coaches suspended in the air. Now, the copper was blackened and, in many places, melted; dripping down and frozen. This was as Frau Canzler had just told us, that the molten copper dripped on to the people escaping from the cellars underneath. The Saints lining the roof, most of them, had lost their heads; one held out a battered cross, bent downwards. The rows of beheaded Saints, black against the sky, made an extraordinary pattern. The clock on the Schloss tower had stopped at 2.20 (presumably on the morning of 14 February 1945).

It was, said my wife, enough to make you weep. It was, even though I had not seen Dresden in its perfection, and she had.

We walked along the Brühlterrassen, the terraces overlooking the Elbe, and out over the Elbe road bridge. One of the bridges downstream had still not been rebuilt. Later, we visited Dresden-Neustadt and saw (what we had not seen from the train) that all the buildings appeared to be either of new construction or burnt-out ruins still to be removed; and what had appeared to be parks were in fact spaces where the shells of buildings had been demolished and debris largely taken away. There were pleasure steamers at the landing bridges, a rivercraft towing a barge under the road bridge, and a police check at the crossroads (which I dodged, although I had a proper permit to visit Dresden).

A particularly well-informed person, whom I shall call 'Aunt Theresa', told us:

I lived in Dresden for some years, but was not there on the night of the bombing. However, I visited it soon after and can tell you what I saw. The main roads had been reduced to narrow pathways between mountains of rubble; the minor roads and vanished completely. The heat produced by the fire-storm was 3,000 degrees. Sandstone can bear 1,200 degrees only: therefore the Frauenkirche, built of sandstone, fell in on itself next morning. It cost two million marks just to move the rubble. In the Kreuzkirche were many valuable paintings; only one remained after the fire, and that was darkened with smoke and burning.

No death toll figures were announced until after the war. First official figure was at least 25,000 killed; later this was corrected to at least 45,000 killed. However, the churchwarden of the Kreuzkirche, who was in a position to know, told me that he understood that one quarter of the population died — that is, 250,000 killed. This figure is believed in Dresden today [1958] to be correct. The presence of refugees and soldiers added immeasurably to the casualties. I believe the official figures were deliberately understated because the real ones would breed hatred.

The question of 'Open City' is still debated. However, the military facts were: (a) Dresden was full of military stores, virtually the last depot left to the German army; (b) Dresden was the assembly area for last-ditch reinforcements, such as men from convalescent depots, etc.; (c) Dresden was the rallying point for military fugitives from broken and dispersed units.

This was the highest case I was to hear made for Dresden as a target of military importance, but of course the military complex was mainly well outside the city centre. Further, it did not fit the basic Bomber Command justification. Hilary St George Saunders in the official *The Royal Air Force 1939-1945*, volume III, published by HMSO in 1954, wrote:

The destruction in Germany was by then (mid-March) on a scale which might have appalled Attila or Genghis Khan . . . Dresden itself, the 'German Florence' and the loveliest rococo city in Europe, had ceased to exist. The exact number of casualties will never be known, for it was full of refugees at the time . . . Such devastation as had been inflicted on Dresden left Harris quite unmoved: the town was a centre of government and of ammunition works and a key city in the German transport system. His method of bringing about 'the progressive destruction and dislocation of the German military, industrial and economic systems' had in his view not only been right and proper, but also successful, and had shortened the war. This was, in his view, the primary consideration.

When we left Dresden in 1958 it was first class on a Polish express, and in the compartment were three men returning from an important conference at Katowice. One claimed to be a writer of some kind, another an engineer in a factory, the third a Communist trade union official. The man who said he was a writer was obviously dying to speak to someone from England. He said that he himself spoke a little English, but as the conversation grew more interesting, so his English got better and better until it was not merely perfect but of a standard equal to that used in the diplomatic service. They were all surprised to hear about the social services in England now, and of workers with cars and TV.

Then the trades union official (formerly a Nazi, now a Communist) started to put forward a complicated argument about the murder of Field Marshal Rommel allegedly involving a senior member of the current government of

West Germany, which I recognized as the latest Party dogma. I feared that to mention the case of Trotsky might be stretching free speech a bit far. After all, we had been warned never to express an opinion on anything while in the DDR in case some 'agent' overheard; and these men were not your local secret policemen from the SSD, they must be at least middle-echelon government. I was saved by the train. We had got on twenty minutes before it left Neustadt station and it was now approaching Dresden Hauptbahnhof. I said: no doubt all governments go in for assassination occasionally, which may or may not be justified, but at least assassination of a government policy-maker is discriminate killing, whereas that . . . And I pointed out of the window.

Nearly thirteen years before, a little boy perhaps two years old had been found wandering among the burnt or dis-membered bodies piled up on the platforms of the Haupt-bahnhof, into which our train now drew. Eventually he came into the care of a nursing sister, who took the child and kept it as her own, and when she married a decorator, her husband was happy to keep the boy, although he didn't think it wise to adopt him. They lived near Bitterfeld in the DDR, not far from Dresden. For two decades after the war they kept inquiries going through the International Red Cross, in case the boy's parents were still alive. The Red Cross came to publish search leaflets bearing photographs and descriptions under the heading 'WHO KNOWS US?' of these pathetic lost, abandoned or orphaned children still unclaimed from the war so long ago.

In October 1964 a family who had fled from a farm near Breslau on 28 January 1945 and were now living in West Germany saw one of these photographs. The face was the absolute image of their son Gotthard! All that remained of this family was the father, Poldi B, his wife, and their two eldest sons, Pius and Gotthard. They had trekked all the way west, very slowly, with horses and cart, but had kept ahead of the Red army and reached safety. But they had never heard again of the rest of the family who had gone ahead by train, via Dresden. This party had consisted of the weaker members: four very small children, of whom the youngest was a boy named Siegfried; the uncle, Nikolaus B; a nanny; a children's nurse; and Erika. Erika's last letter had been postmarked Dresden, 12 February 1945, and had ended: 'I hope we will reach our goal and please write soon. I am dying of homesickness for some post from you. God bless. Kiss. ERIKA.'

The letter arrived much later at the house of Erika's parents in Wiesbaden. A search for the missing party had already been started by a brother of Nikolaus while the father of the children was still trekking with the cart. The sequence of the tragedy could be reconstructed in part by the daughter of the host family in Dresden, who had gone with them to the station and had survived the raid there. Eventually, the corpse of Nikolaus was identified by a pocket-watch found on the body. Many months later, a death certificate for Erika, giving the cause as 'asphyxiation', reached her parents. After that, silence. The nanny, the nurse, and the four little children consumed without trace, somewhere in that holocaust of bombs and fire.

Now it seemed that one might have survived. Poldi, his wife and their two eldest surviving sons went at once into the DDR, to the home near Bitterfeld, and there met a tall young man whose age could have agreed with the date of birth of their youngest son, the missing Siegfried. There certainly was a family resemblance and when he told them his story, of having been found wandering among the corpses in the ruins of Dresden Hauptbahnhof, it seemed very probable that he was Siegfried; but that was not proof. Later a very detailed medical examination showed that he was indeed the missing Siegfried B. Of course, that was not his name now, for his foster parents had given him a name and an approximate date of birth.

The young man had already settled into a career and was in charge of a small post office. Should he give up this secure position and should he go over to the West and face totally new, unknown circumstances? Should he stay with his foster parents — or join his real parents? His decision was to rejoin his real parents and try to get into a university. Erika's brother said:

His foster parents completely approved of his decision, and to this day his true parents are bound in deep friendship to the foster parents. For him, it wasn't easy, but he went on to complete his studies of literature and the theatre. This sort of fate is certainly not unique and it certainly can't have been the most tragic case which occurred in this time of incredible tragedies. It is just that one feels the sadness of it all when one is affected personally, although many millions suffered in those decades. And it still happens.

The next time we came to Dresden, in December 1980, it was by road, driving east through the night, with snow on the high ground. We picked up the Autobahn by Chemnitz (long since renamed Karl-Marx-Stadt), Hitler's old, two-lane motorway, not well repaired and not quite complete even now (for example, a gap over a ravine where one two-lane track had never been built). West of Dresden, we turned off to the right just before the bridge which carries the motorway over the Elbe towards the Polish border and Breslau. A hundred yards or so down the right-hand road was the first sign in black and yellow, 'DRESDEN'!

The Polish border we knew was closed. True to form,

once again a trip behind the Iron Curtain had coincided with a tense situation there. The Soviets had reacted to the revolt by the Polish trade unions by massing tank armies (according to the newspapers — there was no sign of it here) and by introducing a new currency exchange regulation designed to hit the West Germans (and which hit us as well). Still, here we were, fifty miles from Poland, thirty miles from Czechoslovakia, and the Iron Curtain 170 miles behind us; driving down the road to Dresden at cockcrow, early enough to secure a parking space in the Altmarkt.

This time, no permit was necessary, whereas in 1958 we had to apply and were granted one only on condition that we 'drew the correct conclusions' (although it was not stated what these were). And whereas in 1958 guards with tommy-guns had been everywhere, now instead there were the results of *détente* — teenagers wearing jeans and T-shirts inscribed 'TRENTON', mid-Atlantic programmes on DDR television — Nana Mouskouri, Boney M, Elsa the Lioness (dubbed into German), and the first awkward attempts to attract tourists.

Whereas Chemnitz with its many smoking chimneys was clearly an industrial town, in Dresden we passed through a dock area and some industrial premises on the outskirts (with some traces of 1945 bomb damage), but no industry in the centre (just as in 1945). Instead of getting off the train at Hauptbahnhof and walking up the Pragerstrasse to the Altmarkt, this time we parked the car in the Altmarkt and walked down Pragerstrasse to Hauptbahnhof (before taking a tram to the Zoo). It was a dark day, with black clouds, but the rain kept off.

Apart from the Schloss and a few other buildings, the centre of Dresden had been entirely rebuilt; but not as it had been before. There were many stores and hotels, with much modern architecture, with extensive open spaces, often under grass; a not unpleasing solution to the problem of rebuilding a once close-constructed city. But this gave me considerable problems, as the task I had set myself was, having already amassed the stories of many witnesses, to see for myself roughly where they had lived and then trace how and by what routes they had fled to safety. For instance, where did Margret Freyer live, and where did Cenci die? How far was it, on the ground, from Hauptbahnhof to the Technical High School, the way that the invalid Gisela-Alexandra Moeltgen had followed? And how far from there to Tiergartenstrasse and the Zoo, where Otto Sailer-Jackson (who had afterwards died in poverty) had been forced to shoot the ape with no hands? And how large was the Grosser Garten, where Erika Simon saw her mother turning over dead children or bits of dead children in her desperate search for Erika's little brother, Jürgen?

Even lunch turned out to be research, for it was in a cellar restaurant below ground. The food was good and very cheap, but for me the atmosphere was creepy, for this was exactly the sort of place where hundreds had been trapped under burning or collapsing buildings and been suffocated.

Afterwards, as we walked across the Altmarkt towards the Kreuzkirche, a group of small boys ran after us, asking 'Where do you come from?' (By our dress, we were clearly foreigners.) I felt embarrassed and very conscious of the charred corpses heaped up here on the grids thirty-five years ago. But when my wife replied 'England', the boys cried out in astonishment and delight, 'Grossbritannien!' as if they had captured a couple of rare specimens.

This time we were able to enter the Kreuzkirche, which had been repaired but still showed some signs of the bombing. The verger pointed out to us the partly fire-stained painting of the crucifixion which hung over the altar, left exactly as it was on the morning of 14 February 1945, after the Lancasters had finished with it. The effect of the fire had been to stain and darken the lower part of the cross and the foreground of the picture, so that Christ in His agony rose high out of the stains of the fire-storm, looking down at the bomb-chopped stonework of the pillars in the nave. Recent wreaths, now wilting a little, had been placed on the blackened stones of the Frauenkirche. This church is to be preserved in its ruined state, as a reminder, as had been done with another church in Berlin.

The rebuilding of the Zwinger was complete, but that of the Schloss not yet begun; greenery ran up its walls and bushes grew on bare windowsills. The clock was still stopped and my wife noticed how at one window at the side of the building, the blackout blind was still in place, where it must have been pulled down on the evening of 13 February 1945, as the lights went on all over Dresden for the last time for a long time.

There are plenty of tourist booklets now, giving all the facts and figures. The one written by Herbert Wotte and Siegfried Hoyer, published in 1978, gave the casualties as 35,000 killed, 'mainly women, children and old people'. The one compiled by Jürgen Rach, and Erwin and Inge Hartsch, published 1977, stated:

When it was already clear that Dresden would be in the Soviet Occupation Zone of Germany, English and American bomber squadrons raided the city on the night of 13/14 February 1945, although there was no military necessity for this action. The idea was that the Red army should find a dead city when it entered Dresden. Dresden, in the form in which it had evolved in the course of the centuries, was totally destroyed in that night of terror. More than 35,000 died a ghastly death . . . Of the total of 220,000 dwellings, 80,000 were totally destroyed and only 45,000 remained undamaged. More than 250,000 people lost their homes − this is equivalent to the present population of Magdeburg. In the centre of the city there was a devastated area of some fifteen square kilometres in extent, larger than the built-up area of the city in 1890.

In the DDR the officially accepted figure for the Dresden dead is a minimum of 35,000. That is, for certain at least 35,000 dead. The true maximum figure is impossible to compute, and estimates as high as a quarter of a million dead are still believed by many people. Having walked many devastated areas in many countries, including at one end of the scale of ruin Dresden and Hamburg and at the other Southampton and Portsmouth, a death-toll range of about 35–45,000 seems more consistent with the extent of the actual area destroyed, bearing in mind that there was a fire-storm. In Hamburg, also a fire-stormed city, the official minimum figures accepted six years after the war were 48,000 in the 1943 raid-sequence and a total of 55,000 for the entire war. In Dresden, however, there was the additional factor of an extraordinarily high density of population, mostly ill-protected, because of the exodus of refugees from Silesia. Many of these unfortunate people would leave no trace behind them. The figure of 35,000 for one night's massacre alone might easily be doubled to 70,000 without much fear of exaggeration, I feel. But no one will ever know for certain.

Some of the Dresden treasures were destroyed or lost, and many more were damaged, but there the story had a happier ending. As the DDR guidebooks now state:

Red army soldiers and Soviet art specialists recovered the treasures of the Dresden collections which had been hidden by the Nazi leaders in underground workings . . . Between 1955 and 1958, in a magnificent act of friendship, the Soviet Union returned a total of some 1.5 million treasures, which it had preserved for mankind, to the German Democratic Republic.

Possibly this grand gesture was not unconnected with the East German revolt of 1953, and a need to conciliate the population, resentful at the continued removal of German production (including uranium from the mines of the Erzgebirge) so long after the war.

A better augury for peace, because at a much lower level than that of governments, was the attitude of a German ex-soldier to whom I talked in the DDR in 1958. He had fought on the East Front throughout, from 1941 on, and talked of waves of 'human sea' attacks, only the first wave of Russians being armed. It was, he told me, 'sickening' to shoot them down. Eventually, there were so many Russians to so few Germans that it was impossible to shoot them all down. He saw young boys, with coat-sleeves too long for their arms, wandering dazed and weaponless among the German positions, and old men also — all expected to pick up rifles or tommy-guns from the dead and so continue the Stalin offensive.

That man's pity for his former enemies, on a front where the fighting had been as merciless as its winters, made one a little less pessimistic about the nature of the human race.

Sources and Acknowledgements

Sources and Acknowledgements

My thanks must go first of all to the eye-witnesses who offered their testimony especially for this book.

In Germany at the time, willingly or unwillingly

Ayling, Edward   4 R. Sussex Regt, POW El Alamein

Beyer, Edith   Working housewife

Beyer, Eva   Baker's assistant, 17 (now Mrs Smith)

Canzler, Frau   Housewife

Daniel, Dora   Hairdresser

Daniel, Holm   Baby, 3½ months

Daniel, Walter   Crippled ex-soldier

Eichhorn, Hugo   CO SS-Pioneer A.u E. Regt 1

Fehrentheil, Claus von   Wounded SS Officer, patient in hospital

Freyer, Margret   24

Haine, Dr Frank   Civilian internee

Hennicke, Marianne   Schoolgirl, 12, Refugee

K——family   Refugees

Kühnemund, Gerhard   Hitler Youth leader, 15

Leclair, Henry J.   106 US Division, POW Ardennes

Lehmann, Susanne   Schoolgirl, 11 (now Frau Pates)

Mann, Charlotte   Part-time war worker, 36

Meyers, Jack   64 Med Regt RA, POW Western Desert

Moeltgen, Gisela-Alexandra   Housewife (Invalid)

Pieper, Ruth   Hotel secretary, 21 (now Mrs Leach)

Ploski, J.   Polish Officer, POW Warsaw

Prasse, Hildegarde   War widow, 27 (1 child)

Richter, Anneliese   Schoolgirl, 15 (now Mrs Loat)

Rosenberger, Maria   Refugee (now Frau Riedel)

Simon, Erika   Schoolgirl, 11 (now Frau Wittig)

Smith, Clyde   82 US Airborne Div, POW Normandy

Stiller, Charlotte   Housewife (6 children)

Taylor, Edward G.C.   2 Para Bn, POW North Africa

Thiel, Hilde   Refugee housewife (3 children)

Thiel, Walter   Army Officer

Tornow, Eva   Housewife (3 children), (now Frau Studeny)

Vonnegut, Kurt   106 US Division, POW Ardennes

Waehmann, Annemarie   Photographer, 20, patient in hospital

Wingate, Rex   REME, POW Crete

Over Germany at the time, under orders

Akehurst, Ray   W/T Op, Lancaster

Driver, F/O 'Alan'   Navigator, Lancaster

Goldie, Peter   Rear gunner, Lancaster

Hall, Harold W.   Radio Op, B-17 Fortress

Hill, Paul   Flight Engineer, Lancaster

Keran, Lyle E.   Co-Pilot, B-17 Fortress

McCosh, Bernard   Mid-upper gnr, Lancaster

Manuel, H.R.   Co-Pilot, B-17 Fortress

Mitchell, Gordon   Navigator, Lancaster

Moore, Ken   Mid-upper gnr, Lancaster

Peterburs, Col. Joseph A.   Fighter pilot, P-51 Mustang

Sebade, Dale   Tail gunner, B-17 Fortress

Smith, W/Cdr Maurice   Master Bomber, Mosquito

Stewart, William C.   Ball-turret gnr, B-17 Fortress

Wesselow, S/Ldr Peter de   Master Bomber, Lancaster

I must express my gratitude to the Goethe-Institut, London, and the Public Library, Hayling Island, for their invaluable assistance in obtaining books; to the West Sussex County Records Office, Chichester, for making available to me Ted Ayling's diary; to the Albert F. Simpson Historical Research Centre, Maxwell AFB, Alabama, for help in obtaining documents; to '8th AF News' and 'VFM Magazine' for help in obtaining American witnesses, and to Tom Glasgow Jr, North Carolina, and Douglass Mc-Queen Jr, Alabama, for additional assistance; to Siegfried Noack, Osnabruck, for much information regarding the Sarrasani Circus, events in the telephone exchange, and the state of the bridges immediately after the raid; to Hugo Eichhorn for additional information regarding the bridges in the last days of the war, when some were blown by the Germans; and to the following authors, publishers and agents for permission to quote from works written in many cases by eye-witnesses to the events described:

Mr Joseph W. Angell, USAAF Historical Division, *Historical Analysis of the 14—15 February 1945 Bombing of Dresden*, 38 pages.

The Associated Press for AP report from SHAEF, 16 February, 1945.

Mr Ted Ayling for unpublished MSS *Eleven More Months: a Journal of a Private Soldier* (copy deposited with West Sussex County Records Office).

Jonathan Cape Ltd for *Slaughterhouse-Five* by Kurt Vonnegut.

Cassell Ltd for *The Legacy of Lord Trenchard* by W/Cdr H. R. Allen, 1977.

Collins Publishers for *The Navy at War* by Captain S.W. Roskill, and *Like It Was* by Malcolm Muggeridge, 1981.

Fodor's Modern Guides for *Fodor's Guide: Germany*, Hodder & Stoughton, 1974.

David Higham Associates Ltd for *Bomber Offensive* by Sir Arthur Harris, Collins, 1948; *War Over England* by A/Cmdre L.E.O. Charlton, Longmans, 1936; *Piece of Cake* by Geoff Taylor, Peter Davies, 1956.

Her Majesty's Stationery Office for *History of the Second World War: The Strategic Air Offensive Against Germany, 1939–1945* by Sir Charles Webster & Noble Frankland, 1961; and *Royal Air Force 1939–1945* by Hilary St George Saunders, 1954.

A.D. Peters & Co Ltd for *The Towers of Trebizond* by Rose Macaulay, Collins, 1956.

Martin Secker & Warburg Ltd for *The Goebbels Diaries: The Last Days* translated by Richard Barry, edited by Hugh Trevor-Roper, 1978; and *No Jail For Thought* by Lev Kopelev, translated by Anthony Austin, 1977.

Sidgwick & Jackson Ltd for *With Malice Towards None* by Cecil King.

The University of Chicago Press for a reprint from *The Army Air Forces in World War II* by W. F. Craven & J. L. Cate, 1951 & 1965.

Weidenfeld (Publishers) Ltd for *Inside the Third Reich* by Albert Speer, 1970.

Although every effort was made, it has not been possible in all cases to locate the owners of copyright, especially where photographs taken during the closing stages of the war were concerned. I am particularly grateful to those witnesses who were able to loan photographs from their own collections.

Bibliography

Bibliography

Pre-War Prophecies from the Author's Early Bookshelves

THE BROKEN TRIDENT by E.F. Spanner (Spanner, 1929)

WAR IN THE AIR, 1936 by Major Helders (Hamilton, 1934?)

WAR FROM THE AIR by Air Commodore L. E. O. Charlton (Nelson, 1935)

WAR OVER ENGLAND by Air Commodore L. E. O. Charlton (Longmans, 1936)

THE CHOSEN INSTRUMENT by Captain Norman Macmillan (Bodley Head, 1938)

AIR RAID by John Langdon-Davies (Routledge, 1938?)

WHAT HAPPENED TO THE CORBETTS by Nevil Shute (Heinemann, 1939)

(Douhet's AIR SUPREMACY is summarized by Charlton in WAR FROM THE AIR)

American Documentation

THE ARMY AIR FORCES IN WORLD WAR II: VOL. III by W.F. Craven & J.L. Cate (University of Chicago Press, 1951 & 1965)

HISTORICAL ANALYSIS OF THE 14–15 FEBRUARY 1945 BOMBINGS OF DRESDEN by Joseph W. Angell (USAAF Historical Division)

SLAUGHTERHOUSE FIVE: OR THE CHILDREN'S CRUSADE by Kurt Vonnegut (Cape, 1970)

British Documentation

BOMBER COMMAND (HMSO, 1941)

BOMBER COMMAND CONTINUES (HMSO, 1942)

ROYAL AIR FORCE 1939–1945: Vol. III by Hilary St George Saunders (HMSO, 1954)

HISTORY OF THE SECOND WORLD WAR: THE STRATEGIC AIR OFFENSIVE AGAINST GERMANY 1939–1945: four vols. By Sir Charles Webster & Noble Frankland (HMSO, 1961)

BOMBER OFFENSIVE: THE DEVASTATION OF EUROPE by Noble Frankland (Purnell, 1969)

BOMBER OFFENSIVE by Marshal of the RAF Sir Arthur Harris (Collins, 1947)

No. 5 BOMBER GROUP RAF by W. J. Lawrence (RAF, 1951)

PIECE OF CAKE by Geoff Taylor (Davis, 1956)

THE EIGHTH PASSENGER by Miles Tripp (Heinemann, 1969)

THE LEGACY OF LORD TRENCHARD by Wing Commander H. R. Allen (Cassell, 1972)

PORTAL OF HUNGERFORD by Denis Richards (Heinemann, 1978)

WITH PREJUDICE by Lord Tedder (Cassell, 1966)

BOMBER COMMAND by Max Hastings (Joseph, 1979)

DISTURBING THE UNIVERSE by Freeman Dyson (Harper & Row, 1979)

THE SHADOW OF THE BOMBER: THE FEAR OF AIR ATTACK & BRITISH POLITICS, 1932–1939 by Uri Bialer (Royal Historical Society, 1980)

THE DESTRUCTION OF DRESDEN by David Irving (Kimber 1963/64)

CONFESSIONS OF A SPECIAL AGENT by Captain Jack Evans (Hale, 1957)

WITH MALICE TOWARDS NONE by Cecil King (Sidgwick & Jackson)

LIKE IT WAS: THE DIARIES OF MALCOLM MUGGERIDGE ed. John Bright-Holmes (Collins, 1981)

THE NAVY AT WAR by Captain S. W. Roskill RN (Collins)

THE FLEET WITHOUT A FRIEND by John Vader (NEL, 1971)

West German Documentation

DER TOD VON DRESDEN by Axel Rodenberger (Franz Müller-Rodenberger, 1953)

DRESDEN IM LUFTKRIEG by Götz Bergander (Böhlau, 1977)

THE BOMBING OF GERMANY by Hans Rumpf (Muller, 1963) German ed. 1961: DAS WAR DER BOMBENKREIG

INSIDE THE THIRD REICH by Albert Speer (Weidenfeld & Nicolson, 1970)

THE GOEBBELS DIARIES: THE LAST DAYS ed. Hugh Trevor-Roper (Secker & Warburg, 1978)

East German Documentation

BILDDOKUMENT DRESDEN: 1933-1945 by Kurt Schaar-schuch (Herausgaben vom Rat der Stadt Dresden, 1945)

DER DRESDNER ZWINGER by Hubert Georg Ermisch (Sachsen Verlag, 1953)

ZERSTÖRUNG UND WEIDERAUFBAU VON DRESDEN by Max Seydewitz (Kongress-Verlag, 1955)

DIE DRESDNER KUNSTCHÄTZE by Ruth & Max Seydewitz (VEB Verlag der Kunst)

DER KNABE IM FEUER by Daniel Hoffmann (Evangelische Verlagstalt, 1957)

INFERNO DRESDEN by Walter Weidauer (Dietz Verlag, 1966)

DRESDEN by Jürgen Rach, Dr Erwin & Dr Inge Hartsch (VEB F. A. Brockhaus Verlag, 1977)

DRESDEN: TOURIST STADTFÜHRER–ATLAS by Herbert Wotte & Siegfried Hoyer (VEB Tourist Verlag, 1978)

ARCHITEKTURFÜHRER DDR BEZIRK DRESDEN by Walter May, Werner Pampel & Hans Konrad (VEB Verlag für Bauwesen, 1978)

LÖWEN – MEINE BESTEN FREUNDE by Otto Sailer-Jackson (Mitteldeutscher Verlag, 1978)

Soviet Documentation

DIE STADT DIE STERBEN SOLLTE by Helmut Welz (Militär-Verlag DDR, 1972)

BEFREIUNG 1945: EIN AUGENZEUGENBERICHT by Stefan Doernberg (Doetz Verlag, 1975)

NO JAIL FOR THOUGHT by Lev Kopelev (Trans. Anthony Austin), (Secker & Warburg, 1977)

Other Catastrophes

HAMBURG: 800 A.D. – 1945 A.D. by J. K. Dunlop (Control Commission Germany, 1948)

THE NIGHT HAMBURG DIED by Martin Caidin (Ballantine, N.Y., 1960)

THE BATTLE OF HAMBURG by Martin Middlebrook (Lane, London, 1980)

DAS GESICHT DER HANSESTADT HAMBURG: 1939–1945 by F. Werner (Eckardt & Messtorff, Hamburg, 1945)

HAMBURG: TÜR ZUR WELT by O. E. Kiesel (Broschek, Hamburg, 1950)

GESANG IM FEUEROFEN by Hermann Claasen (Schwann, Dusseldorf, 1947)

BRITISH ZONE REVIEW (various issues)

SOLDIER MAGAZINE (various issues)

Index

Index

TRUE WAR—NOW AVAILABLE IN GRANADA PAPERBACKS

Len Deighton
Bomber	£1.95	☐
Fighter	£1.95	☐
Blitzkrieg	£1.95	☐
Declarations of War	£1.25	☐

Norman Mailer
The Naked and the Dead	£2.50	☐

Alfred Price
The Hardest Day	£1.95	☐

Leon Uris
Battle Cry	£1.95	☐

Tim O'Brien
If I Die in a Combat Zone	£1.25	☐

Leslie Aitken
Massacre on the Road to Dunkirk	95p	☐

Edward Young
One of Our Submarines	£1.95	☐

Solomon Speckou
The Alderney Death Camp	£1.50	☐

G.S. Graber
The History of the SS	£1.50	☐

William Manchester
Goodbye Darkness	£1.95	☐

Richard Deacon
A History of British Secret Service	£1.95	☐

GF2081

All these books are available at your local bookshop or newsagent, and can be ordered direct from the publisher.

To order direct from the publisher just tick the titles you want and fill in the form below:

Name _____

Address _____

_____

Send to:
Granada Cash Sales
PO Box 11, Falmouth, Cornwall TR10 9EN

Please enclose remittance to the value of the cover price plus:

UK 45p for the first book, 20p for the second book plus 14p per copy for each additional book ordered to a maximum charge of £1.63.

BFPO and Eire 45p for the first book, 20p for the second book plus 14p per copy for the next 7 books, thereafter 8p per book.

Overseas 75p for the first book and 21p for each additional book.